Soft News Goes to War

Soft News Goes to War

PUBLIC OPINION AND

AMERICAN FOREIGN POLICY IN THE

NEW MEDIA AGE

MATTHEW A. BAUM

PRINCETON UNIVERSITY PRESS

PRINCETON AND OXFORD

Third printing, and first paperback printing, 2006
Paperback ISBN-13: 978-0-691-12377-6
Paperback ISBN-10: 0-691-12377-2

The Library of Congress has cataloged the cloth edition of this book as follows

Baum, Matthew, 1965–
Soft news goes to war : public opinion and American foreign policy in the new media age /
Matthew Baum.
p. cm.
Includes bibliographical references and index.
ISBN 0-691-11586-9 (alk. paper)
1. Television broadcasting of news—United States.   2. Magazine format television programs—
United States.   3. United States—Foreign relations—Public opinion.   I. Title.
PN4888.T4B34 2003
70.1'95—dc10   2002044718

British Library Cataloging-in-Publication Data is available

This book has been composed in Times Roman

Printed on acid-free paper. ∞

pup.princeton.edu

Printed in the United States of America

3   4   5   6   7   8   9   10

TO JEE AND TÉA

FOR MAKING MY LIFE A WONDERFUL

ADVENTURE

CONTENTS

PREFACE   ix

CHAPTER ONE
War and Entertainment   1

   Appendix. Defining "Attentiveness"   15

CHAPTER TWO
Soft News and the Accidentally Attentive Public   18

   Appendix. Locating Changes in Cognitive Costs and Benefits 53

CHAPTER THREE
"I Heard It on *Oprah*"   57

   Appendix. Content Analysis Coding Form   95

CHAPTER FOUR
Bringing War to the Masses   97

   Appendix 1. On Using Opinionation as an Indicator of Attentiveness 133
   Appendix 2. Variable Definitions   138
   Appendix 3. Statistical Tables   144

CHAPTER FIVE
Tuning Out the World Isn't as Easy as It Used to Be   156

   Appendix 1. Data Sources and Variable Definitions   195
   Appendix 2. Testing for Floor and Ceiling Effects   200
   Appendix 3. Comparing Korea, Vietnam, and the Persian Gulf War 202
   Appendix 4. Statistical Tables   204

CHAPTER SIX
Rallying Round the Water Cooler   212

   Appendix 1. Variable Definitions   223
   Appendix 2. Statistical Tables   225

CHAPTER SEVEN
Soft News and World Views: Foreign Policy Attitudes of the
Inattentive Public   229

   Appendix. Statistical Tables   259

CHAPTER EIGHT
Soft News, Public Opinion, and American Foreign Policy:
The Good, the Bad, and the Merely Entertaining   269

   Appendix. Statistical Tables   292

NOTES   295

REFERENCES   330

INDEX   345

A COLLEAGUE once confided in me, with some apparent embarrassment, that watching *Entertainment Tonight* was, for him, a "guilty pleasure." In this, he is far from alone. Millions of Americans routinely watch this and other entertainment-oriented "soft news" TV programs as an escape from the stresses of their daily lives, or from the seemingly endless stream of bad news offered by most traditional news outlets. Yet, for many Americans, soft news shows are, at least sometimes, more than temporary escapes from reality. And for some, such shows are their primary, if not sole, source of news about the nation and the world. With a few notable exceptions, however, scholars and journalists have by and large failed to treat the soft news media seriously. This book attempts to do just that, by systematically investigating the effects of soft news coverage of certain types of political issues, most notably military conflicts, on public opinion, particularly among those Americans who are uninterested in politics and typically eschew traditional sources of news.

Most of this book was completed prior to the tragic events of September 11, 2001. Yet, 9/11, the 2001 invasion of Afghanistan, the 2003 war with Iraq, and the War on Terrorism, in general, all highlight the many continuing challenges and threats facing our nation in the post–Cold War era. They also illustrate the urgent need for the public to come to grips with the world beyond the two great oceans that have, until very recently, allowed Americans to remain relatively aloof from many global problems. Of course, a prerequisite for better understanding the myriad challenges facing the global community is a willingness to pay attention to information about the world. And, as we shall see, for better or worse, the soft news media may be playing a surprisingly prominent role in this process.

This is not a book about 9/11. But my findings hold implications for the questions of *what*, and *how*, the public has learned about the myriad changes in American foreign policy since the day terrorists crashed airplanes into the World Trade Center and the Pentagon. While it is certainly true that nobody *needed* to rely on *Entertainment Tonight,* Jon Stewart, Jay Leno, or Oprah Winfrey, to learn about 9/11—after all, media coverage of these events was virtually ubiquitous for several months—it is equally true that viewers of these programs, along with a variety of other entertainment-oriented talk shows and TV newsmagazines, were exposed to a great deal of information about 9/11 and its aftermath. Indeed, for a time, 9/11 was the primary topic of most soft news shows. This, in turn, begs the question of what, if any, distinct effects might arise from relying on such decidedly apolitical programs for information about serious national or international political issues and events.

The events of 9/11 were in many ways unique. But they were *not* unique in attracting the attention of the soft news media. Indeed, I shall demonstrate that soft news outlets have covered virtually every major U.S. foreign policy crisis over at least the past decade. And the evidence I present in this book suggests that the dramatic proliferation of entertainment-oriented informational television programming over the past two decades has had substantial effects on public awareness of these events, as well as a handful of other similarly high-profile political issues. As we shall see, this rising awareness, primarily among individuals not normally inclined to follow politics or foreign affairs, holds potentially far-reaching implications for public attitudes toward politics and foreign policy, and hence for public policy outcomes.

Acknowledgments

I have been fortunate to receive tremendous support and assistance from a large number of exceptional individuals who have facilitated my research in countless ways. In particular, I shall be forever indebted to David Lake, chair of my Ph.D. dissertation committee at UC San Diego, for taking me under his wing almost as soon as I entered graduate school. He is without question the individual most responsible for my development as a scholar. His patience, encouragement, and advice on wide-ranging topics, including many issues directly related to this book, have been, and continue to be, an important source of guidance and inspiration.

I am also extremely grateful to Sam Kernell, who served as a de facto second adviser throughout my years at UCSD. His relentless optimism and support for my work, combined with his unique insights and substantive critiques, played truly fundamental roles in my development as a scholar. Without his advice and support, this book, much of which is based on work contained in my doctoral dissertation, would never have been written.

I am indebted to Neal Beck, for patiently teaching econometrics to a student who entered graduate school as a virtual mathematical illiterate. I could not have undertaken most of the statistical work in this book without his guidance. While I fear I never mastered asymptotic theory to his satisfaction, I left graduate school far less inept at quantitative analysis than when I arrived.

There are many others to whom I am indebted. My other dissertation committee advisers, Miles Kahler, Paul Papayouanous, and Michael Schudson, offered consistent support and valuable critiques of my dissertation. They showed remarkable patience in reading and commenting on my work, even as I deposited one verbose draft after another on their doorsteps. Barbara Walter—who was essentially an unofficial seventh committee member—read and commented on multiple drafts of several chapters, helped me frame my project in a manner appealing to funding agencies and search committees, and offered constant encouragement and support. For all of these reasons, and for her friendship, I am grateful to her.

At UCLA, Marty Gilens, Tim Groeling, Deborah Larson, David Sears, and John Zaller each read and offered valuable comments on various chapters or complete drafts of this manuscript. Martie Hazelton, Barbara Koremenos, and Amy Zegart have been terrific junior faculty colleagues and friends, and have served as important intellectual sounding boards for many of my often-half-baked ideas. Jamie Druckman was also extremely generous with his time, reading and providing valuable comments on multiple drafts of various chapters in the book. I am also grateful to Robert Entman, James Hamilton, and Shanto Iyengar for their invaluable advice and feedback on the manuscript.

More generally, I have benefited enormously from the outstanding intellectual environments at UCSD and UCLA, due in large measure to my interactions with their exceptional faculties and graduate students. At UCSD, many of my cohorts played integral roles in my graduate school experience and, directly or indirectly, in this research, including Greg Bovitz, Scott Basinger, Andrea Campbell, Jennifer Collins, Chris Denhartog, Greg Freemen, Guadalupe Gonzales, Allen Hicken, Eric Magar, Angela O'Mahony, Lorelei Moosebrugger, and Marc Rosenblum (and others I am doubtless forgetting at the moment).

I am grateful to Phil Gussin for coordinating the work of my research assistants on several of my content analysis investigations. I wish to thank Scott Hoaby, Angie Jamison, Elizabeth Stein, and Eric Zusman for research assistance, and Paul Rosenthal for locating and procuring much of the data for my content analyses. I am also grateful to Barbara Osborn for providing some extremely difficult to obtain data on Nielsen ratings, and to Marde Gregory for arranging interviews with soft news TV producers.

I thank the UC Institute on Global Conflict and Cooperation for supporting my research for two years through a dissertation fellowship, and especially Bettina Halvorsen for her excellent work in administering the fellowship, which made the whole process seem (to me) unbelievably smooth and efficient. I also thank Michael Dimock, Research Director at the Pew Research Center for the People and the Press, who repeatedly responded to my requests for access to data critical for my empirical testing. I rely heavily throughout this book on the Pew Center's truly impressive collection of public opinion survey data. Libbie Stephenson and Marty Pawlocki, at the UCLA Institute for Social Science Research's Social Science Data Archive, also helped me gather a great deal of public opinion data, particularly in the late stages of my research. I am grateful for their time and efforts on my behalf. I also benefited from the helpful comments and suggestions of several anonymous reviewers, as well as from the invaluable assistance throughout the editorial and production process of Chuck Myers, Linny Schenck, and Cindy Crumrine at Princeton University Press.

Portions of several chapters of this book were published previously in the *American Political Science Review* ("Sex, Lies, and War: How Soft News Brings Foreign Policy to the Inattentive Public," 96, no. 1: 91–109, March 2002) and *International Studies Quarterly* ("The Constituent Foundations of the Rally-round-the-Flag Phenomenon," 46, no. 2: 263–98, June 2002). This material is reprinted herein with the permission of Cambridge University Press and Blackwell Publishers, respectively.

Finally, I am especially grateful to my family; to my mother, Carolyn Baum, for encouraging me to follow my heart, and to my father, Richard Baum, for teaching me many of the skills that I have finally been able to bring to bear with, hopefully, some measure of success. I am also grateful to my sister, Kristen Baum, who never ceases to amaze me with her ability to offer subtle insights on virtually any topic, including some contained in this book.

Though she has no understanding of the profound influence she has had on my life, I have no adequate words to describe the inspiration I have gained from my brand new daughter, Téa Rhee Baum, except to say that watching the exhilaration and joy with which she greets every new experience in her life brings the same to every day of mine. Lastly, I am grateful beyond words to my wife and best friend, Jeeyang Rhee Baum, for her constant support, for serving as my primary intellectual sounding board, and for her seemingly boundless patience and understanding in the face of my frequently excessive single-minded obsession with my work. Without her encouragement, understanding and support, this book would simply never have happened. It is to my wife and daughter that whatever I accomplish in life, including this book, is dedicated.

Soft News Goes to War

War and Entertainment

> It started with the Gulf War—the packaging of news, the graphics, the music, the
> classification of stories . . . Everybody benefited by saturation coverage. The more
> channels, the more a sedated public will respond to this. . . . If you can get an
> audience hooked, breathlessly awaiting every fresh disclosure with a recognizable
> cast of characters they can either love or hate, with a dramatic arc and a certain
> coming down to a deadline, you have a winner in terms of building audience.[1]
>
> —*Danny Schechter, former producer, CNN and ABC's* 20/20

ON AUGUST 20, 1998, just three days after President Clinton testified before a
federal grand jury regarding his alleged affair with Monica Lewinsky, the
United States launched a series of cruise missile strikes against six suspected
terrorist sites in Afghanistan and Sudan. The Clinton administration justified the
strikes as retaliation for terrorist attacks against the U.S. embassies in Kenya
and Tanzania two weeks earlier, for which it blamed suspected terrorist mastermind Osama Bin Ladin.

Due both to its extraordinary timing and to widespread public concern over
terrorism, the cruise missile attack captivated the nation. The strikes began at
1:30 P.M. EST; by that evening—long before the next morning's newspapers hit
the stands—almost three-quarters of the public had heard about them.[2] In a
survey conducted the next day, fully 79 percent of respondents claimed to have
followed the story "very" or "fairly" closely.[3] Indeed, according to the Pew
Research Center for the People and the Press, public interest in this event ranks
among the top 10 percent of all major news stories (through August 2001) since
Pew began compiling its News Interest Index in 1986.

A great many people undoubtedly learned about the missile strikes from traditional television news programs. After all, on a typical evening, between 6
and 8 million households watch each of the major network news broadcasts.
And over the next week, the three major networks' evening newscasts combined presented fully sixty-nine stories on the subject. Still others learned about
the strikes from local TV news or cable news networks. Yet, unlike coverage of
foreign policy events of decades past, traditional TV news programs and newspapers were not alone in reporting the story. In addition to these and other hard
news outlets, a variety of entertainment-oriented, soft news programs also covered the missile strike story.[4]

On the evening of the missile strikes, such decidedly apolitical programs as

Entertainment Tonight, Access Hollywood, and *Extra! The Entertainment Magazine* (henceforth *Extra*), to name only a few, featured the attack as their lead story. The missile strike story also dominated the late-night talk shows, including *The Tonight Show, Politically Incorrect, Late Night with Conan O'Brien,* and the Comedy Central Network's *Daily Show.* The next day's daytime talk shows (e.g., *The View*) also featured discussions about the events, as did that evening's entertainment newsmagazine shows. And far more viewers, in turn, regularly watch soft news programs than all of the all-news cable networks combined.[5] Indeed, depending on which programs one counts as soft news outlets, nearly as many watch soft news shows as watch the network evening news. For instance, about 6 million, and sometimes even more, households typically tune in to *Entertainment Tonight,* while over 5 million watch a typical broadcast of *The Tonight Show.*[6] This suggests that television viewers were nearly as likely to encounter the missile strike story on *Entertainment Tonight, The Tonight Show,* or a variety of other soft news shows, as on a network newscast.

Does it matter where people learned about the missile strikes? In fact, coverage by the major networks differed in potentially important ways from that of the soft news media. While the networks focused heavily on the tactics and strategy of the attacks, as well as on their likely ramifications for the fight against global terrorism, soft news coverage focused primarily on a single theme: the uncanny parallels between real-world events and a relatively obscure (until then) movie called *Wag the Dog.*

In the film, an incumbent president in the midst of a reelection campaign is accused of molesting a young girl in the White House. As media interest in the story begins to spike, and his poll numbers consequently begin to plummet, the president responds by hiring a mysterious political operative (played by Robert DeNiro) to devise a means of distracting the public's attention from the emerging sex scandal until after the election. DeNiro enlists the aid of a top Hollywood movie producer (played by Dustin Hoffman). Together, they devise a plan to "produce," in a studio, a phony war in Albania.[7] Despite protestations by the Albanian government that there is no war, the media and public unquestioningly accept the manufactured war scenario, and the public dutifully rallies round the flag. The sex scandal is forgotten, and the president easily wins reelection.

Using Lexis-Nexis, I reviewed transcripts from twelve soft news programs.[8] I found that in the week following the attacks, thirty-five out of forty-six soft news stories on the subject (or 76 percent) addressed the Wag-the-Dog theme, repeatedly raising the question of whether the president might have launched the missile strikes in order to distract the nation from the Lewinsky scandal. While stories about *Wag the Dog* were ubiquitous in the soft news media, traditional news programs were far less enamored with this conspiratorial aspect of the story. During that same period, the three network evening news programs, combined, mentioned *Wag the Dog* or Monica Lewinsky in only eleven of sixty-nine stories (or 16 percent) on the missile strikes.

In numerous opinion polls, upwards of 75 percent of the public expressed support for the attack. In the same polls, the vast majority of Americans indicated they did not believe the strikes were merely a ploy to distract the nation's attention from the Lewinsky scandal. Yet, as many as 40 percent, including 25 percent of self-described Democrats, also indicated they *did* believe distracting the nation was *at least one of the considerations* motivating the president.[9] And these suspicions appear to have been most widespread among the less-educated segments of the population, perhaps not coincidentally the primary consumers of soft news (Davis and Owen 1998; Pew Research Center 1996, 1998b, and 2000).[10]

One survey (*Star Tribune* 1998), conducted in the immediate aftermath of the attack, found that respondents with less than a twelfth-grade education were nearly twice as likely as their counterparts possessing a college or postgraduate degree (60 vs. 31 percent) to believe that the president's decision to order the missile strikes was influenced "a great deal" by his political problems stemming from the Lewinsky scandal.[11] Many of these people doubtless required no external prompting to recognize the parallels between real world events and the fictional events portrayed in *Wag the Dog*, nor to judge the president's motivations accordingly. Yet, in this instance, for at least some of those who did not draw such connections on their own, the soft news media may have done it for them.

The media and public responses to the Afghanistan-Sudan missile strikes illustrate a number of potentially important changes that have taken place over the past several decades in how the mass media cover major political stories, like foreign policy crises, and as a result, in how and what the public learns about such stories. This book is about such changes, and their consequences for public opinion and foreign policy.[12]

Prior to the 1980s, the public learned about politics, particularly foreign policy, primarily from newspapers or the nightly newscasts of the big three broadcast networks, or, moving back a bit further in time, from radio newscasts or meetings of civic organizations. Today far fewer Americans participate in socially oriented civic organizations (Putnam 2000), and political information is available across a far broader array of media outlets and formats, many of which bear only a superficial resemblance to traditional news venues. Indeed, the Afghanistan-Sudan case also suggests that given the mass media's—particularly television's—status as the primary, if not sole, source of political information for the vast majority of the American people, changes in mass media coverage of foreign policy are almost certain to affect how at least some segments of the public understand and evaluate the political world. Indeed, many politically inattentive Americans actively avoid politics and foreign policy, except when covered by their favorite soft news programs. And, as the Afghanistan-Sudan case further illustrates, such individuals may receive information in the soft news media that differs substantially, even dramatically, from that presented in more traditional news outlets.

Ultimately, a change in public perceptions of foreign policy may have important implications for public policy. Scholars have long pondered the barriers to information and political participation confronting democratic citizens. The traditional scholarly consensus has held that the mass public is woefully ignorant about politics and foreign affairs (Converse 1964; Almond 1950; Delli Carpini and Keeter 1996), and hence, with rare exceptions, only relatively narrow segments of the public—the so-called attentive public or issue publics—pay attention to public policy or wield any meaningful influence on policy makers (Rosenau 1961; Key 1961; Cohen 1973; Graebner 1983). By, in effect, democratizing access to information about at least some political issues, soft news coverage of politics challenges this perspective, at least in part.

If a substantial portion of the public that would otherwise remain aloof from politics is able to learn about high-profile political issues, like foreign crises, from the soft news media, this may both increase the diversity (or heterogeneity) of public opinion (Krause 1997; Baum and Kernell 2001) and expand the size of the attentive public, at least in times of crisis. And research has shown that intense public scrutiny, when it arises, can influence policy makers, both in Congress and the White House (Ostrom and Job 1986; Bosso 1989; Powlick 1995; Baum 2000a; Rosenau 1961; Key 1961).

Moreover, as the Afghanistan-Sudan case implies, the *nature* of the political information people consume can influence the substance of the opinions they express (Zaller and Feldman 1992; Iyengar and Kinder 1987; Key 1961). Because the information these new, transient members of the attentive public glean from soft news may differ significantly from that consumed by the traditionally attentive public, soft news coverage may potentially influence not only the extent (i.e., breadth) of public opinion regarding a given political issue, like a foreign crisis, but also its form (i.e., valence and diversity). Such changes, in turn, may influence public policy, both by affecting outcomes at the ballot box and by altering a president's calculus concerning the likelihood of sustaining public support for his policy initiatives.

Along these lines, it is important to bear in mind that even if an issue, such as the Afghanistan-Sudan cruise missile attack, is not intrinsically salient to an individual or she does not truly understand it, if the issue penetrates her consciousness to even a limited degree, it may nonetheless influence her opinions or attitudes, or even her political behavior. Such influence may be either direct, as a response to the information received and the issue to which it pertains, or perhaps indirect, through the information's relationship to other issues or values that the individual *does* consider personally important. In the former case, an individual may develop an opinion regarding an issue about which she had not previously given much thought. Even if this opinion is not deeply held and the issue is not particularly important to the individual, it may still have public policy ramifications if a political entrepreneur, like a journalist or politician, *primes* the issue (brings it to the forefront of attention) during an election period (Miller and Krosnick 1996; Iyengar 1990, 1993; Iyengar and Kinder 1987). For instance, an individual who knows and cares little about foreign policy, and paid only limited attention to the U.S. intervention and withdrawal from Somalia, may nonetheless at election time factor the president's performance with respect to Somalia into her overall evaluation of the president's competence if a political entrepreneur reminds her of the apparent failure of the president's Somalia policy.

In the latter case, some aspect of an issue with which an individual is largely uninterested may also be linked, by a political entrepreneur, to another issue or value about which she cares more deeply. This process is known as *framing* (Iyengar 1991; Druckman 2001a, 2001b; Entman 1991, 1993; Khaneman and Tversky 1984; and many others). For instance, an individual may be untroubled by an illicit presidential affair with a White House intern, yet may hold strong feelings about the ethical and legal significance of lying under oath to cover up the affair. Such an individual may be attentive to the affair story because of its salacious nature. Yet, a political entrepreneur may be able to exploit that attentiveness by refocusing the individual's attention from the salacious details of the affair—which may have little political meaning for the individual—and toward the postaffair coverup. Hence, an individual's opinion about an issue may influence her attitudes or behavior, even if she does not consider it intrinsically important.

Indeed, the Afghanistan-Sudan attack and its aftermath highlight a number of intriguing questions. To what extent and under what circumstances do entertainment programs convey news about serious political issues? What types of public affairs topics appeal to such programs? How and why does the content of such coverage differ from that found in traditional news sources? Who is likely to be watching when an entertainment-oriented program covers a political story, and why? Has soft news coverage systematically influenced public opinion regarding select political issues, including foreign policy crises, in meaningful ways? Finally, how might such changes affect public policy outcomes? These are the primary questions I address in this book.

WATER-COOLER EVENTS AND THE SOFT NEWS MEDIA

Many political issues—including presidential policy initiatives, local or state elections, economic shocks, major debates in Congress, and the like—are covered at length by the news media and, hence, assume a relatively high public profile, at least for some period of time. Yet, a few issues, such as the Afghanistan-Sudan cruise missile strikes, defy comparison to most other political stories. These are issues, like the Monica Lewinsky scandal, the Persian Gulf War, and the post-9/11 war in Afghanistan, that occasionally transcend normal political discourse to become media "events." Throughout the book, I refer to such issues as "water-cooler events," meaning that they are the topics of spontaneous conversations around the water coolers at workplaces across the nation.

I argue that the rise of a new class of entertainment-oriented, quasi-news and information programs, which I refer to collectively as the *soft news media* has had the unintended effect of increasing the likelihood that, like the Afghanistan-Sudan missile strikes, a given foreign policy crisis will become a water-cooler event. They have done so by attracting greater public attentiveness to foreign crises than that achieved by comparable crises in previous decades, particularly among segments of the population not typically interested in politics or foreign policy. Recall that in the Afghanistan-Sudan case, many Americans appear likely to have learned about the cruise missile strikes not from network newscasts, but from soft news programs. And the demographics of the soft news media suggest that this latter group is disproportionately composed of individuals who are relatively uninterested in politics or foreign affairs (Davis and Owen 1998).

Though the term *soft news* is widely employed by media scholars (e.g., Hamilton 2003; Patterson 2000; Kalb 1998a; Scott and Gobetz 1992), no commonly accepted definition exists. Patterson (2000, 3) observes that soft news has been defined, variously, as a residual category for all news that is not "hard," as a particular vocabulary in presenting the news (e.g., more personal and familiar, and less distant or institutional), or as a set of story characteristics, including the absence of a public policy component, a sensationalized presentation, human-interest themes, and an emphasis on dramatic subject matter, like crime and disaster. Though admittedly imprecise, for my purposes, the final definition—based on the aforementioned story characteristics—appears most useful for distinguishing the soft news media from traditional news outlets.

While virtually all news- or information-oriented media present at least *some* stories possessing some or all of the above characteristics, only a subset focus *primarily* on such material, largely (though not necessarily entirely) to the exclusion of traditional—local, national, or international—political or public policy topics and themes. And it is these latter media outlets with which I am concerned. Clearly, in at least some instances, the difference between soft and hard news is one of *degree* rather than *kind*. And a few media outlets (e.g., local TV news, network TV newsmagazines) are not easily categorized as belonging unambiguously in either category.[13] Still, with a few notable exceptions, the differences are fairly stark.

By my definition, a diverse array of program formats qualify as soft news outlets, ranging from network newsmagazine shows to cable and syndicated entertainment newsmagazine shows, to tabloid newsmagazine shows, to daytime and late-night talk shows. These various program formats, along with their core audiences, obviously differ in many important respects. Yet, they share in common three factors that are central to my investigation. First, as we shall see, they all focus *primarily* on soft news topics and themes. Second, their audiences tend to be relatively uninterested in politics (Hamilton 2003; Pew Research Center 1996, 1998b, 2000). And third, as we shall also see, their audiences, unlike those of most traditional news outlets, tune in with the *primary* goal of being entertained, rather than enlightened (Pew Research Center 1996, 1998b, 2000; Prior 2003).

While my predominant focus is on television, this definition also encompasses additional media outlets, including *some* talk radio programs, as well as supermarket tabloid newspapers and a wide variety of specialty magazines. I nevertheless focus primarily on television because, as noted by Neuman, Just, and Crigler (1992, 114), television "can break the attention barrier for issues of low salience. . . . Newspapers and magazines are better sources for new information when the audience is already motivated to pay attention" (see also Patterson 1980).

The soft news media increase the likelihood that a given issue will become a water-cooler event by increasing many individuals' exposure to information about select high-profile political issues, including foreign policy crises, that involve scandal, violence, heroism, or other forms of sensational human drama. And, as shall become apparent in subsequent chapters, it does so *without* necessarily increasing the public's overall appetite for foreign policy or politics in general. Indeed, the Afghanistan-Sudan missile strikes—a dramatic use of military force in the midst of a presidential sex scandal—involved many of the previously described elements, each of which was effectively exploited by the soft news media.

To explain this phenomenon, I develop an *incidental by-product* model of information consumption (e.g., Popkin 1994), based on a standard expected utility model (Riker and Ordeshook 1968). I assume that individuals attempt to derive as much benefit from the information they consume as they are able, given the finite volume of information they can consume, as well as the inherent trade-off between consuming a given piece of information and doing other things within a given time period. Given this assumption, the model becomes a simple cost-benefit decision rule (to be delineated in the next chapter).

In employing an expected utility model, I necessarily incorporate a variant of the rational-actor assumption in my argument. Political scientists, psychologists, economists, communication scholars, and others continue to debate the appropriateness of this assumption, at least in its stronger forms (e.g., Green and Shapiro 1994; Munck 2001). Yet it is important to bear in mind that my use of the rationality assumption is far more modest than that typically debated in the literature. In fact, while expected utility jargon gives the appearance of presuming precision, I do not assume that individuals are cunning, perfectly informed utility maximizers. Rather, all I assume is that people have goals (which may be as basic as seeking to be entertained) and act to achieve their goals as best they can, given their circumstances. In the context of media consumption, I assume only that people know what they like and weigh the pros and cons of consuming a given media product on the basis of how it stacks up against what they like. Hence, for purposes of this book, I remain agnostic concerning the validity or appropriateness of stronger variants of rational-choice theory.

In short, I argue that the public has grown increasingly attentive to foreign crises in recent years, relative to comparable events in prior decades, and that this trend is attributable, at least in significant part, to a previously underappreciated, yet important, characteristic of such events. That is, like celebrity murder trials and sex scandals, foreign crises are easily framed as compelling human dramas. Hence, such events are relatively more likely than most political issues to become water-cooler events. I attribute this evolution primarily to market-driven efforts by television broadcasters (and, to a lesser extent, other media outlets) to make certain types of news appealing to viewers who are uninterested in politics. In other words, broadcasters have sought to reduce the perceived costs for many individuals of attending to select varieties of news and information, including, but not limited to, foreign crises. By altering the cost-benefit calculus for typical individuals, the rise of the soft news media has, without necessarily increasing the public's overall appetite for political news, nonetheless increased the likelihood that typical individuals will attend to *select* high-profile political issues, primarily those possessing characteristics—such as violence, heroism, scandal, a readily-identifiable villain, and the like—amenable to framing as dramatic human interest stories.

THE MEDIA'S EVOLVING INFLUENCE ON PUBLIC OPINION REGARDING FOREIGN POLICY

For many decades, social psychologists and sociologists believed the media had only "minimal effects" on public opinion and behavior (Lazarsfeld, Berelson, and Gaudet 1948; Hovland, Lumsdaine, and Sheffield 1949; Berelson, Lazarsfeld, and McPhee 1954; Campbell et al. 1960). Contemporary scholars have challenged this perspective, finding that the media does influence public opinion in important ways—through priming, framing and agenda setting (Iyengar and Kinder 1987; Iyengar 1990, 1993; Miller and Krosnick 1996; Bartels 1993; and others)

Similarly, while acknowledging widespread public ignorance about politics in general, and foreign policy in particular (Almond 1950; Campbell et al. 1960; Converse 1964; Rielly 1995; Delli Carpini and Keeter 1996; Sobel 2001), scholars have increasingly come to view the public as rational, capable of employing informational shortcuts to make reasoned judgments based on limited factual knowledge (Page and Shapiro 1993; Page, Shapiro, and Dempsey 1987; Popkin 1994; Sniderman 1993; Sniderman, Brody, and Tetlock 1991). Additional research (Jentleson 1992; Oneal, Lian, and Joyner 1996) has shown that, despite its relative ignorance about foreign policy, the public, by relying on heuristic cues, is able to develop "pretty prudent" opinions about it.

Nonetheless, while the predominant views concerning the media and the public have undergone substantial revision, the vast majority of the scholarly literature assumes that, in spite of a well-documented "information revolution" in the mass media, the relationship between the media and the public has remained static throughout the post–World War II era. And, indeed, previous studies (e.g., Delli Carpini and Keeter 1996) have found that the mass public, at least in terms of factual political knowledge, has remained largely unchanged over the past half-century. This implies that changes in the media, however dramatic, have largely failed to affect the public's awareness or understanding of politics. Yet the absence of change in factual knowledge does not necessarily imply a comparable stasis in public *awareness* or *perceptions* of politics and foreign policy. And no theory adequately addresses whether or how changes in the mass media might in fact alter public perceptions of politics in general or foreign policy in particular.

In this book, I challenge the conventional wisdom of an unchanging relationship between the media and the public. I argue that past empirical findings suggesting that changes in the mass media have not affected the public's knowledge about politics and foreign policy have failed to capture meaningful changes in this relationship, and, as a result, in public opinion regarding foreign policy. I shall demonstrate that the media's influence on public opinion has evolved in the post–World War II era, resulting in an increase in the likelihood that the public will be *attentive* to certain high-profile political issues—notably among them foreign policy crises involving the actual or potential use of military force. I shall further demonstrate that such changes hold important implications for the *substance* of public opinion, again, particularly with regard to foreign policy and, ultimately, for public policy outcomes.

WHY FOCUS ON FOREIGN POLICY CRISES?

The conditions described in this study are general, and so not unique to foreign policy. Indeed, my argument also applies to a fairly narrow range of domestic political issues. For instance, the Monica Lewinsky scandal represents perhaps the quintessential non-foreign-policy illustration of a political story receiving intensive coverage by the soft news media. And the scandal also perfectly demonstrates my incidental by-product model in action. During the first week of the scandal, the major networks broadcast more stories about the scandal than about Princess Diana in the week following her death (J. Scott 1998). Yet, the *Los Angeles Times* reported that in the week following the first reports of the president's affair with a White House intern, ratings for the nightly network news broadcasts of ABC, CBS, and NBC increased hardly at all, by only about 6 percent. This compares to *dramatic* increases in ratings—in some instances upwards of 60–70 percent, for a variety of soft news programs (Lowry 1998). Indeed, in the first week following the breaking of the Lewinsky story, tabloid newsmagazine programs like *Hard Copy* and *Inside Edition* accounted for roughly one-third of all television coverage of the scandal (Lowry 1998).

Additionally, while the soft news media have traditionally ignored most traditional political issues, including electoral politics (for reasons addressed in chapter 2), in 2000 this changed, as appearances by presidential candidates on predominantly entertainment-oriented television programs emerged as a mainstream political strategy. And, in the aftermath of the election, the ballot-counting controversy in Florida received intensive coverage by the soft news media. I discuss this development in greater detail in the concluding chapter.

Given that the soft news media may engage in "feeding frenzies" on many kinds of issues, and seem increasingly disposed to do so, why focus on foreign policy? The answer, in short, is that while my argument has broad implications, foreign policy is the area of political news coverage most significantly and consistently affected by the soft news media, and the *only* such news area broad enough to sustain systematic over-time analyses. For instance, major presidential scandals—to say nothing of presidential *sex* scandals—are exceedingly rare.[14] And the soft news media discovered foreign crises long before their recent focus on presidential politics. Foreign policy therefore represents the best available domain for understanding the more general changes in media (particularly television) treatment of news and their effects on public opinion. Hence, while I freely illustrate the applicability of my argument to other domains whenever the opportunity arises, I focus primarily on foreign policy, particularly foreign military crises.[15]

In fact, as we shall see, foreign crises have consistently proven more appealing to the soft news media, and hence more likely to become water-cooler events, than have most other political issues. There are several reasons for this. First, foreign crises are more likely than most political issues to be viewed by the media, elites, and the public as being of exceptional importance and thereby to transcend traditional partisan boundaries. It is this combination of high importance and (relative) nonpartisanship that has led to such issues being labeled "high politics" by the popular press. The broad acceptance of this notion is evident in the oft-cited cliché that politics "stops at the water's edge."[16] As a result, public interest in foreign crises is less likely than most other political issues to be affected by the heightened public cynicism in recent years regarding partisan politics (Dionne 1991; Putnam 1995).

Second, beyond celebrity murder trials or sex scandals, few issues are as likely to focus the media's, and by extension the public's, attention as the prospect of large-scale violence and the potential deaths of large numbers of Americans at the hands of a clearly identifiable villain. Yet Americans know and care less about foreign than domestic affairs (Sobel 2001, 1989; Kegley and Wittkopf 1996; Rielly 1995; Graber 1984, 1997). Moreover, in the post–Cold War era, in the absence of a perceived direct threat to the nation's survival, the public has increasingly tuned out from foreign affairs (e.g., Holsti 1996; Moisy 1997). This trend has by and large persisted even in the aftermath of 9/11 (Kurtz 2002). Not coincidentally, foreign affairs coverage has also steadily declined since the end of the Cold War (Hoge 1997; Moisy 1997; *Media Monitor* 2000; Shaw 2001).[17] These trends, combined with the fact that most noncrisis foreign news is typically ignored entirely by the soft news media, make a trend toward *increased* attentiveness to foreign crises—both pre- and post-9/11— particularly striking, as well as counterintuitive.

WHAT IS ATTENTIVENESS?

Defining and measuring attention has proven a highly elusive endeavor. Writing nearly a century ago, Edward B. Titchener (1908) observed:

The discovery of attention didn't result in any immediate triumph of experimental method. It was something like the discovery of a hornet's nest: The first touch brought out a whole swarm of insistent problems. . . . The discovery of a reliable measure of attention would appear to be one of the most important problems that await solution by the experimental psychology of the future.[18]

Reflecting on Titchener's observation over seventy year later, Kinchla (1980, 214, emphases in original) notes that little changed in the ensuing decades. He thus comments: "Unfortunately, the hornets Titchener referred to are still on the wing. There still is not any widely accepted definition of, or method of measuring, *attention*." Kinchla goes on to argue that attention "should *not* be thought of as a single entity. It seems more useful to assume that a variety of cognitive mechanisms mediate selectivity in information processing." Indeed, according to Wickens (1980, 239), attention is not an objective *thing*. Rather, it is an "inferred construct," used to describe a relationship between the relative costs in performance when multiple tasks are undertaken simultaneously (for a similar perspective, see Kahneman 1973).

With this cautionary note firmly in mind, I briefly enter the hornet's nest; absent reasonably precise definitions of my key variables, both the veracity of the theory and validity of the empirical evidence would be justifiably suspect. At the same time, though partly grounded in social and cognitive psychology, this book is about politics. More precisely, the purpose of this book is to improve our understanding of the influence of one element of the mass media on the political process, through its effects on public opinion. In order to maintain this focus, some compromises are necessary. A large literature in experimental psychology is devoted to defining and measuring attention. My purpose is not to challenge, nor even necessarily to contribute to, this literature. Indeed, as I discuss below, many of the theories concerning attention remain highly controversial, and this book will do little to resolve these debates. Instead, I draw on this literature in the hopes of offering sufficiently precise definitions and operationalizations to allow the reader to both understand the distinctions drawn in the theory and to evaluate the empirical evidence brought to bear in supporting it.

Rather than developing a novel nomenclature for my theory, I rely upon commonly employed, and hence more familiar, terminology. Of course, any widely used technical jargon necessarily carries with it the baggage of its previous usage. My project is particularly plagued by such difficulties. As the above quotations suggest, the extant literature includes numerous, sometimes contradictory, definitions and interpretations of the phenomena I am addressing. In an effort to avoid the pitfalls of imprecise terminology, I offer the following, admittedly imperfect, definition for my primary dependent variable, *attentiveness: to be cognizant of an object, and selectively process information about it.* Following Kinchla (1980, 214), I define *selective* as: "the degree to which one may choose to process specific sources of information and ignore others."

Hence, by this definition, attention derives its meaning in the context of a trade-off between multiple possible information sources (Kinchla 1980; Wickens 1980; Navon and Gopher 1980). In more common parlance, this means simply that directing one's focus more toward one object requires focusing less on some other object or objects. Operationally, by my working definition, to be attentive to something, such as a foreign policy crisis, implies that, at a minimum, in addition to being exposed to it and processing sufficient information to be cognizant that it exists, an individual must watch, listen to, or read (i.e., process) *some* additional information about it. Greater attentiveness, in turn, simply implies processing more information.

This brief discussion clearly does not do justice to the voluminous literature on attention. Still, my definition of *attentiveness* comes into somewhat clearer focus when, for instance, one compares and contrasts it with other, conceptually similar, psychological constructs, such as *cognizance* and *salience*. In the interest of maintaining a focus on the principal arguments presented in the book, however, I defer further explication of the meaning of attentiveness to the appendix to this chapter, where I refer the interested reader.

PLAN OF THE BOOK

The book proceeds as follows. In chapter 2, I delineate my theory of how the relationship between the media and the public has evolved over the past half-century. I begin by investigating the typical individual's *expected benefit* from information about politics. I consider how people in their daily lives go about determining which types and quantities of information warrant their attention, and conclude that, for most people, the expected benefit from political information has remained largely unchanged over the past half-century.

Given largely constant expected benefits, I turn my focus to the *expected costs* of consuming political information. Here I explicate several processes that may reduce the expected costs for typical individuals of attending to information about foreign crises. In doing so, I summarize the evolution of television news in the post–World War II era and the resulting changes in television coverage of politics. A combination of technological, economic, and regulatory changes have resulted in what might best be termed a "direct marketing" revolution in political coverage on television. The net effect has been to make certain types of political information extremely cheap.

Leading the way in this media "revolution" are a wide variety of soft news outlets, which have proliferated dramatically over the past two decades. Many soft news programs, to varying degrees, *look* like traditional newscasts, yet offer viewers very different types of information. Some soft news outlets feature stories about celebrities; others focus on crime or various forms of sensational human drama. While they usually steer clear of politics, when dramatic political events occur, like military conflicts, such programs all cover them, albeit, as we shall see, differently so from the traditional news media. Hence, in recent years, broadcasters have actually captured a larger number of viewers who will now watch television programs that occasionally present information about politics, including foreign crises, even if they are not particularly interested in politics or foreign policy. The seemingly paradoxical effect is that even though fewer American express an interest in foreign affairs in the post–Cold War era—even after 9/11—a wider spectrum of the American public is now attentive to specific international events, or crises, than ever before.

In chapter 3, I turn to a series of content analysis investigations, comparing the contemporary mass media with that of the 1950s and 1960s, as well as comparing the *manner* in which the soft and hard news media cover foreign policy crises. I show that in recent years, whenever the United States deploys or employs military force abroad, soft news outlets routinely cover the story, frequently at some length. Yet they do so in very different ways from those of traditional news outlets. I also compare the breadth and depth of soft and hard news coverage of a series of foreign crises since the 1960s, focusing upon comparisons of several major foreign policy crises that took place in the 1960s with comparable events that took place in the 1990s.

Chapter 4 presents a series of statistical investigations into the relationship between soft news consumption and public attentiveness to a series of high-profile foreign crisis issues. Here I seek to determine if, ceteris paribus, individuals who consume soft news are systematically more attentive to foreign crises than are their counterparts who do not. I also investigate whether any such patterns are uniform, across the public, or whether the relationship between exposure to soft news and attentiveness varies across different segments of the population. I find that soft news coverage of foreign crises matters primarily for politically inattentive individuals, who might otherwise avoid *any* exposure to news about foreign policy.

In chapter 5, I shift my focus from the correlates of attentiveness to specific foreign crises, to long-term trends in public opinion regarding foreign policy crises. I consider whether the relationships identified in chapter 4, combined with the over-time increases in soft news coverage of foreign crises identified in chapter 3, can account, at least in part, for trends in public attentiveness to a variety of U.S. military interventions and other related foreign policy engagements from the 1950s through the 1990s.

Demonstrating a causal link in a time-series context is extremely difficult under the best of circumstances. It is rarely possible to account for all potentially competing explanations for virtually any trend one might discover. My investigations are no exception. In fact, I am particularly plagued by a relative scarcity of data appropriate for tracing trends in public attentiveness to foreign crises, and by the obvious and stark differences in the events I seek to compare—including myriad differences in the economic, political, and social circumstances surrounding such events across time.

Nevertheless, in this chapter I attempt to make the most of a far-less-than-ideal situation by compiling as much circumstantial evidence as I have been able to obtain, from a variety of sources and regarding a wide range of foreign crisis issues. For instance, I begin by comparing public attentiveness to the Korean, Vietnam, and Persian Gulf Wars. This comparison exemplifies the difficulties noted above. These wars differed profoundly in countless ways, including both the conduct of the conflicts themselves, and the social and political contexts within which they took place. Hence, virtually any effort to draw comparisons across the three wars is vulnerable to the criticism that it is impossible to rule out any number of alternative explanations for *whatever* patterns I find.

My response to this general critique is not to deny the uniqueness of each war, nor to assert that they are in many respects comparable, but instead to attempt to draw extremely limited comparisons, involving circumstances that appear analogous in the most critical respects. For instance, in several instances, in comparing the Vietnam and Persian Gulf Wars, I concentrate on the earliest years of Vietnam, before it became unpopular, and when U.S. troop deployments and casualty rates were similar to those experienced during the Gulf War. My goal with this and subsequent analyses in this chapter is to build as convincing a circumstantial case as possible by demonstrating that my proposed explanation(s) for the trends I identify is more plausible than most other obvious alternatives. While none of the investigations in this chapter produces anything approaching a "smoking gun" (definitive evidence of a causal relationship), my hope is that, viewed in tandem, they add up to a convincing circumstantial case in support of my causal argument.

In chapter 6, I shift my focus to an in-depth case study of one widely studied manifestation of public opinion regarding foreign policy: the "rally-round-the-flag" phenomenon (Mueller 1970, 1973; Brody and Shapiro 1991; Brody 1991; Baum 2002a; and many others). This is the tendency of the public to rally behind presidents—manifested as short-term spikes in their job approval ratings—immediately following sudden, high-profile foreign policy events. I find that the changing media environment over the past several decades, and resulting changes in public perceptions of foreign policy, appear to have potentially consequential implications for the rally phenomenon. Specifically, I show that more Americans joined opinion rallies in the 1980s and 1990s than did so in the 1950s and 1960s. And those more likely to rally now than in the past are the very citizens most dependent on soft news outlets for information about a foreign crisis.

Next, in chapter 7, I consider an additional implication of my theory for public opinion regarding foreign policy. Specifically, I argue that due to the *nature* of soft news coverage of foreign crises, politically inattentive individuals who consume soft news are likely to be more skeptical of U.S. foreign policy—particularly when it involves multilateral engagements—as compared to their counterparts who either do not consume soft news or are more politically engaged. And, in fact, my various statistical investigations in this chapter all point in a single direction, toward an *inverse* relationship, primarily among politically inattentive or relatively uneducated Americans, between soft news consumption and support for a proactive or internationalist U.S. foreign policy.

Finally, in chapter 8, I consider the role of the Internet, a topic I largely ignore—or at most treat as a control variable—throughout the book. I then consider a variety of broader implications of my findings for public opinion and for U.S. politics and foreign policy. In doing so, I broaden my focal lens beyond foreign policy, in order to consider the effects of soft news on high-profile domestic political issues, including the 2000 presidential election and the Monica Lewinsky scandal. Many readers will not be surprised to learn that soft news coverage of the Lewinsky scandal influenced public opinion. Yet, perhaps a bit more surprisingly, I find that the soft news media also influenced public opinion regarding the 2000 election. I also present evidence that not only does exposure to soft news influence *attentiveness* to particular foreign crises, but it can also enhance viewers' factual knowledge about them. I then discuss the possibility that because enhanced public scrutiny raises the political risks associated with policy failure, presidential crisis decision making may be influenced in important ways—manifested through increasingly risk-averse policy choices—by enhanced public attentiveness to their overseas activities. I conclude by offering conjectures concerning a few of the many possible implications of the soft news revolution for America's democracy.

APPENDIX: DEFINING "ATTENTIVENESS"

There is substantial debate in the experimental psychology literature concerning whether individuals possess a single overarching "pool" of attention resources or multiple, more task-specific attention resources. A primary distinction between these two perspectives concerns the relative trade-offs required to process a given piece of information, or to pay attention to something. If individuals possess a single, finite resource pool, which is accessed whenever an individual processes a piece of information, then paying attention to one thing necessarily detracts from one's ability to pay attention to something else. In other words, performance suffers when individuals attempt to undertake more than one attention task at the same time. The extent to which performance suffers depends on how much a given attention task draws down one's resource pool. This, in turn, varies with the difficulty of the task. Hence, the trade-off required to perform multiple simple tasks is smaller than that required to undertake multiple difficult or complex tasks.

If, in contrast, individuals possess multiple resource pools, which are oriented toward different types of tasks, then drawing from one resource pool may or may not degrade one's ability to perform a second, simultaneous attention task. If the two tasks draw from different pools, then the individual may suffer no performance degradation at all. In this case, there would be no trade-off. (Of course, if the two attention tasks draw from a common resource pool, then the trade-off returns.) Researchers have found evidence supporting both perspectives. For a review of the arguments and evidence on both sides of this debate, see Kinchla 1980; Wickens 1980; and Khaneman 1973.

As we shall see in the next chapter, my theory assumes that there are indeed attention trade-offs. It does not, however, require that such trade-offs be universal; merely that under normal circumstances, individuals do face some trade-offs in allocating their finite attention resources. This view appears broadly consistent with both theoretical perspectives, neither of which deny the existence of attention trade-offs under many, if not all, circumstances. Indeed, the multiple resource hypothesis accepts that trade-offs are necessary when an individual undertakes multiple tasks that are likely to draw on a common resource pool. One example of this might be watching television and reading, both of which depend on visual information processing.

Regardless of one's view with respect to the aforementioned debate, it is important to distinguish my definition of attentiveness from other similar, yet conceptually distinct, psychological constructs. As I have defined it, attentiveness occupies a conceptual middle ground between two widely employed constructs borrowed from social psychology: *cognizance* and *salience*. To be cognizant of an issue means simply to know that it exists, and nothing more. After all, an individual must know an issue exists before she can decide whether to attend to it. By itself, however, cognizance seems unlikely to have meaningful behavioral consequences. If an individual is aware that an issue exists, yet neither cares about nor follows it, then it seems relatively unlikely that the issue will influence her political attitudes or behavior (Campbell et al. 1960). Hence, *cognizance*, by itself, appears to represent a less intensive, and less purposive, form of interaction with an object than does attentiveness.

Salience, in contrast, carries an implication of personal importance or urgency (Smith, Bruner, and White 1956, 35), which, relative to attentiveness, implies a *more* purposive and intensive interaction with an object. It also implies intrinsic interest. As will hopefully become clear in chapter 2, my incidental by-product model holds that individuals are sometimes willing to attend to information about an issue, even if they are *not* actively seeking it (i.e., they are not intrinsically *interested*). This, in turn, becomes more likely as the information or performance trade-off (i.e., the *selectivity*) required to be attentive to a given object declines.

The distinction between attentiveness and salience, or interest (for my purposes, *interest* and *salience* are essentially synonymous) requires further clarification. It seems less than obvious that an individual could be attentive to an issue with which he or she is entirely uninterested. Nonetheless, *attentiveness* and *salience* are not synonymous. An individual might pay attention to information about an issue, say a war, not because she is interested in or cares about the war, its implications, or its outcome. Rather, it may simply be the case that the *presentation* of the war in the media is emotionally exciting (i.e., entertaining) or the person discussing the war on the radio or television might be intrinsically interesting to the individual (e.g., a celebrity). Hence, an individual may pay attention to information about the war, not because she is interested in the war itself, but rather because she is interested either in being entertained or in listening to the person presenting the information. Hence, salience and attentiveness, though certainly related, are not equivalent. An individual can be attentive to an object without being interested in it.

To further clarify the distinctions between cognizance, attentiveness, and salience, I briefly consider the propensity of individuals to manifest opinions about a given object at each level of interaction with the object. While an individual must become aware of an object before attending to it, cognizance, by itself, may be insufficient for an individual to form an opinion about the object. To form an opinion, an individual must pay attention to some information about the object beyond mere recognition of its existence. Yet one can certainly pay enough attention to form an opinion without truly *understanding* the object or determining that it is particularly important. And, as noted, *salience* implies personal importance. So, for instance, though attentiveness does not necessarily require one to have an opinion, if one is attentive to an object, one is more likely to have an opinion about it than if one is merely cognizant that it exists. Such an opinion may not, however, be particularly important to an individual. Salience, in turn, requires that any opinion about the object be of some personal importance.

Of course, even a personally important, or salient, opinion may not be accurate. Knowledge or understanding requires that any such opinion be both contextually and factually accurate. Hence, there is an important distinction between *knowing* about (or understanding) an issue and *thinking* that one knows about (or understands) an issue. Indeed, an individual may spend many hours watching news programs about a given issue on television, yet retain primarily false, or perhaps technically accurate but tangential, information about it. While most observers would agree that such an individual is *attentive* to the issue, few would equate this with possessing knowledge or understanding.

It is also important to point out that the single dimension upon which I have placed these several constructs is itself a construct, and a rough one at that. It seems unlikely that an individual will attend to sufficient information about an issue to acquire true understanding unless that issue is at least somewhat salient to her, for whatever reason. Yet salience (or interest) and knowledge (or understanding) are clearly not linear quantities that rise and fall in tandem with one another. More salience does not necessarily lead, monotonically, to greater knowledge. We may have a better understanding about an issue that is only somewhat salient to us than about another issue that is highly salient. Numerous factors, such as the accessibility of information or its complexity, intervene between salience and knowledge. Nevertheless, it remains unlikely that an individual will pay sufficient attention to acquire true understanding of an issue unless he or she is at least *somewhat* interested in it. Hence, for purposes of this book, I treat attentiveness as lying somewhere between cognizance or awareness, on the one hand, and salience or personal importance, on the other.

Soft News and the Accidentally Attentive Public

> What we have is a new media culture where the exact same dynamics . . . are at
> work whether the story is about a sex scandal or whether it's a life-and-death
> story about a war.[1]
>
> —*Steven Brill, Editor-in-Chief*, Brill's Content

SCHOLARS HAVE long recognized that people who are not interested in politics often get their news from sources quite different from those of their politically engaged counterparts (Chaffee and Kanihan 1997; Key 1961). While alternative news sources for the politically uninvolved have long been available, the last two decades have witnessed a dramatic expansion in the number and diversity of entertainment-oriented, quasi-news media outlets, which I have referred to collectively as the soft news media.

Political analysts and scholars have mostly ignored the soft news media. And, indeed, most of the time these media eschew discussion of politics and public policy, in favor of more "down-market" topics, like celebrity gossip, crime dramas, disasters, or other dramatic human-interest stories (Hamilton 2003; Patterson 2000; Kalb 1998a). Yet, on occasion, the soft news media *do* convey substantive information concerning a select few high-profile political issues, prominent among them foreign policy crises. This suggests that the proliferation of soft news outlets may have meaningful implications for public opinion concerning politics, including foreign policy. In this chapter, I develop a theory intended to determine, as precisely as possible, the nature of such implications.

My purpose is not to challenge previous empirical studies (e.g., Delli Carpini and Keeter 1996) that have found no evidence of change over the past half-century in the American public's factual knowledge about politics. Nor do I address whether or not the public's *understanding* of politics or foreign affairs has increased during the same period (Rosenau 1997, 1990). Rather, I focus upon the public's average propensity to *pay attention* to information about foreign military crises, as well as about a select few other types of political issues possessing similar characteristics, which I describe below.[2] I argue that in an era in which television is the primary, if not sole, source of news and information for a large majority of the public (Moisy 1997; Stanley and Niemi 1994; Lichty and Gomery 1992; Briller 1990; Bower 1985; Dimock and Popkin 1997), one result of a dramatically changed television environment over the past two decades is that despite a generally unchanged appetite for political news, a broader segment of the public is attentive to *some* television outlet with the *potential* to provide information about political issues, such as foreign crises.[3] And this development, I shall further argue, is not without consequence.

My theory draws upon a standard expected utility model, which takes the usual form, $PB - C$. The B term in this equation represents the expected *benefit* to an individual derived from carrying out a given activity, such as voting (Riker and Ordeshook 1968) or watching the president on television (Baum and Kernell 1999).[4] This is discounted by the P term, which is the *probability* that the individual will actually gain the benefit, should she elect to carry out the activity. The product of B and P represents the total expected benefit to the individual for carrying out the activity. This is then compared to the C term, or the expected *costs* of undertaking the activity. The C term consists of both *opportunity* costs (other activities that must be foregone in order to undertake the current activity) and *transaction* costs (i.e., the effort that must be exerted to undertake the activity). If the expected benefits exceed the expected costs (i.e., $PB > C$), the individual will anticipate a net gain in utility from conducting the activity—in this instance paying attention to information about a foreign crisis—and will therefore do so. Otherwise (if $PB < C$), the individual will anticipate a net loss in utility from conducting the activity, and will refrain from doing so.[5]

In the course of explicating my theory, I investigate both the expected costs and benefits of paying attention. I begin by considering how individuals in their daily lives go about determining which types and quantities of information warrant their attention, focusing on the benefit side of the ledger. I then investigate an alternative explanation for increased public attentiveness to foreign crises: a decline in the expected costs of paying attention. Here I introduce several mechanisms that appear potentially capable of reducing the expected costs for typical individuals of paying attention to information about foreign crises.

Next, I review a series of technological, economic, and strategic changes in the television marketplace that, in combination, have altered the cost-benefit calculus for typical individuals and the incentive structure facing television broadcasters. I conclude with a brief discussion of the class of issues that are particularly likely to appeal to soft news programmers, and so to become water-cooler events: *crises*. This latter discussion also briefly considers several factors that make a given crisis issue more or less likely to actually become a water-cooler event. Before turning to the theory, however, I first introduce an apparent paradox in American public opinion regarding war: one I shall argue that my theory can resolve, and which I investigate empirically in subsequent chapters.

A PARADOX OF PUBLIC OPINION

A Public Less Interested in, yet More Attentive to, War

In the fall of 1970, America was embroiled in a sixth year of the most controversial military conflict in its history, in Vietnam. To that point, the war had claimed the lives of nearly 54,000 Americans, provoking unprecedented turmoil at home.[6] Increasing numbers of Americans took to the streets in opposition to the war, and many draft-age men burned their draft cards in protest of what they considered an unjust military conflict. Richard Nixon had been elected president two years earlier based in part on the promise of a "secret plan" to end the war, a plan that had not yet materialized. When interviewers for the 1970 American National Election Study (NES) asked Americans how important the Vietnam War was to them personally, fully 70 percent responded that it was *very* important. In spite of this, when asked how much attention they were paying to the war, less than half (46 percent) claimed to be paying "a good deal" of attention, while 15 percent claimed not to be following the war at all.[7]

In January 1991, the United States became embroiled in its first large-scale military conflict since the end of the Vietnam War, in the Persian Gulf. In sharp contrast to Vietnam, this war ended in a dramatic and decisive American victory. Given the confluence of the 1990 election and the Persian Gulf crisis, the NES prepared a special extension of its usual election-year survey in order to query Americans regarding the Gulf crisis and war. When asked how important the war was for them personally, 63 percent responded that it was *very* or *extremely* important—7 percent fewer than in 1970.[8] At least in these surveys, Americans in 1991 appear to have considered the Gulf War similarly, or slightly less, important as their counterparts in 1970 considered Vietnam.

Given the similar importance that NES respondents ascribed to Vietnam and the Gulf War, one might anticipate they would have paid comparable attention to the two conflicts. Yet when asked how much attention they had paid to the Gulf conflict, fully 90 percent—nearly twice as many as in 1970—claimed to have paid "quite a bit" or "a great deal" of attention. And only 2 percent of 1991 respondents claimed to have paid "very little" attention to the Gulf War, also a sharp decline from 1970.

A great deal of survey evidence corroborates this surprising anecdotal finding. For instance, figure 2.1 compares the percentage of Americans who failed to offer an opinion—here employed as indicating a lack of attentiveness—when asked whether or not they approved of how presidents Johnson, Nixon, and G. H. W. Bush, respectively, conducted the two conflicts.[9] This question was asked repeatedly, in nearly identical form, throughout both the Vietnam (1965–73, $N = 86$) and Persian Gulf (August 1990–September 1991, $N = 41$) conflicts.

Far more Americans were consistently willing to express an opinion during the Persian Gulf crisis and war than at any time during the Vietnam War.[10] The mean rate of "don't know" responses during the entire period 1965–73 was twice that of the thirteen months of the Gulf crisis covered in this figure (14.5 versus 7.25 percent). If the years with the lowest average "don't know" rate from the Vietnam War era (1968 and 1972) are contrasted with the overall average from the Persian Gulf crisis, the Vietnam era "don't know" rates are still 62 and 41 percent higher, respectively.[11] In fact, on only one of eighty-six surveys between 1965 and 1973 was the "don't know" rate as low as the overall *average* for the thirteen months of the Persian Gulf crisis covered in figure 2.1.[12]

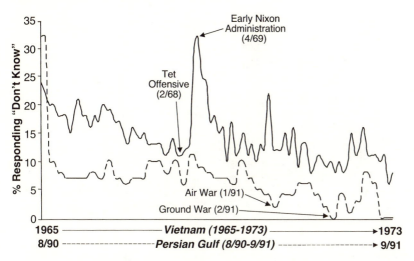

FIGURE 2.1. "Don't Know" Response Rates: Vietnam vs. Persian Gulf
    QUESTION: Do you approve or disapprove of the way President [Johnson/Nixon/
Bush] is handling the situation in [Vietnam/the Persian Gulf]?

    Americans were also repeatedly asked whether it was a mistake for the coun-
try to enter the wars in Vietnam and the Persian Gulf, as well as in Korea.
Figure 2.2 presents the distribution of "don't know" responses to this latter
question. A stark pattern emerges, with the largest percentage of "don't know"
responses coming at the extreme low end of the scale for the Gulf War (meaning that most Gulf War surveys had *low* "don't know" rates), at the high end for
Korea (meaning that most Korean War surveys had *high* "don't know" rates),
with Vietnam lying in between, but closer to Korea than to the Gulf War.
    Overall, the mean level of "don't know" responses during the Persian Gulf
War (5.3 percent, $N = 12$ surveys, 1991) was approximately one-third of that
from the near-identical question asked repeatedly during Korea (15.3 percent,
$N = 13$ surveys, 1950–53), and less than one-half of that recorded during Vietnam (12 percent, $N = 23$ surveys, 1965–71).[13] (In chapter 5, I discuss various
issues surrounding my comparison of these very different military conflicts.)
    These data suggest Americans paid substantially more attention to the Per-
sian Gulf crisis than to either Vietnam or Korea. Yet since the end of the Cold
War they have declared themselves in countless public opinion surveys to be
less concerned with foreign affairs than at any time since World War II, even in
the aftermath of 9/11 (Kurtz 2002). Figure 2.3 shows the annualized trend, from
1945 to 2000, in the percentage of the public mentioning issues pertaining to
foreign affairs, when asked by the Gallup Poll to name the most important
problem facing the nation. Figure 2.3 also presents the percentage of the public
specifically naming the Korean (March 1952 and June 1952) and Vietnam Wars
(1965–73), and the Persian Gulf crisis and war (August–December 1990 and
January–March 1991).

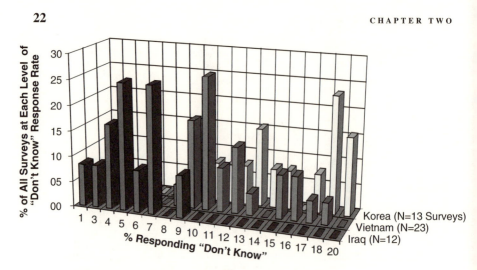

FIGURE 2.2. Distribution of "Don't Know" Response Rates, by War
QUESTIONS: (A) Do you think the United States made a mistake in going into
the war in Korea, or not? (B) In view of the developments since we entered the
fighting in Vietnam, do you think the U.S. made a mistake sending troops to fight
in Vietnam? (C) Do you think the United States made a mistake in [getting
involved in the war in/sending troops to fight against] Iraq, or not?

These data indicate that in the 1950s and 1960s, about half of the public
regularly mentioned issues relating to foreign affairs; in the 1990s, the corresponding average was fewer than 8 percent. And, even at the peak of public
interest in the Gulf War, when 97 percent of Americans claimed to be following
the conflict[14]—far more than ever attended to Vietnam—only a little more than
a third of the public (37 percent) rated the Gulf War as "the most important
problem facing the nation," slightly less than the overall average percentage
rating Vietnam as such in sixteen Gallup surveys conducted between 1966 and
1969 (39 percent).[15]

Figure 2.4 presents additional evidence that foreign affairs did not appear to
be of greater concern to typical Americans in the 1990s than in prior decades.
The figure tracks respondents from the General Social Survey (GSS), conducted
annually by the National Opinion Research Council (NORC) between 1974 and
1994. Respondents were asked to rate a series of six countries on a − 5 to + 5
scale, with + 5 indicating that the respondent "likes a given country very
much," − 5 indicating that the respondent "dislikes the country very much,"
and − 1 or + 1 indicating relatively neutral feelings. The overall mean scores
for six countries (Russia, China, Egypt, Israel, Japan, and Canada) are included
in the summary trend lines in the figure. Combined, these nations represent a
cross-section of America's allies and rivals.[16] Figure 2.4 presents two trends.
The first simply tracks respondents' average level of *disaffection*, over time,
toward the six countries during the entire range of years. For the second trend,

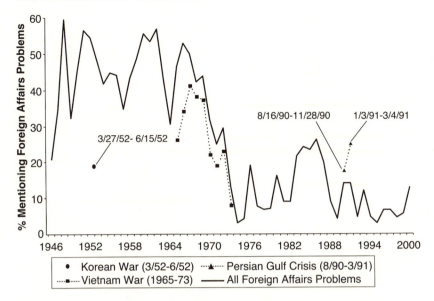

FIGURE 2.3. Annualized Trends in Percentage of Public Mentioning Foreign Affairs Issues in Gallup's "Most Important Problem Facing the Nation" Surveys, 1946–2000

QUESTION: What do you think is the most important problem facing this (the) country today?

SOURCES: (1) Niemi, Mueller, and Smith 1989, pp. 42–43; (2) Lexis-Nexis Academic Universe; (3) Mueller 1994, pp. 44–45

NOTES: (1) Minor variations in question wording were used in several of these surveys (see Niemi, Mueller, and Smith 1989); (2) Gulf crisis figures represent averages of August–December 1990 and January–March 1991. Gulf crisis surveys conducted for Gallup, *L.A. Times*, CBS/*NY Times*, ABC/*Washington Post*, *Time*/CNN and *Washington Post*; (3) Because Gallup asked the "most important problem" question only twice in 2000—both times in close proximity to U.S. military conflicts involving Iraq and Kosovo—I include seven non-Gallup polls (by CBS, NPR, and The Pew Research Center) in the 2000 average.

measuring *strength of affect*, I collapse the 10-point scale into a 5-point scale, with 0 indicating the most neutral feelings toward the six countries and 4 representing the strongest feelings—positive or negative. If Americans were more engaged with foreign policy in the 1990s than in earlier decades, one would expect the latter trend line to curve upward and the former to curve in either direction, but *not* to remain flat. In fact, neither curve displays a significant trend in either direction. Other than a brief downward shift in disaffection in 1991, most likely attributable to the multinational Persian Gulf War alliance and the collapse of the Soviet Union, the two curves remain largely flat.

At least according to the data presented in figures 2.3 and 2.4, individuals in the 1990s appeared substantially *less* worried about foreign affairs problems and no more affectionate or passionate toward foreign countries than were prior generations.[17] This presents an apparent paradox. Why would far more Ameri-

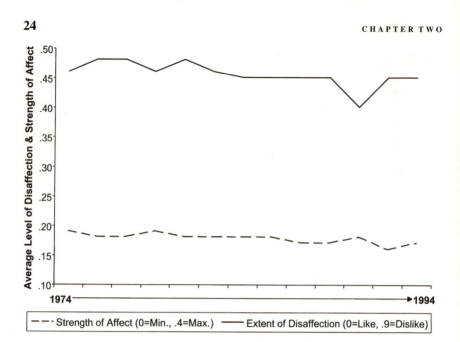

FIGURE 2.4. Trends in Average Level of Disaffection & Strength of Affect toward Foreign Countries, 1974–1994

QUESTION: How far up the [like/dislike] scale or how far down the scale would you rate the following countries?

The following six countries are included in both indexes: Russia, China, Egypt, Israel, Japan, and Canada.

SOURCE: General Social Surveys, 1974–1994

cans pay close attention to a war in 1991 than to a war two decades earlier that the contemporary publics considered more, or at least similarly, important, particularly at a time when Americans appeared to be losing interest in foreign affairs?

Resolving the Paradox

Unlike Vietnam, the Persian Gulf War crossed over from the traditional news media to the entertainment media to an unprecedented extent, and in near-real time. Mark McEwen, co-host of *CBS This Morning*, observed during a February 18, 1991, broadcast—while bombs were still dropping on Baghdad—that "the Gulf War has now reached prime-time television. . . . It's making itself felt in the plots of some of our favorite shows." The program's entertainment reporter, Steve Kmetko, added that thanks to technological advances allowing real-time coverage of war, episodic television programs were able to respond to real-world events in near-real time. As a result, even popular sitcoms and prime-time drama shows worked Gulf War–related issues directly into the plots of their weekly episodes. For instance, commenting on a Gulf War–related episode, Gerald McRainey, star of the network sitcom *Major Dad*, observed: "This show was necessary. We couldn't—we couldn't avoid doing it." Kmetko explained that the Gulf War appealed to entertainment-oriented programs because "both comedy and drama are based on conflict."[18] Recently, the Pentagon has begun referring to this sort of blending of fictional entertainment with real-world military issues and operations as "militainment" (de Moraes 2002).

How might this purely entertainment-oriented television coverage of the Gulf War help to explain the paradox of public attentiveness to Vietnam and the Persian Gulf War? One last anecdote, concerning the media's reaction to the stock market crash of October 27, 1997, will help answer this question. A few days after the crash, Public Radio International's *Marketplace* show—a daily business-analysis program broadcast nationwide—assessed the implications of a one-day 554-point, or 7.2 percent, drop in the Dow Jones Industrial Average. The program's anchor, after recalling an incident that morning in which a painter on the street had inquired "all about the market details," asked David Johnson, the program's regular stock market commentator, what he thought were the implications of the crash for the "real" economy. Johnson replied that most of the time "Main Street" ignores the daily happenings on Wall Street and in the financial markets in general. Yet, he pointed out, this was different. The market crash had grabbed Main Street's attention unlike any other Wall Street event in recent memory. How did he know this? Because, he said, "It was on everybody's tongues. . . . Rosie O'Donnell was talking about it. . . . It was certainly the center of the universe for a while" (*Marketplace*, October 31, 1997).

Johnson based his conclusion about the stock market on the breadth of media attention to the issue, which expanded well beyond the network evening news to include, among other outlets, Rosie O'Donnell's daytime entertainment-oriented talk show. I argue that an analogous *broadening* of media coverage of foreign military crises explains why the public was more attentive to the Persian Gulf War than to Vietnam. Simply stated, due to a series of economic and technological changes in the mass media, particularly television, even as the American people declare themselves in countless opinion polls to be *less* concerned with foreign affairs in the post–Cold War era than at any time since World War II, they are nonetheless becoming *more* attentive to a select few political issues, prominent among them foreign policy crises.

LEARNING ABOUT FOREIGN CRISES FROM THE SOFT NEWS MEDIA

A Model of Individual Information Consumption

This section evaluates both elements (benefits and costs) of the expected utility model. I then consider how individual decision processes and strategic media practices have combined to increase public attentiveness to foreign policy crises. I begin with a consideration of the expected benefits associated with paying attention to political information.

THE BENEFITS OF PAYING ATTENTION

In recent years, the traditional view of the typical citizen as "muddle-headed (lacking constraint) or empty-headed (lacking genuine attitudes)—or both" (Sniderman 1993; 47) has been challenged by what Sniderman (1993) terms "the New Look." Proponents of this view (Page and Shapiro 1992; Page, Shapiro, and Dempsey 1987; Sniderman, Brody, and Tetlock 1991; Sniderman 1993; Popkin 1994; Lupia and McCubbins 1998; and many others), while recognizing that most people possess limited factual political knowledge, argue that they are nonetheless capable of making reasoned decisions, based upon cognitive shortcuts, or heuristics, derived from life experiences and cues from trusted leaders or experts. Popkin (1994) terms this "low information rationality." According to this perspective, while people may not have evolved into "ambulatory encyclopedias" (Lupia and McCubbins 1998, 18), they are nonetheless capable of fulfilling their democratic responsibilities. Indeed, several studies (Jacobsen 1996; Jentleson 1992) have found that in recent history, where the mass public and elites have been at odds over public policy, such as in Vietnam, the public has usually been "right."

To the extent that individuals indeed make efficient use of limited information to arrive at reasoned decisions, it is unclear why citizens today ought to differ from prior generations in their ability to understand and evaluate the political environment. Thanks to the information revolution, vastly more information is available to typical individuals today compared to prior decades. Yet "low information rationality" suggests that this may be of limited practical consequence. In fact, one can easily imagine that if the information revolution has any effect at all, it might well be to produce greater confusion, as more individuals approach a state of information overload in which their decision-making capacity might actually erode.

Recent scholarship in cognitive psychology, however, suggests this latter concern is unwarranted. To understand why, it is important to recognize that information is not equivalent to knowledge. By itself, information is analogous to junk mail; just because one receives a hundred times as much junk mail today compared to earlier decades does not mean that one reads, or pays attention to, a hundred times more mail. Most is merely ignored or summarily discarded, treated as so much noise. For information to become knowledge, or to facilitate one's ability to form an opinion, it must be attended to, processed, and integrated into one's attitudes. Moreover, because attending to new information is costly—we ignore many other information stimuli to focus on any given piece of information (Wechtel 1967; Sniderman, Brody, and Tetlock 1991; Popkin 1994; Conover and Feldman 1984; Hamilton 2003; and many others)—individuals must economize on that to which they attend (Page and Shapiro 1992; Popkin 1994; Page, Shapiro, and Dempsey 1987; Sniderman 1993; Sniderman, Brody, and Tetlock 1991; Moon 1990; Simon 1979; and many others). Individuals therefore tend to pay attention only to information they believe is likely to result in beneficial, or useful, new knowledge (Lupia and McCubbins 1998), and for which the expected benefit outweighs the expected costs.[19]

As a result, it is not necessarily relevant that far more data are available in an era of cheap information, as individuals can simply raise an ever-higher perceptual screen with which to filter out the vast majority of that to which they are exposed. In fact, substantial empirical research has found no measurable increase over the past half-century in average levels of factual knowledge about (Delli Carpini and Keeter 1996) or interest and participation in politics (Niemi and Junn 1998; Nye, Zelikow, and King 1997; Rosenstone and Hansen 1993; Baum and Kernell 1999; Bennett 1986). Indeed, the evidence presented earlier in this chapter suggests this is precisely what has happened.

Similarly, for typical individuals, the marginal benefit of acquiring additional data about a given issue in order to increase one's confidence in a decision clearly declines as more data are accepted. Beyond some threshold, an individual has gathered all the information necessary to reach a decision with an acceptable degree of certainty. As the marginal benefit of continuing to pay attention begins to decline, individuals are increasingly likely to turn their attention elsewhere. Figure 2.5 illustrates the diminishing marginal benefits of paying attention to a given object as more and more information about it is accepted. In this hypothetical example, once the individual achieves 75 percent confidence in her opinion, she ceases paying attention to additional information about the object. For this hypothetical individual facing this hypothetical decision, 75 percent certainty is good enough.

This suggests that individuals today need not fundamentally differ from prior generations in their interactions with the political environment. While the volume of junk mail (i.e., raw information) confronting typical individuals today may vastly exceed that available in previous decades, the vast majority is, as has always been the case, simply ignored. Like their counterparts in prior decades, contemporary individuals pay attention to enough information to reach a decision with an acceptable degree of confidence, at which point they simply screen out any unneeded additional data and turn their attention elsewhere. For individuals who consider politics of little value, this threshold may be quite low.

According to this model, the primary difference between individuals in previous decades and today is that the latter individuals are likely to encounter more information and so, out of necessity, make greater use of their perceptual filters. Ironically, barring substantially expanded cognitive capacity, it seems likely that if typical individuals failed to filter out, or ignore, the excessive information stimuli to which they are exposed, information overload might have caused average levels of political knowledge to have *fallen* in the information age.

Most importantly, if paying attention to information is costly, and if individuals today have a similar, finite, capacity for paying attention—which can be devoted to news about politics or anything else—as did their counterparts in previous decades, then there remain only two plausible explanations for any increased public attentiveness to politics or foreign policy. Either the perceived benefit of information about foreign crises has increased or, alternatively, the cognitive cost of paying attention to such information may have declined. Sep-

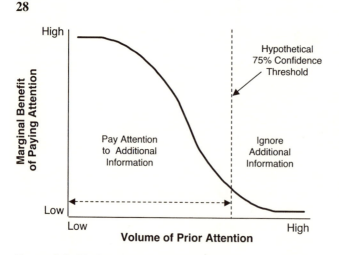

FIGURE 2.5. The Marginal Benefit of Paying Attention as a Function of Volume of Prior Attention to a Given Object

arately or in combination, these two possibilities appear capable of producing an increase in public attentiveness to select political issues, such as foreign crises.

Upon reflection, however, the first possibility seems implausible. The previously cited empirical evidence clearly shows fairly consistent levels of factual political knowledge among the American public since World War II. This suggests that people's perceptual filters have remained effective. Individuals appear not to have changed in their strategies for coping with the political environment (beyond, perhaps, more frequently employing their perceptual filters). Moreover, not only has the public's interest in foreign affairs failed to increase since World War II, but there is also substantial evidence that the public has retained a fairly constant overall appetite for politics in general. For instance, figure 2.6 plots over-time trends in NES respondents' self-reported interest in government and public affairs (1964–2000) and political participation (1956–2000). The former curve trends slightly downward, while the latter curve remains fairly flat. This suggests that NES respondents in the 1990s were no more, and perhaps modestly less, interested in public affairs and no more likely to participate in electoral politics than were their counterparts in the 1950s and 1960s.

These data, combined with well-documented trends toward increased public apathy (Bennett 1986) and cynicism about politics (Nye, Zelikow, and King 1997; Dionne 1991; Rosenstone and Hansen 1993; Miller 1974), suggest it is highly unlikely that the typical individual's expected benefit from political information in general, or information about foreign affairs in particular, has increased. In fact, this evidence suggests that, for most individuals, the overall expected benefit from political information is likely to have remained fairly stable, or perhaps even fallen somewhat. Therefore, to the extent that the public is more attentive in recent years to select political issues, such as foreign crises, we must look elsewhere for our explanation.

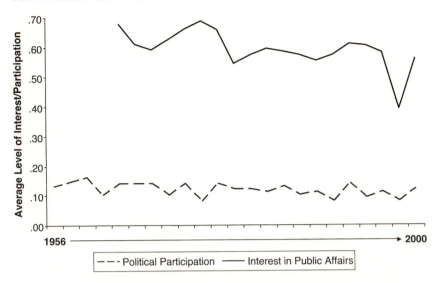

FIGURE 2.6. Trends in Levels of Interest in Public Affairs and Political Participation in
NES Surveys, 1956–2000

Interest in Public Affairs index is based on the following question: How often do
you follow what's going on in government and public affairs? Responses are coded:
0 = hardly at all, .33 = only now and then, .67 = some of the time, and 1 = most
of the time.

Political Participation index is based on the following five questions: (1) Did you
talk to people about voting? (2) Did you attend political meetings? (3) Did you work
for a party or candidate? (4) Did you wear a campaign button or sticker? and (5) Did
you give money to a party or candidate? I created an index by adding together the
responses from all five questions—each of which is coded 1 for a "yes" response and
0 otherwise—and normalizing the resulting scale to a 0–1 interval, where 1 represents
maximum participation.

THE COSTS OF PAYING ATTENTION

I now turn to the second possible explanation: a decline in the cognitive cost of
paying attention to information about foreign crises. Many individuals perceive
politics as offering little in the way of personal benefits. In fact, as cynicism
about politics and the complexity of modern life (Putnam 2000) have increased
over the past few decades, more Americans have opted to largely tune out
politics (S. Bennett 1986; Broder 1994).

Of course, for most Americans, there are *some* political issues that are of
interest under at least *some* circumstances. For instance, a largely apolitical
senior citizen may pay close attention to a congressional debate on privatizing
social security. Many Americans, however, are not interested in most of the
day-to-day political happenings in Washington or in their state capitals. Such
individuals tend to pay attention to politics only when a particularly high-profile
debate arises involving an issue with respect to which they perceive themselves
as having a personal stake. For many individuals, such occasions can be quite

infrequent. For these people, then, when it comes to most political issues, the costs of paying attention usually exceed the expected benefits, thereby rendering paying attention *not* cost-effective. The availability of twenty-four-hour news channels—like CNN, MSNBC, CNBC, and Fox—is unlikely to increase the amount of political information attended to by such individuals, who will simply ignore the increased volume of "junk mail" to which they may be inadvertently exposed in the course of channel surfing.[20]

As noted, the cognitive costs of paying attention can be usefully grouped into two categories: opportunity and transaction costs. Opportunity costs represent the inherent trade-off between paying attention to a piece of information and devoting one's attention to other things. For instance, by watching a given television program, an individual forecloses the option of watching another program or devoting that period of time to another activity, like playing baseball. Whenever an individual elects to pay attention to one piece of information, he or she pays the opportunity cost of *not* paying attention to, or doing, something else. Transaction costs, in turn, represent the time and effort required to undertake a given activity, such as paying attention to information about a foreign crisis. The more time and energy required to carry out the activity, the greater the transaction costs.

If the opportunity or transaction costs associated with paying attention to information about certain political issues, such as foreign crises, have declined, this could account for increased public attentiveness to such issues. Indeed, my argument regarding individuals' capacity to screen out (ignore) excessive information suggests that for an uninterested individual to *avoid* screening out political information, its cost would have to approach zero, thereby removing any incentive to filter it out. I shall argue that with respect to political information, the soft news media are far more likely than traditional news outlets to accomplish this. I now consider both opportunity and transaction costs in greater detail.

Beginning with the former, given the extremely low value to many individuals of news about politics in general or foreign policy in particular, the only way they are likely to pay attention to such information is if the trade-off required is negligible, thereby removing any incentive to ignore it. One means of mitigating the perceived trade-off might be to attach, or *piggyback*, high-cost political information to low-cost entertainment-oriented information. Piggybacking would allow individuals to learn about politics passively (Zukin with Snyder 1984), even if they are neither interested in the subject matter nor motivated to learn about it (Zukin with Snyder 1984; Blumler and McQuail 1969; Wamsley and Pride 1972; Fitzsimmons and Osburn 1968; Robinson 1974). Political information might thus become a *free* bonus, or an *incidental by-product*, of paying attention to entertainment-oriented information.[21]

In earlier decades, in deciding which media to consume, individuals frequently confronted the choice of watching the evening news or reading a newspaper to learn about politics or of watching entertainment-oriented programming. For many individuals, entertainment almost always trumped news about politics (as it continues to do today).[22] The opportunity costs of paying attention to political news were simply too high. In effect, piggybacking might, on occasion, render any trade-off between being entertained and learning about politics moot by, in effect, transforming a select few of the major political issues of the day *into* the entertainment that people seek.[23]

This does not, however, imply that transforming news into entertainment will affect all viewers similarly. Indeed, survey evidence (e.g., *Media Monitor* 1997a; Pew Research Center 1998b) indicates that most people who consume traditional news do so primarily (albeit not exclusively) to learn about the issues of the day.[24] This suggests that increasing the entertainment value of news is unlikely to significantly affect these individuals' attentiveness to political news. Indeed, such individuals have *already* determined that political news is worth their time and effort. Watching soft news shows is unlikely to affect this calculus, even if they occasionally cover political issues. Rather, only individuals who would not otherwise be exposed to politics are likely to be affected by encountering political coverage in the soft news media or by piggybacking.

Yet, even for these latter, politically uninterested individuals, piggybacking is only possible if information about a political issue can be attached to entertainment-oriented information *without* increasing the costs of paying attention or undermining the entertainment value of the program. This involves transaction costs. Along these lines, research in cognitive psychology has found that for an attitude to influence an individual's opinion, it must be both *available* (stored in memory) and *accessible* (readily retrievable from memory) (Aldrich, Sullivan, and Borgida 1989; Ottati and Wyer 1990; McGuire 1969, 1973; Fazio 1989). Media coverage, in turn, is the single most important factor in determining which issues and attitudes become highly accessible to the mass public, at least temporarily (Iyengar 1990, 1992; Krugman and Hartley 1970).[25] The process of rendering an issue accessible by exposing an individual to significant amounts of information about it is known as *priming* (Iyengar 1990, 1993; Miller and Krosnick 1996; Iyengar and Kinder 1987).[26]

Greater accessibility, in turn, means lower transaction costs. In effect, once a media outlet primes an issue, like a foreign crisis—and most likely also *frames* (e.g., Ansolabehere, Behr, and Iyengar 1993; Druckman 2001a, 2001b; Gamson and Modigliani 1987) it in easily understandable terms (which I refer to as *cheap framing*)—the issue, along with the individual's attitudes toward it, becomes increasingly accessible.[27] This process then reduces the incremental costs of paying attention to *additional* information about the issue. Along these lines, Lisa Gregorish, executive producer of Reality Programming, Telepictures, at Fox, and producer of the tabloid news program *Extra*, observed that, upon encountering a story like the U.S. bombing of Iraq on a soft news program, an individual will feel "plugged into it already" if he or she later encounters additional information about the issue on a traditional news program, and may therefore be more willing to watch the traditional news version of the story.[28]

Communications scholars, in turn, have identified a number of frames that are widely employed in explaining issues in the news. For instance, Neuman,

Just, and Crigler (1992) identify a number of common frames that are readily recognized and understood by most individuals. These include "us versus them,"[29] "human impact," "powerlessness,"[30] "economic" and "morality" frames. To this list, Powlick and Katz (1998b) add an "injustice" frame (which is similar to "morality"). Indeed, Graber (1984) found that several of these common frames—"human impact," "morality," and "injustice"—resonated strongly with her interview subjects and frequently informed their political judgments.[31]

The use of cognitive frames that are highly accessible for typical individuals (i.e. cheap framing) is likely to have two primary effects. First, paying attention to news that employs a highly accessible frame requires less cognitive energy than attending to such information presented in a traditional news format (e.g., newspaper or network news). Such information is, after all, cheap. Indeed, absent cheap framing, piggybacking would almost certainly fail. Second, receiving some cheap information about an issue, such as a foreign crisis, *primes* the issue. This reduces the marginal transaction costs of paying attention to additional information later on, as an individual's attitudes about the issue become increasingly accessible. Having been provided a *context* within which to evaluate information about an issue, an individual will likely find subsequent discussions of it less confusing and more compelling, and thus presumably less costly to focus upon. In fact, if, through cheap framing, information about a political issue can be piggybacked to low-cost and high-benefit entertainment-oriented information, any transaction costs associated with paying attention to the political information are virtually eliminated.[32]

Initial exposure to information about an issue, such as a foreign crisis, in a cheap information format also makes it easier to incorporate subsequent bits of information into a preexisting "causal narrative" (Popkin 1994, 72–73; see also Holyoak and Thagard 1995 on the role of "analogic reasoning"). A causal narrative is an informational shortcut whereby individuals create "scripts" or "scenarios" (i.e., contexts) about issue areas, general beliefs, and values. The narrative is a basic storyline concerning how the individual feels about a given issue area. Subsequent information related to that issue area is evaluated through what Popkin calls a "goodness-of-fit test"—that is, an assessment of how the new information relates to the individual's preexisting beliefs, or narrative, concerning that issue. Information consistent with the pre-existing narrative is more easily incorporated and hence is subsequently more accessible.[33]

Most individuals construct mutually inconsistent causal narratives, which, though co-existing, rarely come into contact with one another. Reconciling multiple conflicting narratives requires expending substantial cognitive energy, and is thus costly (Tetlock 1985, 1986; R. Smith 1993). Complex issues that cannot be related to a readily accessible frame are relatively likely to prime potentially contradictory narratives. In contrast, issues that are easily explained through reference to the most widely held cognitive frames (e.g., morality, human impact, etc.) are less likely to prime conflicting causal narratives, thereby reducing a person's need to expend cognitive energy for reconciling potentially conflicting narratives. As a result, ceteris paribus, individuals are more likely to prefer to pay attention to cheap information rather than to more complex or morally ambiguous information. Along these lines, Smith, Bruner, and White (1956, 261) argue that a basic human requirement in dealing with the world is "a need to minimize surprise." So, for instance, relative to a soft news program, a viewer is more likely to encounter in a traditional news outlet a complex presentation of information concerning a given issue (Hamilton 2003) that may weigh the relative merits of multiple perspectives, or place the issue into a broader policy context. This increases the likelihood of a "surprise," and makes such information more costly.[34]

As the previous comment by Lisa Gregorish implied, once some cheap information about an issue, such as a foreign crisis, succeeds in grabbing an individual's attention, that individual is more likely to pay attention to *additional* information about the issue, perhaps in a traditional news format. In other words, once the issue has been primed by a cheap information source, the pertinent causal narrative(s) will subsequently be more readily accessible, thereby making it less difficult (i.e., less costly) to incorporate additional, related information (Iyengar 1990), even if it is relatively more complex, like that presented by traditional news programs (Hamilton 2003). Hence, cheap information sources can serve, in effect, as "gatekeepers" with respect to more costly information sources.

I argued earlier that people will pay attention to news only when the expected benefits outweigh the expected costs of doing so. And I presented evidence that the expected benefits of attending to politics, including foreign policy crises, have remained relatively constant throughout the post–World War II era. In contrast, my review of the cost side of the ledger suggests that if, as I have conjectured, the soft news media have in recent years engaged in cheap framing and piggybacking, they may have substantially reduced the expected costs of paying attention to foreign crises. This, in turn, might help account for any trend toward increased public attentiveness to foreign crises. (In the Appendix to this chapter, I discuss the theoretical rationale for locating the changes described herein on the cost, rather than the benefit, side of the expected utility ledger.) In the next section, I demonstrate that television broadcasters have, in fact, systematically and aggressively engaged in both strategies.

Technological Innovation and the Pressures of the Marketplace

A DIRECT MARKETING REVOLUTION IN TELEVISION

The previous discussion suggested that a decline in the cognitive costs of paying attention to information about foreign crises might help explain increased public attentiveness to such events. This, however, begs the question of *why* the costs of such information might have declined. In this section, I address the latter issue. I present evidence that television broadcasters have indeed, in recent years, systematically employed cheap framing and piggybacking strategies, in tandem, with the apparent effect of reducing the cognitive costs of paying attention to information about select high-profile political issues, including foreign crises.

Kalb (1998b) observes: "For the past 20 years, we have been the beneficiaries—or the victims—of a vast technological revolution that has transformed the way we get and process information." Indeed, over the past several decades, the mass media—including television, radio, and some elements of the print media[35]—have undergone what is best described as a revolution in direct marketing. Yet, while all three media formats have evolved in similar ways (in at least some respects), innovations in television broadcasting, due to its overwhelming dominance in American culture, hold far more important implications for American society than changes in either the radio or print media. Hence, the following discussion focuses primarily on television.[36]

The television industry has evolved over the past fifty years from an oligopoly to a competitive market. In the 1950s and 1960s, television was dominated by the three broadcast networks, which presented political information primarily through their largely undifferentiated network evening news programs. Referring to the pre-1980 period, one senior network executive recalled "when viewers turned on the TV set, they had five choices, and the networks were three of them . . . [and they] collectively accounted for about 90 percent of the television audience" (Lowry 1997). The only other options available to consumers were listening to the radio or reading a newspaper or magazine. The audience simply had nowhere else to go, and was therefore essentially "captive" (Baum and Kernell 1999).

When most viewers received only a few channels, virtually all programming—news and entertainment—competed for the same audience. As a result, programming converged to the lowest common denominator, as risk-averse broadcasters attempted to provide the type of programming assumed to attract the largest possible portion of the overall audience.[37] Program differentiation was considered risky and economically inefficient (Webster and Lichty 1991).

Absent any significant competition, the major networks faced little economic pressure to earn a profit from their evening news broadcasts. In December, 1962, William Paley, creator of CBS, told a group of CBS correspondents "You guys cover the news; I've got Jack Benny to make money for me" (Kalb 1998a, 10). Along these lines, an official at the Federal Communications Commission (FCC) I interviewed recalled that in the early years of television, broadcasters did not anticipate earning a profit from their nightly newscasts, which were limited to fifteen minutes per evening. Rather, they considered performance-oriented entertainment programming as their primary source of income.[38] News was a loss leader (Hallin 1991; Grossman 2000), seen primarily as a civic responsibility or a means of buying respectability (Auletta 1991; Kalb 1998a; Hess 1998; Grossman 2000). Along these lines, NBC News Vice President David Corvo commented: "In the past . . . the news divisions were not expected to make the kind of money they are expected to make now. . . . They put forward their news divisions as a way of showing they were doing public service" (Committee of Concerned Journalists 1998b). Indeed, broadcasters were required by the FCC to include specific minimum quotas of news and public affairs programming in their schedules.[39] In a 1960 report, for instance, the FCC explicitly defined news programming as a "major element . . . necessary to the public interest" (Federal Communication Commission 1998).

In contrast, the growth over the past several decades of cable television, satellite broadcasting, and, most recently, the Internet, combined with a relaxed regulatory environment, has created a highly competitive media marketplace (Patterson 2000).[40] The rise of cable television represents perhaps the single most important technological innovation responsible for facilitating this changing role of news programming (Baum and Kernell 1999).[41] Between 1969 and 2002, the number of American households subscribing to cable expanded from about 6 percent to almost 70 percent. The average number of channels available to cable subscribers has also expanded dramatically, from less than fifteen in 1983 to seventy-four in 2000 (Webster and Lichty 1991; Bednarski 2001). Thanks to fiber optics and digital satellite broadcasting, many individuals now receive well in excess of one hundred channels. Combined, these developments represent an explosion of consumer choices.[42]

The increasingly competitive television environment forced broadcasters to adapt their programming strategies. The optimal strategy was no longer to exclusively attempt to reach a preponderance of the overall television audience, but rather to attract a loyal segment, or "niche," of the audience (Webster and Lichty 1991).[43] As a result, as the number of competitors increased, programming—including that of the major networks—grew more differentiated.[44] This changing environment was reflected in a comment by CBS chairman and CEO Michael H. Jordan: "Yes, we want to hold on to journalistic and other standards. But I don't aspire to that Paleyesque role. This is a business" (Kalb 1998a, 10). Indeed, in 1984, in response to emerging changes in the norms of the media marketplace, and at the behest of the broadcast industry, FCC regulations mandating minimum levels of news and public affairs content were overturned (FCC 1998).[45]

Television has always depended on advertising dollars for its survival. Yet, broadcasters did not begin to recognize that news—at least beyond *local* news—could be a highly profitable enterprise until the early 1980s (Kalb 1998b; Zaller 1999), not coincidentally the period when cable and video technology became widely accessible. After all, news is far less expensive to produce in large quantities than original entertainment programming (Davis and Owen 1998; Kalb 1998a, 1998b).

For instance, one original episode of the NBC newsmagazine *Dateline* costs about $500,000. This contrasts with the approximately $13 million price tag for a single episode of NBC's hit drama series *ER* at the peak of its popularity (Bark 1998). By examining the Nielsen ratings and advertising costs for these two programs, we can translate these per-episode costs into a cost per viewer. A typical episode of *ER*, at the time television's top-rated original series, attracted an average of about 14.6 million households between September 1998 and September 1999. In that same period, an average of about 9.3 million households tuned in to *Dateline*.[46] *Dateline* thus attracted roughly 64 percent of the audience of *ER*. Simple division, however, reveals that NBC spent nearly seventeen times more money per household for *ER* (about $0.89), than for *Dateline* (about $0.053). Thirty seconds of advertising on *ER* costs almost 3.8 times as much as on *Dateline* ($565,000 versus $150,000) (Graham 1997; Bark 1998). Yet, additional division reveals that NBC must air twenty-three thirty-second commercials during an episode of *ER* before breaking even on its $13 million investment. In contrast, NBC earns a profit in its fourth commercial aired during *Dateline*.

To estimate how much advertising revenue these programs actually earn, I monitored an episode of *ER* (aired on March 24, 2000). During that episode, NBC broadcast twenty-four commercials between the opening and closing credits, thereby barely surpassing the break-even point. (The networks typically broadcast between twenty and thirty commercials per hour in prime time). If we take twenty-four commercials as the norm, then a typical *Dateline* episode would earn a profit of $3.1 million ($3.6 million gross, less $500,000 for production). This compares to a profit of $560,000 for *ER* ($13.56 million gross, less $13 million for production). Even if we assume the maximum of thirty commercials per episode, *Dateline* still nets $200,000 more than *ER*. This suggests that newsmagazines such as *Dateline* are a greater programming value for network investments.[47] Moreover, it is far easier to create another *Dateline*-like program, with an audience comparable to that for *Dateline*, than it is to reproduce *ER*, along with the show's extraordinary popularity.[48] These data are summarized in Table 2.1.

Like any business enterprise, the news business had little choice but to respond to a changing marketplace. To be profitable it was necessary to capture and maintain a substantial audience, much of which was not interested in large doses of dispassionate reporting of the political issues of the day. Hence, for news, like entertainment programming, to become a profit center for television networks, it needed to appeal to a large enough audience to attract significant advertising revenue. Merely cloning traditional network evening newscasts across more channels and time periods was unlikely to broaden audience appeal, unless the entertainment value of such programming could be enhanced.

In their efforts to make news profitable, the networks were able to draw upon a proven model of the successful blending of news and entertainment. Local television news producers had long since discovered the financial benefit of making news entertaining.[49] So, as market competition increased, the programming strategies of profit-conscious news organizations increasingly came to resemble those of the entertainment media (Picard 1998). In other words, when news organizations sought to find new ways to reduce the cognitive costs to viewers of consuming news, they did so by making it look more like entertainment and by seeking to provide channels and programs catering to virtually every type of taste and preference. Warren Littlefield, president of NBC entertainment, thus noted: "One challenge for broadcasters is to figure out who you [the viewer] are and to be true to who you are" (Hofmeister 1997).

TABLE 2.1. Cost Effectiveness for NBC of *Dateline* vs. *ER*

	Dateline	*ER*
Production cost per episode (1998)	$0.5 million	$13 million
Average audience, 9/98–9/99 (households)	9.3 million	14.6 million
Average cost per household	*$0.053*	*$0.89*
Cost per 30-second commercial (1997–98)	$0.15 million	$0.565 million
Typical commercials per episode (3/24/00)	24	24
Profit for one episode given 24 commercials*	$3.1 million	$0.56 million
Profit given maximum of 30 commercials*	$4 million	$3.8 million

*Represents gross income, less production cost, per episode.

The net effect is that traditional news programming has been supplemented, and in some respects supplanted, by a variety of new types of entertainment-oriented informational programs, which I have collectively termed the soft news media. Relative to traditional news programs, soft news outlets place a greater emphasis on episodic human-interest-oriented stories with highly accessible themes—themes that are particularly suitable for cheap framing. Conversely, the soft news media are far less likely than their traditional news counterparts to employ *thematic* frames, which provide a broader context for understanding the causes and consequences of a given issue or event, but which also tend to be more complex and, hence, less accessible for politically uninterested individuals.[50]

In other words, whereas traditional news programs report the news in order to *inform* the audience, at least in some significant measure, the soft news media seek almost exclusively to *entertain* the audience. Recognizing a limited public demand for political news, television broadcasters responded by transforming news into an inexpensively produced form of entertainment.[51] Indeed, regarding her programming strategy for Fox's soft news programs, Gregorish commented: "To me it's all about disseminating information in the most entertaining fashion."[52]

THE RISE OF THE SOFT NEWS MEDIA

Two examples of the dramatic proliferation of the soft news media are entertainment and tabloid TV newsmagazines and daytime and late-night talk shows. Where Johnny Carson once enjoyed a virtual monopoly in late-night TV talk, the late-night airwaves have grown cluttered in recent years with such *Tonight Show* rivals as David Letterman, Conan O'Brien, Bill Maher, and others. Even popular "shock" radio hosts, like Howard Stern and Don Imus, have their own TV talk shows. And in the daytime, the genre pioneered by Phil Donahue in the 1980s has proliferated to the point where today over a dozen talk shows, ranging from *The Jenny Jones Show* to *The Oprah Winfrey Show*, air daily on broadcast television.[53] Entertainment and tabloid newsmagazine shows, in turn, pioneered in the late 1980s by *A Current Affair*, now dominate the early-evening hours. Some of these programs (e.g., *Extra* and *Access Hollywood*) air several times per day.[54]

One example of an arguably less clear-cut program format, in turn, is the network TV newsmagazine. While such programs do cover hard news issues, particularly when major events arise, recent content analysis studies have found that they focus *primarily* on soft news topics, like celebrity profiles and crime dramas. For instance, a content analysis of stories on *60 Minutes* between January and June 1998 (Kalb 1998b) revealed that 60 percent of the sixty-two segments aired addressed soft news topics (i.e., celebrity profiles, "can you believe?" investigative reports, or lifestyle pieces), while only 13 percent dealt with traditional hard news topics (most of which, interestingly, involved foreign policy). Zaller (1999), in turn, finds that between 1968 and 1998, the score for *60 Minutes* on a news quality index he developed fell by over half. And the news quality score for *60 Minutes greatly* exceeded those of its competitors (like *Dateline* and *20/20*).

A 1998 study (CCJ 1998a) found that five prime time network newsmagazines—*20/20, 48 Hours, 60 Minutes, Prime Time Live* and *Dateline*—devoted a combined total average of just 5.5 percent of their coverage during the fall season of 1997 to topics relating to either government, military/national security policy, foreign affairs, education, or the economy. In sharp contrast, they devoted nearly half of their total airtime to stories pertaining to entertainment and celebrities, personality profiles, crime or human-interest topics. During the same period, the corresponding averages for network news stories (ABC, CBS and NBC) were 35 percent of airtime devoted to the aforementioned *hard* news topics and just 12 percent devoted to the above *soft* news topics. Overall, government and foreign affairs were the two most common topics on network evening newscasts, while the top topics on network newsmagazines were crime, human interest, and personality/profile. Finally, along the same lines, a content analysis by Hamilton (2003) found that network newsmagazine programs placed far greater emphasis on dramatic human-interest topics and themes than did traditional national newscasts.

And this genre has expanded dramatically. Prior to 1980, *60 Minutes* was the only prime-time network newsmagazine on television. Since that time, particularly over the past decade, *60 Minutes* has attracted increasing competition. The major networks have begun to routinely offer newsmagazines in prime time virtually every evening. In fall 1998, for instance, the three primary broadcast networks combined offered ten prime-time hours per week of newsmagazines, and CNN added four additional hours per week of such magazines (Weinstein 1998).

Perhaps the best evidence of the prominence of the soft news media is the dramatic proliferation of the types of stories favored by soft news programs. According to one content analysis investigation, conducted by the Center for Media and Public Affairs (*Media Monitor* 1997b), the most popular topics for tabloid television programs include crime and violence, natural disasters, and socially deviant or self-destructive individual behavior. A second study (Media Monitor 2000), found that the number of network news stories about murder increased fivefold between 1990 and 2000. A third study (*Media Monitor* 1997b) found that stories about popular culture have also dramatically increased in frequency. Finally, a 1998 study by the Committee of Concerned Journalists (CCJ 1998b) concluded that celebrity, scandal, gossip, and other "human interest" stories have increased as a share of total media coverage over the past twenty years from 15 to 43 percent.

GIVING THE PEOPLE WHAT THEY WANT

Not surprisingly, while all news outlets strive to match their programming content to the interests of their audiences (Hamilton 2003), the types of frames emphasized by the soft news media tend to mirror average individuals' perceptions of issues in the news to a greater extent than is the case in traditional news outlets. Neuman, Just, and Crigler (1992) found that in explaining a series of news stories, their interview subjects differed substantially from the traditional news media in the relative emphasis placed upon the previously noted series of highly accessible cognitive frames, reproduced in table 2.2.

As one might expect, those most frequently mentioned by the interview subjects are, due to their broad accessibility, featured more prominently in soft news programming. "Human impact" was the most widely employed cognitive frame among Neuman, Just, and Crigler's interview subjects. This frame was employed by the interview subjects twice as frequently as by the traditional news media. As previously discussed, the soft news media, unlike traditional news outlets, heavily emphasize the human impact frame. And "morality," which was mentioned nearly four times more often by individual interview subjects as by the traditional news media, is also a common theme of soft news programming. The aforementioned content analysis of tabloid news programs (*Media Monitor* 1997a) found that such programs regularly frame their stories in *moralistic* terms, passing judgment on the central actors in more than half of the stories examined in the study.

These same themes—human impact and morality—are prevalent in most major foreign policy crises (as well as in some domestic political events), which make such events highly amenable to episodic storylines incorporating cheap framing and piggybacking. Hence, it is not surprising that soft news programs would cover such issues. And in chapter 3, I present evidence that soft news programs do in fact present substantial coverage of foreign policy crises, and do so almost exclusively in an episodic manner. This suggests that the previously described changes in news programming have potentially important implications for media coverage of foreign policy, as well as a select few domestic political issues. Indeed, by making news about certain high-profile political issues accessible, the soft news media increase the likelihood that politically inattentive individuals will pay attention to, and learn about, them (Eveland and Scheufele 2000).

TABLE 2.2. Cognitive Frames Emphasized by News Media and Individuals

Frames	% Emphasis by News Media	% Emphasis by Individuals
Conflict	29	6
Moral values	4	15
Economics	16	21
Powerlessness	33	22
Human impact	18	36

Source: Neuman, Just, and Crigler 1992, 75.

Why Entertainment Shows Cover Politics and Foreign Policy

WHAT SELLS? THE INCENTIVES OF SOFT NEWS PROGRAMMERS

While, like traditional news outlets, soft news programs do appear to regularly cover foreign crises, they do not necessarily do so in the same manner or for the same reasons. Soft news programs cover foreign crises, as well as a select few domestic political issues, because, in addition to the usual stories of infidelity, crime, and other dramatic, human-interest-oriented topics, certain aspects of foreign crises—those involving the potential or actual use of military force—contain many of the elements that appeal to their audiences. Hence, soft news shows can entertain their audiences by exploiting dramatic themes borrowed from select political events.[55] And rather than focus on the more arcane aspects of a crisis, like military tactics or geopolitical ramifications, soft news programs frame the issues in terms appealing to their entertainment-seeking viewers, who may not be interested in learning about military strategy or international politics.

The Persian Gulf War was the first large-scale U.S. military conflict of the information age, and it became the quintessential water-cooler event. The soft news media rapidly recognized that the Gulf crisis represented an ideal "soap opera" for their program formats, one that would likely earn substantial ratings. Gregorish explained the appeal of the Gulf War, and the aspects of the war that were, and were not, appealing to soft news programs:

> Because there are so many of our guys over there, there are going to be those poignant stories of the families waiting for word, sitting back here, when it's on our turf. It's the domestic angle. . . . There are the Schwarzkopfs of the world, and the Colin Powells. . . . Those are really interesting guys and they are calling all the shots, so I [will] probably do in-depth profiles on them; "who are these guys?" But when it comes to every single detail of what's going on, that's not [our mission]. You have to know who you are.[56]

Hence, the massive coverage of the Gulf War by nonnetwork news programs—including that of the major networks themselves (e.g., morning variety shows and prime-time TV news magazines), local news broadcasts, daytime and late-night talk shows, entertainment and tabloid news programs and various cable networks—arguably set in motion a spiral of attention resulting in greater and more sustained public attentiveness to the Gulf War than to any other event in U.S. polling history (at least until the O. J. Simpson trial).

Gregorish offered a similar rationale for soft news coverage of other, more recent foreign crises. Of Operation Desert Fox, the December 1998 U.S. and UK bombing campaign against Iraq, she commented that it provided "great pictures" and "sensational value."[57] Regarding the same conflict, Barry Berk, supervising producer of the entertainment news program *Access Hollywood*, reflected: "Does it come under the general guidelines of what *Access Hollywood* is about, covering a war? No. A war certainly isn't entertainment. It's got nothing to do with Hollywood. [But] celebrities were talking about it. . . . It's great drama. It's a good media story."[58]

Commenting on the intense soft news coverage of an incident in which a U.S. pilot was shot down over Kosovo during the spring 1999 NATO air war against Serbia, Gregorish observed that because it was a survival story, culminating in a dramatic rescue, "it's every single thing you're looking for that makes up a good story."[59] With respect to the same incident, Berk added: "It's a dramatic story for all of us. It's a human-interest story for all of us. It's got everybody's attention. But they'll [traditional news programs] approach it from the military side, what's being done. And we'll go after the Hollywood producer and is he going to try to make something out of this story, make it into a movie. That's a different approach."[60]

As the preceding discussion should make clear, the appeal of foreign crises for soft news programmers does *not* lie in their *international* or *political* nature. In describing the general characteristics that make a story attractive to a soft news program, Gregorish commented: "Simplicity transcends everything usually. Simplicity with great pictures or a riveting storyteller or nicely choreographed and packaged will always win out."[61] It is not a coincidence that sex scandals and salacious murder trials, when they arise, tend to dominate soft news programs. Such topics are readily understandable within a basic intuitive context, or causal narrative, which for most individuals is readily accessible. Moreover, such issues easily lend themselves to presentation in moralistic and judgmental terms, which are, as noted, a specialty of the soft news media.

These factors, in combination, give an issue a high degree of potential entertainment value. When asked why the soft news media presented extensive coverage of the Monica Lewinsky scandal, Gregorish commented, "[The scandal] had everything. It had sex. It had power. You name it; it had all the ingredients that were saucy, that make it . . . a sensational story."[62] Hence, it is not surprising that the Lewinsky scandal is located fairly high up—at the 86th percentile (through August 2001)—on the Pew Research Center's aforementioned news interest index, which has tracked news stories that have been closely followed by the public since 1986.

Indeed, the stark contrast between public interest in Bill Clinton's Whitewater scandal relative to the Monica Lewinsky sex scandal illustrates the importance of these qualities. The Whitewater investigation involved numerous complex issues that could not be easily summarized in a straightforward and emotionally compelling manner. In other words, many people lacked pertinent accessible causal narratives (i.e., a context) through which to process information about financial misdeeds involving an obscure land deal in Arkansas. President Clinton's infamous relationship with Monica Lewinsky, in contrast, was readily explainable to typical Americans in a few words: the president cheated on his wife, got caught, and lied about it. Moreover, the most widely recognizable issues of morality, including adultery and deceit, were at the center of the scandal. Thus, even when all of the network news programs intensely covered the Whitewater controversy for extended periods of time, soft news programs, and even local television newscasts, largely ignored the investigation, and overall public interest in the Whitewater affair remained fairly low. This issue never became a water-cooler event, reaching no higher than the 57th percentile on the Pew Research Center's news interest index. Commenting on the absence of soft news coverage of Whitewater, Gregorish explained:

> The more convoluted the scandal, the more difficult it is for people to understand, the more they distance themselves and the more I don't think the [soft news] media will take it on. Just because there are so many [elements to the scandal] . . . you have to speak tangentially almost. It's not a real cut and dried beginning, middle, and end story. You have to get into so much minutiae and so much detail that it's lost on the average person.[63]

In contrast, as previously noted, soft news media coverage of the Monica Lewinsky scandal was consistently intense. This was the quintessential water-cooler event. Berk commented, "It's good TV. It's what people were talking about. What was the buzz? And that's all people were talking about was Lewinsky. It's like covering the Simpson trial." Berk contrasted this with the Whitewater scandal, about which he observed:

> It's not our story. It's a pure political story, involving the President of the United States and the First Lady, and it's a money scandal. And that's just not what we're about. If you took it apart, and dissected it, and said "okay, is this what *Access Hollywood* is about, or *Entertainment Tonight*?" [the answer is] No. There's just no reason to do it. It's not the kind of story that . . . our clients, our stations, buy our show [for]. . . . It's really not even an editorial decision. It's something that is not even considered.[64]

Hence, not surprisingly, the soft news media offered extensive coverage of the Lewinsky scandal, and many such outlets were rewarded with unprecedented boosts in their ratings.[65] One news content monitoring report found that in the week following the January 21 breaking of the story, there were 142 scandal-related reports on tabloid newsmagazine programs, including *Hard Copy* and *Inside Edition*. As noted in chapter 1, such programs accounted for about one-third of all coverage in the first week of the scandal (Lowry 1998).

How does this relate to foreign crises? Simply stated, most individuals possess accessible causal narratives pertaining to issues surrounding the use of military force. Indeed, few issues are greater attention grabbers than the potential for mass violence and the possible deaths of large numbers of their fellow citizens at the hands of a clearly identifiable villain. Like sex scandals and celebrity murder trials, military conflicts lend themselves well to cheap framing ("morality plays" involving "good vs. evil" and "us vs. them") through episodic storylines, and thus tend to prime individuals' readily accessible causal narratives. Along these lines, political columnist Norah Vincent, writing in the *Los Angeles Times*, offered the following observation about the public and media fascination with American-born Taliban fighter John Walker Lindh and with Pat Tillman, an all-American football star who passed up a multimillion dollar NFL contract to join the army and fight in Afghanistan:

> Americans love a morality tail, especially one that's been taken from real life. We like facile categories of good and bad, and we like creating fiery male leads to drop neatly into them. That's why the drama now unfolding before us regarding 21-year-old American Talib John Walker Lindh and 25-year-old football-star-turned-army-recruit Pat Tillman could have been written for the screen by Tom Clancy (Vincent 2002).

As one would expect, soft news programmers (as well as, of course, their hard news counterparts) prefer stories that they believe will capture and sustain their audience's interest. And by presenting emotionally compelling issues with readily understandable themes in unambiguous, moralistic terms, a producer or reporter can improve the odds that a given story will interest her audience.[66] Figure 2.7 illustrates the decision calculus of a producer or journalist in attempting to determine which stories to cover.

The two curves shown at figure 2.7 represent two different types of news story. The curve labeled "complex issue" represents a news item not easily framed in widely accessible terms. The Whitewater scandal exemplifies this type of story. Note that as the volume of news provided by the media increases, the marginal audience appeal curve for typical viewers remains fairly flat, and marginal costs continually outweigh marginal benefits $(C > B)$. Only when a fairly large volume of information is presented in the media does the marginal audience appeal curve begin to rise more rapidly, eventually surpassing the point where expected marginal costs are equivalent to the expected marginal benefits of paying attention $(B = C)$. As more information is presented, individuals are more likely to encounter it, and thereby begin to develop a context for understanding the story. Since typical individuals will only pay attention when $B > C$, the media must provide a great deal of information before typical consumers will begin to consider the story worthy of their attention. This type of story is not particularly attractive to programmers, especially those in the soft news media.

In contrast, the curve labeled "compelling issue" represents a story that is of immediate interest to the audience, who find it worthy of attention even before very much information is accepted (i.e., $B > C$). Such a story (e.g., a sex scandal or military conflict) is easily framed in widely accessible terms, and

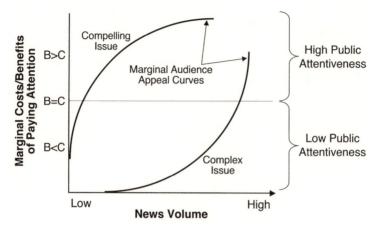

FIGURE 2.7. Evolution of Audience Appeal for Different Issue Types as Function of Expected Costs and Benefits of Paying Attention

hence, typical individuals need not expend a great deal of time or cognitive energy to understand what the story is about or why it is of interest. For this latter type of story, the benefits of paying attention (B) continue to outweigh the corresponding costs (C) even after a relatively large amount of information is accepted. For obvious reasons, programmers, especially those in the soft news media, will generally prefer to cover this type of story.

AND THE (SOMETIMES) COMPLEMENTARY INCENTIVES OF POLITICAL ELITES

Numerous studies have documented the central role played by elite opinion-makers—the "prestige press" (B. Cohen 1963), policy makers, and business leaders—in shaping the nation's political discourse, including determining which political issues are presented to the public in any depth or detail (e.g., Holsti 1996, 1992; Holsti and Rosenau 1979; Zaller 1992; Page, Shapiro, and Dempsey 1987). And political elites frequently find it in their own interest to frame the issues involved in a foreign crisis—particularly one involving the potential or actual use of force—in stark, moralistic and emotionally compelling terms, thereby providing ready-made frames, albeit perhaps unintentionally, suitable for soft news programs.

For instance, a president hoping to appear resolute in a crisis with another country may wish to demonstrate to the adversary that his domestic population supports his policies and would stand behind him should the use of force become necessary. By framing a crisis as a battle of good versus evil and priming such basic values as "patriotism," a president can render a potentially confusing and complex dispute more readily understandable (and, presumably, justifiable) for many individuals. This is particularly significant because most people, including even most political sophisticates, rely on simple heuristic cues and cognitive shortcuts in determining which policies to support or oppose. For instance, rather than thoroughly scrutinizing the issues and arguments surrounding a given policy, many people instead look to trusted leaders or experts for signals regarding the wisdom of the policy (Sniderman, Brody, and Tetlock 1991; Sniderman 1993; Popkin 1994; Page, Shapiro, and Dempsey 1987).

Framing a crisis in simple, emotionally compelling terms offers a political leader the twin potential benefits of increasing (*a*) the likelihood that the public will pay attention and (*b*) the likely level of support for her policies. For example, during the Persian Gulf War, President G.H.W. Bush likened Saddam Hussein to a modern day Hitler, which provided the public with a stark, moralistic good-versus-evil frame through which to view the conflict. President Clinton and Secretary of State Madeleine Albright similarly vilified Serbian President Slobodan Milosevic. And, more recently, the G. W. Bush administration has employed similar moralistic terms in vilifying Osama Bin Laden, the presumed mastermind of 9/11. Below, I present a few examples of statements by political elites seeking to frame America's adversaries as the embodiment of evil.

U.S. War against Taliban and Al-Qaeda Global Terror Network

We will rid the world of evil doers. (President George W. Bush, *NBC Nightly News*, September 16, 2001)

We've never seen this kind of evil before, but the evildoers have never seen the American people in action before either, and they're about to find out. (President George W. Bush, *CBS Evening News*, September 16, 2001)

Kosovo Air War

Slobodan Milosevic is a war criminal the likes of which Europe has not seen since the days of Adolf Hitler. (Representative Eliot Engel [Dem., New York], *NBC Nightly News*, May 26, 1999)

Do you think the Germans would have perpetrated the Holocaust on their own without Hitler? Was there something in the history of the German race that made them do this? No. We've got to—we've got to get straight about this. This is something political leaders do. And if people make decisions to do these kinds of things, other people can make decisions to stop them. (President Bill Clinton, *NBC Nightly News*, May 13, 1999)

Persian Gulf War

[Saddam Hussein is] Hitler revisited. But remember when Hitler's war ended, there were the Nuremberg trials. (President George H. W. Bush, *CBS Evening News*, October 15, 1990)

Saddam Hussein has more tanks, more planes . . . than Adolf Hitler had when Chamberlain came back with that infamous piece of paper, peace in our time. And those of us who've had to go to bat—you know—at a time in need, feel strongly that our younger generation not forget the lesson we learned, in spades, at that time. (Representative Robert Michel [Rep., Illinois, House Minority Leader], *CBS Evening News*, January 10, 1991)

As a result, for many individuals, paying attention to information about a foreign crisis potentially involving military force, once it has been framed by elites in stark, moralistic terms, represents a relatively low-cost proposition. Because military conflicts are naturally presentable in such terms, and because elites frequently seek to exploit this tendency and therefore speak about military conflicts in moralistic terms, war represents an ideal subject for soft news outlets. So, relative to other political issues—such as the state of the economy, health care, environmental policy initiatives, or international trade—military conflicts are more likely to be covered by the soft news media and perhaps also to become water-cooler events.

SUMMARY AND HYPOTHESES

Driven by market competition and the relatively low cost of producing soft news, broadcasters are finding human interest and other entertainment values in places where their predecessors saw only dry news. One implication is that soft news, as opposed to traditional news programming, may actually increase the likelihood that typical individuals—particularly those not normally interested in politics—will be exposed to information about at least *some* of the major issues of the day, especially those that become water-cooler events, albeit in a format that is less public-policy-oriented and less apt to provide a context for understanding an issue.

Under normal, everyday circumstances, these developments might not result in a public more attuned to political issues than were earlier generations. Given well-documented increases in political apathy and cynicism about politics, it is not surprising to find that typical individuals are no more interested in politics than their parents or grandparents were. This suggests that individuals have reacted to the explosion of available information by becoming increasingly selective regarding what information warrants their attention. Most of the time, the highly segmented modern television marketplace presumably allows individuals to *escape* news and information more effectively than in prior decades. Soft news programs, for instance, generally avoid such "mundane" political topics as foreign affairs, in favor of more salacious issues like celebrity sex scandals, murder trials, and fashion shows. Hence, with minimal effort, television viewers can remain blissfully uninformed about the day-to-day political issues facing the nation, including foreign policy.

When, however, potential water-cooler events emerge—and cross over from network evening newscasts to the soft news media—a far broader audience will likely confront such issues, albeit perhaps as the subject of an entertainment-oriented talk show or entertainment newsmagazine show. Moreover, unlike the relatively arcane or complex presentation of political information offered by traditional news outlets, soft news programs will focus on aspects of such issues of interest to their particular niche of the viewing audience.

For instance, during the Persian Gulf War, while CNN and the major net-

works filled the airwaves with graphic images of precision bombs and interviews with military experts, the daytime talk shows hosted by Oprah Winfrey,
Geraldo Rivera, and Sally Jesse Raphael, as well as the original tabloid TV
newsmagazine, *A Current Affair*, focused on episodic stories of the personal
hardships faced by spouses of soldiers serving in the Gulf and on the psychological trauma suffered by families of Americans being held prisoner in Iraq as
"human shields." In this context, learning about the war was an incidental by-
product of seeking entertainment (e.g., human drama or a fight between good
and evil). War-related information was effectively piggybacked to entertainment-oriented information, and thereby made available to viewers at virtually
no additional cost. In other words, when *The Oprah Winfrey Show* presented a
program dealing with the Gulf War, substantive information about the war was
"piggybacked," via cheap framing (e.g., human impact and injustice), to information presented primarily for its entertainment value. In choosing to watch
Oprah, viewers also, at no additional cost, received substantive information
about the Persian Gulf War.[67]

The incidental nature of soft news coverage of foreign crises is illustrated in
the following comment by Barry Berk of *Access Hollywood*, regarding that
program's rationale for covering some foreign crisis issues, despite the program's primary mission of providing their audience with information about
movies and celebrities:

> I think rather than just say [to a celebrity], "Why did you like that script?" or "Why do
> you want to make this movie?" . . . it's a way to get to know the celebrities better.
> And let [the audience] know there's another level there; that they [celebrities] do have
> opinions; that they're citizens and they're parents, and they have concerns. And they
> get very upset about the prospect that we're bombing Iraq. Or "good for them, I'm
> glad we're going in there." You know, they have opinions. I think people find that
> interesting.[68]

Hence, when a foreign crisis emerges, the numerous programming formats
that comprise the modern television marketplace may focus their diverse lenses
upon a single issue, albeit varying aspects of that issue. When the mass media
unify their focus, I expect the contemporary public, in the aggregate, to be
significantly more attentive to such an issue, compared to the publics of prior
decades. In today's news environment, when an issue crosses over from traditional news outlets to the soft news media, politically uninterested citizens are
far more likely to be exposed and pay attention to the issue—as an incidental
by-product of seeking entertainment—relative to most typical political issues,
which rarely reach beyond traditional news programming.

Most importantly for my theory, this mechanism does not depend on any
overall increase in the public's interest in or knowledge about politics or foreign
affairs.[69] Indeed, the basis for predicting increased attentiveness is entirely independent of the expected benefit for typical individuals of political information
in general or information about foreign affairs in particular. Once someone is
exposed to an issue in her preferred programming format, her cost-benefit cal-

culus for paying attention to additional information about the issue is altered. For such an individual, this issue is no longer a typical mundane, and perhaps baffling, political news item.

Numerous hypotheses, ten of which are presented below, follow from the theory. These can be divided into hypotheses pertaining to soft news programming (supply side) and those pertaining to public reactions to soft news programming decisions (demand side). The latter group are further subdivided into individual-level predictions and predictions pertaining to aggregate, over-time trends. The hypotheses are as follows:

A. SOFT NEWS PROGRAMMING

H_1 The soft news media will regularly cover U.S. foreign crises involving the potential or actual use of military force.

H_2 The soft news media will offer substantially less coverage of most other (less dramatic or more partisan) political issues that do not meet the criteria outlined above for facilitating cheap framing and piggybacking.

H_3 As the soft news media have proliferated and matured over the past decade, the extent of soft news coverage of foreign crises will have increased.

B. PUBLIC REACTIONS TO SOFT NEWS PROGRAMMING

B_1. Individual-Level Hypotheses

H_4 People consume soft news in order to be entertained, not to learn about politics or foreign policy.

H_5 People who watch soft news programs will be more attentive to particular foreign crisis issues and events (and other highly accessible issues) than will people who do not.

H_6 Soft news consumption will be most strongly positively related to foreign crisis attentiveness (or attentiveness to other similarly accessible issues) among the *least* politically engaged members of the public, and this relationship will weaken as political engagement increases.

H_7 Attentiveness to other, less dramatic, or more partisan political issues will *not* be significantly related to exposure to soft news.

H_8 People who attend to information about a political issue in a soft news context are more likely to subsequently pay attention to the issue in a traditional news context (the Gateway Hypothesis).

B_2. Over-Time Aggregate Trend Hypotheses

H_9 Public attentiveness to foreign crises has increased, over time, especially among individuals who are *least* inclined to follow political issues or foreign affairs. Hence, the positive relationship between political engagement and attentiveness to foreign crises has weakened, over time.

H_{10} The trends described in H_9 will be weaker for other, less dramatic or more partisan, political issues.

Each of these hypotheses, along with various other related hypotheses introduced along the way, is tested at length in subsequent chapters.[70] Before turning to the empirical tests, however, I first briefly define and discuss the concept of a crisis—the type of political issue I have implicitly labeled as most likely to appeal to the soft news media—and its relationship to water-cooler events. In doing so, I hope to offer further insight into which issues, or *types* of issues, are most likely to cross over from the traditional to the soft news media and thereby command significant public attention, possibly even becoming water-cooler events.

WHAT ARE CRISES AND WHEN DO THEY BECOME WATER-COOLER EVENTS?

According to the theory outlined above, at least when it comes to covering politics, the soft news media prefer to cover issues involving unusually high drama—in a word, *crises*. This, of course, begs the question of what exactly constitutes a crisis. According to dictionary definitions (e.g., *Merriam-Webster's Tenth New Collegiate Dictionary*), a crisis implies a specific, decisive situation or event, taking place within a well-defined, or focused, time or period. In other words, a crisis must be *focused* and *specific*. Neuman (1990), in turn, defines a crisis as a major national problem involving fairly "clear-cut beginnings, middles and ends." Yet, while issues meeting these definitions may constitute crises, they will not necessarily become water-cooler events. To do so, an issue must not only constitute a crisis, but it must do so in dramatic fashion.

A *dramatic* crisis, of course, by definition entails a high degree of drama. And, as any writer will testify, drama is facilitated by—though it does not always require—the element of surprise. Hence, for our purposes, a useful working definition of a dramatic crisis is as follows: *a specific, focused issue or event involving a major national problem that emerges suddenly and unexpectedly and has a readily identifiable beginning, middle, and end.* Such issues are particularly likely to become water-cooler events. And while not all such issues involve foreign policy, foreign policy disputes involving the potential or actual use of military force represent a class of issues that are particularly likely to satisfy this definition. In fact, as the quotation at the start of chapter 1, from a former producer of ABC's *20/20*, suggests, this definition perfectly describes the Persian Gulf War, the quintessential foreign policy water-cooler event.

Still, not all water-cooler events emerge overnight as dramatic crises. Some may originate not from specific events at all, but rather from issues that have persisted in the public consciousness for a long period of time, but which, for whatever reason, temporarily move to the political center stage. Examples include the state of the economy (e.g., inflation and unemployment), the war on drugs, or the war on poverty.[71] These are perennial concerns for typical Americans. Most of the time, however, they do not dominate elite, media, or public conversations. Yet, occasionally such issues temporarily achieve crisis proportions and become water-cooler events, as was the case with unemployment during the Great Depression, the ballot recounting process in Florida in the aftermath of the 2000 presidential election, and, more recently, the corporate corruption scandal of 2002.

The 2000 presidential election, in turn, clearly demonstrates that not every issue that becomes a water-cooler event can be readily characterized as a crisis. Not coincidentally, the 2000 election was the closest (and hence most *dramatic*) campaign in at least four decades. In some respects, presidential elections appear to satisfy Neuman's (1990) definition of a crisis (clear-cut beginning, middle, and end). Indeed, a presidential election might best be thought of as a relatively short-term national problem, which *may* rise to the level of water-cooler event (by taking on the urgency of a dramatic crisis for a short period of time). In the immediate aftermath of this historically close election, this appears to be just what happened. Other examples of water-cooler events that may not qualify as crises, at least as defined above, include the Elian Gonzales emigration case and the controversy surrounding President Clinton's last-minute pardons upon leaving office.

In fact, not all water-cooler events emerge from traditional political issues at all. For instance, the death of Princess Diana—clearly a water-cooler event—represents a *non*political story that was nonetheless transformed by the media into a dramatic crisis. Even so, in this instance, the news media—hard and soft—framed much of their coverage of Diana's death around various more-traditional political issues (the dangers of a celebrity-obsessed culture, the loss of a prominent spokesperson on the issue of civilian casualties caused by land mines left over from military conflicts, etc.). In this way, an event that was intrinsically nonpolitical was nonetheless transformed in the public mind into a dramatic political crisis, and subsequently became a water-cooler event.

Still, not even every dramatic crisis becomes a water-cooler event. Figure 2.8 graphically illustrates several paths along which issues may evolve in the process of either succeeding or failing to achieve water-cooler event status. This figure demonstrates the complexity of the path for a given issue from the point where it first emerges on the political landscape to the point where it may ultimately become a water-cooler event. Even strong emphasis by political elites and the mass media are not sufficient to assure water-cooler event status, as there is no guarantee that the public will respond to such cues. Indeed, saturation coverage of a dry or overly complex story seems unlikely to raise public interest so that it rises to the level of water-cooler event. At some point along the way, the public must show signs of rising interest in the story. Otherwise—as indicated by the many paths leading to low public interest—profit-oriented news organizations will most likely drop the story before it ever has the opportunity to cross over to the soft news media, let alone become a water-cooler event.

Media coverage of the Savings and Loan debacle of the 1980s—even after it broke into the headlines—is a case in point. Of the nearly nine hundred major news stories included on the Pew Research Center's aforementioned list of

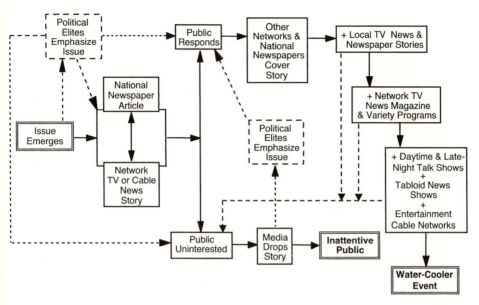

FIGURE 2.8. Model of Media Dissemination of and Public Attentiveness to Political Issues

news stories that attracted significant public attention (between 1986 and August 2001), the Savings and Loan scandal—which was followed closely by 26 percent of the public—peaked in August 1989 at the 62nd percentile. This means that perhaps the single largest financial debacle in U.S. history barely ranks in the top 40 percent of major news stories over the past one-and-a-half decades. Most likely due, at least in part, to its complexity, this scandal, which by some estimates cost U.S. taxpayers somewhere between $500 billion and $1 trillion, never captured the public's imagination. In sharp contrast, 36 percent of the public claimed to have closely followed the 1992 congressional check-bouncing scandal, which cost the taxpayers exactly nothing. This places the latter, far less complex, but also far less consequential, scandal considerably higher on Pew's list, at the 84th percentile. Apparently, at least in these cases, simplicity trumped severity.

Indeed, there may be many mitigating factors, such as other issues competing for the media and public spotlight, which prevent any given issue from attracting substantial public attention, regardless of the best efforts of media or political elites. In fact, an informationally conducive environment might be considered a virtual *necessary* condition for an issue to become a water-cooler event. Yet, it is difficult to precisely define an "informationally conducive" environment, except to note that it is unlikely to be characterized by simultaneously competing candidate water-cooler events. After all, the attention capacities of the media and the public are limited. Even this circumstance, however, is by no means absolute. One water-cooler event may arise and rapidly replace a previous such event in the media. Hence, it is certainly possible that an issue may become a water-cooler event even in the presence of another, contemporaneous high-profile event competing for media and public attention. Nonetheless, as my discussion in this chapter indicates, consumer demand, as well as journalists' expectations regarding consumer demand, remain critical in determining whether a given issue will "cross over" to the soft news media and perhaps subsequently evolve into a water-cooler event.

CONCLUSION

In this chapter, I have argued that due in part to the increasing prevalence of soft news outlets, foreign military crises—as well as some other issues which are decidedly not "high politics"—are increasingly likely to attract the attention of typical individuals. In general, issues that can be readily framed in stark and dramatic terms, thereby priming widely accessible frames, without generating significant cognitive conflict between simultaneously accessible yet contradictory causal narratives, are most likely to be covered by the soft news media. Such issues are thereby most likely to attract the attention of even politically uninterested individuals. These are the issues that occasionally become water-cooler events.

A direct marketing revolution in television has systematically altered the cost-benefit calculus for a large segment of the public, which is not predisposed to follow politics. By transforming mundane political coverage into entertainment, the soft news media have successfully employed piggybacking and cheap framing strategies in order to capture a substantial segment, or niche, of the television audience. This has the perhaps unintended effect of increasing the likelihood that politically uninterested individuals will be exposed to information about those political issues that cross over from hard to soft news outlets.

I have described the class of issues most likely to become water-cooler events as "dramatic crises" because these events typically possess the several characteristics necessary to appeal to the soft news media. Nonetheless, not all crises, nor even all dramatic crises, are covered by the soft news media or become water-cooler events. Indeed, it seems unlikely that there exists any full-proof formula for determining ex ante which issues will pass this attentiveness threshold. Rather, given the extraordinary complexity of the modern political, media, and public opinion environments, perhaps the best we can hope for in the near term is an improved understanding of the various factors that raise or lower the probability that a given issue or event will capture the public's imagination.

While the theory developed in this chapter is potentially applicable to a range of political issues that constitute crises, at least temporarily, foreign policy events involving the actual or potential use of military force represent a class of issues particularly likely to fit this description. Indeed, the propensity of the soft news media to cover foreign crises, combined with the dramatic proliferation of soft news outlets in recent years, has significantly increased the likelihood that a given foreign crisis will command sufficient and sufficiently widespread public attention to become a water-cooler event. In the next chapters, I turn to multiple empirical tests of my theoretical predictions.

APPENDIX: LOCATING CHANGES IN COGNITIVE COSTS AND BENEFITS

My model locates changes in public attentiveness on the cost, rather than the benefit, side of the ledger (with respect to *political* information). This decision may appear somewhat arbitrary. After all, doesn't soft news make politics fun, thereby raising the expected benefit of consuming political news? Clearly, in one sense, this is, on its face, true. And, admittedly, locating the change on the benefit side would have little effect on the overall argument. Yet, to understand why I have chosen to locate the aforementioned changes primarily on the cost side of the ledger, it is important to bear in mind the precise nature of the costs and benefits under consideration.

Recall that the incidental by-product model holds that any political information piggybacked to the entertainment-oriented information presented by soft news programs remains largely, though perhaps not exclusively, *incidental*. Hence, the anticipated benefit of *learning about politics*, per se, does not factor into the viewer's decision to pay attention to soft news shows. (Moreover, I assume that, for typical individuals, the expected benefit of *entertainment* is fairly high and the expected cost fairly low.) Rather, through piggybacking and cheap framing, the expected cost of *learning about politics*, in the course of being entertained, may be reduced to near zero, effectively dropping out of the equation.

Stated differently, the theory concerns the marginal costs and benefits of paying attention to a given issue for purposes of entertainment, not enlightenment, in an environment in which, regardless of its perceived intrinsic benefit, the marginal cost of gaining some modicum of "enlightenment" (loosely defined) collapses to essentially zero. This is an important, albeit subtle, distinction. So, if low-benefit political information can be attached to higher-benefit entertainment-oriented information, without adding to the total cost of attending to that information, then even an individual who is not intrinsically interested in politics may nonetheless be willing to pay attention. It is therefore not necessary for the theory that the expected benefit of political information rises when presented in a soft news context. So long as the cost is effectively zero, and the *entertainment* benefit of a piece of information exceeds zero, any change in expected benefits of learning about politics (which, by definition, cannot be lower than zero) are essentially superfluous. The converse seems far less plausible, as the expected benefits of consuming *political information*, per se, must be weighed against variations in expected costs.

A related issue concerns the possibility of diminishing marginal benefits, over time, to paying attention, even to *entertainment*-oriented information. After all, even the most compelling issues eventually run their course. If benefits diminish over time, themselves eventually approaching zero, this could undermine the effects of falling marginal costs. Yet, the costs of paying attention seem likely to fall most sharply during the *early* stages in the issue attention cycle, at the very time that benefits (attributable to perceived *entertainment* value) are increasing most rapidly. Stated differently, marginal costs are likely to decline, while marginal benefits increase (or remain flat), early on, when the issue is relatively new to an individual (as he or she is first discovering the issue's beneficial entertainment value). In contrast, after an individual reaches a saturation point for information pertaining to the issue, and it ceases to be enjoyable to continue paying attention, marginal benefits may decline rapidly, while marginal costs will either cease to decline or, if the opportunity costs of continuing to pay attention increase to a greater extent than any continuing decline in transaction costs, begin to rebound.

This conjecture is easily substantiated. As the quotation that opened this book suggests, the primary purpose of soft news programming is to attract *and hold on to* an audience. Given the intrinsic interest in sustaining an audience's interest, it follows that broadcasters will attempt to maximize the marginal benefit derived by their target audience from paying attention to their coverage of a given story *for as long a period as possible*. If this becomes impractical, the story will most likely be dropped. So long as their respective audiences respond, however, the soft and hard news medias will provide more information. As Neuman (1990, 163) notes, the news media are notorious for "feed[ing] on themselves, reporting on the issues which seem to be catching on." Neuman (1990) refers to this as "audience-contingent effects." Moreover, the bulk of any decline in the expected costs of paying attention is likely to take place as soon as a given issue crosses over from the traditional to the soft news media. After all, the soft news media specialize in presenting information in an emotionally compelling, entertaining, and hence low-cost, format.

After this point, marginal changes in expected costs are likely to remain small so long as the soft news media persist in covering the issue. The marginal cost curve thus falls sharply early on, as soon as a story "catches on" (Neuman 1990) and then remains fairly flat.[72] The marginal benefit curve, in contrast, if it varies at all, is likely to *rise* fairly rapidly early on, as soon as the soft news media begin covering an issue. It is at this stage that a typical individual will encounter an accessible frame through which to evaluate the issue. The benefit curve then remains relatively constant, until an issue has largely run its course, at which point it begins to fall, while marginal opportunity costs may begin to rise. At some point, a typical individual will begin to lose interest in acquiring yet another piece of information about an issue. At this point, benefits (i.e., entertainment value) decline while opportunity costs remain fairly constant, or perhaps begin to increase somewhat.

If opportunity costs do eventually rise, this increase might outweigh any continued decline in transaction costs. If so, marginal costs would be more accurately represented as a U-shaped curve. Nevertheless, the basic story, and its implications for the theory, are unaffected by the shape of the marginal cost

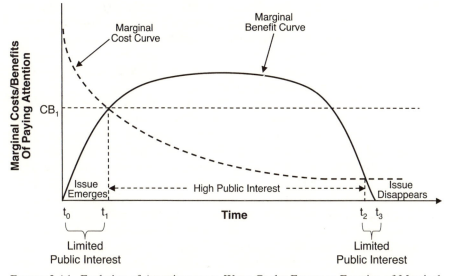

FIGURE 2.A1. Evolution of Attentiveness to Water-Cooler Events as Function of Marginal Costs and Benefits of Paying Attention

curve in the latter stages of an issue's evolution, so long as it is initially downward sloping. Hence, for convenience, in figure 2.A1 I represent the marginal cost curve as diminishing, over time, and then remaining flat. (In other words, for simplicity, I assume that opportunity and transaction costs eventually cancel each other out.)

Regardless of the shape of the marginal cost curve, until an issue approaches its "saturation point," where it has received fairly high and sustained levels of public scrutiny, ceteris paribus, marginal costs seem likely to diminish more than marginal benefits (which, with respect to entertainment value, will tend to rise or remain relatively stable). Advertising researchers refer to this saturation phenomenon as "ad wear-out" (Naples 1979). Figure 2.A1 presents the evolution of the marginal cost and benefit curves for a hypothetical water-cooler event.

Between time t_0 and t_1, when the issue first emerges in the media and in the public's consciousness, the marginal costs of paying attention fall fairly rapidly, while the marginal benefits of paying attention rise equally rapidly. Nevertheless, so long as the issue is primarily covered by network news and other traditional news programming, the marginal costs for many individuals will outweigh the marginal benefits of paying attention. Downs (1972) refers to the earliest stages of an issue-attention cycle as the "preproblem stage." This is the period where the issue exists and may be covered to a limited extent, but has not yet captured the sustained attention of the media or public. This pattern continues until the issue moves beyond the network news to nontraditional news outlets, including the soft news media.

After the soft news media begin covering the issue, at about time t_1, the two curves cross at the point where marginal costs are equivalent to marginal benefits (CB_1), at which point the politically inattentive public begins to pay attention. Downs refers to this as the "discovery stage." He argues that this stage is frequently accompanied by a mass euphoric optimism that the problem can be resolved. Note that the marginal benefits (i.e., entertainment value) continue to increase, while the marginal costs continue to fall, as the issue receives more, and more broad-based coverage in the media.

Eventually, the issue reaches the "plateau," where the two curves are farthest apart. At this point, both curves flatten out as, according to Downs, the public begins to recognize that the "problem" is not easily solved and is, in fact, quite complex and likely to persist. After this point, the issue enters the "decline" stage, and the benefit curve begins to reverse, as the public is saturated with coverage of the issue and begins to lose interest in acquiring additional information (as the issue loses its "entertainment value"). Between times t_1 and t_2, the marginal benefits of paying attention outweigh the marginal costs. This continues until the marginal costs and benefits of consuming additional information are again equivalent, at time t_2—the point where both curves again cross the line at CB_1. Between time t_2 and time t_3, the public rapidly loses interest in the story, until after time t_3, which Downs refers to as the "post-problem" period, the story disappears from the media and public consciousness altogether.

CHAPTER THREE

"I Heard It on *Oprah*"

> We're trying desperately to hold onto an ever-shrinking audience, as far as the big commercial networks are concerned. . . . We're reaching out more and more for people who believe there are three-headed cows. . . . I'm part of the process of trying to find a larger audience of people who've never really cared about news . . . And to get them, we have to do things that we didn't ever used to do before.
>
> —*Sam Donaldson, anchor of ABC News, on CNN* Reliable Sources
> (*October 10, 1999*)

SEVERAL MONTHS before the United States launched air strikes (on October 7, 2001) against Afghanistan and the Al Qaeda terrorist network, I received an anonymous e-mail petition—which, to that point, had amassed more than two hundred signatures—asking recipients to express their outrage over the mistreatment of women by the ruling Taliban regime in Afghanistan. The author of the petition indicated that he or she had been moved to take action by a series of horrific anecdotes presented in the media. By itself, this is unsurprising. What caught my attention, however, was the source of the anecdotal stories, which, according to the petition, was not the *New York Times* or the network evening news. Rather, the author learned about the alleged atrocities committed by the fundamentalist regime in Afghanistan from Oprah Winfrey, who, it turns out, had broadcast a series of programs in recent years devoted to the plight of women in countries ruled by autocratic regimes.

This, of course, is merely an anecdote. By itself it does not demonstrate that foreign policy is a regular topic of the soft news media. In the course of this chapter, I provide more systematic evidence. Specifically, I substantiate, as systematically as possible, three of my hypotheses, as well a key assumption embedded in the theory. Beginning with the last, the hypothesized relationship between soft news coverage of foreign crises and public attentiveness to such crises makes sense only if a substantial portion of the American public routinely watches soft news TV programs. I therefore begin this chapter by offering evidence, in the form of public opinion surveys and Nielsen ratings, that the American people, particularly those relatively uninterested in politics or foreign affairs, do indeed consume a great deal of soft news.

Hypothesis 1 predicts that soft news programs will offer significant coverage of foreign crises. In order to set the stage for the empirical tests conducted in subsequent chapters, it is first necessary to demonstrate that the soft news media do actually cover foreign crises on a regular basis and that television coverage of foreign crises has, over time, changed in meaningful ways. For if the soft news media do not typically cover these events, or if they do so no more today than in prior decades, then it is unlikely that they could influence public attentiveness to foreign crises or contribute to any attentiveness trends.

Hypothesis 2, in turn, predicts that soft news programs will offer far less coverage of more traditional or partisan political issues, which lack the necessary ingredients for appealing to the soft news audience or for becoming watercooler events. Finally, Hypothesis 3 predicts that given the proliferation of the soft news media over the past decade, soft news coverage of foreign crises will have expanded commensurately.

This chapter substantiates each of these hypotheses through a series of content analysis investigations that, together, demonstrate that the soft news media: (1) offered substantial coverage of a series of U.S. foreign policy crises during the 1990s; (2) offered far less coverage of a series of other, *less* dramatic or *more* (intrinsically) partisan political issues during the same time period; and (3) covered foreign crises in a qualitatively different manner than did traditional news outlets. I conclude with a case study comparing television and print media coverage of the Vietnam and Persian Gulf Wars. This comparison highlights the dramatic changes in the breadth and depth of media coverage of war between the 1960s and the 1990s. Taken together, the evidence presented in this chapter suggests that the nature and extent of soft news coverage of foreign crises may indeed have important ramifications for public attentiveness to and attitudes about U.S. foreign policy, especially among individuals for whom a soft news outlet represents their primary, or even sole, source of news about politics.

AMERICA'S ADDICTION TO TV AND SOFT NEWS

Over the past several decades, countless studies and public opinion polls have revealed an unmistakable trend toward the public's increased reliance on television and declining reliance on newspapers as a source of news and information about politics and public affairs (Bower 1985; Briller 1990; Moisy 1997; Bogart 1991; Webster and Lichty 1991; Lichty and Gomery 1992; Roper Center Online 1998; Dimock and Popkin 1997; and many others). These trends are reflected in falling newspaper subscription rates (Bogart 1991) and in rising percentages of survey respondents naming television as their primary and most trusted source of news and information (e.g., Roper Center Online 1998, Pew Research Center, various years).[1] In fact, the studies cited above represent only a small sample of the overwhelming evidence suggesting television has in large measure replaced newsprint as the nation's predominant and most trusted source of news.

The public's reliance on television is particularly stark during major crises. For instance, in early January 1991, when asked to name their primary sources of news about "the latest developments in the Persian Gulf," 82 percent of respondents to one survey (Princeton Survey Research Associates 1991) selected television, more than twice as many as mentioned newspapers (40 percent), and vastly more than mentioned radio (15 percent) or magazines (4 percent).[2]

And America's TV news addiction extends beyond traditional notions of what constitutes "news," and even beyond traditional forms of news programming. Indeed, Americans also have a strong appetite for soft news, especially on television. In one April 1998 survey, a larger percentage of respondents (78 percent) reported watching television newsmagazines such as *60 Minutes*, *20/20*, or *Dateline* either "sometimes" or "regularly" than reported watching the network evening news (67 percent) (Pew Research Center 1998b).[3] In the same survey, nearly as many respondents reported watching tabloid news programs such as *Hard Copy* or *Inside Edition* (47 percent) as CNN (57 percent). And the self-reported tabloid audience was as large or larger than that for CNBC (39 percent), MSNBC (32 percent), ESPN (40 percent), Fox (47 percent), or the three network morning variety programs (*CBS This Morning*, *Good Morning America*, and *The Today Show*) combined (42 percent). An additional 35 and 28 percent of respondents, respectively, reported watching *Entertainment Tonight* and daytime TV talk shows. Indeed, Lisa Gregorish, of Fox, recalled that as producer of *Hard Copy*, she was surprised to learn that for many viewers the show was their primary, if not sole, source of "news."[4]

Two years later (Pew Research Center 2000), the overall picture remained, in most respects, virtually unchanged. The most noteworthy difference was a 9-percentage point *decline* in the percentage of respondents who reported watching network evening newscasts (from 67 to 58 percent). The self-reported audience for soft news held fairly steady in 2000, with 31 percent of respondents reporting that they watched daytime talk shows, like *The Oprah Winfrey Show* or *The Rosie O'Donnell Show*. The corresponding percentages for *Entertainment Tonight* and network TV newsmagazine shows were 36 percent and 72 percent, respectively. Self-reported viewing of all-news cable networks in 2000—including CNN (55 percent), CNBC (42 percent), Fox (45 percent), and MSNBC (38 percent)—also differed only modestly from 1998.

The 1998 Pew Research Center survey also offers evidence suggesting that entertainment-oriented programming can influence which political issues capture the attention of typical individuals. Consistent with the incidental by-product theory, almost two-thirds of respondents reported that one significant factor in determining which news-oriented programs they watch is whether a given program "stirs your emotions." Similarly, over 70 percent placed a premium on news that "is enjoyable and entertaining," while 80 percent preferred news programming that "has news personalities who present the news in a caring way."[5]

The data presented thus far are aggregate totals. Yet news consumption, both soft and hard, differs dramatically across different groups of Americans. For instance, according to the 2000 NES, respondents who received the *lowest* possible score on the interviewer's 5-point scale assessing respondents' level of political information report watching daytime TV talk shows about twice as frequently as their counterparts who received the *highest* score. In sharp contrast, the *least* politically informed respondents report watching about 127 percent *less* national news on network television, as compared with the *most* politically informed respondents.

These same patterns emerge if we differentiate NES respondents by education level, rather than political information (though the latter differences are somewhat larger for talk shows and smaller for network news watching). Similarly, in one survey of media consumption habits (Pew Research Center 1998a), respondents who did not graduate from high school report watching tabloid newsmagazine programs and daytime talk shows on television about 40 and 144 percent more often, respectively, than their counterparts with a college or postgraduate degree. Nielsen ratings for some of the most popular soft news programs, disaggregated by education, mirror these survey results. In October 2002, for instance, the combined average ratings for several popular tabloid/entertainment news programs (*Entertainment Tonight, Access Hollywood, Extra*, and *Inside Edition*) and daytime talk shows (*The Oprah Winfrey Show, Live with Regis and Kelly, Dr. Phil*, and *Caroline Rhea*) were 27 and 33 percent higher, respectively, among households headed by an adult lacking a college education, compared to college-educated households. In contrast, college-educated respondents in the aforementioned 1998 survey (Pew Research Center 1998a) reported watching national network news and *The News Hour with Jim Lehrer* 18 and 62 percent more often, respectively, than their counterparts who did not graduate from high school.[6]

Some additional insight into the differences between hard and soft news audiences can be discerned from the demographic breakdowns of the TV audience at different times of the day and evening. For instance, according to Nielsen Media Research, as of July 2002, only about 40 percent of adult viewers watching network television between the hours of 11:00 P.M. and 1:00 A.M.—a time slot during which late-night entertainment talk shows dominate the airwaves—attended *any* college. And a typical daytime (9:00 A.M. to 4:00 P.M.) television viewer is even less likely to have attended college (36 percent). By comparison, the corresponding figures for the network Sunday morning political interview programs *Meet the Press* (NBC) and *Face the Nation* (CBS) are 60 and 53 percent, respectively. In other words, according to these data, typical adult *Meet the Press* viewers are 50 and 67 percent more likely to have attended at least some college, compared to their counterparts watching late-night and daytime TV, respectively. Adult *Face the Nation* viewers, in turn, are, on average, 33 and 47 percent more likely, respectively, to have attended some college, compared to their late-night and daytime TV-watching counterparts.[7]

While this survey and demographic evidence is suggestive, we can better estimate the overall size of the audience for soft news outlets by reviewing the Nielsen ratings for these programs. At table 3.1, I present the average Nielsen

TABLE 3.1. Nielsen Ratings for Select "Hard" and "Soft" News Programs (Various Periods, 2002)

Program	Rating/Households	Program	Rating/Households
Tabloid/Entertainment TV Newsmagazines		**Network Newsmagazines**	
Entertainment Tonight	6.3/6,722,000[a]	60 Minutes (CBS)	9.7/10,350,000[c]
Inside Edition	3.5/3,735,000[d]	60 Minutes II (CBS)	8.2/8,750,000[d]
Extra	2.9/3,100,000[a]	Dateline (NBC)	7.9/8,429,000[c]
Access Hollywood	2.9/3,100,000[d]	20/20 (ABC)	6.3/6,722,000[c]
Daytime Talk Shows		**Cable News Networks (Average Daily Audiences)**	
The Oprah Winfrey Show	6.7/7,149,000[a]	Fox	1.3/1,400,000[d]
Dr. Phil	5.0/5,335,000[d]	CNN	.86/921,000[d]
Live with Regis and Kelly	3.9/4,161,000[a]	MSNBC	.49/528,000[d]
		CNBC	.20/213,000[d]
Late-Night Talk Shows		CNN Headline News	.20/213,000[d]
The Tonight Show with Jay Leno (NBC)	5.1/5,441,000[e]	**Cable News Shows**	
The Late Show with David Letterman (CBS)	4.2/4,481,000[e]	Larry King Live (CNN)	1.0/1,086,000[b]
Late Night with Conan O'Brien (NBC)	2.0/2,074,000[b]	The Fox Report with Shephard Smith (Fox)	.80/854,000[b]
		The O'Reilly Factor (Fox)	.74/794,000[b]
Network News Shows		Newsnight with Aaron Brown (CNN)	.61/654,000[b]
NBC Nightly News	7.3/7,789,000[c]	Hannity & Colmes (Fox)	.57/611,000[b]
ABC World News Tonight	6.9/7,362,000[c]	Crossfire (CNN)	.57/605,000[b]
CBS Evening News	5.9/6,295,000[c]	Wolf Blitzer Reports (CNN)	.4/448,000[b]
Meet the Press (NBC)	3.6/3,841,000[b]	The News with Brian Williams (MSNBC)	.3/315,000[b]
Nightline (ABC)	3.2/3,414,000[b]	Hardball with Chris Matthews (MSNBC)	.2/261,000[b]
This Week (ABC)	2.6/2,774,000[b]		

Note: In 2002, one ratings point was equivalent to approximately 1.067 households and one household was equivalent to approximately 1.33 viewers.
[a]September 2001 through February 2002
[b]January through March 2002
[c]October 2002
[d]November 2002
[e]December 2002

ratings for a variety of soft news programs during various periods in 2002 (depending on accessibility of ratings data). These are contrasted with ratings for network evening newscasts, network political talk shows and all-news cable network shows.[8]

According to these data, in late 2002, more households typically watched *Entertainment Tonight* (*ET*) and *The Oprah Winfrey Show* than watched the *CBS Evening News*.[9] On multiple occasions between 2000 and 2002, both of these soft news shows have attracted audiences in excess of 8 million households (or over 10 million viewers). Moreover, in most markets, *ET* airs opposite one of its own primary competitors, *Access Hollywood* and *Extra*, both of which, in late 2002, typically attracted about 3.1 million households.[10] Hence, depending on whether or not one assumes a 100 percent overlap in audiences for programs broadcast at different time slots, these three programs alone typically reach between about 11 and 14 million unique households per day (or between 14.6 and 18.6 million unique viewers).

The audiences for network newsmagazines are frequently even larger. Indeed, CBS's *60 Minutes* and *60 Minutes II*, NBC's *Dateline*, and ABC's *20/20* each routinely attract larger audiences than network evening newscasts. The typical audiences for the various all-news cable networks are tiny by comparison. During November 2002, for instance, a *combined* average of fewer than 3.3 million households watched the five major all-news cable networks—CNN, Fox, CNBC, MSNBC, and HLN—at any given time, about the same as the lowest-rated tabloid/entertainment news program included in table 3.1, and slightly over half of the audience for the lowest-rated network newsmagazine show. Ratings for cable news typically spike during major domestic or international crises. Yet the single largest audience in the history of cable news— January 17, 1991, when 5.4 million households watched the start of the Gulf War on CNN (Noah 1997)—was smaller than the *average* audience for the *lowest*-rated network evening newscast in 2002.

In the first quarter of 2002, approximately 1.1 million households tuned in to a typical prime-time broadcast of the highest-rated cable news program at the time, *Larry King Live*. This represents only a tiny fraction (15 and 16 percent, respectively, in table 3.1) of the average audiences for *The Oprah Winfrey Show* and *Entertainment Tonight*. Indeed, the audiences for *Oprah* and *ET* frequently rival, and sometimes exceed, those of the top dozen cable news programs *combined*.[11]

Nielsen ratings for individual programs can vary widely, depending on a range of factors, such as the time of year, the topic of a paticular broadcast, the popularity of competing programming, and others. Hence, the data in table 3.1 represent only a series of snapshots. Nevertheless, viewed as a whole, these data, combined with the survey evidence presented above, strongly suggest that the audience for soft news outlets is quite large, both in an absolute sense, and relative to network and cable news programming. Finally, though my focus is primarily on television, these consumption patterns extend to elements of the radio (e.g., talk radio) and print (e.g., news magazines) media as well.[12]

TRENDS IN TV COVERAGE OF 1990s U.S. FOREIGN POLICY CRISES

How Frequently Do Soft News Shows Cover Foreign Crises?

That many Americans watch soft news programs demonstrates only that such programs have the *potential* to influence public opinion regarding foreign policy, not that they actually do so. The political relevance of the soft news media depends on the extent to which such programs actually cover political issues, like foreign crises. In this section I show that soft news TV outlets—including network newsmagazines, talk shows, and entertainment and tabloid newsmagazine shows—have indeed offered substantial coverage of a variety of U.S. foreign policy crises over the past decade.

And such coverage of political issues appears not to have gone unnoticed by soft news viewers. For instance, according to a May 1996 survey by the Pew Research Center, one-fourth of respondents indicated that they learn about politics "sometimes" or "regularly" from late-night talk show hosts, such as David Letterman and Jay Leno. Among respondents under thirty years of age, the figure rises to 40 percent. An additional 13 percent of respondents, and 20 percent of respondents under age 30, claimed to learn about politics from MTV. Along these lines, *Washington Post* columnist and political and media commentator Howard Kurtz (1999) commented:

> A growing segment of the population is tuning in to politics through a different cultural channel—Leno's raunchy routines on "The Tonight Show" or "Don Imus" down-and-dirty ridicule on the radio or movie stars opining about the nation's woes on "Politically Incorrect." Fans of these shows get more than just sharp-edged satire. Whatever their degree of irreverence, these programs impart serious information amid the yuks. And their effect on public opinion is not to be taken lightly.

Evidence of soft news coverage of foreign crises abounds. *Hard Copy*, for instance, produced *at least* one program devoted to the U.S. intervention in Somalia in October 1993 and also covered U.S. missile strikes in Iraq in a September 1996 broadcast.[13] *Hard Copy* has also presented *at least* three broadcasts (per intervention) addressing the U.S. interventions in Bosnia and Haiti, a second program addressing Somalia in July 1995, and four additional programs addressing the ongoing series of U.S. crises with Iraq.[14]

A similar pattern of soft news coverage was apparent in a January–February 1998 crisis between the United Nations Security Council (led by the United States) and Iraq concerning Iraq's failure to cooperate with UN weapon inspectors. For instance, on February 21, 1998—while UN Secretary General Kofi Annan was attempting to negotiate a diplomatic settlement in Baghdad—*Extra* broadcast an interview with a Pentagon official addressing the likely role of "smart bombs" in any U.S. air strikes against Iraq. A search of transcripts from several prominent daytime television talk shows indicated that during the January–February 1998 crisis with Iraq, Oprah Winfrey discussed the crisis in two broadcasts, and Geraldo Rivera's daytime talk show did so in three broadcasts.

Even celebrity-oriented *Access Hollywood* presented a segment devoted to the crisis with Iraq (on March 4, 1998).[15]

In an effort to identify more systematic evidence of soft news coverage of foreign crises, I searched program transcripts from a variety of soft news programs for coverage of the Persian Gulf War and the ongoing series of postwar crises with Iraq, as well as four other large-scale U.S. military operations in the 1990s—in Somalia, Haiti, Bosnia, and Kosovo. Table 3.2 presents the results for nine prominent talk shows, eight entertainment and tabloid newsmagazine outlets (spanning cable and broadcast television), and one popular syndicated radio program.

Network newsmagazine shows have also provided extensive coverage of each of the above conflicts. While these programs are somewhat more prone to cover political issues than, say, entertainment newsmagazine shows, as noted in chapter 2, they focus *primarily* on soft news topics. Consequently, table 3.2 also includes the results from a search of transcripts, using Lexis-Nexis, for five network television newsmagazine shows. Additionally, for purposes of comparison, I also include the results of a Lexis-Nexis search for soft news coverage of several more traditional political issues.

These figures represent the average number of different broadcasts of each category of soft news program in which a given crisis was discussed or featured. It is important to point out, however, that due to limited availability of transcripts, the unwillingness of some programs that I contacted directly to provide the requested information, the recent start-dates of several of the programs and cancellation of several others, these figures are incomplete, and so are intended only to be suggestive.

Despite the aforementioned limitations in the data, each of the soft news program categories in the table appears to have offered substantial coverage of these foreign policy crises. This supports Hypothesis 1. The magnitude of coverage of foreign crises by the soft news media is more easily seen in figure 3.1, which presents the total volume of coverage of two major U.S. military crises, involving Iraq and Bosnia, by four soft news programs over the past several years.

It is not immediately obvious where precisely the threshold lies beyond which coverage of foreign crises by soft news programs should be deemed "significant." In this sense, the figures in table 3.2 and figure 3.1 are difficult to interpret. To facilitate such an assessment, as well as to search for trends in the extent of soft news coverage of foreign crises, figure 3.2 tallies the magnitude of soft news coverage of two early-1990s U.S. military interventions (Somalia and Haiti) and two mid-to-late-1990s military interventions (Bosnia and Kosovo). The figure compares coverage of the four crises in the soft news media with coverage over the same time period on *ABC's World News Tonight* broadcast.

Several points can be discerned from figure 3.2. First, each of these four categories of soft news programs offered significant coverage of these foreign crises. Indeed, the combined number of daytime and late-night television talk show broadcasts addressing Bosnia or Kosovo is equivalent to nearly 70 percent of the total number of broadcasts mentioning these interventions on ABC's *World News Tonight*. These same programs offered roughly 54 percent as many broadcasts as *World News Tonight* mentioning Somalia or Haiti (combined).[16] The corresponding figures for coverage of Bosnia and Kosovo by the entertainment news programs listed in table 3.2 are similar to those for the talk shows. Indeed, one entertainment newsmagazine, *Extra*, mentioned Bosnia in nearly half (44 percent) as many separate broadcasts as *World News Tonight*.

The above comparisons focus on soft and hard news *broadcasts*. Yet network newscasts may be more likely than soft news outlets to include multiple stories in a single broadcast. If we replicate the prior comparisons, this time employing the total number of *stories* (including multiple stories per broadcast) on *World News Tonight*, the combined total number of separate *broadcasts* of the TV talk shows listed in table 3.2 mentioning the U.S. interventions in Bosnia and Kosovo is equivalent to more than half of the total number of *stories* on *World News Tonight* mentioning those conflicts. These same programs offered roughly 40 percent as many broadcasts as the total number of stories on *World News Tonight* addressing Somalia and Haiti. And the number of separate broadcasts mentioning Bosnia presented on *Extra* is equivalent to 40 percent of the total number of *World News Tonight* stories mentioning Bosnia. Hence, even when we account for the possibility of multiple stories per broadcast on network news programs, the volume of soft news media coverage continues to appear quite substantial.

Additionally, while the figures for the network newsmagazines seem relatively modest at first glance, when one considers that most of these programs are broadcast only once or twice per week, on average, compared to nightly broadcasts of network evening newscasts, the magnitude of coverage by network newsmagazines appears far more impressive. Moreover, unlike the network news broadcasts, most of the soft news programs included in table 3.2 have only existed for a portion of the period covered in figures 3.1 and 3.2, thereby biasing these figures in favor of ABC's network newscasts. Taken together, these figures indicate that while soft news programs do not cover foreign crises nearly as intensely as network evening newscasts do, they nonetheless offer substantial amounts of such coverage.

Finally, as predicted by Hypothesis 3, the data in figure 3.2 suggest that soft news coverage of foreign crises has increased substantially over time. Comparing soft news coverage of the two interventions that took place in the first half of the 1990s with the two interventions that took place in the latter half of the decade, we see sharp over-time increases in coverage, particularly among entertainment TV newsmagazines and cable soft news programs, two programming formats that expanded dramatically during the 1990s. And, in fact, the substantial expansion in the number of prime time hours of television devoted to newsmagazines on all of the major networks (see chapter 2), including the cable news networks, suggests that future foreign crises are likely to receive even greater soft news coverage than those crises included in table 3.2.

TABLE 3.2. Partial Listings of "Soft" News Coverage of 1990s U.S. Foreign Crises and Other Political Issues[a]

						Number of Separate Broadcasts Addressing Issue						
Program	Gulf War	Somalia	Haiti	Bosnia	Iraq (1992–99)	Kosovo	1996 Primaries	1998 Elections	Regulate Tobacco	NAFTA	WTO	Lewinsky Scandal
Network Newsmagazines												
Dateline NBC[b]	—	4	8	17	52	13	4	4	1	1	0	16
20/20[c]	42	3	4	8	20	10	0	1	0	0	0	4
Primetime Live[d]	36	8	4	11	16	—	3	0	0	1	0	3
48 Hours[e]	2	3	4	3	8	1	2	2	0	0	0	2
60 Minutes[f]	14	4	8	17	51	16	2	1	1	2	2	2
Averages	23.5	4.4	5.6	11.2	29.4	10.0	2.2	1.6	0.40	0.80	0.40	5.4
Late-Night TV Talk Shows												
Jay Leno[g]	—	—	39	25	102	14	48	0	0	15	0	45
David Letterman[h]	—	4	20	32	88	21	35	1	0	27	0	37
Conan O'Brien[i]	—	3	22	14	53	4	23	0	0	25	0	30
Politically Incorrect[j]	—	—	—	19	55	15	31	1	5	0	1	34
Averages	—	3.5	27.0	22.5	74.5	13.5	34.3	0.50	1.3	16.8	0.25	36.5
Daytime TV Talk Shows												
Oprah Winfrey[k]	3	6	8	8	4	—	—	—	—	0	—	—
Rosie O'Donnell[l]	—	—	—	3	4	10	—	1	0	0	0	1
Regis and Kathie Lee[m]	—	5	7	10	18	7	0	0	0	4	0	6
Geraldo Rivera[n]	6	3	5	40	13	—	0	0	0	0	0	29
Phil Donahue[o]	—	37	26	59	58	—	5	—	—	0	0	—
Averages	4.5	12.8	11.5	24.0	18.4	8.5	1.7	0.33	0.0	1.0	0.0	12.0
Network TV Soft News												
Extra[p]	—	—	16	116	62	8	1	1	0	0	0	24
Entertainment Tonight[q]	—	—	4	16	7	2	0	1	0	0	0	15
Inside Edition[r]	—	—	4	11	24	3	2	1	0	1	1	28
A Current Affair[s]	4	4	1	8	7		2			0	0	

Cable TV Soft News

Program											
E! Network[t]	—	3	26	6	3	2	0	0			36
Black Entertainment Television[u]	—	23	3	12	6	0	0		2	1	8
Comedy Central's Daily Show[v]	—	—	3	21	16	—	1	1	3	0	11
MTV News[w]	—	7	11	4	7	19	1	0	2	0	5
Averages	3.0	11.0	10.8	10.8	8.0	7.0	0.50	0.25	1.75	0.25	15.0

Radio Programs

Program											
Howard Stern Show[x]	—	18	47	32	13	2	1	0			28

Note: "—" indicates either that a given program was not on the air at the time of a given event or that transcripts were unavailable.

[t] A majority of the data included in this table was acquired through on-line searches of Lexis-Nexis. According to Lexis-Nexis, only select transcripts are available on-line, and many of these are available only as abstracts, rather than as complete text transcripts. Hence, all figures acquired through searches of Lexis-Nexis must be considered incomplete. Moreover, many of the programs in this table were not covered by Lexis-Nexis before the mid-1990s. I acquired crisis coverage information (through October 1998, thereby excluding Kosovo and the December 1998 crisis with Iraq) regarding *The Oprah Winfrey Show* and *Extra* through telephone interviews with representatives from those programs. Figures for the Persian Gulf War are taken from daily program listings in the *Los Angeles Times* between January and March 1991, which only sporadically include program topics. These figures almost certainly understate the true extent of coverage.

[b] Coverage of Iraq begins in October 1997; coverage of Bosnia is from 1994 to 1998; coverage of Haiti is from 1994 to 1995; and coverage of Somalia is from December 1992 through October 1993. Kosovo coverage is from March 24 to June 11, 1999.

[c] Coverage of Bosnia is from 1993 to 1996; coverage of Somalia is from 1992 and 1994; coverage of Haiti is from 1992 and 1994; and coverage of Kosovo is from March 24 to June 13, 1999.

[d] Coverage of Bosnia is from 1993 to 1995; coverage of Somalia is from 1991 to 1994; and coverage of Haiti is from 1994 and 1995.

[e] Coverage of Bosnia is from 1994 and 1995; coverage of Somalia is from 1992 and 1993; coverage of Haiti is from 1994 and 1995; and coverage of Kosovo is from April 15, 1999.

[f] Coverage of Bosnia is from 1993 to 1997; coverage of Somalia is from 1992 and 1993; coverage of Haiti is from 1993 to 1996; and coverage of Kosovo is from March 16 to June 22, 1999. Three of the broadcasts addressing the Kosovo conflict are from *60 Minutes II*, a weekday spinoff of the original *60 Minutes* program.

[g] Coverage of Bosnia is from 1993 to 1995; coverage of Haiti is from 1994 to 1995, with one program in 1996; and coverage of Iraq is from 1993 to 1998. Kosovo coverage is from March 26 to June 14, 1999.

[h] Coverage of Somalia is from 1993 to 1994 (Letterman's debut was in August 1993). Coverage of Bosnia is from 1994 to 1997; coverage of Haiti is from 1994 to 1995; and coverage of Iraq is from 1993 to 1999. Kosovo coverage is from March 29 to June 11, 1999.

[i] Coverage of Somalia is from October and December 1993. Coverage of Bosnia is from 1994 to 1996; coverage of Haiti is from 1993 to 1995; and coverage of Iraq is from 1994 to 1999. Kosovo coverage is from March 29 and April 9, 1999.

TABLE 3.2. *Continued*

[j]*Politically Incorrect* appeared on the Comedy Central cable network through 1996, after which it moved to a late-night time slot on ABC. Coverage of Iraq is from 1996 through May 1999; coverage of Bosnia is from December 1995 through 1997; coverage of Kosovo is from March 24 to June 15, 1999.

[k]Coverage of Iraq is from January 1995, February 1998, March 1998, and June 1998; coverage of Bosnia is from 1995 to 1998; coverage of Haiti is from 1994 to 1995; and coverage of Somalia is from December 1992 through June 1993.

[l]Kosovo figures are from March 23 to June 10, 1999. Iraq and Bosnia figures are from 1997 to 1998.

[m]Coverage of Somalia is from September and October 1993; coverage of Haiti is from October 1993 to October 1994; coverage of Iraq and Bosnia is from February 1994 through December 1998; coverage of Kosovo is from March to June 1999.

[n]Figures are from Geraldo Rivera's now-defunct daytime talk show, and do *not* include coverage in Rivera's more recent political-news-oriented programs (e.g., *Rivera Live*). Coverage of Somalia is from December 14 and 28, 1992, and August 9, 1995; coverage of Bosnia is from 1995 to 1998; coverage of Haiti is from May 1994 to May 1996; and coverage of Iraq is from 1993 to 1998.

[o]Figures are from the *Posner and Donahue* talk-show program (1991 through October 1995), which was a follow-up to Phil Donahue's long-running daytime talk show. Coverage of Iraq is from October 1991 to May 1995; coverage of Bosnia is from 1995; coverage of Somalia is from 1992 to 1993; and coverage of Haiti is from 1994.

[p]*Extra*, which originated in 1994, later changed its name to *Extra! The Entertainment Magazine*, and then subsequently reverted to its original name. Most of the information regarding *Extra* in this table is from a telephone interview with Extra Assignment Desk Assistant to the Managing Editor Abbie Melton (November 13, 1998). Data from 1999 were obtained through on-line searches of Lexis-Nexis. These figures are from the period 1994 to May 1999. The program also broadcast, between 1994 and 1998, 94 stories relating to terrorism (domestic and international) and 32 stories addressing the Middle East peace process. Coverage of Iraq is from 1996 to 1998; coverage of Bosnia is from 1996 to 1998; and coverage of Haiti is from 1994. Coverage of Kosovo is from March 29 to May 18, 1999.

[q]Coverage of Iraq is from 1995 to 1999. Coverage of Bosnia is from 1995 to 1997, with the exceptions of one program in December 1994 and two in December 1993. Coverage of Haiti is from September 1994 to May 1995. Coverage of Kosovo is from April and June 1999.

[r]Coverage of Iraq is from 1993 to 1998; coverage of Bosnia is from 1995 to 1998; coverage of Haiti is from May to September 1994; coverage of Kosovo is from March 5 and 24, 1999, and April 19, 1999.

[s]Transcripts from *A Current Affair* are available, beginning in 1993, on Lexis-Nexis. The program was canceled in 1996. Figures for Iraq are from April 1995 to February 1996; figures for Bosnia are from 1994 to 1996; figures for Somalia are from October 1993.

[t]E! is the cable Entertainment network. These figures are from three entertainment-oriented programs: *E! News Daily*, *E! News Weekend*, and *The E! Gossip Show*. Coverage of Bosnia is from 1995 to 1997 (with one story on October 20, 1993). Coverage of Haiti is from April 22, 1994, May 15, 1995, and February 27, 1997; and coverage of Iraq is from December 8, 1997, and April 28, 1998. Kosovo coverage is from April 9 and May 10, 1999.

[u]These figures are from two programs: *BET Tonight* and *BET News*. BET's coverage of Bosnia, Iraq, and Kosovo is from the period March 1996 to May 1999. BET's coverage of Haiti is from 1994 to 1996.

[v]Coverage of Iraq is from December 1996 through 1998. Coverage of Bosnia is from October 1996 through 1997. Coverage of Kosovo is from February 18 to June 14, 1999.

[w]These figures are from several MTV programs, including *MTV News*, *MTV 1515*, and *MTV Music News*. Coverage of Iraq is from October 11, 1994; coverage of Bosnia is from 1994 to 1996; coverage of Haiti is from 1994 to 1995; coverage of Kosovo is from March 20, April 6, and May 31, 1999.

[x]Coverage of Iraq is from 1996 to 1999; coverage of Bosnia is from 1995 to 1996; coverage of Kosovo is from January 19 to June 15, 1999.

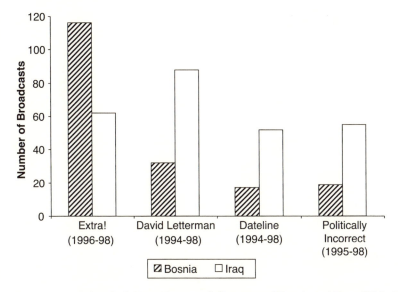

FIGURE 3.1. Select Soft News Programs' Coverage of Bosnia and Iraq, 1994–1998

It is, of course, possible that the increases shown in figure 3.2 could be artifacts of differences between the interventions themselves. For instance, Somalia and Haiti are each poor, Third World nations, of little strategic importance to the United States in the post–Cold War era. Bosnia and Kosovo, in contrast, are in the heart of Europe, which remains central to American foreign policy. News organizations, both hard and soft, may have considered the latter two crises more newsworthy by virtue of their geographic location. If so, we should observe comparable differences in the volume of coverage by traditional news sources. This, however, is not the case. While soft news programs increased their coverage from Somalia and Haiti, on the one hand, to Bosnia and Kosovo, on the other, by anywhere from 44 to 377 percent, ABC's *World News Tonight* offered only 14 percent more coverage of the latter pair of crises. These figures suggest a disproportionate trend toward greater soft news coverage, relative to coverage of foreign crises by the traditional news media—once again supporting my third hypothesis.[17]

As predicted by Hypothesis 2, the story is quite different for soft news coverage of other, less-dramatic or more overtly partisan political issues. For instance, a content analysis of soft news coverage of the Republican presidential candidates during the 1996 primaries, shown in table 3.2, found, with several exceptions, far less coverage of the primaries than of any of the foreign crises included in the table.[18] I also conducted content analyses for soft news media coverage of the 1998 state and federal election campaigns (January 1–November 3, 1998), the 1998 debate in Washington over tobacco regulation (January 1–December 31, 1998), and the Monica Lewinsky scandal (January 21–April 30, 1998).[19] Additionally, to see if the distinction I have drawn between foreign

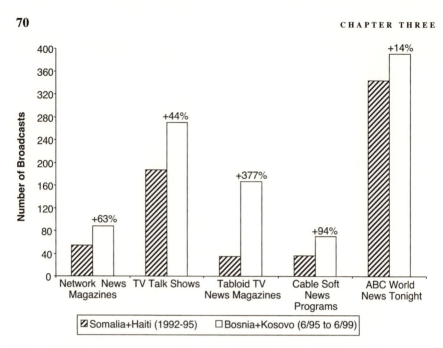

FIGURE 3.2. Trends in Soft News Coverage of Foreign Crises, Early-to-Mid vs. Mid-to-Late 1990s

crises and other foreign policy issues is valid, I conducted content analyses of soft news coverage of NAFTA and the World Trade Organization (WTO) (January 1, 1992–February 29, 2000).[20] Due to their relatively greater complexity and the absence of easily identifiable moral "heroes" or "villains," these latter two foreign affairs issues seem relatively unlikely to have appealed to the soft news media.

Each of these issues was covered at length by the traditional news media. For instance, a Lexis-Nexis search of the same time frame, employing the identical search terms as my soft news searches, returned 58 stories related to the 1998 elections on ABC's *World News Tonight*. The corresponding figures for the *CBS Evening News, NBC Nightly News,* and *The News Hour with Jim Lehrer* were 36, 45, and 56 stories, respectively. The tobacco search terms, in turn, returned 30 tobacco-related stories on ABC's *World News Tonight*. The corresponding figures for the *CBS Evening News, NBC Nightly News,* and *The News Hour with Jim Lehrer* were 22, 29 and 30 stories, respectively. This suggests that at least the *traditional* news media considered these issues to be of significant interest. The results from my keyword searches of soft news media outlets are shown in the final columns of table 3.2.

To an even greater extent than the 1996 presidential primaries, the soft news programs listed in the table appear hardly to have noticed the 1998 elections, while soft news coverage of the tobacco debate approached zero. And, with the sole exception of NAFTA-related humor on three late-night talk shows (almost exclusively in the context of presidential humor), these soft news outlets all but ignored NAFTA and the WTO.[21] In sharp contrast, most of the soft news programs listed in table 3.2 provided substantial coverage of the Lewinsky scandal.[22] Taken together, these results offer strong support for each hypothesis.

Do the Soft and Hard News Media Cover Foreign Crises in Different Ways?

Just because the soft news media cover foreign affairs does not necessarily mean that they do so differently from the traditional news media. Yet, if such coverage by soft news outlets *does* differ qualitatively from that offered by the hard news media, this may have important implications for public attitudes regarding foreign policy, at least under some circumstances. Hence, I now investigate *how* soft news programs cover foreign policy crises. As we shall see, the content of foreign crisis coverage by soft news programs frequently differs significantly from that of the traditional news media. Learning about politics or foreign policy from the soft news media is therefore not necessarily equivalent to doing so via traditional news outlets, especially if the soft news media are an individual's *only* source of news about an issue.

I begin this section by presenting the results of a content analysis investigation into the qualitative differences between the coverage of foreign crises by the soft and hard news media. Then, in order to give the reader a clearer sense of the flavor of soft news coverage of foreign crises, I present a series of anecdotes, intended to flesh out some of the differences as well as some of the similarities, in how the soft and hard news media cover such issues and events.

COMPARING SOFT AND HARD NEWS COVERAGE OF U.S. FOREIGN CRISES, 1992–1999

With the help of several research assistants, I acquired and analyzed thirty-eight soft news reports concerning a variety of U.S. foreign policy crises in the 1990s from the following tabloid and entertainment newsmagazine shows: *Extra, Access Hollywood, Inside Edition, Entertainment Tonight, Hard Copy,* and the Comedy Central Network's *Daily Show.* My research assistants and I also coded fifty-five randomly selected traditional news reports on the same topics (during roughly the same time periods) from the following programs: ABC's *World News Tonight, CBS Evening News, NBC Nightly News,* and CNN's early-evening newscasts. In this section I review my principal findings from this analysis. The raw data employed in this investigation, including the sources, dates and durations of the reports and their topics, are summarized in table 3.3. (The questionnaire employed by the coders is presented in the appendix to this chapter.)

One obvious potential criticism of this comparison can be immediately dismissed when we look at table 3.3. That is, the soft and hard news reports are, on average, nearly identical in length: 2:38 for the soft news reports and 2:56 for the hard news reports.[23] Hence, it is clearly not the case that the soft news reports represented mere passing mentions of the crisis or conflict at issue in the context of unrelated stories. Rather, in every instance, the soft and hard news

TABLE 3.3. Soft and Hard News Reports Included in Content Analysis Investigation

Date	Duration	Program	Topic
Traditional News Programs			
12/25/92	2:06	CNN *Prime News*	Somalia
12/31/92	4:56	CNN *Prime News*	Somalia
1/3/93	2:27	*CBS Evening News*	Somalia
1/12/93	1:14	*CBS Evening News*	Somalia
1/24/93	2:15	CNN *Prime News*	Somalia
3/10/93	2:27	CNN *Prime News*	Somalia
3/25/93	2:05	*CBS Evening News*	Somalia
5/1/93	3:42	*CBS Evening News*	Bosnia
6/18/93	3:33	ABC *World News Tonight*	Somalia
7/1/93	2:03	CNN *Prime News*	Somalia
10/2/93	2:03	CNN *Prime News*	Somalia
10/4/93	2:02	*CBS Evening News*	Somalia
10/5/93	3:16	ABC *World News Tonight*	Somalia
10/7/93	2:15	*CBS Evening News*	Somalia
10/20/93	2:02	*CBS Evening News*	Somalia
9/26/94	3:53	ABC *World News Tonight*	Haiti
9/26/94	3:51	ABC *World News Tonight*	Haiti
9/30/94	4:50	CNN *Prime News*	Haiti
9/30/94	2:14	ABC *World News Tonight*	Haiti
10/1/94	5:36	CNN *Prime News*	Haiti
10/1/94	3:21	*CBS Evening News*	Haiti
6/10/95	5:14	ABC *World News Tonight*	Bosnia
6/11/95	2:25	CNN *Prime News*	Bosnia
6/12/95	2:04	CNN *Prime News*	Bosnia
6/12/95	3:33	ABC *World News Tonight*	Bosnia
6/12/95	3:48	*CBS Evening News*	Bosnia
6/12/95	7:24	CNN *Prime News*	Bosnia
12/1/95	2:59	ABC *World News Tonight*	Bosnia
12/1/95	2:47	ABC *World News Tonight*	Bosnia
12/31/95	2:16	*CBS Evening News*	Bosnia
1/22/96	3:54	ABC *World News Tonight*	Bosnia
1/24/96	2:49	CNN *Prime News*	Bosnia
1/25/96	2:05	CNN *Prime News*	Bosnia
12/19/97	5:03	ABC *World News Tonight*	Iraq
1/30/98	2:27	CNN *Prime News*	Iraq
2/28/98	2:02	*NBC Nightly News*	Iraq
8/20/98	2:20	*NBC Nightly News*	Cruise missile attacks on Afghanistan & Sudan
8/20/98	2:03	*CBS Evening News*	Cruise missile attacks on Afghanistan & Sudan
8/21/98	2:57	CNN *Prime News*	Cruise missile attacks on Afghanistan & Sudan
8/22/98	2:09	*CBS Evening News*	Cruise missile attacks on Afghanistan & Sudan

TABLE 3.3. *Continued*

Date	Duration	Program	Topic
8/24/98	2:20	ABC *World News Tonight*	Cruise missile attacks on Afghanistan & Sudan
12/16/98	2:21	ABC *World News Tonight*	Iraq
12/17/98	2:00	*CBS Evening News*	Iraq
12/18/98	19:43	CNN *Prime News*	Iraq
12/18/98	2:15	*NBC Nightly News*	Iraq
2/15/99	2:58	*CBS Evening News*	Kosovo
3/6/99	3:42	CNN *Prime News*	Kosovo
3/15/99	3:11	ABC *World News Tonight*	Kosovo
3/27/99	3:21	*NBC Nightly News*	Kosovo
4/8/99	2:52	*NBC Nightly News*	Kosovo
4/10/99	2:18	*CBS Evening News*	Kosovo
5/25/99	2:09	ABC *World News Tonight*	Kosovo
6/29/99	2:04	*CBS Evening News*	Kosovo
1/29/99	3:40	ABC *World News Tonight*	Kosovo
4/29/99	2:29	CNN *Prime News*	Kosovo
Soft News Programs			
7/24/94	2:39	*Hard Copy*	Bosnia
9/27/94	5:26	*Inside Edition*	Iraq
9/27/94	5:32	*Inside Edition*	Haiti
6/13/95	7:45	*Inside Edition*	Iraq
04/01/96	2:16	*Inside Edition*	Bosnia
07/02/97	3:13	*Inside Edition*	Bosnia
2/27/98	2:00	*Entertainment Tonight*	Iraq
3/4/98	2:44	*Access Hollywood*	Iraq
8/18/98	3:23	*Access Hollywood*	Cruise missile attacks on Afghanistan & Sudan
8/20/98	3:03	*Extra*	Cruise missile attacks on Afghanistan & Sudan
8/20/98	2:20	*Access Hollywood*	Cruise missile attacks on Afghanistan & Sudan
8/21/98	2:39	*Access Hollywood*	Cruise missile attacks on Afghanistan & Sudan
8/21/98	2:34	*Extra*	Iraq
8/21/98	3:26	*Extra*	Osama Bin Laden
8/21/98	2:29	*Extra*	Iraq
8/22/98	1:44	*Daily Show*	Cruise missile attacks on Afghanistan & Sudan
8/23/98	2:15	*Entertainment Tonight*	Cruise missile attacks on Afghanistan & Sudan
8/25/98	2:27	*Access Hollywood*	Interview with George H. W. Bush (regarding Gulf War)
8/26/98	2:39	*Extra*	South Africa nightclub bombing
8/27/98	2:09	*Extra*	South Africa nightclub bombing
8/27/98	0:51	*Access Hollywood*	South Africa nightclub bombing

TABLE 3.3. *Continued*

Date	Duration	Program	Topic
8/28/98	1:12	*Access Hollywood*	South Africa nightclub bombing
9/7/98	3:05	*Extra*	Terrorism
9/10/98	7:18	*Extra*	Osama Bin Laden
12/17/98	1:35	*Extra*	Iraq
12/17/98	1:33	*Extra*	High-tech weapons
12/18/98	1:42	*Entertainment Tonight*	Iraq
12/18/98	1:55	*Extra*	Iraq
12/18/98	1:02	*Access Hollywood*	Dangers to journalists of covering wars
3/24/99	1:33	*Inside Edition*	Afghanistan
3/24/99*	2:35	*Extra*	Kosovo
3/29/99	2:15	*Extra*	Kosovo
3/29/99	2:02	*Extra*	Iraq
3/29/99	0:21	*Access Hollywood*	Kosovo
4/5/99	2:26	*Extra*	Kosovo
4/5/99	2:16	*Extra*	Kosovo
4/5/99	2:37	*Extra*	Kosovo
4/5/99	1:32	*Extra*	Kosovo

*Estimated air date (precise date was unavailable).

stories focused exclusively (or at least predominantly) on the foreign policy topic noted in table 3.3.

The data were divided between written transcripts and videotaped segments. Nevertheless, the coders agreed on over 85 percent of all coding decisions for both soft and hard news programs. And there were no significant differences in inter-coder reliability between written transcripts and videotaped reports.[24]

My results clearly demonstrate that the soft news media cover foreign policy crises quite differently from traditional news outlets. Table 3.4 summarizes my key findings. The first five questions address the prevalence of episodic and thematic frames in soft and hard news coverage of U.S. military interventions. *Episodic* frames emphasize the experiences or reactions to events of a specific individual or small group (e.g., a family), without providing a broader context for understanding the story. An example would be a story about the reactions of a family to news that their son or daughter has been seized as a prisoner of war. A *thematic* frame, in contrast, provides a broader context, explaining why a given conflict occurred or discussing the broader issues involved in the conflict (Iyengar 1991).

The results indicate that compared to traditional national newscasts (ABC, CBS, NBC, and CNN), soft news outlets have a far lower probability of employing a thematic frame, such as describing the origins of the conflict (.08 vs. .44, $p < .001$), noting whether the conflict began prior to U.S. involvement (.00 vs. .24, $p < .001$), or identifying the countries and groups involved in the conflict

TABLE 3.4. Content Analysis of Soft versus Hard News Coverage of U.S. Military Operations, 1992–1999

	Soft News	Hard News	Soft News Difference
Use of Episodic and Thematic Frames			
Probability report discussed origins of conflict	.08	.44	−0.38***
Probability origins of conflict described as beginning prior to U.S. involvement	.00	.24	−0.24**
Probability report mentions a country, faction, or group as an adversary/antagonist in conflict	.21	.55	−0.34*
Probability report featured an individual, family, or small group(s)	.95	.69	+0.26***
Probability report featured the issue or conflict as a whole or the circumstances surrounding the conflict	.16	.69	−0.53***
Cues from Credible or Noncredible Sources			
On average, how many members of president's party sourced per report?	0.15	0.60	−0.45***
On average, how many members of opposition party sourced per report?	0.05	0.09	−0.04
On average, how many experts (including senior military officers) sourced per report?	0.44	0.78	−0.34^
On average, how many celebrities sourced per report	0.77	0.00	+0.77**
Support for U.S. Decision Makers			
Probability report includes comment by celebrity *critical* of U.S. decision makers	.30	.00	+0.30***
Probability report includes comment by member of president's party *supportive* of U.S. decision makers	.11	.24	−0.13^
Probability report suggests conflict has good chance of being resolved through U.S. action	.00	.11	−0.11**
Comparisons to U.S. Foreign Policy Failures			
Probability report mentioned a past U.S. foreign policy crisis/conflict	.45	.25	+0.20^^
On average, how many of past foreign policy crises/conflicts mentioned per report represented clear U.S. foreign policy failures?	0.45	0.15	+0.30^^
On average, how many comparisons per report to Vietnam War?	0.16	0.00	+0.16**

^̃$p < .10$, ^̂$p < .07$, *$p < .05$, **$p < .01$, ***$p < .001$

(.21 vs. .55, $p < .05$).[25] More generally, soft news reports are far less likely (.15 vs. .69, $p < .001$) to feature discussion of the conflict or crisis as a whole or the circumstances surrounding the conflict or crisis. The exception to this latter pattern concerns the likelihood of drawing analogies to past U.S. interventions and other foreign policy experiences, which is far more common in soft news outlets (.45 vs. .25, $p < .06$). Conversely, while episodic frames are quite common in hard news coverage, appearing in 69 percent of the hard news reports investigated in this study, they are virtually ubiquitous in soft news coverage. Fully 95 percent of all soft news reports employed episodic frames, focusing primarily on the experiences of an individual, family or small group. The difference in prevalence of episodic frames between soft and hard news programs is statistically significant at the .001 level.

Moreover, in referencing past U.S. military activities, soft news outlets were three times as likely as their hard news counterparts to draw comparisons between the current crisis and past U.S. foreign policy *failures*, such as terrorist attacks against U.S. interests abroad or the Vietnam War (.45 vs. .15, $p < .05$).[26] Sixteen percent of all soft news reports, accounting for nearly one-fifth of *all* soft news mentions of past U.S. foreign policy conflicts, drew comparisons to arguably the single most traumatic and high-profile U.S. foreign policy failure of the twentieth century, the Vietnam War. This compares to *zero* mentions of Vietnam across all fifty-five traditional news broadcasts. Not surprisingly, this difference is also statistically significant, at the .01 level.

In not a single report investigated in this study did a soft news outlet suggest or imply that whatever issue or problem prompted U.S. involvement was likely to be successfully resolved through U.S. military action. The corresponding probability that a hard news report would suggest that a U.S. intervention might be successful was 11 percent—also quite low, but far from zero. Once again, the difference between soft and hard news reports in the likelihood of anticipating a U.S. success is statistically significant at the .01 level.

Finally, in covering U.S. military operations, the traditional news media are far more prone than their soft news counterparts to feature comments by individuals likely to possess significant and accurate information about the U.S. policy. This difference spans members of the president's party (on average, 0.60 presidential party members per hard news report vs. 0.16 per soft news report, $p < .001$), opposition party members (0.09 vs. 0.05, insig.) and expert commentators (0.78 vs. 0.45, $p < .07$).

Instead, the soft news media emphasize commentary by sources far less likely to possess important and accurate information regarding the U.S. policy at issue. In particular, comments by celebrities were featured in soft news coverage more frequently than comments by all three of the other groups combined. On average, soft news programs featured 0.79 celebrities per report, while traditional news reports included *no* celebrities whatsoever. This difference is again statistically significant ($p < .01$). The latter difference is potentially important because it seems quite likely that, on average, the opinions of celebrities will carry less weight with most viewers than, for instance, the opinions of policy experts or members of the administration conducting the policy. There are, of course, certainly *some* celebrities, like Oprah Winfrey or Rosie O'Donnell, whose opinions are highly credible among their fans. And, to the extent that some soft news viewers *do* consider the opinions of celebrities as credible cues, it is worth noting that in those instances where celebrities took any discernable position on the U.S. conflict at issue—which was the case in about 37 percent of the soft news reports—they were statistically significantly ($p < .001$) more likely to *criticize* U.S. decision makers than to support them. Overall, the probability of a critical comment in a soft news report was .30, while that of a supportive comment was .18. In contrast, a typical hard news report was more likely than a typical soft news report (.24 vs. .13, $p < .09$) to include a *supportive* comment from a member of the president's party. Taken together, these data identify stark differences in the coverage of U.S. foreign policy between the soft and hard news media—differences, in each instance, that are consistent with the theory.

Of course, a quantitative analysis comparing the extent to which the soft and hard news media emphasize different styles or themes does not by itself paint a particularly vivid picture of the substantive differences in soft and hard news coverage of foreign crises. Painting such a picture requires moving from the macrolevel analysis presented above (i.e., comparing averages across large numbers of reports) to the microlevel (i.e., comparing individual instances of soft and hard news reports on similar topics). In the hopes of offering the reader a clearer sense of exactly how the soft and hard news approaches to covering foreign crises differ in specific instances, I next present a series of illustrative anecdotes, as well as several narrower content analyses of specific events, drawn from a variety of U.S. military engagements from the 1990s.

A FEW ILLUSTRATIVE EXAMPLES OF SOFT AND HARD NEWS MEDIA COVERAGE
OF FOREIGN CRISES

Some, even many, of the themes presented by soft news shows can also be found in traditional news programs. Yet as my content analysis revealed, on average, soft news programs differ significantly from their hard news counterparts in terms of their relative degree of emphasis on such themes, and in their far greater reliance on episodic, rather than thematic, frames. For instance, in their coverage of U.S. military involvement in Bosnia, traditional news programs discussed a variety of story lines, including the ethnic cleansing of Bosnia's Muslim population by Bosnian Serbs, the nature of U.S. military involvement, including the risk of becoming bogged down in "another Vietnam," as well as diplomatic efforts aimed at resolving the conflict and the origins of the civil war in Bosnia. In contrast, many soft news programs devoted a disproportionate share of their coverage to the travails of fighter pilot Scott O'Grady, who was shot down by Bosnian Serbs over enemy territory on June 2, 1995. Captain O'Grady managed to survive for five days on a diet of insects and grass, after which he was able to send a radio signal that was picked up by NATO forces, who subsequently launched a successful rescue mission. O'Grady's story of heroism and survival behind enemy lines represented an ideal made-for-soft-news tale of human drama, and, not surprisingly, the soft news media offered saturation coverage of the story. Soft news reporting—including that by such programs as *Dateline, Entertainment Tonight, Extra, A Current Affair*, and all of the late-night talk shows, to name only a few—emphasized the story of O'Grady's travails behind enemy lines, as well as the reactions of his family and friends, ranging from their responses to the news that he had been shot down, to receiving word that he had been rescued, to the hero's welcome he received upon returning home.

To determine the nature and extent of soft news coverage of Bosnia in June 1995, I reviewed Lexis-Nexis transcripts from twelve soft news programs for which the appropriate data was accessible.[27] I found that of thirty-five total broadcasts across these twelve shows which addressed the conflict in Bosnia, 30 (or 86 percent) featured the O'Grady story. Of course, traditional news programs also covered the story. The difference is that, in the latter case, this was merely one of *many* story lines, whereas, for many soft news programs, this was the *only* story (or one of a very few similarly dramatic story lines). The three major networks, combined, covered the O'Grady story in only thirteen out of fifty-seven (or 23 percent) June 1995 national news broadcasts that addressed Bosnia.

The disproportionate emphasis on individual (i.e., episodic) stories of danger and heroism by soft news programs is not limited to the case of Bosnia. For instance, on April 1, 1999, during the NATO air war in Kosovo, Serbian forces captured three U.S. servicemen: Steven Gonzales, Andrew Ramirez, and Christopher Stone. Over the next several days, a variety of soft news programs, ranging from *Extra* to *Inside Edition* to *The Rosie O'Donnell Show* to *Dateline*, featured related stories involving several typical soft news themes. Such stories included discussion of the possibility that the captured servicemen might be tortured and their likely psychological responses to torture, as well as the reactions of family members and friends at home, including the proliferation of yellow ribbons in the soldiers' home towns. Indeed, this latter theme—the reactions of family members at home to the travails of U.S. servicemen facing extraordinary risks abroad—along with *heroism* (i.e., stories of individuals overcoming long odds), are perhaps the two most prevalent themes in soft news coverage of foreign crises.

In order to get a clearer sense of the similarities and differences in coverage of the Kosovo story by soft and hard news programs, I asked a research assistant to review network news coverage of the Kosovo air war in close proximity to the capture of the three U.S. servicemen. He reviewed the *CBS Evening News* on April 3, 1999, two days after the servicemen were captured. In watching the newscast, I asked my research assistant to record the topics of the several related stories, as well as the types of themes and frames employed in covering the war. I reviewed the same newscast in order to verify my research assistant's findings.

CBS's coverage of Kosovo on this particular evening included some of the same topics and themes as the aforementioned soft news programs, particularly—and not surprisingly—the emphasis on the plight of the POWs. Yet, for the *CBS Evening News*, this was but one of many themes. Most of the broadcast that evening was devoted to the conflict in Kosovo. Reports on the POWs ranged from a discussion of the broader events and conditions leading to their capture, to President Clinton meeting with military families, to interviews with the families and friends of the POWs. The dominant frames in these broadcasts might best be described as *conflict*, meaning that the reports described events on the battlefield largely in descriptive, rather than normative, terms, as well as *human drama*, which tended to be more normative.

Unlike the soft news media, however, *CBS Evening News* coverage was not limited to the POW story. The broadcast also covered the issue of ethnic cleansing, presented excerpts from interviews with President Clinton and a senior Serbian official on a variety of topics (including, but not limited to, ethnic cleansing and the plight of the POWs), as well as reporting on the magnitude of U.S. airpower in the region, allied strategies and tactics, and the overall status of the war. Hence, while there were certainly many parallels between soft and hard news coverage in the aftermath of the capture of the three U.S. servicemen, coverage by the hard news media was predictably far more diverse and employed thematic frames to a far greater extent.

Only four months earlier, in December 1998, the United States and Great Britain had launched Operation Desert Fox, a four-day bombing campaign over Iraq. *Inside Edition* covered the air strike campaign in three separate programs, two of which addressed the dangers of domestic terrorism, while the third told the story of Staff Sgt. Jeff Berry of the U.S. Air Force, who was forced to postpone his planned wedding due to his deployment to the Persian Gulf. *Access Hollywood*, in turn, focused on the curious timing of the air strikes, which took place on the eve of President Clinton's impeachment trial in the Senate. This same *Wag the Dog* theme also dominated coverage on Comedy Central's *Daily Show*, as well as that of late-night talk shows, including *The Late Show with David Letterman, The Tonight Show with Jay Leno*, and *Late Night with Conan O'Brien*. *Extra*, in turn, covered the air strike campaign in twelve segments, across six separate broadcasts. Each segment focused on either the reactions of celebrities (including the rapid rise to celebrity status of NBC reporter Donatella Lorch), the threat of domestic terrorism, or the seemingly curious proximity of the air strikes to the president's impeachment trial. Coverage by the network newsmagazines—including *Dateline, 20/20, 48 Hours*, and *60 Minutes*—was somewhat more varied, but also included large doses of the *Wag the Dog* theme, as well as extended discussions of the risks of domestic terrorism.

Once again, to compare coverage of Operation Desert Fox across differing news formats, I asked my research assistant to review a variety of soft and hard news programs from a randomly selected day during the four-day air strike campaign. He focused on the evening of December 18, the third day of Desert Fox. He viewed five programs from that evening, four from CBS and one from

NBC. These included the *CBS Evening News*, the early and late local news broadcasts of Los Angeles CBS affiliate KCBS, *The Late Show with David Letterman*, and *Extra*. As before, he recorded the topics of the broadcasts, while paying close attention to the types of themes and frames employed in reporting on the airstrike campaign. I again reviewed the programs in order to verify my research assistant's findings.

On that particular evening, the *CBS Evening News* presented a special one-hour broadcast. Most of the broadcast was devoted to President Clinton's impending impeachment trial in the Senate and to Operation Desert Fox. Out of a total of fourteen reports on the two issues, nine dealt with the impeachment trial or related issues, and five dealt with the situation in Iraq. Of the nine scandal-related stories, only two made any reference whatsoever to the situation in Iraq, and both of these were merely passing references, having little to do with the primary story themes. Rather, the primary themes emphasized in these stories were the administration's strategy in preparing for the impeachment trial and the related partisan conflict between Democrats and Republicans. There was also a story about *Hustler* publisher Larry Flint's investigation into alleged marital infidelity by Republican House Speaker Bob Livingston.

The five stories on Operation Desert Fox, in turn, made absolutely no mention of the Lewinsky scandal or the impeachment trial. Instead, they focused on describing the progress of the air strike campaign. Themes included several stories highlighting U.S. military power (e.g., a reporter reviewing, from the deck of an aircraft carrier, the types of weapons used in Desert Fox), discussions of allied military strategy, and coverage of international protests against the air strikes. The dominant frames employed in these broadcasts might best be described as *power* and *conflict*, both of which were largely thematic in nature. (The difference here is that in the former case, the stories emphasized the overwhelming military dominance of the U.S. and NATO, while in the latter case, as previously noted, the stories merely described events on the battlefield.)

Local news broadcasts drew a much clearer connection between the impeachment trial and the situation in Iraq. In one story, for instance, the reporter talked about "two battlefields: one in Baghdad, one in the capital. . . . the difference is that the president is in charge of one and not the other." Despite this linkage, however, local news reports rarely questioned the president's motives. In fact, most of the impeachment-related coverage made only passing reference to the conflict in Iraq. And, *none* of the stories on Operation Desert Fox made *any* reference whatsoever to the impeachment trial. In reporting on the air strikes, local news coverage, to a greater extent than the national news, emphasized dramatic visuals, and included reports about U.S. military power and Saddam Hussein, the latter of which exemplifies the propensity of local news to couch a war story in "good versus evil" or "hero versus villain" terms.

Finally, clear qualitative differences were apparent between coverage of Desert Fox in the soft news media and that on national and local news broadcasts. In covering the conflict, that evening's episode of *Extra*—which I mentioned above—focused on profiling NBC reporter Donatella Lorch, with an emphasis on her live reporting from Baghdad. The report showed visuals of Lorch dressed in battle fatigues and helmet, while simultaneously showing her mother watching Lorch's reporting and worrying aloud about the dangers she was facing. The anchor commented on how "she looks so much like her mom." The report offered no significant commentary on the conflict itself, but instead focused on Lorch's emergence as a media celebrity. The predominant (unambiguously episodic) frame employed in the story was what Neuman, Just, and Crigler (1992) refer to as *human impact*, in this instance with an emphasis on family and celebrity.

David Letterman, in turn, devoted much of his monologue that evening to jokes explicitly connecting the two events. Overall, about half of Letterman's jokes drew a direct linkage between the impeachment trial and Operation Desert Fox. (For instance, Letterman quipped that President Clinton had prepared for the war by helping an intern hide underneath a desk.) In sum, as we move "down market"—from the *CBS Evening News*, to local TV news, to the soft news media—we observe a steady movement toward drawing explicit linkages between the impeachment trial and Desert Fox, along with greater emphasis on personal stories (i.e., episodic frames) and sensational or dramatic themes.

Similar themes prevailed in soft news coverage of the Persian Gulf War. For instance, as noted in chapter 2, between January and March 1991, a variety of soft news programs, including the daytime talk shows hosted by Oprah Winfrey, Geraldo Rivera, and Sally Jesse Raphael, as well as tabloid news programs like *A Current Affair*, featured (episodic) stories on the families of servicemen and -women stationed in the Middle East, including families of individuals being held as "human shields" in Iraq. The same programs also emphasized other, related themes, including the travails of American prisoners of war, the threat of terrorism in the United States, and the effects of the war on celebrities, families, and children.

More recently, virtually all soft news programs offered extensive coverage of the events surrounding 9/11 and its aftermath. Figure 3.3, for instance, tracks the monthly trends in the percentages of *all* stories broadcast on two soft news outlets, *Extra* and *Inside Edition*, devoted to issues related to 9/11, from September 12, 2001, through August 2002. For purposes of comparison, the figure also presents the corresponding trend over the same time period for ABC's *World News Tonight*. Interestingly, these data indicate that, at least in terms of relative intensity of 9/11-related coverage, the trends for the two tabloid programs largely mirrored that of the network news.[28]

And, once again, soft news coverage emphasized accessible themes and episodic frames, including individual examples of heroism or personal tragedy and the role of celebrities. For instance, during its 17 broadcasts between September 12 and October 3, 2001, *Extra* presented a total of 64 "news" feature segments, all but seven of which dealt in some way with 9/11. Of these 57 9/11-related stories, nearly two-thirds involved either the reactions or involvement of celebrities (22 stories, or 39 percent) or accounts of individual survival and heroism (14 stories, or 25 percent).[29] The former set of stories addressed topics ranging

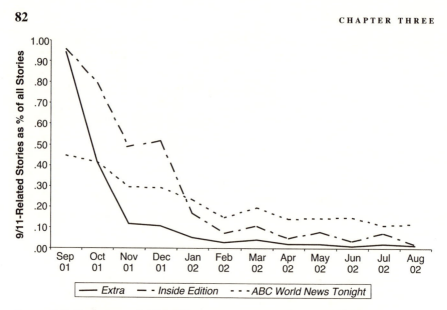

FIGURE 3.3. Percentage of All Stories on *Extra, Inside Edition,* and ABC's *World News Tonight* Related to 9/11 or Its Aftermath, September 2001–August 2002
SOURCES: Vanderbilt Television News Archive (http://tvnews.vanderbilt.edu/); http://www.insideedition.com; and http://www.extratv.com

from the efforts of celebrities to raise funds for the victims of the terrorist attacks to the effects of the attacks on the movie industry. The latter set of stories focused primarily on the efforts of firefighters and rescue workers, including profiles of individual firefighters. The remainder of this program's 9/11-related coverage featured a variety of human-interest stories, such as that of one woman whose husband was missing and presumed dead, and who gave birth to a new baby who "will never meet his daddy" (September 24, 2001), as well as tips for talking to children about the tragedy (September 22, 2001).

A similar pattern prevailed on *Inside Edition,* which featured topics relating to 9/11 in 85 percent of all stories broadcast between September 12 and October 31, 2001 (166 out of 196 total stories).[30] And, just as on *Extra,* nearly 60 percent of *Inside Edition's* coverage during that period featured episodic stories of heroism, personal tragedy, or survival (66 stories, or 40 percent) or the reactions of celebrities and the entertainment industry (31 stories, or 19 percent). The former set of stories featured such topics as profiles of individuals killed in the World Trade Center and their surviving family members, stories about the birth of babies of 9/11 victims, and profiles of passengers aboard hijacked Pan Am Flight 93, who died following an apparent effort to storm the cockpit and regain control of the aircraft. One *Inside Edition* story, for instance, broadcast on September 28, 2001, profiled a window washer at the World Trade Center who was missing and presumed dead, and featured the reactions of his family members.

The latter set of stories featured such topics as efforts by Jay Leno's wife to publicize the plight of women in Afghanistan (September 27), actress and singer Jennifer Lopez's alleged post-9/11 fear of traveling to New York City to promote her new fashion line (October 30), a variety of celebrity and entertainment-industry fund raisers for the benefit of 9/11 victims (e.g., October 3), and the repeated cancellation and rescheduling of the Emmy Awards (October 8). The remaining 9/11-related stories ranged from profiles of Osama Bin Laden and the 9/11 hijackers, to coverage of the Florida anthrax scare, to general coverage of the domestic terrorism threat and related investigations, to stories about how Americans were coping with post-9/11 trauma. Not surprisingly, the vast majority of these stories were episodic in nature.

Consistent with research cited in chapter 2, unlike traditional news programs—which sought, admittedly with varying degrees of success, to retain at least a modicum of objectivity—many soft news outlets made no such effort to appear unbiased in their coverage. For instance, in an interview on the Fox news network (November 24), John Walsh, host of *America's Most Wanted*, a program devoted to profiling the most wanted criminals in America, indicated that the U.S. government had asked him to devote an episode to profiling the terrorists suspected of masterminding 9/11, as well as other attacks against U.S. targets. He noted that the program enthusiastically agreed, and subsequently set out to the Persian Gulf city of Dubai, capital of the United Arab Emirates, to pursue the suspects. Explaining why the program was filming in the Middle East, he did not hesitate to pass moral judgment on the suspects, commenting, "We'll go wherever we have to go to find these cowards."

Even before September 11, 2001, terrorism was a regular theme of soft news coverage of foreign affairs. Indeed, virtually all of the soft news programs reviewed in table 3.2 have presented stories on terrorism. For example, according to Lexis-Nexis, excluding post-9/11 coverage, *Extra* has devoted over twenty-five program segments to the subject. One such episode, broadcast on March 24, 2001, discussed threats by Spanish terrorists against Hollywood celebrity Antonio Banderas, as well as similar threats against other celebrities, including Russell Crowe and Pierce Brosnan. *Inside Edition*, in turn, has presented sixteen feature segments (in sixteen separate broadcasts) related to terrorism.

Terrorism coverage by these two programs, as well as that of many other soft news programs, is almost entirely episodic, typically following major terrorist events—ranging from the bombing of Olympic Park in Atlanta during the 1996 Summer Olympic Games, to the 1998 bombing of U.S. embassies in Kenya and Sudan, to thwarted millennium-related terror attacks in Seattle and Los Angeles. Soft news terrorism coverage has focused on such themes as the nature and extent of domestic threats, including the dangers of nuclear, chemical, and biological weapons, as well as profiles of suspected terrorist mastermind Osama Bin Laden. In a January 2000 broadcast, for instance, talk show host Rosie O'Donnell, in the course of a celebrity interview, discussed at length her fear, and that of her family and friends, of millennium-related terrorism. The threat to America of millennium-related terror attacks was also featured in a round-table discussion on the daytime talk show *The View* in late December 1999. In fact, another prominent soft news theme is the reaction of celebrities to terrorist incidents. For instance, *Access Hollywood* and *Entertainment Tonight* presented several stories on the reactions of Hollywood celebrities to a terrorist bombing of a Planet Hollywood, a restaurant chain owned by several prominent Hollywood celebrities, in South Africa on August 25, 1998.

Network newsmagazines, in turn, have offered extensive, and also largely episodic, coverage of domestic and international terrorism. NBC's *Dateline* and ABC's *20/20* presented terrorism-related features in forty-nine and forty-one separate broadcasts, respectively, *before* 9/11. And *60 Minutes* and its sister program, *60 Minutes II*, combined, have featured terrorism in nearly three hundred stories over the past decade (once again, prior to the events of September 11, 2001). These stories have addressed themes similar to those noted above, ranging from stories of heroism and survival following specific terrorist attacks, to interviews with the families of victims of terrorism, to profiles of suspected terrorists and their sponsors, including Saddam Hussein and Osama Bin Laden. One example of the latter theme appeared in a January 19, 1996, segment of *20/20*, entitled "The Assassin—An American Who Killed for Iran." This story profiled an American citizen named David Belfield, a self-described world terrorist, recruited by Islamic fundamentalists to be an assassin for Iran. At the time of the broadcast, the FBI had been searching for Belfield, who had fled to Iran, for over fifteen years. A second example is a June 10, 2001, episode of *60 Minutes*, which featured the story of a father's efforts to sue the government of Iran for supporting the terrorist organization suspected of sponsoring a suicide attack in Israel in April 1995, in which his daughter, a twenty-year-old student, was killed.

Finally, to test the validity of my hypothesis that the soft news media will tend to eschew partisan politics, I investigated how several soft news programs covered the Monica Lewinsky scandal. This represents a particularly difficult test for my argument, as the Lewinsky scandal was a profoundly partisan affair, ultimately degenerating into a nearly unprecedented—at least in recent decades—degree of partisan warfare in the Congress. (Recall, for instance, First Lady Hillary Clinton's assertion during an interview on *Good Morning America* that she and her husband were victims of a "vast right-wing conspiracy.") I conducted keyword searches, using Lexis-Nexis, to determine how many soft news media stories on the Lewinsky scandal had a clear partisan component. Specifically, I looked for stories that mentioned the word "Lewinsky" plus either "Democrat" or "Republican."

The first program I searched was *Access Hollywood*. My search returned 175 "hits" (each representing a program segment in which "Lewinksy" was mentioned). These 175 hits spanned 90 episodes, indicating that the program covered the Lewinsky scandal in 90 distinct episodes between 1998 and 2000. Of these, *not a single story* mentioned either "Democrat" or "Republican." The same was true for *Entertainment Tonight*, for which my search returned 306 "hits," spanning 118 episodes. Again, this indicates that *Entertainment Tonight* covered the Lewinsky scandal in 118 separate broadcasts, while apparently—at least within these often abridged transcripts and transcript summaries—mentioning neither "Democrat" nor "Republican" *even once*. A search of *Extra*'s coverage of the scandal, in turn, produced 202 hits, spanning 115 separate broadcasts, of which only two mentioned the word "Democrat"—in both instances entirely incidentally to the scandal—and none of which mentioned the word "Republican."

Interestingly, when I changed the additional search terms (beyond "Lewinsky") from "Democrat or Republican" to "Congress or House or Senate," a search of *Extra* returned 40 hits, spanning 34 separate broadcasts. For *Access Hollywood* and *Entertainment Tonight*, the corresponding figures were 20 hits, spanning 15 broadcasts, and 27 hits across 19 broadcasts, respectively. In other words, *Extra*, *Access Hollywood*, and *Entertainment Tonight* referenced the role of the Congress in the Lewinsky scandal on a fair number of occasions, but apparently did so *exclusively* in nonpartisan terms.

In contrast, a search of ABC's *World News Tonight* revealed that the program mentioned "Lewinsky" 510 times over the same time period, spanning 188 separate broadcasts. Of these hits, 142 mentioned "Republican" or "Democrat," spanning 86 separate broadcasts. In other words, 28 percent of all "hits," across 46 percent of all broadcasts addressing the Lewinsky scandal, also mentioned either "Democrat" or "Republican" in the same story.

Lexis-Nexis transcripts are often incomplete—frequently limited to only abstracts of program topics—and hence some of the stories may have mentioned search terms that are not picked up by my rather narrow searches. Yet this does not necessarily bias my results in favor of *World News Tonight* relative to the soft news programs, or vice versa. That said, it is the case that soft news transcripts are more frequently incomplete than transcripts for network newscasts, often, as noted, representing mere abstracts of a given broadcast. This latter difference *could* potentially bias my results. Still, even this latter difference cannot account for the dramatic discrepancy between mentions of "Congress or House or Senate," on the one hand, and "Democrat or Republican," on the other, within the soft news transcripts. Hence, while the absolute figures may be imperfect, the relative comparisons do appear to represent a reasonable illustration of the stark differences in how the soft and hard news media covered the Lewinksy scandal. In fact, these data resoundingly support my expectations concerning the relative absence of partisan or divisive frames in the soft news media.

These results also mirror my findings from a second content-analysis investigation, reported elsewhere (Baum 2002b), in which I compared soft and hard news coverage of the 2000 presidential election. I found that in interviewing the presidential candidates, the hosts of entertainment-oriented talk shows (e.g., Oprah Winfrey, Rosie O'Donnell, Regis Philbin, Jay Leno, David Letterman and others) rarely ever mentioned political parties or other partisan themes. They also rarely mentioned substantive policy issues or compared the issue positions of the major candidates. In sharp contrast, Sunday morning political talk shows, as well as network and cable news shows, were intensely partisan in their candidate interviews, and were far more likely than entertainment-oriented talk shows to compare and contrast candidate positions on the issues. Indeed, the latter pattern (high levels of partisanship and a high propensity to contrast candidate issue positions) was prevalent throughout the campaign coverage of traditional national news programs.

VIETNAM AND THE PERSIAN GULF WAR

I conclude this chapter with a comparison of newspaper and television coverage of the Vietnam War (in February 1968, in the immediate aftermath of the Tet Offensive of January 30, 1968) and the Persian Gulf War (in February 1991, at the height of the "air war"). Gelb and Betts (1979) note that television coverage of the Vietnam conflict reached unprecedented levels of intensity and volume in the aftermath of the Tet Offensive. I therefore consider this an optimal period for comparing Vietnam with the Persian Gulf War. This analysis, which indirectly tests Hypothesis 3, consists of several parts, including a comparison of the extent of presidential rhetoric concerning the two conflicts, as well as investigations into the breadth and depth of coverage of the two wars by the *New York Times*, *USA Today*, national network TV news, and network affiliated local TV newscasts.

Presidential and Newspaper Emphasis on Vietnam and the Gulf War

As previously discussed, the two wars clearly differed in numerous respects.[31] Yet they were similar in two respects that are particularly important for my purposes. First, as the evidence presented in chapter 2 indicates, the contemporary publics considered the two conflicts similarly important national problems. Second, as we shall see, the contemporary "prestige" presses appear to have devoted comparable attention to both conflicts.

One clear predictor of the likely volume of television coverage of a given event is the degree of importance attributed to it by the nation's political leaders and by the prestige press. To estimate the former, I compare the volume of rhetoric devoted to the two wars by Presidents Johnson and G.H.W. Bush, respectively. Intense coverage by the *New York Times*, in turn, is fairly good evidence that an issue is considered important by the nation's political elite, and vice versa. Hence, in order to determine the relative importance attributed to these two conflicts by the prestige press and political elite, I compare the volume of editorial and front-page coverage of Vietnam and the Gulf War in the *New York Times* in February 1968 and February 1991. This represents an important control: if the political elite considered the Gulf War significantly more important than Vietnam, then it would be unsurprising to find greater media attention to the more recent conflict.

I begin by comparing the relative urgency of the two conflicts as perceived by the contemporary presidents, Johnson and G.H.W. Bush. Specifically, I compare the number of mentions by the respective presidents of "Vietnam" and "Iraq" in the *Public Papers of the President* (1998). Presumably, ceteris paribus, the more urgent a president considers an issue, such as a war, the more likely he is to devote his attention to it, both in private and in public. In 1968, the year of the Tet Offensive (and, as previously noted, the high point for television coverage of the Vietnam War), President Johnson mentioned (either verbally or in writing) Vietnam 614 times in the *Public Papers of the President*. This represents about 51 mentions per month, or 1.7 per day. In contrast, during the Gulf War (January–March 1991), President G.H.W. Bush mentioned Iraq 173 times, equivalent to 58 mentions per month, or about 1.9 per day. Hence, on a mentions-per-day basis, President G.H.W. Bush in 1991 spoke or wrote publicly about Iraq slightly more often (+11 percent) than President Johnson spoke or wrote about Vietnam in 1968.

Indeed, when one considers that the Tet Offensive did not span the entire year 1968, and hence, part of the period included in this measure was *relatively* calm, while the Persian Gulf crisis/war was in high gear throughout the entire January–March 1991 period, these figures appear to be biased in favor of the Gulf War. Nonetheless, despite the relatively greater intensity-per-day of war-related events during the Gulf War period, on a per-day basis, President G.H.W. Bush's public discussion of the Gulf War in the January–March 1991 period barely surpassed that of Johnson's public discussion of Vietnam during the entire year of 1968.

If we limit the Vietnam analysis to the most intense month of the Tet Offensive, February 1968, President Johnson's public discussion of Vietnam, on a per-day basis, substantially exceeds President G.H.W. Bush's public discussion of the Gulf War. In that month, President Johnson mentioned Vietnam 70 times, or about 2.4 times per day.[32] This represents about 26 percent more public discussion of Vietnam, relative to the Gulf War. Given these relative emphases by the two presidents, if all else were equal, one might anticipate greater media coverage of Vietnam, at least in February 1968, than of the Gulf War in early 1991.

Still, while media coverage of a given issue typically fluctuates in tandem with variations in presidents' public emphasis on the issue, this relationship is far from perfect. Hence, I separately estimate the relative importance of the two wars from the perspectives of the contemporary elite presses. To do so, I review both editorial and front-page coverage in the *New York Times* during both periods. Beginning with the former, I employ the degree of editorial emphasis placed upon a given topic as a gross indicator of the relative importance of that topic to the newspaper's editorial board. In effect, I am here employing the priorities of the *New York Times* editorial board as a proxy for those of the elite (or prestige) press. While this is admittedly a far from perfect measure of the overall priorities of the prestige press, it is a common approach in media studies. To the extent that the contemporary publics and prestige presses viewed these two wars as similarly "important," one might reasonably anticipate, ceteris paribus, comparable media and public attention to the two wars.

Comparing *New York Times* editorials from 1968 and 1991 is, admittedly, a potentially risky proposition. After all, by February 1968, the *New York Times* had been reporting and editorializing about the Vietnam War for several years. By contrast, the Persian Gulf crisis/war was only in its seventh month in February 1991. Hence, it may simply be the case that by February 1968, the *New York Times* was less inclined to report or editorialize intensively in response to Vietnam-related events than might have been the case in the war's early years. Yet, as noted, the Tet Offensive was a singularly dramatic event in the war, and played a critical role in galvanizing opposition to the war among many media and political elites. Hence, it seems at least as likely that the *New York Times* would write *more* about the Tet Offensive in 1968 than would have been the case several years earlier, when its political, if not military, significance would have been less clear. Given my relatively narrow purposes, I therefore consider this to be a reasonable, albeit admittedly imperfect, comparison.

In order to measure the editorial priority placed upon each issue by the *New York Times*, I tally the number of editorials presented in February 1968 and February 1991 dealing with Vietnam, the Gulf War, or closely related topics. In February 1968, the *New York Times* ran a total of ten editorials that dealt, either directly or peripherally, with the Vietnam conflict. In February 1991, the *Times* ran fourteen editorials dealing in any way with the Gulf War. By this crude indicator, the *New York Times* editorial board appears to have placed approximately 29 percent *less* emphasis upon Vietnam than upon the Gulf War during the highest profile periods of these two conflicts.

I turn next to front-page coverage of the two conflicts in the *New York Times*.[33] Unfortunately, the Lexis-Nexis archive coverage of the *New York Times* begins in January 1969, and hence excludes February 1968. It is, however, possible to compare other periods of the Vietnam War with the Persian Gulf crisis and war.[34] For instance, the data presented in figure 2.1 suggest that the public was more attentive to Vietnam in 1972 than in any other year of the war, including 1968. This is most likely attributable, at least in part, to several high-profile events, including the Paris peace negotiations and the U.S. and South Vietnamese invasion of Cambodia. Whatever the reason, the American public was particularly attuned to Vietnam in 1972. And in that year, the *New York Times* presented 739 front-page stories dealing with the war. This represents an average of 62 stories per month, or about 2 per day.

Interestingly, in February 1991, the *New York Times* ran 62 Persian Gulf War–related stories, *identical* to the average number of stories-per-month on Vietnam during the entire year of 1972. During the period of the Gulf War (January–March 1991), the *Times* ran 190 front-page stories, equivalent to 63 stories per month, or slightly more than 2.1 stories per day. Once again, these figures are nearly identical to the number of stories devoted to Vietnam in 1972. If one considers the entire period of the Persian Gulf crisis and war (at least through the ceasefire in March 1991), the story begins to tilt in favor of Vietnam. Between August 1990 and March 1991, the *New York Times* ran 407 stories relating to Iraq. This represents 51 stories per month, or about 1.7 per day. These latter figures are somewhat lower than the previously cited 1972 figures.

As noted, 1972 was unusual in the extent of public attention to Vietnam, as well as in the volume of media attention. One means of further "stacking the deck" in favor of the Gulf War is to consider multiple years of Vietnam, during which interest in that conflict waxed and waned. After all, the Vietnam War extended over a far longer period of time than the Persian Gulf crisis and war. Over the four-year period from 1969 to 1972, the *New York Times* presented a total of 1,985 front-page stories on Vietnam, representing an average of 42 stories per month, or about 1.4 stories per day. This represents about 18 percent fewer stories per day, on average, than those devoted to the Persian Gulf War between August 1990 and March 1991. These data are summarized in figure 3.4.

It is possible to gain some insight into the changing media environment by broadening our investigation of the print media. I therefore also investigate front-page coverage by *USA Today*. *USA Today*, also a prominent national newspaper in 1991, is a decidedly more "down-market" paper than the *New York Times*. Indeed, many media scholars consider *USA Today* as more-or-less the print equivalent of soft news (though, by my definition, it might not qualify as a soft news outlet). While tabloid newspapers have existed for centuries, there was no equivalent of *USA Today*—a nationwide daily newspaper offering a disproportionate emphasis on soft news topics—during the Vietnam War. And *USA Today* covered the Gulf War extensively. Between August 1990 and March 1991, *USA Today* presented 231 front-page stories on the Gulf crisis and war. This is equivalent to 29 stories per month, or about 1.4 per day. Since *USA Today* is published only on weekdays, this latter figure is perhaps the most pertinent for comparison to the *New York Times*. Indeed, on a per-day basis, *USA Today* offered as much front-page coverage of the Gulf War as the *New York Times* offered regarding Vietnam between 1969 and 1972. And this represents only 18 percent less front-page coverage, on a per-day basis, than the corresponding *New York Times* coverage of the Persian Gulf crisis and war. These data, which suggest a significantly changed print media environment, offer a clue into why the public might have been far more attentive to the latter conflict.

TV Coverage of Vietnam and the Gulf War

To the extent that the above figures reasonably reflect the relative importance placed upon these two events by the news media (elite and otherwise), and given the comparable public emphasis on the two wars by the contemporary presidents, one might expect fairly similar amounts of television coverage of the Gulf War and Vietnam. After all, the largest differential across these comparisons is a fairly modest 29 percent greater editorial emphasis on the Gulf War, relative to Vietnam. As I show below, the differential in television coverage of the two events vastly exceeds this figure.

A proper estimation of the volume of television coverage of the two wars

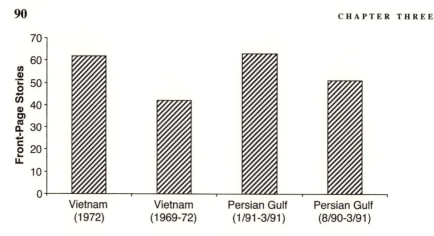

FIGURE 3.4. Number of Front-Page *New York Times* Stories per Month, Vietnam vs. Persian Gulf War

requires consideration of both the breadth and depth of coverage. By *breadth*, I refer to the number of news and informational programs that might potentially cover a given issue. *Depth*, in contrast, refers to the actual extent of coverage of a given issue by a particular program or programs.

Beginning with the latter, I compare network evening news coverage of the two wars. For this analysis, I turn to the Vanderbilt Television News Archive. I focus my analysis on the *CBS Evening News*, which is representative of the three major network evening news programs. Since data for 1968 are unavailable, I once again focus on 1972, another "high point" of public interest in the Vietnam War. In that year, the *CBS Evening News* broadcast a total of 678 stories mentioning Vietnam, equivalent to 62 stories per month, or about 2 per day. During the three months of the Gulf War (January to March 1991), the *CBS Evening News* presented a total of 177 war-related stories, equivalent to 59 stories per month, or, again, about 2 per day. Indeed, on a stories-per-day basis, the *CBS Evening News* presented essentially identical coverage of the two wars. And if we expand the latter search to include the pre-war phase of the Gulf crisis, the figures begin to tilt in favor of Vietnam. Over the entire Gulf crisis and war period (August 1990 to March 1991), the *CBS Evening News* presented a total of 416 stories mentioning Iraq, equivalent to 52 stories per month, or about 1.7 per day. On a stories-per-day basis, this represents 15 percent fewer stories devoted to the Persian Gulf crisis and war (August 1990–March 1991) than to Vietnam (1972). Hence, like the *New York Times*, traditional television news programs appear to have offered comparable coverage of the two wars. These data are summarized in figure 3.5.

In order to estimate the *breadth* of coverage of the Vietnam and the Gulf wars, I reviewed a full month of television listings in *TV Guide* from February 1968 and February 1991. I constructed a scale with which I scored programming from one of the major networks (CBS) in terms of potential news and informational content. Television documentaries, or special reports covering ei-

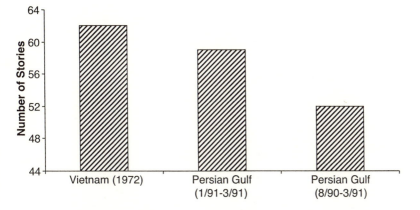

FIGURE 3.5. Number of *CBS Evening News* Stories per Month, Vietnam vs. Persian Gulf War

ther Vietnam or the Gulf War or closely related topics, received 2 points; network newscasts received 1.5 points per half hour; network newsmagazines, local newscasts, and combination news/variety-show programming (e.g., *Good Morning America*) received 1 point per half hour; tabloid or entertainment news programs received 0.5 points per half hour; television talk shows received 0.25 points per half hour, as did "top-of-the-hour" news updates of five minutes or less. I tallied a full month of CBS programming (between 7:00 A.M. and 11:00 P.M.) during both periods. The results of this analysis are summarized in figure 3.6.

The two columns on the left side of figure 3.6 indicate that in February 1991, CBS offered nearly double the volume of *potential* news and informational programming (+ 88 percent) relative to February 1968. Given the explosion of soft news outlets since 1991, which, as I have shown, regularly cover major foreign crises, this latter differential would clearly be far greater in 2003.[35]

While one might reasonably be skeptical of the informational value of entertainment-oriented TV newsmagazines or talk shows, a review of table 3.2 (above) as well as the program listings of several such shows reveals that these programs did in fact devote substantial attention to the Persian Gulf War in January and February 1991. In fact, daily program listings in the *Los Angeles Times* indicate that most of the popular daytime talk shows presented programs dedicated entirely to the Gulf conflict during this period. *Geraldo Rivera* devoted at least six shows solely to the Gulf War; *Sally Jesse Raphael*—a decidedly apolitical talk show host—broadcast at least two such shows, *Oprah Winfrey* broadcast at least three war-related programs, and *Phil Donahue* devoted at least one show to the war.[36] In each case, the topics for each show were only sporadically listed in the daily programming schedules, so the true figures are most likely higher. In addition, Gulf War–related programming was presented on numerous non-news-oriented cable channels, including Nickelodeon, the Family Channel, the

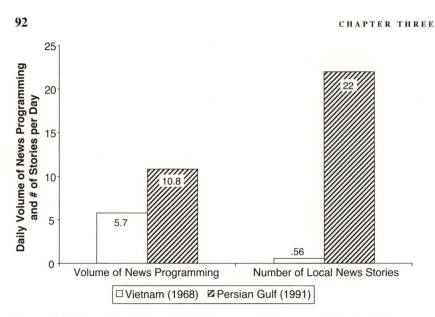

FIGURE 3.6. Potential and Actual Daily Coverage of Vietnam and Persian Gulf Wars by Local TV News, February 1968 vs. February 1991

Arts and Entertainment Network, and MTV, as well as on tabloid news programs, such as *A Current Affair* and *Hard Copy*. (Several, but not all, of these programs are included in the data presented in table 3.2.)

These figures, of course, only scratch the surface of television news coverage, both hard and soft, of the Persian Gulf War. For instance, the major networks' morning variety programs—consisting of a mix of hard and soft news elements—presented Gulf War stories on nearly a daily basis throughout its duration. Between January and March 1991, the NBC *Today* and CBS *This Morning* programs combined presented war-related coverage in 53 separate broadcasts. These same shows covered the Persian Gulf crisis in 45 separate broadcasts between August and December 1990.[37] The January–March 1991 figures suggest that these two morning variety programs each covered the Gulf War during a majority of their daily broadcasts during the course of the war. Moreover, a search of NBC and CBS programming transcripts yielded about 400 programs on the Gulf War, excluding network evening newscasts, between January and March 1991, plus an additional 141 programs on the crisis with Iraq between August and December 1990.[38]

In order to fully substantiate my argument concerning the role of television in general, and soft news in particular, in influencing the overall level of public attentiveness to major foreign crises, it is necessary—albeit perhaps not sufficient—to demonstrate that despite a comparable number of stories on the two wars by the network evening newscasts, a greater overall *volume* (depth) of television coverage was in fact presented in 1991, relative to 1968. The closest approximation to contemporary soft news programming in 1968 was local television news. While my theoretical argument primarily concerns the growth of the soft news media, trends in local TV news tend to parallel—and are in many respects directly related to—trends in soft news coverage. In particular, like soft news media outlets, local TV news has responded to the increasingly competitive television environment by adapting high-profile international events, particularly military conflicts, albeit to a less extreme degree than most soft news outlets, to the sensibilities of audiences that are not necessarily tuning in to learn about foreign affairs (Hamilton 1998). While the "quality" of local news varies widely (Zaller 1999), it has, in most markets, come to resemble soft news programming in its emphasis on dramatic, human-interest-oriented stories. Indeed, local television news inspired the oft-cited cliché "if it bleeds, it leads."

Local news might thus best be characterized as occupying a middle ground between traditional network news and entertainment news programming (though some would no doubt argue that local newscasts are more accurately characterized as pure soft news). I therefore consider such comparisons, though admittedly not ideal, useful for identifying trends in coverage of foreign crises by the non-hard-news media.

Hence, to investigate the *actual* extent of coverage of the two conflicts—beyond traditional national newscasts—I review the local news film registers of a San Francisco, California, CBS affiliate (KPIX) from February 1968 and February 1991, as well as the February 1968 news film registers from two other network-affiliated local newscasts, for which the corresponding 1991 registers were inaccessible.[39] News film registers consist of a list of stories to be covered, and by whom, in each newscast. These registers frequently represent the sole historical record, when video is unavailable, of what a particular news program actually broadcast.

The results of this analysis are even more dramatic than those from my investigation of *TV Guide* listings. As indicated in the two columns on the right side of figure 3.6, during the first eighteen days of February 1968, KPIX broadcast a total of ten stories dealing in any way with the Vietnam conflict—an average of slightly more than one story every two days (0.56 stories per day). In sharp contrast, during the first 18 days of February 1991, KPIX broadcast an average of 22 stories per day dealing with the Gulf War—an almost forty-fold increase over 1968.

I also acquired 1968 news film registers from NBC affiliate WLBT in Mississippi. WLBT's local news programs broadcast a total of four Vietnam-related stories in February 1968. While I was unable to acquire the comparable 1991 registers, the news archivist at the Mississippi Department of Archives and History indicated in a telephone conversation that WLBT had presented "extensive" daily coverage of the Persian Gulf conflict. Additionally, I acquired February 1968 news film registers from CBS affiliate WABI, in Bucksport, Maine. Like WLBT, WABI ran only four Vietnam-related stories in February 1968. Again, while I was unable to acquire WABI's registers from February 1991, it seems highly improbable that their coverage of the Gulf War was so minimal.[40] These results offer some additional indirect support for Hypothesis 3.

While it is certainly possible that part of this difference is attributable to a

greater perceived relative importance, or urgency, of the Gulf War—which un-
folded in a matter of months, as compared to Vietnam, which by 1968 was
more than three years old—by political leaders or the media that was not captured in my previous investigations, it seems highly unlikely that such a differential accounts for the vast disparity in coverage. (Recall the relatively small
differential in the *New York Times* or network news coverage, or of public
presidential rhetoric, and the similar sense of urgency of the contemporary publics in 1968 and 1970 versus 1991.)

Far more plausible an explanation, I believe, is the dramatic change in news-
and quasi-news television programming between the 1960s and 1990s. In 1968,
due at least in part to the absence of inexpensive live satellite feeds and color
videotape footage, most local network affiliates ignored national and international affairs almost entirely—apparently including the Vietnam War—in favor
of truly "local" topics and themes. In sharp contrast, by 1991, local TV newscasts routinely covered high-profile national and international events, albeit
with a heavy emphasis on "local" angles to such stories. And, as the quotation
at the start of the book indicated, the Persian Gulf war was an ideal made-for-
television soap opera, many elements of which—particularly the effects of the
war on communities whose residents were serving in the Gulf—fit perfectly
with the relatively "soft" orientation of local television news (as well as, of course,
with the more exclusively human-interest orientation of the soft news media).

CONCLUSION

This chapter began by presenting evidence that large numbers of Americans
watch soft news programs on a regular basis. I then demonstrated that soft news
programs present substantial coverage of major foreign crises, and that the *nature* of soft news coverage of foreign crises differs substantially from that of
more traditional news outlets.

The implications of the changes in the mass media, most notably television,
described in chapter 2 are particularly visible when a foreign crisis arises of
sufficient magnitude to focus television's many diverse "lenses," thereby becoming a potential water-cooler event. Also evident in this context is the public's increased dependence on a wider variety of media, relative to prior periods
in American history, for its news about such crises, including, notably, the soft
news media. My comparison of Vietnam and the Persian Gulf War indicated
that media coverage of war has dramatically expanded and diversified since the
1960s. Indeed, in recent years, the expansion of television coverage of foreign
crises—including the Gulf War—has extended far beyond traditional network
newscasts to include a vast array of soft news programs, including television
newsmagazines, "human drama"–oriented local newscasts, tabloid or entertainment news programs, as well as daytime and late-night talk shows.

Moreover, the rise of soft news comes at a time when the broadcast and cable
news networks have significantly cut back on their coverage of international
affairs (Hoge 1997; Moisy 1997; *Media Monitor* 2000), suggesting that the

explanation for any increase in public attentiveness to foreign crises must lie elsewhere. Taken together, these developments, combined with the other evidence detailed above, suggest that the soft news media indeed appears capable of contributing to increased attentiveness by the American public to select high profile political issues, including foreign policy crises. It also suggests that Americans whose only meaningful exposure to political information comes from the soft news media will at times be exposed to quite different information from that of their counterparts who follow politics and foreign policy in the traditional news media. In subsequent chapters I explore some possible implications of this latter distinction.

APPENDIX: CONTENT ANALYSIS CODING FORM

1. Did the report discuss the origins of the conflict?

2. If you answer *yes* to question 1, was the crisis described as having origins long before the current actual or contemplated U.S. involvement?

3. Did the report identify a country, faction, or group as an adversary/antagonist in the conflict?

4. Was the crisis presented as one that had a good chance of being resolved through U.S. action?

5. How many members of the U.S. President's political party were sourced in the report?

6. How many members of the opposition political party were sourced in the report?

7. How many experts (includes senior military officers) were sourced in the report?

8. How many celebrities were sourced in the report?

9. How would you characterize the assessment of the U.S. decision-makers offered by those [presidential party members/opposition party members/experts/celebrities]?

    (1) supportive   (2) critical   (3) mixed   (4) none offered

10. Were any past foreign policy crises mentioned in the report? If *yes*, list them below.

    Foreign Policy Crisis   Context

_____   _____

11. For each past foreign policy crisis mentioned in the report, note if the crisis was a reasonably clear-cut success or failure for U.S. foreign policy (or is widely perceived as such by most elites and members of the public), or if it was not clear-cut either way.

12. Did the report focus on, or address the circumstances or involvement of, an individual, family, or other small group?

13. Did the report address the general issues involved in the conflict or crisis that was the subject of the report (as opposed to the effects on, or involvement of, specific individuals, families, or small groups)?

CHAPTER FOUR

Bringing War to the Masses

THE PURPOSE of this chapter is to substantiate my core theoretical prediction: that soft news is an important source of information concerning foreign policy crises, as well as select high-profile domestic political issues, for politically inattentive Americans. To do so, I conduct seven distinct statistical investigations, drawing from a variety of public opinion surveys, aimed at drawing as direct a link as possible between soft news coverage of foreign crises and attentiveness to such crises by consumers of soft news programming.

My goal in conducting multiple investigations is to build as convincing a case as possible for the theory by replicating my tests across a diverse set of data sources and operationalizations of attentiveness. In the course of this chapter, I thus investigate the correlates of public attentiveness to the U.S. interventions (or other involvements) in Bosnia, Lebanon, Panama, and Northern Ireland; to the 1998 U.S. cruise missile attacks against Afghanistan and Sudan, as well as attentiveness to the issue of terrorism; to major foreign-policy-related problems facing the nation; and finally, to the Monica Lewinsky scandal. This allows me to test five of the hypotheses derived in chapter 2—plus several closely related corollaries to those hypotheses—against a diverse array of real-world issues and events.

First, according to Hypothesis 4, people consume soft news programming in order to be entertained, not to learn about politics or foreign policy. Second, given that soft news indeed serves as a meaningful source of information about foreign crises, then according to my fifth hypothesis people who watch soft news programs should be more attentive to foreign crises than people who do not. Third, Hypothesis 6 indicates that because the soft news audience tends not to be particularly interested in politics or foreign affairs, exposure to soft news programs should increase attentiveness to foreign crises most strongly among the *least* politically engaged members of society. Fourth, Hypothesis 7 holds that because most typical political issues do not possess the characteristics that appeal to soft news programmers, they are less likely to be covered by soft news programs. Hence, attentiveness to other, more typical or partisan political issues should *not* be significantly related to exposure to soft news outlets. And fifth, according to my eighth (Gateway) hypothesis, exposure to some information about a foreign crisis in a soft news context tends to enhance attentiveness to crisis-related information in more traditional news contexts.

The results from the statistical investigations in this chapter strongly support each hypothesis, in most instances across multiple, distinct tests. Before turning to my statistical investigations, however, I begin with a brief discussion of the methodology employed in this and subsequent chapters.

Methodology

Throughout my statistical investigations, I have elected to focus upon data from public opinion surveys, in order to place my findings in an unambiguous real-world context. By doing so, I hope to maximize, to the extent possible, the external validity of my results, particularly with respect to the population sample (Cook and Campbell 1979; Sears 1986). After all, it would be difficult to accurately estimate in an experimental context, years after the fact, people's degree of attentiveness to specific, real-world foreign policy crises. While this focus has obvious advantages, it nonetheless raises potential concerns regarding the validity of my various indicators of attentiveness. Moreover, it is more difficult to isolate a specific causal relationship in a survey context, relative to, say, a controlled experiment.

The trade-off between *internal* and *external* validity plagues much of social science research (Cook and Campbell 1979; Sears 1986). Traditionally, social psychologists have primarily employed experimental methods, designed to isolate, to the greatest extent possible, the variables they are investigating from other related, yet distinct, psychological phenomena. The experimental method has a clear advantage over public opinion surveys in that it allows potential confounding factors to be carefully controlled, thereby isolating the variable(s) of interest. Hence, experiments typically have greater *internal* validity than do public opinion surveys. Internal validity, however, frequently comes at a price. That is, by carefully controlling the response environment, experimenters risk reducing the *external* validity of their findings. This means results that obtain in a laboratory may not generalize to the "real world," due to either the differing context in which issues arise or an unrepresentative population of experimental subjects. The decision to employ a given methodology depends upon many factors, such as the primary goal of the research or the appropriateness of the research question for laboratory experiments. For various reasons, both conceptual and practical, I have opted to prioritize the external validity of my evidence. This by no means implies that I am unconcerned with internal validity. Clearly, for evidence to be compelling, it should possess as much of both elements as possible. Rather, this is simply a question of *relative* emphasis, given the necessity of a trade-off, at least to some extent, between the two.

Public opinion surveys are, in many cases, too crude to allow careful measurement of a particular psychological construct or to allow a researcher to distinguish between two similar constructs (like attentiveness and salience). Indeed, none of the indicators of attentiveness employed in this chapter are ideal. Most tap at least partially into the other constructs, like cognizance or salience, discussed in chapter 1. Given the unavailability of an "ideal" indicator, I have opted for a "next-best" strategy, which I refer to as *triangulation*. In other words, in this and subsequent empirical chapters, I conduct numerous tests, using multiple, distinct indicators of my key dependent and independent variables and multiple data environments. Each attentiveness indicator by itself may be insufficiently precise to offer convincing evidence for the theory. Yet, in addition to their many differences, I argue that they each share a common underlying factor: a strong relationship to attentiveness. (In appendix 1 to this chapter, I present evidence in support of this assertion.) Hence, to the extent that the hypothesized relationships emerge across the entire range of statistical tests, the most plausible explanation for such consistently supportive results becomes the one underlying factor—attentiveness—that they all share in common. This, in turn, represents far stronger support for the theory than any single successful test, viewed in isolation. I now turn to my hypothesis testing, beginning with the question of *why* people consume soft news.

WHY PEOPLE WATCH SOFT NEWS

Might some individuals tune in to soft news programs with the explicit intent of learning about foreign crises? Such individuals may reason that when a crisis arises, the soft news media will offer more interesting coverage than network newscasts or newspapers. If so, the incidental by-product model would be irrelevant. Fortunately, polling organizations have asked respondents this very question. One May 1996 survey on public media use habits, conducted by the Pew Research Center for the People and the Press (henceforth Pew Research Center) asked respondents the extent to which they prefer news about entertainment, famous people, crime, national politics, or international affairs (among other topics), as well as whether and to what extent they consume a variety of soft news media. I created an entertainment news index, based on the first three items mentioned above and a soft news index based upon the latter series of questions.[1] If, as predicted by Hypothesis 4, information about politics or foreign crises is being piggybacked to entertainment programming, primarily as an incidental by-product, then we should observe a strong positive relationship between viewers' interest in entertainment-oriented news and consuming soft news media, but *not* between interest in news about national or international affairs and soft news consumption. Figure 4.1 strongly supports this hypothesis.

   Consistent with my incidental by-product model, figure 4.1 indeed shows a strong positive relationship between *interest* in entertainment-oriented news and *consuming* soft news. The entertainment news interest index correlates with the soft news consumption index at an impressive .40. In contrast, the relationship between interest in news about international affairs and consuming soft news is essentially zero ($-.01$), as is the corresponding correlation between soft news consumption and interest in national politics ($-.03$). Most respondents apparently consume soft news primarily for its entertainment value. This strongly suggests that to the extent individuals are receiving any information about politics or foreign policy in the soft news media, they are doing so not by design, but rather as an incidental by-product of seeking entertainment. Any information about foreign affairs appears in these data to be piggybacked to entertainment-oriented news. (For further evidence on this point, see Prior 2003.)

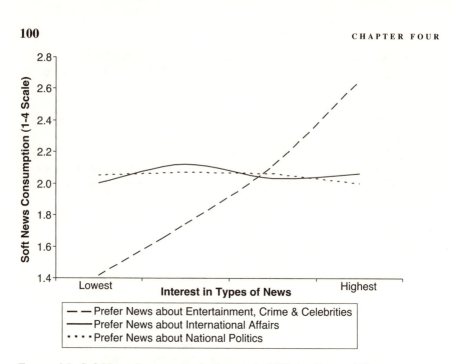

FIGURE 4.1. Soft News Consumption by Interest in Differing Types of News
SOURCE: Pew Research Center, Media Consumption Survey, May 1996

Commenting on viewers' motives for watching programs like *Hard Copy* and *Inside Edition*, Lisa Gregorish, of Fox, observed, "People watch those shows to see a little bit of trash."[2] Barry Berk, of *Access Hollywood*, added: "There's all kinds of people who love this kind of show. It's diversion for them. . . . This is a form of entertainment for them." In particular, he added, focus groups have indicated that people watch *Access Hollywood* because "they want stories about stars and the movies, the process of making a movie, [and] the casting news." In contrast, when asked why *Access Hollywood* might cover a more serious social or political issue, like ethnic diversity on television, Berk pointedly noted: "Do we have a responsibility [to cover social issues]? No. [We covered the diversity story because] it's a good story . . . and people are talking about it." He added, "There are other outlets for [topics like] tobacco and welfare reform."[3]

THE SOFT NEWS MEDIA AND ATTENTIVENESS TO BOSNIA, LEBANON AND TERRORISM

My first investigation into the correlates of attentiveness employs the previously cited May 1996 Pew Research Center survey (1996). In addition to asking respondents which types of television and radio programming, magazines, and newspapers they watch, listen to, and read, the survey also asks whether respondents had followed a series of major political events, including three foreign crisis issues. Additional questions include a series of socioeconomic and demographic items as well as several questions useful for estimating respondents' political knowledge and interest.

As dependent variables, I focus on three variations of the following question, each addressing respondents' interest in a specific crisis-related issue: "Now I will read a list of some stories covered by news organizations this past month. As I read each item, tell me if you happened to follow this news story very closely, fairly closely, not too closely, or not at all closely": (1) "The military conflict between Israel and the pro-Iranian Muslims in Lebanon"; (2) "The passage in Congress of a new law dealing with domestic terrorism";[4] and (3) "The situation in Bosnia." (Because the response categories form a reasonably symmetric ordinal scale, ordered logit is an appropriate estimator.)

The independent variables, in turn, fall into three categories: socio-economic status (age, education, family income, married, white), interest in and knowledge about politics (political knowledge, voted in 1992, political partisanship, approve of president) and media consumption habits (cable subscriber, soft news index, hard news index). The latter variables consist of a broad range of questions concerning respondents' interest in and attention to news and entertainment programming on television and radio, in magazines, on the Internet, and in newspapers. I collapsed these variables into two broad indexes, the first representing the extent of respondents' exposure to traditional, or hard, news sources and topics and the second capturing respondents' exposure to soft news.[5] In addition to the two indexes, I separately control for respondents' level of interest in international affairs news. In table 4.1, I list the components of each index, each of which consists of 4-point scales, with 4 representing the maximum degree of interest or attention.[6] (The key independent variables are defined in appendix 2 to this chapter.)

Most of the items in the respective indexes fall fairly unambiguously in either the "hard" or "soft" category. Yet several are less clear-cut. In particular, some readers might argue that network newsmagazines belong in the hard news category, while local television news is more appropriately characterized as a soft news format. As noted, however, recent studies have found that network newsmagazines primarily cover soft news topics. And local TV news, while it certainly offers large doses of soft news—and is clearly "softer" than, say, network newscasts—*routinely* covers traditional local, national, and international political and policy issues. In fact, according to a study of forty-nine stations in fifteen cities (Rosenstiel, Gottlieb, and Brady 2000), "politics and government" is second only to "crime and law" as the most prevalent topic on local TV newscasts. Hence, at least by my definition, local TV news seems more appropriately characterized as hard news.

Nonetheless, rather than prejudge the proper location of these items, I conducted a variety of tests to determine their appropriate placement in, or exclu-

TABLE 4.1. Items Included in 1996 Pew Research Center Survey Soft and Hard News Indexes[a]

Hard News Index Items	Soft News Index Items
Watch network national news	Watch tabloid news programs
Watch local news	Watch daytime talk shows
Watch business news	Watch network newsmagazines
Watch CNN	Watch MTV
Watch C-SPAN	Read tabloid newspapers
Watch *PBS News Hour with Jim Lehrer*	Follow news about entertainment
Listen to National Public Radio	Follow news about famous people
Listen to news on radio	Follow news about crime
Read business magazines	
Read newsmagazines	
Read daily newspaper	
Follow news about national politics	
Follow news about business & finance	
Follow news/public affairs on internet	

[a]Each item consists of a 4-point scale, with 4 representing *maximum* interest or attention. The hard news exceptions are newspapers and radio, which are coded 1 if the respondent reads newspapers or listen to news on the radio and 0 otherwise.

sion from, my indexes. First, I compared alpha reliability scores with and without the suspect items, and with each item moved to the opposing category. In each case, the reliability scores were highest when the items were located as in table 4.1. (In fact, the alpha reliability scores for the hard and soft news indexes in table 4.1 are a fairly substantial .72 and .66, respectively, and correlate only modestly, at .19.) Next, I reran all of my models with one or both of the suspect items excluded or placed in the opposing index. The results indicated that excluding local news or network newsmagazines had only a modest effect on the reported results, while placing either item in the opposing index consistently *weakened* the results. Further testing also revealed that the results reported below persist in the absence of *any single item* from either index, and, hence, are in no way artifacts of a particular index construction or item.

In order to maintain a focus on the explicit tests of my hypotheses, as well as to avoid an excessively technical presentation of my analyses, following presentation of my first set of results, I discuss throughout the book only the substantive results of theoretical interest in the main text. I present the first set of results in detail in the main text, however, so that the reader will have a clear understanding of the nature of the statistical investigations undertaken throughout the book. Similarly, I employ a comparable (though, depending on availability, not always identical) set of socioeconomic and political controls throughout my statistical analyses. Hence, for subsequent investigations, except where important differences in model specification arise, I do not reiterate in the main text the specific control variables employed in each model. Interested readers are invited to consult the appropriate appendixes for subsequent presentation of the full model specifications, variable definitions and coding, and statistical results from which I derive the substantive findings reported throughout the remainder of the book.

Table 4.2 presents the results from ten multivariate ordered logit analyses. The first six are discussed in this section, while the last four, discussed in the next section, replicate my key findings, using two different surveys and a fourth foreign crisis issue. In order to maintain a focus on my hypothesis testing, as well as for purposes of brevity, I do not discuss in this and subsequent statistical analyses the substantive interpretations of the control variables, but instead concentrate on the key causal relationships that test my hypotheses.[7]

The results from the first, third, and fifth models in table 4.2 indicate that across all three foreign crisis issues, exposure to soft news is positively associated with attentiveness, though the relationships are only statistically significant for the Bosnia and Terrorism models ($p < .05$ and $p < .001$, respectively). Not surprisingly, consumption of hard news is also associated with following each crisis more closely. These results lend support to my fifth hypothesis, which predicts that exposure to soft news should be positively associated with attentiveness to foreign crises.

My sixth hypothesis predicts that exposure to soft news should have the strongest impact among the least politically engaged members of the public. To test this latter hypothesis, as well as to further test Hypothesis 5, it is necessary to conduct an additional set of analyses. For this test, I add an interaction term (Soft news index × International affairs news) in order to determine whether the effects of consuming soft news differ for respondents with differing propensities to follow international events. I present the results of these analyses in the second, fourth, and sixth models in table 4.2. In each instance, the results strongly support my sixth hypothesis, as well as offering additional support for Hypothesis 5. The coefficients on the base categories (Soft news index and International affairs news) and the interaction terms are each in the predicted directions, indicating that among individuals who are relatively uninterested in international affairs, soft news appears to represent an alternative to traditional hard news as a source of information about all three foreign crisis issues. Moreover, the coefficients on the soft news exposure variables are each statistically significant at. 05 or better, while the interaction term is significant in the Terrorism ($p < .05$) and nearly so in the Lebanon ($p < .056$) and Bosnia ($p < .073$) models.[8]

Because logit coefficients are difficult to interpret, at figure 4.2 I translate the coefficients on the key variables into probabilities, with all controls held constant at their mean values.[9] The results indicate that for individuals who report following international affairs "very" or "fairly" closely, exposure to soft news matters little for attentiveness to any of the three foreign crisis issues. Yet, individuals who follow international affairs less closely (representing over one-third of the respondents) *do* appear to attend to each issue through the soft news media. Consistent with my sixth hypothesis, the relationships are strongest for respondents who claim to follow international affairs "not at all closely."

TABLE 4.2. Ordered Logit Analyses of Media Consumption Habits and Attentiveness to Bosnia (1993 and 1996), Lebanon (1996), Terrorism (1996) and U.S. Invasion of Panama (1990)

	Coef. (Std. Err.)									
	Lebanon		Terrorism		Bosnia '96		Bosnia '93		Panama	
	Model 1	Model 2	Model 3	Model 4	Model 5	Model 6	Model 7	Model 8	Model 9	Model 10
Media Consumption										
Soft news index	.018	.097	.063	.148	.036	.161	.312	1.168	.868	1.299
	(.016)	(.049)*	(.017)***	(.047)**	(.017)*	(.053)**	(.143)*	(.558)*	(.131)***	(.421)**
Hard news index	.091	.090	.109	.109	.083	.083	.603	.603	.703	.687
	(.012)***	(.012)***	(.013)***	(.013)***	(.013)***	(.013)***	(.131)***	(.129)***	(.169)***	(.170)***
International affairs news	.891	1.465	.368	.972	.767	1.670	—	—	—	—
	(.086)***	(.334)***	(.081)***	(.327)**	(.087)***	(.356)***				
Cable subscriber	.244	.246	.214	.221	.104	.113	—	—	—	—
	(.137)^	(.137)	(.139)	(.140)	(.139)	(.140)				
SES/Demographics										
Education	−.092	−.096	−.053	−.057	−.038	−.043	.362	.968	.145	.417
	(.040)*	(.040)*	(.041)	(.041)	(.041)	(.041)	(.088)***	(.355)**	(.078)^	(.245)^
Age	.015	.015	.016	.017	.005	.006	.016	.016	.002	.003
	(.004)***	(.004)***	(.004)***	(.004)***	(.004)	(.004)	(.005)**	(.005)**	(.005)	(.005)

	(1)	(2)	(3)	(4)	(5)	(6)	(7)	(8)	(9)	(10)
Family income	−.024 (.033)	−.024 (.033)	−.056 (.033)^	−.056 (.033)	−.018 (.034)	−.019 (.034)	−.022 (.066)	−.011 (.066)	−.181 (.075)*	−.183 (.075)*
Male	.120 (.115)	.122 (.115)	−.114 (.116)	−.117 (.116)	.131 (.119)	.138 (.118)	.499 (.169)**	.521 (.167)**	−.190 (.154)	−.208 (.153)
Married	−.024 (.038)	−.023 (.038)	−.082 (.038)*	−.081 (.038)*	.004 (.038)	.004 (.038)	—	—	—	—
Unemployed	—	—	—	—	—	—	—	—	−.213 (.207)	−.200 (.206)
White	−.152 (.167)	−.173 (.167)	−.302 (.159)^	−.330 (.160)*	−.028 (.177)	−.068 (.178)	.068 (.372)	.001 (.382)	−.015 (.399)	−.027 (.398)
Black	—	—	—	—	—	—	.199 (.523)	.177 (.520)	−.772 (.461)^	−.772 (.459)^
Political Knowledge & Attitudes										
Political knowledge	.155 (.063)**	.151 (.063)*	.133 (.067)*	.129 (.067)*	.086 (.064)	.078 (.064)	—	—	.318 (.065)***	.309 (.065)***
Voted in 1992	.107 (.149)	.109 (.148)	.025 (.143)	.021 (.143)	.026 (.149)	.029 (.149)	.286 (.229)	.295 (.230)	—	—
Partisanship	−.094 (.111)	−.093 (.110)	.038 (.109)	.046 (.110)	−.141 (.110)	−.137 (.110)	—	—	—	—
Party identification	−.007 (.039)	−.009 (.039)	.045 (.039)	.045 (.040)	−.041 (.039)	−.043 (.039)	−.089 (.125)	−.097 (.127)	.137 (.193)	.138 (.191)
Approve of president	.143 (.107)	.141 (.106)	−.005 (.106)	−.009 (.107)	.030 (.106)	.029 (.106)	.046 (.211)	.007 (.211)	.511 (.223)*	.515 (.224)*
Importance of Panama	—	—	—	—	—	—	—	—	.524 (.151)***	.524 (.151)***

Table 4.2. Continued

	Coef. (Std. Err.)									
	Lebanon		Terrorism		Bosnia '96		Bosnia '93		Panama	
	Model 1	Model 2	Model 3	Model 4	Model 5	Model 6	Model 7	Model 8	Model 9	Model 10
Interaction Terms										
Soft news index × international affairs news	—	−.031 (.017)	—	−.032 (.017)	—	−.048 (.018)**	—	—	—	—
Soft news index × education	—	—	—	—	—	—	—	−.246 (.140)^	—	−.128 (.113)
Constant 1	3.759 (.671)	5.217 (1.059)	4.524 (.638)	6.113 (1.054)	2.347 (.656)	4.621 (1.105)	3.760 (.760)	5.860 (1.557)	.683 (.723)	1.546 (1.114)
Constant 2	5.467 (.677)	6.932 (1.069)	6.067 (.649)	7.662 (1.060)	4.163 (.660)	6.459 (1.119)	5.486 (.782)	7.599 (1.589)	2.230 (.675)	3.104 (1.094)
Constant 3	7.248 (.687)	8.711 (1.076)	7.811 (.658)	9.401 (1.061)	6.329 (.673)	8.624 (1.126)	7.188 (.809)	9.312 (1.613)	4.551 (.681)	5.433 (1.102)
Pseudo R^2	.13 (N = 1,319)	.13 (N = 1,319)	.09 (N = 1,307)	.09 (N = 1,307)	.10 (N = 1,322)	.10 (N = 1,322)	.06 (N = 594)	.07 (N = 594)	.11 (N = 1,077)	.12 (N = 1,077)

Note: All models employ White's heteroscedasticity-consistent ("robust") standard errors and probability weighting.
^$p < .10$, *$p < .05$, **$p < .01$, ***$p < .001$

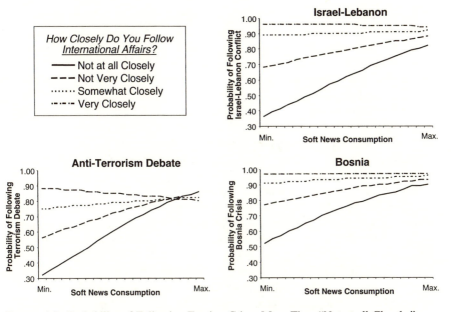

FIGURE 4.2. Probability of Following Foreign Crises More Than "Not at all Closely," as Soft News Consumption and Interest in International Affairs Vary

Hence, I focus on this group. The figure presents three graphics showing the influence of the soft news media on the probability of following *more* than "not at all closely," respectively, the Israel-Lebanon conflict (upper-right quadrant), the terrorism debate (lower-left quadrant), and the war in Bosnia (lower-right quadrant).

Figure 4.2 indicates that among respondents who follow international affairs "not at all closely," as attentiveness to soft news increases from its lowest to highest levels, the probability that they have followed the Israel-Lebanon conflict *more* than "not at all closely" increases by 38 percentage points (from .40 to .78). The corresponding increases for the congressional antiterrorism debate and for Bosnia are 58 percentage points (from .34 to .92) and 47 percentage points (from .46 to .93), respectively.[10]

Figure 4.2 does not reveal *how much* attention respondents paid to the three issues. To estimate the magnitude of the effect of the soft news media, we can observe the *extent* of self-declared attentiveness, as soft news consumption increases. In fact, in these data, a majority of the increase in attentiveness associated with soft news consumption is located in the category representing the probability of following the several issues "fairly closely." This suggests the soft news effect is substantial. As soft news consumption increases, the corresponding probabilities of following the Israel-Lebanon conflict, antiterrorism debate, and Bosnia intervention "fairly closely" increase by 19 (from .09 to .28), 34 (from .08 to .42) and 41 (from .10 to .51) percentage points, respectively.[11] Each of these results clearly supports Hypothesis 6, suggesting that respondents who are uninterested in international affairs are nonetheless exposed to information about all three crisis issues through the soft news media.[12]

My investigations of three distinct foreign crisis issues point clearly in a single direction, toward a strong and direct relationship between exposure to soft news and attentiveness to foreign crises.[13] Moreover, the fact that this finding appears inconsistent with studies—including one based on the identical survey (Rhine, Bennett, and Flickinger 1998)—that have found viewing of entertainment-oriented programming *negatively* associated with political knowledge suggests that attentiveness must be considered distinct from, albeit related to, political knowledge.

These results are less surprising when one considers that each of these topics has been covered at some length by a wide variety of soft news programs. In chapter 3, I presented evidence of soft news coverage of the Bosnia crisis, as well as the general topic of terrorism, so I will not revisit that evidence here, except to reiterate that each topic was covered extensively in the soft news media. Thus far, however, I have not addressed soft news coverage of the Arab-Israeli conflict, including the Israel-Lebanon dispute. And, in fact, the soft news media have offered significant coverage of this issue as well. For instance, according to Lexis-Nexis, *Extra* has broadcast twenty-one feature stories addressing aspects of the Arab-Israeli conflict. Two such stories, in April and May 1996, featured comments by actors Richard Gere and Richard Dreyfus advocating peace in Israel in the aftermath of renewed fighting in Lebanon and acts of terrorism in Israel. Similarly, *Entertainment Tonight* broadcast a story on October 13, 2000, concerning the postponement of filming on a movie starring Robert Redford and Brad Pitt due to violence in the Middle East. Another episode of *Extra*, broadcast in 1997, profiled two American teenage boys visiting Israel with their grandparents, who were caught up in a terrorist suicide bomb attack in a Jerusalem marketplace in which 13 people were killed and 150 injured. The two teenagers became heroes when they saved the lives of two of their Israeli friends, who had gone into the market just before the attack.

In fact, nearly every program discussed in chapter 3 and featured in table 3.2, has covered the Arab-Israeli conflict, including the Israel-Lebanon dispute, in many instances at some length. This coverage has spanned the usual themes and frames of the soft news media, including the aforementioned interviews with celebrities and coverage of individual (episodic) stories of tragedy, heroism, and survival in the aftermath of terrorism. For instance, in March 1996, *Inside Edition* covered a suicide bombing in Tel Aviv by the Palestinian extremist militant group Hamas. In addition to providing some background coverage of the incident, and the threat it posed to the peace process, the segment also profiled several Americans killed in the blast, as well as a victim of a 1995 terrorist attack in Israel. And in a January 1996 broadcast, *Inside Edition* interviewed Jackie Pflug, a survivor of a 1985 hijacking of an Egypt Air flight by Palestinian terrorists. Hence, it is unsurprising that attentiveness to the Israel-Lebanon conflict would be positively affected by soft news consumption.

SOFT NEWS AND NON-FOREIGN-CRISIS ISSUES

The question remains as to whether, as predicted by Hypothesis 7, the above interaction disappears if respondents are asked about an issue covered intensely by the traditional news media but *not* by the soft news media. If the interaction persists, this would suggest that the above relationships may be artifacts of some omitted variable(s), such as, perhaps, greater overall media exposure by soft news consumers. One appropriate political issue for addressing this question is a presidential primary election. Primaries are highly partisan events, in which candidates typically seek to appeal mostly to party activists, who constitute a disproportionate percentage of primary voters, rather than to "mainstream" voters. Hence they are less appealing to a predominantly politically moderate (and cynical) populace, which is more likely to tune in to a general election, in which candidates typically race to the center. Primaries ought therefore to be less amenable than foreign crises, or general presidential elections for that matter, to cheap framing and piggybacking.[14] In fact, as reported in chapter 3, a content analysis of soft news coverage of the Republican presidential candidates during the 1996 primaries found, with several exceptions, far less coverage of the primaries than of any of the foreign crises included in the table.

To test Hypothesis 7, I employed a fourth dependent variable, addressing whether the respondent had followed news about the Republican presidential candidates in the 1996 presidential primary election campaign. As with the previous models, the dependent variable is a four-category scale, measuring the extent to which respondents followed the Republican primaries. The first two models in Table 4.A1 (shown in appendix 3 of this chapter) present the results from two ordered logit analyses employing this dependent variable, with and without the interaction term. I also tested several additional interactions (not shown) between the soft news index and political partisanship and political knowledge. Consistent with Hypothesis 7, soft news proved insignificant across each specification and, as anticipated, the interactions did not emerge. Hence, the soft news media appear in these relationships to contribute to attentiveness to foreign crises, but *not* to the 1996 Republican primaries.

A second survey (Pew Research Center 1998a) allows a more general test of the theoretical distinction I drew above between foreign crises and presidential primaries, which rests upon the differing degrees to which each is amenable to selective framing and piggybacking. As noted, while I focus on foreign crises as a critical test, this distinction is general. If it is valid, we should find positive relationships between exposure to soft news and attentiveness to any political issue easily framed in highly accessible terms. In contrast, for most typical political issues, which tend not to possess this characteristic, we should not find statistically significant relationships. Respondents were asked the same media exposure questions employed in the 1996 Pew Research Center survey (plus questions regarding several newer programs). They were also asked how closely they had followed several high-profile issues, including: (*a*) "allegations of sexual misconduct against Bill Clinton," (b) "the debate in Washington over legislation to regulate the tobacco industry," and (c) "candidates and election campaigns in your state." To further test Hypotheses 5–7, I conducted a series of ordered logit analyses, employing the extent of respondents' attentiveness to each of these issues as dependent variables.

The coding of the dependent variables is identical to that employed above for the 1996 Pew Research Center survey. For these analyses, I constructed hard and soft news indexes similar to those employed previously, and included a similar set of control variables. (The components of the hard and soft news indexes, for which the alpha reliability scores are .75 and .69, respectively, are listed in appendix 2.)[15] My fifth and seventh hypotheses would predict a statistically significant positive relationship between exposure to soft news and attentiveness to the Lewinsky scandal, but not to either the tobacco debate or the 1998 election campaigns. The former issue represents the classic material of soft news: a salacious scandal involving a high-profile public figure. The latter issues, in contrast, are far more complex, (intrinsically) partisan and arcane, and thus less amenable to selective framing and piggybacking.

Compared to general presidential elections, off-year elections typically focus more on particularistic policy issues that are of little interest to many Americans, who perceive the stakes to be much lower. (This, in large part, explains the large drop in voter turnout during off-year elections.) Indeed, the content analysis presented in chapter 3 indicated that the soft news media offered only minimal coverage of the 1998 elections, while soft news coverage of the tobacco debate approached zero. In sharp contrast, most soft news programs covered the Lewinsky scandal intensively. Finally, with respect to the scandal, my sixth hypothesis predicts that the effects of soft news consumption ought to weaken as respondents' intrinsic interest in national politics increases.

The results strongly support each hypothesis across all three dependent variables, with and without an interaction between soft news consumption and respondents' self-declared interest in following news about national politics (see table 4.A2, in appendix 3). As one might expect, given modest soft news coverage, neither attentiveness to the tobacco debate nor to the 1998 election campaigns is significantly related to exposure to soft news, while both are strongly related to exposure to hard news.

In contrast, also as one would anticipate, given intensive soft news coverage, attentiveness to the Lewinsky scandal is strongly related to soft news consumption ($p < .05$ and $p < .001$, with and without the interaction term, respectively). Among the least politically engaged respondents (those who report following news about political figures and events in Washington "not at all closely") as soft news consumption increases from its minimum to maximum values, the probability of following the scandal "fairly" or "very" closely increases by approximately 52 percentage points (from .19 to .71).[16]

And the effects of soft news consumption once again weaken in a stepwise fashion as respondents' intrinsic interest in following national politics rises. At the opposite extreme, among respondents who report following news about political figures and events in Washington "very" closely, a maximum increase in soft news consumption is associated with a far smaller rise of 8 percentage points (from .83 to .91) in the probability of following the scandal "fairly" or "very" closely.[17] Taken together, these results once again offer clear support for my fifth through seventh hypotheses.

Soft News as a Gateway to Traditional News Consumption

Hypothesis 8 holds that in addition to serving as a source of information about foreign crises, the soft news media also serve as a gateway to more traditional sources of news programming. In other words, once an individual is exposed to *some* information about an issue, such as a foreign crisis, in the soft news media, he or she will be more willing to pay attention to *additional* information about the issue in more traditional news formats. Soft news, in effect, provides viewers with a context for understanding the relatively more complex and detailed information presented by traditional news sources (Hamilton 2003). This makes information in a traditional news context relatively more accessible.

It is, of course, possible that the relationship might run in both directions. Individuals who view a story about a given subject on a traditional news program may become more likely to watch additional information about that same subject if they encounter it in a soft news context. This latter relationship, however, seems less likely. Given that, as the previously cited survey data indicate, the primary motivation of most hard news consumers is to become informed about the issues of the day, there is little reason to suppose that watching hard news would make a typical individual more likely to watch an entertainment-oriented soft news program. In other words, it seems relatively less likely that watching a report about a U.S. military intervention on, say, *The News Hour with Jim Lehrer* would induce a viewer to seek out additional information about the intervention on, say, *Hard Copy* or *Entertainment Tonight*.

To test my hypothesis, as well as the possibilities of reciprocal or reverse causality, I investigate whether exposure to soft news is positively associated with consuming hard news, and vice versa. In order to determine whether the causal arrows between soft and hard news consumption run in one or two directions, it is necessary to simultaneously estimate the influence of the former on the latter, and that of the latter on the former. This type of relationship suggests a system of two equations, which can be estimated using three-stage least squares (3SLS).

In the first equation, hard news consumption is the dependent variable, and soft news consumption is a causal variable. The two variables are then reversed in the second equation.[18] Each equation includes a slightly different battery of causal variables, similar to those employed in the prior analyses, as appropriate given each dependent variable.[19] The results, shown in table 4.A3, in appendix 3, indicate that soft news does indeed appear to serve as a gateway to hard news.[20] Among these respondents, as their soft news consumption increases from its lowest to highest values, hard news consumption increases by 44 percent ($p < .001$). In sharp contrast, variations in hard news consumption have no statistically significant effect on soft news consumption. This indicates that consuming soft news does increase people's willingness to consume hard news, but exposure to hard news does not influence the decision to consume soft news. Indeed, this is precisely the pattern predicted by the theory.

These data suggest, consistent with the Gateway Hypothesis, that individuals who happen upon an issue in a soft news context are more likely to "stay tuned" if they encounter it in a traditional news format.[21] These results are, of course, from only one survey. And it is certainly possible that they may be unique to this particular survey. To address this possibility, I conduct a second test of the Gateway Hypothesis, this time replicating the prior 3SLS models with data from a second survey (Pew Research Center 2000), which includes nearly identical media consumption and demographic questions as the 1996 Pew Research Center survey. Hence, for this test, I employ nearly identical model specifications and soft and hard news indexes.[22]

The results, shown in the latter two columns of table 4.A3, essentially replicate those from the 1996 Pew survey; consuming soft news is once again associated with increased hard news consumption, while consuming hard news does not appear in these data to influence soft news consumption. Moreover, the R^2 values for the soft news model (.36) is slightly higher than in the corresponding 1996 model (.28), suggesting that the instrument for soft news consumption is somewhat superior to that employed in the 1996 3SLS model. This strongly suggests that the results from the 1996 survey are not an artifact of one particular survey instrument, and thereby further support the Gateway Hypothesis. While these tests by no means rule out the possibility that, at least in some situations, the traditional news media may serve as a gateway to soft news programming, they do offer substantially greater support for the opposite causal pathway, as predicted by Hypothesis 8, *from* soft *to* hard news.

THE SOFT NEWS MEDIA, OPERATION JUST CAUSE, AND THE CIVIL WAR IN BOSNIA

I next further test my individual-level hypotheses using two *Times Mirror* surveys, one from January 1990 and the other from February 1993 (*Times Mirror* 1990 and 1993). The 1990 poll was conducted in the midst of the U.S. invasion of Panama on December 21, 1989—termed Operation Just Cause—whose stated goal was to oust from power Panama's ruling strongman, General Manuel Noriega. The 1993 poll was undertaken at a time when the Bosnian civil war had expanded to involve fighting between Muslims and Croatians. It was also during this period that NATO forces began flying combat patrols over Bosnia. Hence, like Panama in late 1989 and early 1990, the war in Bosnia attracted substantial media attention in early 1993.

As we have already seen, Bosnia was covered at length in the soft news media throughout the 1990s (recall chapter 3). In the case of the Panama invasion, as previously discussed, crime—including drug-related crime and drug trafficking—is among the most common topics on soft news programs, especially the tabloid newsmagazine shows. Given General Noriega's alleged links to Colombian drug traffickers, Operation Just Cause represented in many ways an ideal topic for the soft news media, combining multiple highly accessible, soft-news-friendly themes—U.S. military intervention, violence, controversy, a readily identifiable villain, crime, drug trafficking, and the like—into a single dramatic storyline highly amenable to episodic framing.

Unfortunately, the Panama invasion took place at a time before transcripts for most soft news programs were accessible. This makes it difficult to determine the extent to which the soft news media covered the invasion. The exceptions are the network TV newsmagazine programs, all of which covered Operation Just Cause at length. At a time when the "war on drugs" was considered a major crisis issue in America, the primary focus of these programs, not surprisingly, was General Noriega's alleged links to Colombian drug kingpins. For instance, in January and February 1990, ABC's *20/20* ran a series of stories, called "Drug War Status Reports," featuring Noriega's alleged drug connections. The other network TV newsmagazine programs on the air at the time, including *48 Hours* and *Primetime Live*, also emphasized the relationship between the Panama invasion and the war on drugs. Hence, while data limitations prohibit a detailed assessment of the soft news media's coverage of the U.S. invasion of Panama, those outlets whose transcripts were available in 1989 do appear to have covered it at length. This suggests that, along with the Bosnian civil war, Operation Just Cause is an appropriate topic for investigating the relationship between soft news consumption and attentiveness to foreign policy crises.

In addition to asking respondents how closely they had been following events in Panama and the Bosnian civil war—with responses again ranging from "not at all closely" to "very closely"—the two surveys asked respondents how often they watched, read, or listened to a variety of news and entertainment media outlets. In both cases, the question format was identical to that employed in the prior investigations in this chapter. As before, I transformed the media consumption questions into two scales, measuring respondents' exposure to soft and hard news, respectively. Table 4.3 lists the items included in each scale, for both surveys.[23]

This analysis essentially replicates that from the prior section, with two noteworthy exceptions. First, unlike the previous analysis, these surveys do not contain any questions that explicitly measure respondents' intrinsic interest in international affairs. Nor do they include any items addressing respondents' political engagement in general. Yet, in order to test my sixth hypothesis, it is necessary to identify an indicator of respondents' level of political engagement. An alternative indicator is respondents' level of education. Education level is certainly far from a perfect indicator of a respondent's propensity to follow politics in general or international affairs in particular. Yet, numerous studies have found education to be closely related to political knowledge and have

TABLE 4.3. Items Included in Soft and Hard News Indexes for 1990 Panama Invasion Survey and 1993 Bosnia Civil War Survey

Hard News Index Items	Soft News Index Items
Read daily newspaper (1990)	Watch TV newsmagazine shows, like *20/20* (1990, 1993)
Watch news programs on TV (1990)	
Listen to news on radio (1990)	Watch *A Current Affair* (1990, 1993)
Read weekly newsmagazines (1990)	Watch *Entertainment Tonight* (1990, 1993)
Read magazines like *Atlantic, Harper's,* or *The New Yorker* (1990)	
	Read personality magazines, like *People* (1990)
Read business magazines (1990)	
Watch Sunday interview/news shows, like *Meet the Press* (1990)	Read tabloid newspapers, like *National Enquirer* (1990)
Listen to National Public Radio (1990)	Watch TV talk shows, like *Oprah, Donahue,* and *Geraldo* (1993)
Watch *The McNeil-Lehrer Report* (1990)	
Watch CNN (1990)	
Watch national network TV news (1993)	
Watch local TV news (1993)	

employed it in statistical analyses as an indicator of political knowledge and engagement (Ault and Meernik 2000; S. Bennett 1995; Converse 1964; Krause 1997; MacKuen 1984).

In fact, education is reasonably closely correlated with political knowledge and engagement. According to one of the previously cited surveys (Pew Research Center 1996), better-educated individuals are more likely to be interested in international affairs and more likely to watch traditional sources of news and information about politics (e.g., network evening news programs) than are their less-educated counterparts. Hence, highly educated individuals are likely to be less dependent upon the soft news media for information about politics. And Hamilton (1998) finds that individuals with a high school education or less report substantially lower levels of interest in a wide range of domestic and international political issues—including the U.S. interventions in Bosnia and Somalia—than their college-educated counterparts. Finally, among respondents to the 1996 NES survey, education and political information are correlated with one another at about .50. Hence, for this analysis, I employ education level as a crude indicator of political engagement in general, and propensity to follow international political events in particular. In order to capture the effects of soft news consumption on respondents at differing levels of political engagement, I interact the soft news index with respondents' education level.

The other noteworthy difference between the current and prior investigations applies only to the 1990 survey. In that instance, an item is available that explicitly measures the perceived importance of the Panama invasion to respondents.[24] By explicitly controlling for personal importance, I am better able to isolate the effects of attentiveness. The remaining causal variables are nearly identical to those employed in my analysis of the 1996 Pew Research Center survey, and I do not revisit them here. The interested reader is invited to consult appendix 2, where the several new control variables are defined.

The results from four logit analyses of the correlates of attentiveness to Bosnia and Panama are shown in the final four columns of table 4.2, introduced in the previous section. In each instance, the first model excludes the interaction term, and so tests my fifth hypothesis, concerning the overall effect of soft news consumption on attentiveness to foreign crises. In order to test my sixth hypothesis, concerning disproportionate effects for the least politically engaged members of the population, the second model then adds the interaction term. The results from both pairs of analyses strongly support each hypothesis. In each instance, the coefficient on the soft news index is correctly signed and statistically significant with or without the interaction term. Once again, for ease of interpretation, I translate the key coefficients from the interaction models into probabilities of following the U.S. invasion of Panama and the civil war in Bosnia with differing degrees of "closeness," as respondents political engagement (proxied by education level) varies.[25]

The results indicate that among the least-educated respondents (i.e., those who did not attend high school), as soft news consumption increases from its lowest to highest levels, the probability of following the U.S. invasion of Panama "very closely" increases by 68 percentage points ($p < .01$). The corresponding effects on the probability of following the invasion "fairly closely," not too closely" or "not at all closely" are declines of 44, 18 and 7 percentage points, respectively ($p < .01$ in each case). For the Bosnia model, among the least-educated respondents, a maximum increase in education is associated with increases of 5, 31, and 18 percentage points in the probabilities of following the civil war "very," "fairly," or "somewhat" closely, respectively, and a 56-percentage-point *decrease* in the probability of following Bosnia "not at all" closely. Each of these results supports my fifth hypothesis.

Consistent with my sixth hypothesis, in both cases the effects of soft news consumption weaken in a stepwise fashion as respondents move up the education ladder. Among the most highly educated respondents (those with a college or postgraduate degree) a maximum increase in soft news consumption is associated with a 30-percentage-point increase in the probability of following the Panama invasion "very closely." The corresponding effects on the probabilities of following the Panama invasion "fairly closely," "not too closely," or "not at all closely," are declines of 22 ($p < .01$), 6 ($p < .01$), and 1 ($p < .05$) percentage point(s), respectively. In the Bosnia model, highly educated respondents vary hardly at all in their attentiveness, regardless of their soft news consumption.

The effects of soft news consumption on the probability of following the Panama invasion "very closely"—the category with the largest soft news ef-

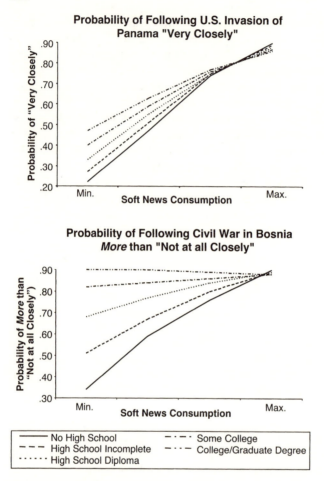

FIGURE 4.3. Probability of Following Panama and Bosnia, as Soft News Consumption and Education Vary

fects—as education varies, are shown in the top graphic of figure 4.3. The bottom graphic then plots the corresponding effects on the probability of following Bosnia *more* than "not at all closely," which, in this instance, as with all of the other foreign crises investigated thus far in this chapter, save Operation Just Cause, is the category with the largest soft news effects.

In each instance, highly educated respondents start out at a much higher level of attentiveness, before leveling off slightly *below* the level of attentiveness of the least-educated respondents who consume maximum quantities of soft news. This represents clear additional support for Hypothesis 6. The reversal between low- and high-education respondents at the highest level of soft news consumption, though modest in magnitude and hence most likely of little substantive importance, raises at least the possibility, once again, that among highly politically engaged individuals, soft news is a distraction, rather than a meaningful source of information.

The differences in the effects of soft news consumption across education groups on attentiveness to Panama, though substantial, are smaller than the corresponding differences identified in the previous section—concerning attentiveness to Bosnia, the congressional antiterrorism debate, and the Israel-Lebanon conflict, all in 1996, and with respect to the Bosnian civil war in 1993. With respect to the former three cases (from 1996), this is presumably attributable, in part, to differences in the available indicators of respondents' ex ante propensity to follow a given foreign policy news story. Education level is clearly a rougher proxy of respondents' general propensity to follow foreign crises than their self-declared interest in news about international affairs.

It is also important to recognize the stark difference in the profiles of the several foreign policy events. While Bosnia, the Israel-Lebanon conflict, and the terrorism debate were certainly of interest to many Americans, only Operation Just Cause involved a large-scale invasion by U.S. ground forces into hostile territory. In 1993, for instance, no American ground forces were in harm's way in Bosnia. And in 1996, though the U.S. involvement in Bosnia did involve large numbers of U.S. ground forces, their mission was peacekeeping, not war fighting. Hence, not surprisingly, Americans, on average, were far more attuned to events in Panama.

In at least this one respect, Operation Just Cause appears to bear a closer resemblance to Operation Desert Storm than to any of the other foreign crises investigated in this chapter. For instance, according to the Pew Research Center's News Interest Index, which, as noted, has tracked public interest in major news stories since 1986, 60 percent of respondents claimed to have followed the Panama invasion "very" closely. As of August 2001, Operation Just Cause was the 19th most closely followed story out of nearly 900 items included in the index, thereby placing in the *top 2 percent* of all news stories since 1986.

According to these data, the level of public interest in the Panama invasion approached that of the Persian Gulf War, which peaked at seventh on the list, with 67 percent of respondents claiming to have followed the war "very" closely.[26] By contrast, the U.S. intervention in Bosnia peaked, in January 1996, at 126th on the list (or the 86th percentile), with 37 percent of respondents claiming to have followed the Bosnia story "very" closely. And in 1993, only 26 percent of the Pew Research Center's survey respondents reported following the civil war in Bosnia "very" closely. This places Bosnia circa 1993 at 327th place on the list (or the 63rd percentile).

If we shift our comparison to the percentages of respondents who claimed to have followed the Panama invasion and the Gulf War *at least* "fairly" closely (i.e., "very" or "fairly" closely), the gap nearly disappears, with 91 percent and 92 percent, respectively, claiming to have followed the two conflicts at least "fairly" closely.[27] This compares to 82 percent of respondents who in January 1996 reported following Bosnia at least "fairly" closely. These data suggest that, as was the case with the Gulf War, the baseline level of exposure to information about Panama among low-information individuals was almost certainly higher than with respect to Bosnia. This presumably explains why the largest variation for the Panama model occurs at the highest attentiveness level ("very closely"), while that for all of the other foreign crises investigated in this chapter, including Bosnia in 1993 and 1996, occurs at the lowest level (*more* than "not at all closely").

In fact, because no comparable media consumption surveys are available from the Gulf War period, media coverage of Operation Just Cause represents perhaps the closest approximation of the feeding frenzy surrounding the Persian Gulf War for which it is possible to explicitly test the influence of soft news consumption on attentiveness. After all, at least according to the Pew Center data, the differential in public interest in the two conflicts is only 7, or 1, percentage point(s) (depending on the interest threshold employed). Though media coverage of Panama was by no means comparable to that of the Gulf War, either in intensity or duration, it was nonetheless extremely intense. In the first fifteen days of Operation Just Cause (December 20, 1989–January 3, 1990), the three major broadcast network evening newscasts presented a combined total of 111 stories related to the invasion, or an average of 7.4 stories-per-day. By comparison, during the first fifteen days of Operation Desert Storm (January 17–31, 1991), the three network evening newscasts presented 146 Gulf War-related stories, or 9.7 stories-per-day.[28] By this admittedly limited yardstick, network evening news coverage of Just Cause was about 24 percent less intense than coverage of Desert Storm; a significant difference to be sure, but hardly overwhelming. Bearing in mind that the soft news media presumably also covered the Gulf War more intensively than they covered Operation Just Cause, this suggests that the soft news media's influence on public attentiveness to the Persian Gulf War *may* have approximated, to at least some extent, the form and magnitude of its corresponding influence during the Panama invasion.

That exposure to soft news outlets leveled the attentiveness playing field across the different education groups, even for such a high-profile event as the Panama invasion, represents particularly impressive evidence of the soft news media's important role in raising the awareness of foreign crises among politically inattentive Americans. Moreover, it is worth reiterating that in the case of Operation Just Cause, these relationships arise after accounting for the perceived importance of the Panama invasion to respondents. In other words, because the 1990 survey allows an explicit control for the salience to the respondent of Operation Just Cause, we can be fairly confident that the relationships illustrated in figure 4.3, with respect to Panama, are capturing variations in attentiveness, and *not* salience (personal importance).

Finally, as an additional test of Hypothesis 7, I employed a third dependent variable from the 1993 survey, addressing whether the respondent had followed news about the state of the U.S. economy. As with the previous models, the dependent variable is a four-category scale, measuring the extent to which respondents followed economic news. The latter two models in table 4.A1 present the results from two ordered logit analyses employing this dependent variable, with and without the interaction term. Once again, consistent with Hypothesis 7, consumption of soft news appears to have no significant effect on respondents' propensity to follow news about the economy. Hence, as expected, while the soft news media do appear in these data to contribute to public attentiveness to U.S. foreign policy crises, they do not wield a comparable effect on attentiveness to the state of the U.S. economy, even in the midst of an economic downturn (as was the case in 1990).

THE SOFT NEWS MEDIA AND THE NORTHERN IRELAND CONFLICT

The United States has been intimately involved for many years in efforts to resolve the civil war in Northern Ireland. Indeed, the Clinton administration played a central role in drafting the Good Friday peace accords of April 10, 1998, and in persuading the various parties to the conflict to sign it. Most importantly for my purposes, the soft news media have presented substantial coverage of the conflict in Northern Ireland. For instance, one episode of the tabloid newsmagazine *A Current Affair* featured a profile of a young Irish girl who spoke about her hopes for peace to Clinton during a presidential visit to Northern Ireland and was subsequently invited to Washington to visit the White House.

Daytime talk shows have also covered the conflict in Northern Ireland. An episode of *The View*, for instance, featured an interview with actress Roma Downey, a native of Northern Ireland, who spoke at length about the peace process. And *Live with Regis and Kathie Lee* discussed efforts by England's Prince Charles to get involved in the Northern Ireland peace process. Network newsmagazines, such as *20/20*, *48 Hours*, and *60 Minutes* have also covered the conflict and peace process. For example, one episode of *60 Minutes* profiled an IRA hit-man-turned-informant named Sean O'Callaghan. Finally, a number of comedy-oriented talk shows, including *The Late Show with David Letterman* and Comedy Central's *Daily Show*, have also covered Northern Ireland. The *Daily Show*, for instance, featured stories lampooning the Good Friday peace accords, as well as the announcement that the Nobel Peace Prize had been awarded to the architects of the accords, David Trimble and John Hume. Hence, while the Northern Ireland peace process is not the archetypal water-cooler event, I believe it is an appropriate foreign crisis issue for further testing my theory.

On July 13–14, 1998, the Gallup Organization conducted a telephone survey (Gallup 1998) to query respondents concerning their news consumption habits, as well as their opinions regarding several major public policy issues, including social security and the peace process in Northern Ireland. I focus on two questions as dependent variables for this investigation, each addressing respondents interest in the Northern Ireland peace process: (A) "In the situation in Northern Ireland, are your sympathies (1) more with the Irish Catholics, or (2) more with the Irish Protestants, (3) [with] both, (4) [with] neither, [or] (5) don't know/not familiar"; and (B) "As you may know, the leaders of the two opposing sides in Northern Ireland have reached a new compromise agreement concerning the governance of Northern Ireland. Are you generally optimistic or pessimistic that this agreement will lead to lasting peace in Northern Ireland? (1) optimistic, (2) pessimistic, (3) don't know/not familiar with."

I transformed the responses into dichotomous variables, coded 0 for responses of "don't know/not familiar (with)" and 1 otherwise. My hypothesis is that public attentiveness, as distinct from factual knowledge, can be reasonably estimated by an individual's willingness to offer an opinion, and vice versa. Moreover, in this instance, "don't know" responses are grouped with "not familiar" responses (the latter arguably being a more direct indicator of *in*attentiveness). In this and subsequent analyses, I refer to the percentage of individuals willing to offer a response to a given survey question, or those *not* responding "don't know" or "no opinion," as the level of *opinionation*. (In appendix 1 to the present chapter, I discuss my use of "don't know" responses as an indicator of attentiveness, and present the results of a series of reliability and validity tests.)

The independent variables for this investigation are similar to those employed in the prior analyses, and I do not review them here, beyond noting that they fall into three general categories: socioeconomic status, political partisanship, and media consumption habits. The latter variables consist of a broad range of questions concerning respondents' consumption of news and entertainment programming on television, radio, in magazines, and in newspapers. As in the prior section, I collapsed these variables into two broad indexes, the first representing the extent of respondents' exposure to hard news and the second capturing respondents' exposure to soft news.[29] In table 4.4, I list the components of each index.[30] (The coding and definitions of the key independent variables are described in appendix 2.)

The results from two logit analyses (shown in table 4.A4 in appendix 3) indicate that exposure to soft news is positively associated with attentiveness to the Northern Ireland peace process ($p < .05$, for both dependent variables). Once again, I convert the coefficients on the soft news index from both models into probabilities of having an opinion, as exposure to soft news varies, with all other independent variables held constant at their mean values.[31] The results indicate that as soft news exposure moves from its lowest to highest levels, the probability of expressing familiarity with the Northern Ireland peace process increases by 25 (from .69 to .94) and 13 (from .86 to .99) percentage points, for Questions A and B, respectively. In each case, these increases in are statistically significant at the .05 level. These results offer clear support for my fifth hypothesis.

Unfortunately, like the previous analysis, this survey does not contain any questions that explicitly capture respondents' intrinsic interest in international affairs. Hence, I again employ education level as a crude indicator of political engagement in general, and the propensity to follow international political events in particular. In order to capture the differing effects of exposure to soft news on different types of respondents, I interact the soft news index with

TABLE 4.4. Items Included in Soft and Hard News Indexes for Northern Ireland Survey

How Often Does Respondent Get News From	
Hard News Index Items	Soft News Index Items
Nightly network news programs	TV entertainment news ahows[a]
Local television news programs	Television talk shows[b]
CNN	Radio talk shows
C-SPAN	TV newsmagazine shows[c]
Public television news	Morning news and interview shows[d]
Cable news other than CNN	
Sunday morning television news shows	
National Public Radio	
National network news on radio	
Weekly news magazines	
Newspapers or national newspapers	

[a]Examples of this type of program include *Hard Copy, Access Hollywood*, and *Entertainment Tonight*.

[b]Examples of this type of program include the *Oprah Winfrey* and *Rosie O'Donnell* shows.

[c]Examples of this type of program include *60 Minutes, Dateline*, and *20/20*.

[d]Examples of this type of program include CBS's *Good Morning America* and NBC's *Today* show.

respondents' education level. (The results from these logit analyses, employing the same two dependent variables, are shown in the second and fourth columns, respectively, of table 4.A3 in appendix 3.) As in the previous section, these latter analyses offer substantial support for Hypothesis 6. Once again transforming the key coefficients into probabilities, figure 4.5 graphically illustrates the relationship between exposure to soft news programming and attentiveness to the Northern Ireland peace process, at different levels of education.

In both cases, exposure to soft news exerts its strongest effect among the least-educated respondents. Indeed, as before, effects of exposure to soft news diminish in a stepwise fashion as respondents move up the education ladder. Among respondents who did not attend high school, as exposure to soft news increases from its lowest to highest values, the probability of being familiar with the Northern Ireland peace process increases by 55 and 54 percentage points for the two dependent variables (Questions A and B, respectively). In contrast, among respondents possessing a graduate degree, a maximum increase in exposure to soft news is associated with modest increases of 5 and 0.3 percentage points in the probability of being familiar with the peace process (again, for Questions A and B, respectively). Overall, a maximum increase in exposure to soft news is associated with a statistically significant increase ($p < .05$ or better) in the probability of being familiar with the peace process among all respondents who did not attend college.[32] This includes about 44 percent of the respondents.

Finally, to test my seventh hypothesis, I reran the previous models, substitut-

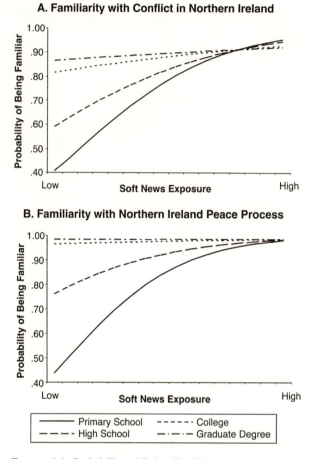

FIGURE 4.4. Probability of Being Familiar with Northern Ireland, as Soft News Consumption and Education Vary

ing two less dramatic, non-foreign-crisis issues as the dependent variables. For these latter analyses, I employed the following two questions: (A) "Which of these statements concerning the Social Security system do you agree with more? (1) It has some problems, but these can be dealt with gradually by Congress over the next few years; (2) It faces serious problems which must be dealt with by Congress in the next year; (3) It has no problems; or (4) Don't know/refused"; and (B) "I'm going to describe some stories involving journalists that have been in the news recently. For each one, please say whether you have heard or read anything about it before now. . . . That the *Cincinnati Inquirer* admitted illegally attaining information on the Chiquita Banana company and paid Chiquita $10 million to settle the company's claims." I transformed the Social Security question into a dichotomous variable, coded 0 for responses of "don't know" or refusals to offer an answer, and 1 otherwise. I coded the Chiquita Banana company question 0 if the respondent had *not* heard or read about the scandal and 1 if the respondent *had* heard or read about it.

The results from four logit regressions—both with and without the interaction with education level—are presented in table 4.A4, in appendix 3. In each instance, both with and without the interaction term, soft news exposure is *not* significantly related to respondents' attentiveness to either the social security debate or the Chiquita Banana incident. Indeed, in all but one of the four models, the coefficients on the soft news index are highly insignificant, and far smaller in magnitude than in either Northern Ireland model. And in the latter model (the sixth model in table 4.A4), while the magnitudes of the coefficients on soft news index and the interaction term are comparable to those in the Northern Ireland models, neither approaches statistical significance. Taken together, these results represent strong additional support for my seventh hypothesis.

THE SOFT NEWS MEDIA AND MAJOR PROBLEMS FACING THE NATION

On May 7–13, 1998, the Pew Research Center conducted a telephone survey ($N = 981$) to query respondents concerning news consumption habits as well as their views regarding the most important problems facing the nation (Pew Research Center 1998b). For this latter question, respondents were asked to specify up to five national problems. As my dependent variable for this investigation, I employ respondents' propensity to mention at least one foreign-affairs-related problem. I therefore collapsed the responses into two categories, coded 1 if respondents mentioned at least one foreign affairs problem and 0 otherwise.

It seems fairly straightforward to extrapolate that if an individual mentions a given issue, or class of issues (e.g., "issues related to foreign policy") in an open-ended question, then that individual has been at least somewhat attentive to the issue or class of issues. By this same logic, mentioning more distinct answers regarding a given issue or class of issues suggests greater attentiveness. Of course, this also likely implies greater personal concern (or salience) with the issue, which is why responses to open-ended questions are, in my view, a more imperfect indicator of attentiveness than some of the other indicators employed in this chapter.[33] Hence, here and in subsequent analyses, when employing this type of indicator, I separately control, wherever possible, for factors that would tend to make a given issue or issue area personally important to a given individual.

My hypothesis here is that attentiveness, as distinct from factual knowledge, can be reasonably estimated by individuals' propensity to recall a foreign affairs issue in an open-ended question. In fact, given the unprecedented domestic political environment at the time of this survey, this is a particularly difficult test of my theory. Due to the Monica Lewinsky scandal, the attention of the American public at the time of the survey was focused sharply inward. As a result, overall, fewer than 5 percent of respondents mentioned even a single foreign affairs issue.

It is important to bear in mind that this analysis differs from many others in this study in that respondents must weigh foreign policy issues *relative* to domestic issues in formulating their responses. The other analyses do not require such comparisons. This is important because of the differing content of hard and soft news and the differing media consumption habits of respondents at different education levels. In each survey included in this study, poorly educated respondents report consuming, on average, significantly less hard news and more soft news than their better-educated counterparts. Hard news, in turn, tends to be heavily oriented toward domestic politics, rather than foreign policy (Moisy 1997). In contrast, for the previously discussed reasons, the opposite bias, in favor of covering dramatic foreign policy events over most domestic political issues, predominates in the soft news media (bearing in mind that this is a comparison of relative proportions, as most political issues are ignored entirely by the soft news media). This suggests, ceteris paribus, that poorly educated individuals who are heavy consumers of soft news (and who do not consume much hard news) are relatively more likely than their hard-news-oriented, better-educated counterparts to mention foreign, rather than domestic, issues when asked to name the most serious problems facing the nation. This was particularly true at the time of this survey, when, as noted, due to the Lewinsky scandal, the traditional news media was focused sharply inward. Hence, in this section, rather than retesting my fifth and sixth hypotheses, I instead test two corollaries to those hypotheses:

$H_{4.1}$ Individuals whose primary sources of news are soft news outlets are disproportionately likely to emphasize those political topics and themes most prevalent in the soft news media; and

$H_{4.2}$ The aforementioned effect should be strongest among the least politically engaged (or educated) individuals, who are least likely to seek out alternative news sources.

The independent variables for this investigation fall into three categories similar to those employed in previous models in this chapter: socioeconomic status, interest in and knowledge about politics, and media consumption habits. The latter variables again consist of a battery of questions concerning respondents' interest in and attention to news and entertainment programming on television, on the radio, in magazines, and in newspapers. As before, I collapse these variables into two broad indexes, the first representing the extent of respondents' consumption of hard news sources and topics and the second capturing respondents' exposure to soft news outlets. Table 4.5 lists the components of each index.[34] (The coding and definitions of the key independent variables are presented in appendix 2.)

The results from four logit analyses employing these indexes—reported in appendix 3, at table 4.A5—once again support Hypotheses 5 through 7. Beginning with the basic model, for ease of interpretation, I again convert the coeffi-

TABLE 4.5. Items Included in Soft and Hard News Indexes for Foreign Policy Problems Survey

How Often Does Respondent Get News From	
Hard News Index Items	Soft News Index Items
Nightly network news programs	TV entertainment news shows[a]
Local television news programs	Television talk shows[b]
CNN	TV newsmagazine shows[c]
C-SPAN	Morning news and interview shows[d]
PBS *News Hour with Jim Lehrer*	Court TV
Cable news other than CNN	MTV News
CNBC	
National Public Radio	
Newspapers or national newspapers	

[a]Examples of this type of program include *Hard Copy*, *Access Hollywood*, and *Entertainment Tonight*.
[b]Examples of this type of program include the *Oprah Winfrey* and *Rosie O'Donnell* shows.
[c]Examples of this type of program include *60 Minutes*, *Dateline*, and *20/20*.
[d]Examples of this type of program include CBS's *Good Morning America* and NBC's *Today* show.

cient on the soft news index into probabilities of mentioning a foreign affairs problem as exposure to soft news varies, with all other independent variables held constant at their mean values.[35] The results indicate that exposure to soft news indeed affects the propensity of survey respondents to mention foreign affairs problems. Respondents who report regularly consuming soft news are substantially more likely to mention a foreign affairs problem (.18) than those who report "never" doing so (.02). This represents a statistically significant ($p < .05$) difference of 16 percentage points. Moreover, while the maximum probability of mentioning a foreign affairs problem (.18) is rather modest, it is important to recall that this survey was conducted at a time when the American public was unusually focused on domestic politics. In fact, the .18 change represents nearly a fourfold increase beyond the overall average likelihood of mentioning a foreign affairs problem in this survey of .047. Hence, these results clearly support Hypothesis 4.1.

In order to test Hypothesis 4.2, I again employ respondents' education level as an indicator of their propensity to follow international affairs.[36] The second model in Table 4.A5, at appendix 3, presents the results of this analysis. In this instance, I add an interaction term (Education × soft news index), intended to capture the differing effects of exposure to soft news on respondents at differing levels of education. Figure 4.5 graphically illustrates the relationship between variations in exposure to soft news and respondents' probability of mentioning a foreign affairs problem, at different levels of education.

As in the previous investigation, exposure to soft news exerts a far stronger effect on the probability of mentioning a foreign affairs problem among less-

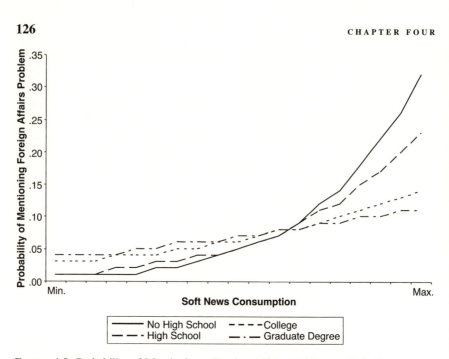

FIGURE 4.5. Probability of Mentioning a Foreign Affairs Problem, as Soft News Consumption and Education Vary

educated respondents. Once again, the effects of exposure to soft news diminish in a stepwise fashion as respondents move up the education ladder. Among respondents who completed only primary school (an eighth-grade education), as exposure to soft news increases from its lowest to highest values, the probability of mentioning a foreign affairs problem increases by 28 percentage points ($p < .05$). The corresponding increase among respondents possessing a graduate degree is a statistically insignificant 11 percentage points. Overall, a maximum increase in exposure to soft news produces a statistically significant ($p < .10$ or better) decline in the probability of mentioning a foreign affairs problem among all respondents who did not complete a four-year college degree (though, as noted, the magnitude of the substantive effect diminishes as education increases).[37] This includes about 69 percent of the respondents to this survey. Moreover, as anticipated, at the highest level of soft news consumption, the least-educated respondents are indeed more likely to mention a foreign affairs problem than were their better-educated counterparts. These results support Hypothesis 4.2.

In order to test whether the significant results reported above were sensitive to variation in the definition of a "foreign affairs problem," I recoded the dependent variable so that mentions of foreign aid were treated as *non*-foreign-affairs responses. It is unclear whether Americans view foreign aid as primarily an economic or a security-related issue area. Since my theory primarily concerns national security issues, foreign aid is perhaps the most ambiguous category of foreign policy issue. In fact, recoding the dependent variable in this manner alters the results only modestly; the coefficients on the key variables all remain similar in magnitude and significance (see the final two columns of table 4.A5).[38] Hence, my results do not appear overly sensitive to the coding rule with respect to foreign aid. Taken together, the results from this analysis once again offer clear and consistent support for Hypotheses 4.1 and 4.2.

Soft News and Non-Foreign-Policy Problems Facing the Nation

While the patterns described thus far appear highly robust, they are, with but one exception (the Lewinsky scandal), limited to a single dimension: foreign affairs. Yet, Hypotheses 4.1 and 4.2 are not limited to foreign crises. Rather, they predict that soft news consumers, especially those who are not intrinsically interested in politics, ought to be more attentive than their non-soft-news con-suming counterparts to *any* theme or topic that is prevalent in the soft news media, such as crime, morality, or scandal.

Hence, before concluding this section, I briefly investigate the propensity of different groups of respondents to mention as the nation's most important prob-lem issues pertaining to any of the following subjects, which are prevalent in soft news media coverage of politics: national defense/international issues, crime/justice, morality/family values, scandal/corruption, or terrorism.

Of course, it is possible that consuming soft news would similarly influence respondents' propensity to mention other types of issues. (Overall, about 34 percent of respondents mentioned one of the aforementioned issue areas as the nation's most important problem.) Yet my theory would predict that respon-dents' propensity to mention other, less accessible types of issues, which are not prevalent in the soft news media, should *not* be influenced by soft news consumption. Hence, this analysis also tests the following corollary to my sev-enth hypothesis:

H$_{4.3}$ The propensity to emphasize other, less dramatic, or partisan political issues will *not* be significantly related to exposure to soft news.

Below at table 4.6, I divide respondents into four groups: low education/low soft news consumption, low education/high soft news consumption, high educa-tion/low soft news consumption, and high education/high soft news consump-tion. I define "low" education as not having attended college. "High" education, in turn, indicates that the respondent attended at least *some* college. "Low" soft news consumption is defined as one standard deviation below the mean level of soft news consumption in the survey. "High" soft news consumption, in turn, is defined as one standard deviation above the mean. As before, I employ educa-tion as an indicator of political engagement.

Based on these categorizations, table 4.6 compares the propensity of each group of respondents to mention as the nation's most important problem topics pertaining to any of the aforementioned issue areas, as well as, separately, the propensity of each group to mention issues pertaining in any way to the state of

TABLE 4.6. Probability of Mentioning Major Problems Related to Predominant Themes of Soft News Media or the State of the U.S. Economy, by Education and Soft News Consumption

Issues Prevalent in the Soft News Media			
	Soft News Consumption		
	Low	High	Difference
Education			
12th grade or less	.19 (9/46)	.36 (30/84)	.17
At least some college	.36 (30/86)	.38 (26/68)	.02
Issues Pertaining to State of U.S. Economy			
	Soft News Consumption		
	Low	High	Difference
Education			
12th grade or less	.17 (8/46)	.18 (15/84)	.01
At least some college	.10 (9/86)	.13 (9/68)	.03

the domestic U.S. economy. Here, I employ the state of the economy as exemplary of the type of issue not typically covered by the soft news media. Overall, only about 16 percent of the respondents mentioned *any* issues pertaining to the U.S. economy as the nation's most important problem. This is presumably attributable to the timing of the survey, which took place in the midst of a sustained period of economic growth. Nonetheless, the economy remains a frequent topic of traditional news outlets, and, hence, is an appropriate topic for contrasting soft and hard news coverage.

The results in table 4.6 indicate that among respondents without a college education, those who do not consume much soft news are about half as likely as their more-frequent soft-news-consuming counterparts to mention major problems pertaining to the most prevalent soft news themes (.19 vs. .36, respectively). In sharp contrast, among respondents with a college education, soft news consumption matters hardly at all in their propensity to mention problems pertaining to such themes (.36 vs. .38, respectively). Turning to the propensity to mention problems pertaining to the state of the U.S. economy, in this instance, respondents' consumption of soft news has almost no effect *regardless* of their level of education. Among respondents without a college education, the propensity to mention an economy-related issue as the nation's most important problem increases by only 1 percentage point (from .17 to .18), as soft news consumption increases from one standard deviation below the mean to one standard deviation above the mean. And among college educated respondents, the corresponding effect of consuming soft news is only slightly larger, an increase of 3 percentage points (.10 vs. .13). This suggests that soft news consumption does indeed matter more—especially among individuals who are not highly educated—for those types of issues that tend to be covered by the soft news media.

Additionally, hard news consumption had a much weaker effect than soft news consumption on respondents' propensity to mention the aforementioned soft new topics, and a modest positive effect on their propensity to mention an issue pertaining to the economy. And, in contrast to the effects of soft news consumption on respondents' propensity to mention typical soft news topics, the latter patterns were strongest among respondents with a college education. Among respondents who did not attend college, those who consume a great deal of hard news were only 1 percentage point more likely to mention economic problems (.14 to .15), while among their college educated counterparts, the corresponding increase, though still modest, was nonetheless larger (4 percentage points, from .10 to .14). Finally, hard news consumption had much weaker effects than soft news consumption on respondents' propensity to mention soft news topics, regardless of their education level. Among respondents without a college education, hard news consumers (again, defined as at least one standard deviation above the mean consumption level) were 11 percentage points more likely to mention one of the aforementioned soft news topics (.43 vs. .32), a substantially smaller difference than the corresponding effect of consuming soft news. Among college-educated respondents, the effect was nearly zero (.36 vs. .35). Taken together, these figures once again support all three hypotheses (4.1, 4.2, and 4.3).

Wagging the Dog? Monica Lewinsky and the 1998 U.S. Cruise Missile Attacks against Afghanistan and Sudan

This book began with an anecdote concerning the August 1998 U.S. cruise missile strikes against suspected terrorist sites in Afghanistan and Sudan. In the final section in this chapter, I explore this U.S. foreign crisis more systematically. In particular, I investigate whether individuals who were attentive to the Monica Lewinsky scandal were more attentive to the cruise missile attacks than those who were not attentive to the Lewinsky scandal. The theory predicts that individuals will learn about foreign crises as an *incidental by-product* of seeking entertainment. Following the Lewinsky scandal was clearly, for many Americans, a highly entertaining pastime. Indeed, the scandal dominated the soft news media for over a year. The question I ask here is whether, consistent with the incidental learning model, individuals who watched news about the scandal were exposed to information about the cruise missile attacks as an incidental by-product. To investigate this possibility, I employ a Pew Center telephone survey (Pew Research Center 1998c), conducted between August 21 and August 24, 1998.

In addition to asking respondents whether and to what extent they had followed the cruise missile strikes (the dependent variable) and the Lewinsky scandal ("Scandal"), the survey also asked respondents how important they considered the accusation that President Clinton lied under oath about his relationship with Monica Lewinsky ("Scandal importance"), as well as asking a subgroup of respondents whether they believed the decision to launch missile strikes was intended to divert public attention away from the scandal ("Wag the dog").[39] Once these factors are controlled, what remains is respondents' attentiveness to the missile strikes as a function of attentiveness to the scandal, independent of either their interest in the scandal or their views with respect to any possible link between the scandal and the missile strikes. In other words, any remaining relationship between attentiveness to these two issues is effectively *incidental*.

The dependent variable is drawn from the following question: "Tell me if you happened to follow this news story very closely, fairly closely, not too closely, or not at all closely: U.S. military strikes against sites linked to terrorists in Afghanistan and Sudan." I transformed the responses into a dichotomous variable, coded 0 if the respondent followed the missile strike story "not at all" or "a little" closely and 1 if he or she followed it "fairly" or "very" closely.[40] As has been the case throughout my investigations, I also include a variety of controls for respondent's socioeconomic status, partisanship, and political engagement. (All controls, except those defined above, are defined and coded identically to comparable variables in prior models, and hence are not revisited here.)

The results from this analysis, presented in table 4.A6 in appendix 3, indicate that, even after controlling for respondents' intrinsic interest in the Lewinsky scandal and whether they believed the two issues were linked, respondents who were attentive to the scandal were more attentive to the missile strikes. Translating the logit coefficients to probabilities indicates that as respondents move from lowest to highest attentiveness to the scandal, their probability of attending to the cruise missile attacks increases by 24 percentage points, from .69 to .94 ($p < .01$).

If the theory is correct, however, this relationship ought not to be evenly distributed across the respondents. In fact, Hypothesis 6, which predicts the strongest positive relationship between soft news exposure and crisis attentiveness among the least politically engaged members of the public, further suggests that the relationship between attentiveness to the scandal and the missile strikes ought to be strongest among the least politically engaged respondents, who are the heaviest consumers of soft news. This suggests an interaction between political engagement and attention to the scandal, much like those investigated in the previous section. Unfortunately, this survey contains no direct indicator of political engagement. Hence, as before, I rely on a second-best indicator: the respondent's level of education. I thus interact the scandal attention variable with education ("Scandal × education"). The results of this second analysis are also shown table 4.A6. At figure 4.6, I translate the logit coefficients into probabilities of being attentive to the missile strikes for respondents at different levels of education.

Among respondents who did not attend high school, as attention to the Lewin-

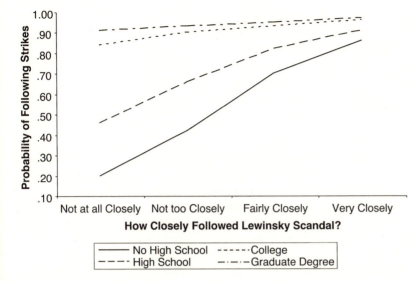

FIGURE 4.6. Probability of Following Missile Strikes as Attention to Lewinsky Scandal and Education Vary

sky scandal increases from its lowest to highest levels, the probability of being attentive to the missile strikes increases dramatically, by 66 percentage points (from .20 to .86). Consistent with Hypothesis 6, the relationship between the two attentiveness indicators weakens in a stepwise fashion as respondents move up the education ladder. The corresponding increases for respondents with high school and college educations, respectively, are 45 and 12 percentage points (from .46 to .91 and from .84 to .96, respectively). Finally, among respondents with a postgraduate degree, attention to the scandal matters hardly at all. Among these highly educated respondents, as attention to the scandal increases from its lowest to highest values, the probability of being attentive to the cruise missile strikes increases by only 6 percentage points, from .91 to .97. These results represent additional, albeit indirect, support for Hypothesis 6.

Unfortunately, this survey does not include questions that would make it possible to determine precisely how respondents were learning about the missile strikes and the scandal. It is possible that they learned about both events primarily from traditional news outlets. Including controls for respondents' evaluation of the importance of the Lewinsky scandal, their propensity to see the two events as related, and their partisan leanings does, however, lead one to suspect that the remaining relationship is not entirely an artifact of watching both events on network or cable news programs or reading about them in newspapers.[41] For instance, considering an issue important seems reasonably likely to be related to whether or not one watches or reads traditional news stories about it.

Moreover, as noted in chapter 2, soft news programs accounted for a substantial portion of overall coverage of the Lewinsky scandal. And, as discussed in chapter 1, the cruise missile strikes were heavily covered in the soft news media. Nonetheless, given the absence of media-use questions in this survey and its limited scope, this evidence, though suggestive, must be interpreted with caution.[42]

CONCLUSION

My investigations into the relationship between exposure to soft news outlets and attentiveness to four different foreign policy crisis issues, as well as to "major problems" pertaining to foreign affairs, established, in each instance, a direct link between media consumption and individual attentiveness to foreign crises. Indeed, each of my three individual-level hypotheses, along with several corollaries to those hypotheses, as well as my Gateway Hypothesis, was supported across multiple statistical tests. Soft news appears in these data to be an important source of information about foreign crises or domestic water-cooler events (e.g., Bosnia, terrorism, the Israel-Lebanon conflict, the Panama invasion, the Northern Ireland peace process, the Monica Lewinsky scandal), but not about other less dramatic or more intrinsically partisan political issues (e.g., Republican primaries, social security, the Chiquita Banana scandal, tobacco legislation, the state of the U.S. economy). Moreover, soft news is particularly influential among those individuals who are not typically inclined to follow politics or foreign affairs. Indeed, one implication of the propensity of soft news programs to favor coverage of foreign crises over other types of political issues was substantiated by the tendency of less-educated (or politically uninterested) soft news enthusiasts to mention foreign policy issues more frequently than domestic political issues when asked to name the most important problems facing the nation. Also consistent with the theory, this pattern did not extend to highly educated (or politically engaged) individuals.

I also found some evidence that, consistent with Hypothesis 8, soft news functions as a gateway to more traditional sources of news about foreign affairs, while the opposite relationship did not emerge. Additionally, some indirect evidence supporting the incidental by-product model was evident in the aftermath of the U.S. bombing of suspected terrorist sites in Afghanistan and Sudan. Among low-education respondents, attention to the Monica Lewinsky scandal—a topic heavily covered in the soft news media—was strongly positively related to attention to the missile strikes. Also consistent with the model, this relationship weakened as respondents moved up the education ladder.

Finally, the relationships identified in this chapter run directly counter to other studies that have found a *negative* relationship between viewing entertainment-oriented TV programming and traditional measures of political knowledge. That my attentiveness indicators produced results quite different from the usual indices based upon factual or partisan knowledge represents some additional evidence that attention is indeed distinct from knowledge or understanding. I believe a clear distinction must be drawn between possession of general factual knowledge about politics, on the one hand, and attentiveness to politics or foreign affairs, on the other. Simply stated, there is an important difference between *thinking* that one knows about a given issue and actually knowing about, or understanding the issue. When one examines the former, as I have attempted to do, the pattern that emerges differs sharply from the oft-cited inverse relationship between interest in entertainment-oriented TV programming and political knowledge.

To the extent that individuals make political decisions on the basis of what they *think*, rather than what they actually *know*, a broadening of public attention to foreign crises is almost certainly not without practical political implications. Indeed, the evidence presented in this chapter suggests that by attracting public attention to the highest profile political issues, the proliferation of the soft news media may represent an important, if as yet not fully appreciated, political phenomenon. In subsequent chapters, I consider several potential political implications of soft news media coverage of foreign policy crises, as well as other high-profile political issues and events. But first, in the next chapter, I turn to a series of tests of my over-time hypotheses, investigating trends in public attentiveness to a series of foreign crisis issues from the 1950s through the 1990s.

APPENDIX 1: On Using Opinionation as an Indicator of Attentiveness

Opinionation is one of my key, though by no means sole, indicators of attentiveness. While opinionation and attentiveness are not necessarily perfectly synonymous, I argue that they are closely related and that opinionation may be appropriately employed as an indicator, albeit imperfect, of attentiveness. Ceteris paribus, the more attentive one is to a given issue, the more likely one is to be willing to express an opinion about that issue, if queried, and vice versa. Moreover, the more attentive an individual is to an issue or class of issues, the more opinions or considerations he or she is likely to have about the issue or class of issues. Similarly, the greater the aggregate public attentiveness to an issue, the greater ought to be the percentage of the public willing to express an opinion on the issue and the more unprompted opinions typical individuals ought to be willing to express about it (in open-ended questions).[43]

In operationalizing opinionation as the willingness of survey respondents to respond to a given survey question, I hypothesize that responding "no opinion" or "don't know" represents a lack of attentiveness to the issue. Page and Shapiro (1983), for instance, argue that attentiveness can be most directly, though not perfectly, measured by the proportion of respondents answering "don't know" or "no opinion" to survey questions. A low proportion of "no opinion" or "don't know" responses is, they assert, evidence of attentiveness, and vice versa (see also Powlick and Katz 1998b).[44] As I discussed in the appendix to chapter 1, attentiveness represents a *somewhat* lower information threshold than salience, and a *far* lower threshold than knowledge or understanding. It is relatively unlikely—though not impossible—that individuals will fail to express an opinion about an issue that is important (i.e., salient) to them or about which they have significant knowledge. Indeed, as I discuss below, a more plausible concern regarding the external validity of opinionation comes from the other end of the continuum: the possibility that opinionation is a better indicator of cognizance than attentiveness.

It is possible that a deep sense of ambiguity may provoke a "don't know" response from a respondent who cares passionately about an issue. Yet it seems more likely that individuals will express an opinion about an issue even if it is *not* particularly salient to them, assuming they have paid some measure of attention to it. Hence, opinionation seems likely to be a better indicator of attentiveness than personal importance (or salience). Nonetheless, it remains possible that "don't know" or "no opinion" rates might also reflect ambiguity— in either the question or the mind of the respondent—or ambivalence regarding the appropriate answer, rather than attentiveness. Ambivalence or ambiguity, in turn, might result from such factors as general cynicism about politics or relatively bitter partisan debate surrounding a given issue. The former factor might cause respondents to condemn all policy options and simply tune out from politics, while the latter might cloud the political signals an individual is accustomed to receiving from political leaders.

And one can imagine elite debate having the opposite effect as well, due perhaps to a rise in the intensity of political messages in a bitter partisan environment (Nicholson, Segura, and Woods 1999). Louder political signals in a contentious environment may simply be easier to receive by individuals who are not necessarily intrinsically interested in following politics. At the same time, it is possible that highly politically aware individuals are more likely to respond "no opinion" or "don't know" because they suffer greater cognitive conflict in reaching political judgments. Political sophisticates are able to bring more considerations—some of which may conflict with one another—to bear on any given issue (Zaller and Feldman 1992; Tetlock 1984, 1985). Hence, they may be more likely than their less politically aware counterparts to respond "don't know" or "no opinion" due to greater ambivalence regarding the appropriate response. Nevertheless, while it is doubtless true that *some*, "don't know" responses indicate ambivalence, the evidence presented below suggests that opinionation is, under most circumstances, a better indicator of attentiveness than of ambivalence.

For instance, the 1996 and 1998 NES surveys offer significant evidence that "no opinion" and "don't know" responses are a better indicator of unfamiliarity with the object of a survey question than of ambivalence or confusion about how best to respond. Respondents to the preelection wave in 1996 were asked a series of nineteen "feeling thermometer" questions, which ask individuals to rate a political figure on a 0–100 scale, with 100 representing the most-positive feeling toward that individual. Respondents who answered "don't know" were asked whether their answer indicated unfamiliarity with the individual or ambivalence/conflict over the appropriate response. Overall, 76 percent of the 1996 respondents indicated that their "don't know" response meant they were *unfamiliar* with the individual they were being asked to rate.[45] In 1998, the corresponding average, also across nineteen feeling thermometer questions, was a remarkably similar 75 percent indicating *unfamiliarity*, rather than ambivalence or uncertainty.[46] These results are particularly impressive when one considers that survey respondents tend to be reluctant to admit to being unfamiliar with a high-profile individual.

Of course, familiarity, which in this context is synonymous with cognizance, is not identical to attentiveness. It is, however, a necessary precursor to attentiveness. After all, one cannot attend to something without first being aware of its existence. Unfortunately, public opinion surveys rarely allow such a nuanced delineation of the meaning of "don't know" or "no opinion" responses. Indeed, these NES surveys are nearly unique in asking even *one* follow-up question regarding the meaning of "don't know." Hence, "familiarity" is as close as I have been able to come to capturing attentiveness in this survey context. Nevertheless, these results do strongly suggest that, at least most of the time, a response of "don't know" does *not* indicate ambivalence or cognitive conflict.

My strategy for parsing out the difference between attentiveness and cognizance is the same as that for distinguishing between the former construct and salience. By replicating my investigations across various data sets—with some indicators of attentiveness lying closer to salience on the information exposure continuum while others lie closer to cognizance—I can reasonably conclude that, to the extent the results across indicators are comparable, the "true" causal factor must be some element that all indicators share in common, which I argue is attentiveness.

Additional validity and reliability tests, the results of which are shown in table 4.A7, in appendix 3, further support my use of "don't know" and "no opinion" rates. If, as I have argued, attentiveness is a precursor of knowledge or understanding, and if opinionation is a valid indicator of attentiveness, then we should observe a statistically significant relationship between indicators representing the two concepts. One frequently employed indicator of political knowledge included in NES surveys is the interviewer's postinterview estimate of the respondent's level of political information (Baum and Kernell 1999; Zaller 1985, 1992). For this particular test, if a "don't know" response is a valid indicator of inattentiveness, then we should observe an inverse relationship between "don't know" rates and the political information variable.

In fact, the figures in table 4.A7 indicate that, across a series of NES surveys conducted during the Korean, Vietnam, and Persian Gulf Wars (1952, 1968, 1970, 1972, 1990/91), the likelihood of responding "don't know" to a question about the three wars (see appendix 1 of chapter 5, question 2B) was *inversely* and significantly related to the respondent's level of political information.[47] The significant inverse relationships individually suggest that "don't know" rates are a valid indicator of attentiveness. Moreover, the consistent significance over time and across the three wars also suggests that "don't know" rates are reasonably reliable. In other words, the dependent variable appears to be measuring a similar underlying factor, or concept, in each survey.[48]

Another indicator of attentiveness employed above involves the number of mentions of a given issue or class of issues in open-ended questions. One such question, included in nearly every NES survey between 1960 and 1998, asks respondents to name the most important problem facing the nation. Above, I argued that offering more responses to open-ended questions is a reasonable, albeit far from perfect, indicator of greater attentiveness. This suggests that mentioning more "major problems" in open-ended questions indicates greater attentiveness to high-profile political issues. If so, mentioning major problems pertaining specifically to *foreign affairs* should be inversely related to an individual's propensity to respond "don't know" to questions about the Vietnam or Gulf wars. And, in fact, as also shown in table 4.A7, in all Vietnam and Persian Gulf War–era surveys (1968, 1970, 1972, 1990/91), a "don't know" response to the identical war-related question was indeed *inversely* related to the number of mentions of foreign-policy-related issues in the NES open-ended "most important problems facing the nation" question.[49] With but one exception, the coefficients are significant at the .05 level or better in every survey. As before, the significant inverse relationships in all but one survey suggest that "don't know" rates appear to be both reasonably valid and fairly reliable indicators of attentiveness.

Additionally, a principal component factor analysis indicated that respondents' self-declared attention to the Vietnam and Persian Gulf wars loads on a common factor with the propensity to respond "don't know" to the previously noted war-related question—asked in tandem in two NES surveys (1970 and 1991) and employed as a dependent variable in chapter 5—at nearly .40 (the two variables correlate at .22). While these moderate relationships by no means suggest that these two indicators can be considered perfect substitutes, they do indicate that they are reasonably closely related to one another. Indeed, when "don't know" responses to the war related question are regressed on self-declared attention to the two wars, the coefficient on attention is significant at .001 and, by itself, explains about 6.5 percent of the variance in propensity to respond "don't know."

As additional tests of the validity of employing "don't know" responses as an indicator of attentiveness, I conducted a similar analysis with two surveys concerning the Middle East peace process. The first survey was a Gallup poll, conducted on August 12–13, 1997. In addition to asking respondents how closely they had followed "the recent situation in the Middle East involving Israel and the Palestinians," it also asked with whom the respondent's sympathies lie and whether the respondent believed there would ever be a permanent peace between Israel and the Arab nations.[50] I recoded these latter questions to measure respondents' opinionation. In other words, "don't know/refused" responses were coded 1, and all other responses were coded 0. A principal components factor analysis indicates that respondents' degree of attention to the situation in the Middle East loads fairly strongly (.59) on a common underlying factor as the two opinionation questions. Adding education to the factor analysis increases the factor loading to .61.[51] And attention to the Middle East correlates fairly well with opinionation on these two questions and education at .44, .26, and .27, respectively. These results, once again, suggest that opinionation is indeed a reasonable indicator of attentiveness.

The second survey, conducted by CBS on September 18, 1978, the night President Jimmy Carter announced the successful completion of the Camp David Peace Accords between Egypt and Israel, asked respondents whether they had "heard or read anything about the results of the Camp David summit meeting with Egypt and Israel and the United States?" It also asked respondents three questions suitable for assessing their opinionation regarding the Middle East peace process. The first asked whether respondents believed Camp David would lead to a "real" peace settlement, the second asked respondents who they viewed as most responsible for the agreement, and the third queried respondents concerning President Carter's performance during the summit. As before, I transformed the responses to all three questions, so that "don't know/no answer" responses were coded 1 and all other responses were coded 0.[52] A principal components factor analysis indicates that, as before, having heard or read about the Camp David Accord loads fairly strongly (.46) on a common underlying factor as the three transformed opinionation questions. Adding education to the factor analysis raises the factor loading to .51.[53] The three opinionation questions and education correlate reasonably well with whether respondents had heard or read about Camp David, at .27, .25, .25, and .28, respectively.

If opinionation is indeed a valid indicator of attentiveness, then it should be positively correlated with other variables that are positively related to attentiveness. Two likely candidates are education and interest in politics. Much evidence suggests better educated individuals tend to be more attentive to politics in general, and foreign policy in particular.[54] Similarly, individuals who follow political campaigns are, almost by definition, more attentive to politics. Hence, if responding "don't know" is indeed a valid and reliable indicator of a lack of attentiveness, then the likelihood of responding "don't know" should be inversely related to individuals' education level and self-declared attention to political campaigns.

Additional testing, shown in the lower half of table 4.A7, indicates that in *all* of the above-noted NES surveys during the three wars, a "don't know" response to the previously noted war-related question is significantly related, at the .01 level or better, to respondents' attention to political campaigns. The same tests indicated that, also in *each* of the aforementioned surveys, education is significantly and inversely related, at the .01 level or better, to a respondent's likelihood of responding "don't know" to the war-related question.[55] Once again, the consistently significant coefficients, across five NES surveys, suggest that "don't know" rates are indeed a reasonably valid and reliable—albeit admittedly imperfect—indicator of attentiveness.

APPENDIX 2: VARIABLE DEFINITIONS[56]

A. *Pew Research Center May 1996 and May 1998 Media Consumption Poll Variables* (Telephone surveys, $N = 1,751$ and $N = 3,002$, respectively)

All Pew Research Center survey data can be downloaded at: http://www.people-press.org.

DEPENDENT VARIABLES

"Now I will read a list of some stories covered by news organizations this past month. As I read each item, tell me if you happened to follow this news story very closely, fairly closely, not too closely, or not at all closely": (1) "The military conflict between Israel and the pro-Iranian Muslims in Lebanon" (1996); (2) "the passage in Congress of a new law dealing with domestic terrorism" (1996); (3) "the situation in Bosnia" (1996); (4) "allegations of sexual misconduct against Bill Clinton" (1998); (5) "the debate in Washington over legislation to regulate the tobacco industry" (1998) and (6) "candidates and election campaigns in your state" (1998). Coding: 1 = not at all closely, 2 = not very closely, 3 = fairly closely, and 4 = very closely.

POLITICAL INTEREST AND KNOWLEDGE

> *Voted in 1992* (or *1996*): Dummy variable, coded 1 if respondent voted in 1992 (or 1996, in 1998 survey), and 0 otherwise.
> *Political Knowledge* (1996 only): Respondents' levels of political knowledge were estimated through construction of a scale derived from three knowledge-based questions. Respondents were asked if they knew: (*a*) who the Speaker of the U.S. House of Representatives is; (*b*) which political party has a majority in the U.S. House of Representatives; and (*c*) what the federal minimum wage is today. (For the minimum wage question, answers within one category of the correct answer, on a seven-category scale, were coded as correct responses.) Respondents were given one point for each *correct* response, resulting in a 3-point scale, with a score of three representing those *most* politically knowledgeable.
> *Partisanship*: 3-point scale estimating the extent of the respondent's partisanship (from party identification question). Coding: 1 = No Preference, 2 = Independent or Other, 3 = Democrat or Republican.
> *Party Identification*: 5-point scale, coded 1 = Democrat, 2 = Independent, leaning Democratic, 3 = Independent, no preference or other, 4 = Independent, leaning Republican, 5 = Republican.

1996 MEDIA CONSUMPTION (QUESTIONS EMPLOYED IN SOFT AND HARD NEWS INDEXES)

(Note: All media indexes are ordinal scales, based on the sum of all individual items.)

(A) "Now I'd like to know how often you watch or listen to certain TV and radio programs. For each that I read, tell me if you watch or listen to it regularly, sometimes, hardly ever, or never. Network Newscasts; Local Newscasts; CNN; C-SPAN; NPR; TV Newsmagazines; *PBS News Hour with Jim Lehrer*; MTV; Tabloid TV Shows; Daytime TV Talk Shows." Coding: 1 = never, 2 = hardly ever, 3 = sometimes, 4 = regularly.

(B) "I'm going to read you a list of different types of news. Please tell me how closely you follow this type of news either in the newspaper, on television, or on radio . . . very closely, somewhat closely, not very closely, or not at all closely? International Affairs; Political News; Business News; News about Crime; News about Famous People; News about Entertainment." Coding: 1 = not at all closely, 2 = not very closely, 3 = somewhat closely, 4 = very closely.

(C) "Now I'd like to know how often you read certain types of publications. As I read each, tell me if you read them regularly, sometimes, hardly ever, or never. (First,) how about: Tabloid Newspapers (i.e., *The National Enquirer, The Sun* or *The Star*); Newsmagazines; Business Magazines." Coding: 1 = never, 2 = hardly ever, 3 = sometimes, 4 = regularly.

(D) *Daily Newspaper*: Dummy variable coded 1 if respondent reads a newspaper regularly and 0 otherwise.

(E) *News on Internet*: "Do you ever go on-line to get information on current events, public issues and politics? If yes, how often do you go on-line for this type of information . . . every day, 3 to 5 days per week, 1 or 2 days per week, once every few weeks, or never?" Coding: 1 = never, 2 = less than once every few weeks, 3 = every few weeks or 1–2 days per week, 4 = 3–5 days per week or every day.

(F) *Cable Subscriber*: Dummy variable coded 1 if respondent currently subscribes to cable and 0 otherwise. (This question is included as a separate control.)

1998 SOFT AND HARD NEWS INDEX COMPONENTS

Soft News Index: 10-item scale constructed from the identical question format as in the 1996 survey, and including the following items: MTV, Tabloid TV Newsmagazines, Daytime Talk Shows, Court TV, Morning News/Variety Shows, Newsmagazine Shows, *Entertainment Tonight, The National Enquirer*, Howard Stern, and *People* Magazine.

Hard News Index: 13-item scale constructed from the same question format as the soft news index, and including the following items: Nightly Network News Programs, Local Television News Programs, CNN, C-SPAN, National Public Radio, *The News Hour with Jim Lehrer*, CNBC, MSNBC, Fox News, Newsmagazines, Business magazines, *Harper's* Magazine and Daily Newspapers. (The daily newspapers item is a 6-point scale, with respondents receiving one point each for indicating that they read the following newspapers: *New York Times, Wall Street Journal, Washington Post, Los Angeles Times, Herald Tribune*, and *Boston Globe*.)

B. January 1990 Times Mirror *Center Poll Variables* (Telephone survey, $N = 1,207$)

DEPENDENT VARIABLE

"Now I will read a list of some stories covered by news organizations this past month. As I read each item, tell me if you happened to follow this news story very closely, fairly closely, not too closely, or not at all closely. . . . The invasion of Panama." Coding: 1 = not at all closely, 2 = not very closely, 3 = fairly closely, and 4 = very closely.

KEY CAUSAL VARIABLES

Political Knowledge: Respondents' levels of political knowledge were estimated through construction of a scale, derived from five knowledge-based questions about foreign policy. Respondents were asked if they knew: (a) who Colin Powell is; (b) who Vaclav Havel is; (c) whether the Rumanian government had been successfully overthrown by rebels; (d) whether U.S. troops had played a role in the revolution in Rumania; and (e) what had happened to ousted Rumanian president Nicolai Ceausescu. Respondents were given 1 point for each *correct* response, resulting in a 6-point scale, running from 0 to 5, with a score of 5 representing maximum politically knowledge.

Importance of Panama Invasion: "What do you think is the most important news event that happened in the nation or in the world last month—in December?" Responses were coded 1 = Panama invasion, 0 = all other responses.

MEDIA CONSUMPTION QUESTIONS (ITEMS EMPLOYED IN SOFT AND HARD NEWS SCALES)

Soft News Index: 5-item scale constructed from the identical general question format as in the 1996 Pew Research Center Survey, and including the following items: *A Current Affair*; Personality Magazines such as *People* or *US*; *The National Enquirer,* the *Sun*, or the *Star*; *Entertainment Tonight*; and Newsmagazine shows such as *60 Minutes* or *20/20.*

Hard News Index: 10-item scale constructed from two question formats. The first is the same as the soft news index, and included the following items: CNN; National Public Radio; *McNeil-Lehrer*; Newsmagazines; Business Magazines; *Harper's, Atlantic*, or *The New Yorker* Magazines; Sunday Morning News Shows, like *Meet the Press*. The second format asked respondents the following three questions: (1) "Do you get a chance to read a daily newspaper just about every day, or not?" (2) "Do you happen to watch any TV news programs regularly, or not?" and (3) "Do you listen to the news on the radio regularly, or not?" The latter questions are dichotomous variables, which I rescaled, for consistency, as follows: "yes" = 4 and "no" = 0.

C. July 1998 Gallup Media/Social Security Poll Variables (Telephone survey, N = 619)

DEPENDENT VARIABLES

(A) "In the situation in Northern Ireland, are your sympathies: (1) More with the Irish Catholics, or (2) more with the Irish Protestants, (3) both, (4) neither, (5) don't know/not familiar"; (B) "As you may know, the leaders of the two opposing sides in Northern Ireland have reached a new compromise agreement concerning the governance of Northern Ireland. Are you generally optimistic or pessimistic that this agreement will lead to lasting peace in Northern Ireland? (1) Optimistic, (2) pessimistic, (3) don't know/not familiar with." Coding: 0 = don't know/not familiar with, 1 = all other responses.

MEDIA CONSUMPTION (QUESTIONS EMPLOYED IN SOFT AND HARD NEWS INDEXES)

(A) "Now, I would like to ask you some questions about the media. As you know, people get their news and information from many different sources, and I would like to ask you where you get YOUR news and information. I will read a list of sources, and for each one, please tell me how often you get your news from that source: every day, several times a week, occasionally, or never. First, how often do you get your news from: Newspapers, National Newspapers, Nightly Network News Programs, Morning News and Interview Programs, CNN News or CNN Headline News, Cable News other than CNN, C-SPAN, Public Television News, Local Television News, National Public Radio, National Network News on Radio (other than NPR), Radio Talk Shows, Television Talk Shows, Half-Hour TV Entertainment News Programs." Coding: 1 = never, 2 = occasionally, 3 = several times a week, 4 = every day.

(B) "And how often do you get your news from each of the following WEEKLY sources of news: every week, several times a month, occasionally, or never. First, how often do you get your news from: Weekly Newsmagazines, Television News Programs on Sunday Mornings, TV Newsmagazine Shows during the Evenings." Coding: 1 = never, 2 = occasionally, 3 = several times a month, 4 = every week.

POLITICAL PARTISANSHIP

Liberal-Conservative: "How would you describe your political views?" Coded: 1 = very conservative, 2 = conservative, 3 = moderate, 4 = liberal, 5 = very liberal.

Party Identification: Coded: 1 = Republican, 2 = Independent, leaning Republican, 3 = Independent, 4 = Independent leaning Democratic, 5 = Democrat.

SOFT AND HARD NEWS INDEX COMPONENTS

Soft News Index: TV Entertainment News Shows; Television Talk Shows; Radio Talk Shows; TV Newsmagazine Shows; Morning News and Interview Shows (e.g., *Good Morning America*).

Hard News Index: Nightly Network News Programs, Local Television News Programs; CNN, C-SPAN; Public Television News; Cable News other than CNN; Sunday Morning Television News Shows; National Public Radio; National Network News on Radio; Weekly Newsmagazines; Newspapers or National Newspapers.

D. May 1998 Pew Research Center Believability of Media/People Survey (Telephone Survey, $N = 981$)

POLITICAL INTEREST AND KNOWLEDGE

Registered to Vote: Dummy variable, coded 1 if respondent is currently registered to vote, and 0 otherwise.

Awareness of Political Figures: The respondent's level of awareness of political figures was estimated through construction of an additive scale, derived from a series of questions asking respondents to rate the "believability" of the following nine individuals: Al Gore, Newt Gingrich, Colin Powell, Bill Gates, Janet Reno, Madeleine Albright, Ted Turner, Rush Limbaugh, and Pat Robertson. Respondents were asked to place half of the above individuals on a 1–4 scale, with 4 representing maximum believability. (All respondents rated Al Gore.) Respondents were also offered the opportunity to indicate that they "never heard of" the individual. For the summary indicator, respondents were given 1 point for each individual they were willing to rate on the 1–4 scale and 0 points for each "never heard of" response, resulting in a 5-point scale (running from 0 to 4), with a score of 4 representing *maximum* awareness of national political figures. Responses of "can't rate" were coded as missing data. (I employed the same question to construct a "trust" scale. Because the two scales are highly collinear—as they are constructed from the same variable—they could not both be included in the same model. Since the *Awareness* variable consistently outperformed the *Trust* variable, I elected to include only the former variable in the final model specification.)

Partisanship: 4-point scale estimating the extent of the respondent's partisanship (drawn from party identification question). Coding: 0 = No preference, other, don't know, and not leaning to either party, 1 = Independent, not leaning to either party, 2 = Independent, no preference, other or don't know, but does lean toward either Democrats or Republicans and 3 = Democrat or Republican.

Party Identification: 5-point scale, coded 1 = Democrat, 2 = Independent, leaning Democratic, 3 = Independent, no preference or other, 4 = Independent, leaning Republican, 5 = Republican.

MEDIA CONSUMPTION

"Now I'd like to know how often you watch or listen to certain TV and radio programs. For each that I read, tell me if you watch or listen to it regularly, sometimes, hardly ever, or never." Coding: 1 = never, 2 = hardly ever, 3 = sometimes, 4 = regularly.

Network Newscasts; Local Newscasts; CNN; CSPAN; NPR; TV Newsmagazines; *PBS News Hour with Jim Lehrer*; MTV; Tabloid TV Shows (e.g., *Hard Copy, A Current Affair*, or *Inside Edition*); Daytime Talk TV (e.g., Ricki Lake, Jerry Springer, or Jenny Jones); Court TV; Morning TV Variety Programs (e.g., *Today Show, Good Morning America*, or *CBS This Morning*); Other All News Cable Channels (e.g., Fox News Channel or MSNBC).

Daily Newspaper: Dummy variable coded 1 if respondent reads a daily newspaper regularly, and 0 otherwise.

APPENDIX 3: STATISTICAL TABLES

TABLE 4.A1. Ordered Logit Analyses of Media Consumption Habits and Attentiveness to Republican Primary Elections (1996) and the State of the U.S. Economy (1993)

| | Coef. (Std. Err.) | | | |
| | Primaries | | Economy | |
	Model 1	Model 2	Model 3	Model 4
Media Consumption				
Soft news index	.021 (.017)	.062 (.044)	.148 (.143)	−.009 (.546)
Hard news index[a]	.081 (.014)***	.081 (.014)***	.433 (.143)**	.433 (.144)**
Cable subscriber	.074 (.140)	.074 (.140)	—	—
SES/Demographics				
Education	.063 (.040)	.060 (.040)	.321 (.110)**	.207 (.376)
Age	.003 (.004)	.003 (.004)	.015 (.006)*	.015 (.006)*
Family income	.005 (.032)	.004 (.032)	.100 (.068)	.099 (.068)
Male	.179 (.119)	.178 (.119)	−.016 (.180)	−.022 (.181)
Married	.020 (.036)	.019 (.036)	—	—
White	−.157 (.167)	−.171 (.168)	−.132 (.327)	−.117 (.332)
Black	—	—	−.405 (.472)	−.401 (.472)

Political Knowledge & Attitudes			
Follow national political news	.688 (.093)***	.990 (.342)**	—	—
Political knowledge	.126 (.062)*	.122 (.063)*	—	—
Voted in 1992	.253 (.138)^	.253 (.138)	.571 (.241)*	.572 (.241)*
Partisanship	.203 (.112)^	.205 (.112)		
Party identification	.173 (.038)***	.172 (.038)***	−.066 (.137)	−.065 (.137)
Approve of president	.011 (.104)	.008 (.104)	−.017 (.249)	−.008 (.249)
Importance of Panama	—	—	—	—
Interaction Terms				
Soft news index × national politics	—	−.016 (.017)	—	—
Soft news index × education	—	—	—	.047 (.142)
Constant 1	4.295 (.633)	5.019 (.957)	.740 (.821)	.362 (1.579)
Constant 2	5.833 (.641)	6.559 (.971)	2.169 (.802)	1.790 (1.555)
Constant 3	7.836 (.657)	8.561 (.984)	4.257 (.807)	3.878 (1.555)
Pseudo R^2	.11	.11	.06	.06
	(N = 1,322)	(N = 1,322)	(N = 595)	(N = 595)

Note: All models employ White's heteroscedasticity-consistent ("robust") standard errors and probability weighting.

[a]"Hard News Index for "primaries" model excludes "interest in national politics" and includes "interest in international affairs."

^p < .10, *p < .05, **p < .01, ***p < .001

TABLE 4.A2. Ordered Logit Analyses of Likelihood of Being Attentive to Traditional Political Issues and a Domestic Water-Cooler Event

	Coef. (Std. Err.)					
	'98 Elections		Tobacco		Lewinsky	
	Model 1	Model 2	Model 3	Model 4	Model 5	Model 6
Media Consumption						
Soft news index	.005 (.016)	−.014 (.047)	−.020 (.015)	.024 (.047)	.054 (.016)***	.108 (.047)*
Hard news index	.949 (.158)***	.945 (.159)***	1.059 (.164)***	1.067 (.165)***	.227 (.163)	.237 (.164)
Cable subscriber	−.138 (.143)	−.138 (.143)	.000 (.144)	−.001 (.144)	−.045 (.148)	−.044 (.149)
SES/Demographics						
Age	.008 (.004)*	.008 (.004)*	.003 (.005)	.003 (.005)	.006 (.005)	.006 (.005)
Education	.033 (.046)	.033 (.046)	.024 (.047)	.025 (.047)	−.022 (.044)	−.023 (.044)
Family income	.054 (.037)	.055 (.037)	−.005 (.037)	−.009 (.037)	.004 (.036)	−.000 (.036)
Male	−.211 (.128)	−.209 (.128)^	−.105 (.128)	−.112 (.128)	.117 (.126)	.110 (.127)
Married	−.041 (.041)	−.041 (.041)	.041 (.043)	.041 (.043)	.048 (.040)	.047 (.040)
White	−.013 (.191)	−.015 (.191)	.459 (.192)*	.466 (.193)*	.162 (.198)	.166 (.198)

Political Knowledge & Attitudes						
Follow national political news	—	.468 (.330)	—	.952 (.305)**	—	1.213 (.316)***
Voted in 1996	.546 (.153)***	.547 (.153)***	−.146 (.155)	−.146 (.156)	−.273 (.154)	−.271 (.155)^
Partisanship	.215 (.081)**	.216 (.081)	.122 (.079)	.119 (.079)	.153 (.085)	.147 (.085)^
Party identification	.047 (.042)	.047 (.042)	−.023 (.042)	−.022 (.041)	−.031 (.043)	−.030 (.043)
Approve of president	−.285 (.157)	−.287 (.156)	−.021 (.156)	−.016 (.156)	−.442 (.151)**	−.434 (.151)**
Interaction Term						
Soft news index × follow national politics	—	.007 (.017)	—	−.016 (.016)	—	−.020 (.016)
Constant 1	3.769 (.558)	3.399 (1.051)	2.514 (.544)	3.344 (1.025)	1.755 (.517)	2.774 (.993)
Constant 2	5.088 (.572)	4.717 (1.064)	3.833 (.547)	4.665 (1.030)	3.197 (.524)	4.225 (1.005)
Constant 3	7.013 (.591)	6.644 (1.072)	5.896 (.563)	6.728 (1.036)	5.182 (.538)	6.209 (1.007)
Pseudo R^2	.11	.11	.08	.08	.08	.09
	(N = 1,048)	(N = 1,048)	(N = 1,049)	(N = 1,049)	(N = 1,045)	(N = 1,045)

Note: All models employ heteroscedasticity-consistent ("robust") standard errors and probability weighting.

^$p < .10$, *$p < .05$, **$p < .01$, ***$p < .001$

TABLE 4.A3. Three-Stage Least Squares Estimation of Influence of Soft News Exposure on Hard News Consumption, and Influence of Hard News Exposure on Soft News Consumption

| | Coef. (Std. Err.) | | | |
| | 1996 | | 2000 | |
	Hard News Model	Soft News Model	Hard News Model	Soft News Model
Media Consumption				
Soft news index	.244 (.046)***	—	.279 (.037)***	—
Hard news index	—	.004 (.102)	—	.013 (.051)
Interest in political news	.090 (.013)***	—	.079 (.012)***	—
Interest in news about local government	—	—	.011 (.011)	—
Interest in news about international affairs	.054 (.013)***	—	.056 (.011)***	—
Interest in business news	.075 (.011)***	—	.103 (.011)***	—
Interest in science news	.021 (.011)^	—	.022 (.011)*	—
Interest in entertainment news	—	.128 (.017)***	—	.224 (.012)***
Interest in celebrity news	—	.125 (.017)***	—	—
Interest in crime news	—	.087 (.019)***	—	.100 (.013)***
Regularly follow national news	—	—	.123 (.020)***	—
Regularly follow international news	—	—	.028 (.021)	—

SES/Demographics							
Age	.002	(.001)***	−.001	(.001)	.002	(.0006)***	−.0003	(.0007)
Education	.050	(.007)***	−.060	(.011)***	.027	(.007)***	−.072	(.007)***
Family income	.035	(.005)***	−.007	(.009)	.027	(.005)***	−.005	(.006)
Male	.048	(.020)*	−.034	(.029)	.072	(.020)***	−.211	(.021)***
White	−.030	(.029)	−.278	(.038)***	−.045	(.027)^	−.314	(.029)***
Married	−.003	(.006)	−.005	(.009)	−.030	(.018)^	−.015	(.022)
Political Knowledge & Attitudes							
Political knowledge	.032	(.011)**	−.046	(.016)**	—		—	
Voted in 1992/1996	.085	(.024)***	−.115	(.033)***	−.041	(.032)	−.008	(.038)
Partisanship	−.046	(.018)**	.009	(.026)	.013	(.012)	.046	(.014)***
Party identification	.003	(.006)	−.020	(.009)*	.005	(.005)	.008	(.006)
Approve of president	−.026	(.017)	−.003	(.024)	—		—	
Constant	.412	(.140)**	1.863	(.162)***	.254	(.110)*	1.693	(.084)***
R^2	.37		.28		.36		.36	
	(N = 1424)		(N = 1424)		(N = 2297)		(N = 2297)	

Note: All models employ White's heteroscedasticity-consistent ("robust") standard errors and probability weighting.

^p < .10, *p < .05, **p < .01, ***p < .001

TABLE 4.A4. Logit Analysis of Attentiveness to Northern Ireland, as Soft News Consumption and Education Vary

	Coef. (Std. Err.)							
	N. Ireland (Question A)		N. Ireland (Question B)		Social Security		Chiquita Banana	
	Model 1	Model 2	Model 3	Model 4	Model 5	Model 6	Model 7	Model 8
Media Consumption								
Soft news index	.656	1.576	.850	2.003	.176	2.653	−.274	−.111
	(.331)*	(.804)*	(.374)*	(1.019)*	(1.119)	(1.730)	(.231)	(.851)
Hard news index	−.270	−.285	.179	.198	−.827	−.770	.819	.814
	(.349)	(.343)	(.490)	(.482)	(1.139)	(.917)	(.332)**	(.333)**
SES/Demographics								
Education	.225	.526	.506	.917	.176	1.146	.196	.247
	(.093)*	(.281)	(.135)***	(.355)**	(.497)	(.911)	(.081)*	(.261)
Age	−.008	−.004	.033	.038	.109	.135	.063	.064
	(.043)	(.043)	(.051)	(.051)	(.094)	(.096)	(.041)	(.041)
Age^2	.000	.000	−.000	−.001	−.001	−.001	−.000	−.000
	(.000)	(.000)	(.001)	(.001)	(.001)	(.001)	(.000)	(.000)
Male	.485	.474	.434	.442	−.106	.044	.269	.267
	(.285)^	(.286)^	(.411)	(.414)	(.824)	(.748)	(.247)	(.247)
Family income	.099	.100	.076	.074	.614	.594	.057	.057
	(.087)	(.088)	(.117)	(.119)	(.221)**	(.228)**	(.088)	(.088)
Black	−.414	−.458	−2.072	−2.154	.484	.054	−1.124	−1.124
	(.452)	(.445)	(.500)***	(.501)***	(1.657)	(1.394)	(.488)*	(.488)*

Hispanic	.206	.209	.489	.517	—	—	-.735	-.742
	(.591)	(.591)	(.781)	(.785)			(.683)	(.664)
Unemployed	-.223	-.324	-1.307	-1.425	-2.176	-2.595	.176	.159
	(.401)	(.406)	(.503)**	(.501)**	(1.221)^	(1.377)^	(.399)	(.410)
Political Attitudes								
Liberal–conservative scale	-.131	-.141	-.531	-.550	.563	.462	-.267	-.268
	(.150)	(.152)	(.208)**	(.210)**	(.530)	(.468)	(.147)^	(.148)^
Party identification	-.033	-.031	.258	.262	-.255	-.231	.148	.149
	(.098)	(.098)	(.139)^	(.140)^	(.216)	(.225)	(.094)	(.094)
Approve of president	.446	.440	.033	.029	-1.480	-1.778	-.050	-.051
	(.321)	(.325)	(.453)	(.464)	(.825)^	(.832)*	(.320)	(.319)
Interaction Term								
Soft news index × education	—	-.154	—	-.217	—	-.471	—	-.025
		(.136)		(.174)		(.300)		(.122)
Constant	-.205	-2.034	-1.760	-3.983	.619	-4.080	-4.762	-5.103
	(1.426)	(1.944)	(1.522)	(2.457)^	(4.264)	(6.024)	(1.281)***	(2.119)*
Pseudo R^2	.06	.06	.20	.21	.33	.36	.09	.09
	$(N = 496)$	$(N = 496)$	$(N = 503)$	$(N = 503)$	$(N = 477)$	$(N = 477)$	$(N = 501)$	$(N = 501)$

Note: All models employ White's heteroscedasticity-consistent ("robust") standard errors and probability weighting.
^p < .10, *p < .05, **p < .01, ***p < .001

TABLE 4.A5. Logit Analyses of Likelihood of Mentioning a Foreign Affairs Problem, as Attention to Soft News and Education Level Vary

	Coef. (Std. Err.)			
	Foreign Aid Counted as Foreign Policy Issue		Foreign Aid *Not* Counted as Foreign Policy Issue	
	Model 1	Model 2	Model 3	Model 4
Media Consumption Habits				
Soft news index	.852 (.362)*	1.645 (.839)*	.671 (.408)^	1.565 (.911)^
Hard news index	−.108 (.384)	−.120 (.381)	.178 (.374)	.165 (.370)
SES/Demographics				
Education	.086 (.111)	.320 (.220)	.172 (.125)	.433 (.274)
Age	.007 (.011)	.007 (.011)	−.003 (.013)	−.002 (.013)
Family income	.019 (.095)	.011 (.094)	−.038 (.106)	−.049 (.109)
Male	.415 (.370)	.397 (.373)	.648 (.438)	.635 (.442)
Urban resident	.596 (.435)	.619 (.448)	.367 (.489)	.387 (.499)
Southern resident	−1.138 (.471)*	−1.162 (.484)*	−2.001 (.671)**	−2.024 (.677)**
Northeast resident	−.604 (.437)	−.624 (.444)	−.652 (.476)	−.673 (.484)

	Model 1	Model 2	Model 3	Model 4
White	−.152 (.469)	−.126 (.471)	−.375 (.543)	−.349 (.544)
Muslim	1.613 (1.231)	1.868 (1.272)	2.713 (1.381)*	2.990 (1.435)*
Christian	.275 (.577)	.307 (.566)	1.060 (.772)	1.113 (.768)
Political Knowledge & Attitudes				
Awareness of political figures	−.361 (.245)	−.387 (.254)	−.674 (.255)**	−.707 (.270)**
Approve of president	.502 (.564)	.505 (.562)	1.700 (.691)**	1.716 (.698)**
Approve of Congress	.776 (.433)^	.780 (.434)^	.871 (.582)	.884 (.582)
Party identification	−.061 (.137)	−.063 (.139)	−.163 (.158)	−.164 (.160)
Partisanship	.047 (.303)	.057 (.301)	.316 (.383)	.334 (.381)
Registered to vote	.363 (.447)	.356 (.441)	.887 (.564)	.861 (.553)
Interaction Term				
Soft news index × education	—	−.176 (.157)	—	−.193 (.169)
Constant	−4.090 (1.812)*	−5.105 (1.871)**	−5.142 (2.344)*	−6.321 (2.420)**
Pseudo R^2	.08	.08	.16	.17
	(N = 630)	(N = 630)	(N = 630)	(N = 630)

Note: All models employ White's heteroscedasticity-consistent ("robust") standard errors and probability weighting.
^$p < .10$, *$p < .05$, **$p < .01$, ***$p < .001$

TABLE 4.A6. Logit Analyses of Attentiveness to Cruise Missile Strikes against Afghanistan and Sudan, as Function of Attentiveness to Lewinsky Scandal

	Coef. (Std. Err.)	
	Model 1	Model 2
Scandal	.768 (.173)***	1.187 (.413)**
Importance of scandal	.442 (.219)*	.454 (.227)*
Wag the dog	−.762 (.417)^	−.738 (.418)^
SES/Demographics		
Age	.016 (.011)	.015 (.011)
Education	.413 (.110)***	.728 (.300)*
Family income	.146 (.102)	.143 (.101)
Male	−.369 (.324)	−.396 (.326)
Married	.621 (.333)^	.636 (.335)^
White	.850 (.383)*	.911 (.380)*
Unemployed	.653 (.389)^	.665 (.382)^
Urban resident	.350 (.148)*	.349 (.150)*
Political Knowledge & Attitudes		
Registered to vote	.859 (.344)**	.896 (.347)**
Party identification	−.166 (.103)	−.167 (.104)
Approve of president	1.088 (.462)*	1.129 (.468)*
Approve of Republican leaders in Congress	−.668 (.366)^	−.694 (.369)^
Interaction Term		
Scandal × education	—	−.115 (.098)
Constant	−6.599 (1.278)***	−7.763 (1.673)***
Pseudo R^2	.26	.27
	($N = 413$)	($N = 413$)

Note: All models employ heteroscedasticity-consistent ("robust") standard errors and probability weighting.

^$p < .10$, *$p < .05$, **$p < .01$, ***$p < .001$

TABLE 4.A7. Logit Analyses of Relationship between Responding "Don't Know" to War-Related NES Questions and Political Information, Mentioning Foreign-Policy-Related "Major Problems," Education, and Attention to Political Campaigns

	\multicolumn{5}{c}{Coef. (Std. Err.)}				
	1952		1968		1970		1972		1990/91
Model Specification 1									
Political information	−.587 (.097)***		−.395 (.056)***		−.393 (.061)***		−.575 (.068)***		−.579 (.116)***
Foreign policy problems	—		−.325 (.117)**		−.342 (.111)**		−.203 (.170)		−.865 (.229)***
Constant	−.428 (.270)		−.184 (.185)		−.235 (.172)		−.699 (.189)***		−1.115 (.301)***
Adj. R^2	.05		.04		.04		.05		.07
	(N = 1,335)		(N = 1,646)		(N = 1,652)		(N = 2,672)		(N = 1,946)
Model Specification 2									
Education	−.103 (.040)**		−.083 (.021)***		−.064 (.020)**		−.056 (.022)**		−.171 (.031)***
Interest in political campaigns	−.474 (.166)**		−.251 (.092)**		−.285 (.085)***		−.451 (.094)***		−.470 (.156)**
Constant	−1.403 (.150)***		−.467 (.226)*		−.508 (.221)*		−1.360 (.243)***		−.626 (.358)ˆ
Adj. R^2	.02		.02		.02		.02		.06
	(N = 1,711)		(N = 1,646)		(N = 1,669)		(N = 2,692)		(N = 1,957)

Note: All models employ heteroscedasticity-consistent ("robust") standard errors.

ˆ$p < .10$, *$p < .05$, **$p < .01$, ***$p < .001$

Tuning Out the World Isn't as Easy as It Used to Be

DEMONSTRATING a causal relationship with respect to long-term trends is exceedingly difficult. There are almost always numerous possible explanations for virtually any aggregate trend, including the change in public attentiveness from Vietnam to the Persian Gulf War described in chapter 2. Moreover, establishing a causal link between individual-level behavior and aggregate trends frequently proves elusive.[1] Yet the findings presented in chapter 4 nonetheless raise the possibility that those individual-level relationships may help account, at least in part, for any aggregate trend toward increased attentiveness to foreign crises.

Data limitations preclude a direct test of the influence of variations in exposure to soft news, over time, on attentiveness to foreign crises. Hence, making the most of the available data, I conduct in this chapter a variety of indirect tests of my two hypotheses concerning over-time aggregate trends. First, if the soft news media are at least partly responsible for any trends toward greater attentiveness, then, given my individual-level findings, Hypothesis 9 predicts that we should observe the most substantial over-time increases in attentiveness among respondents who are *least* inclined to follow politics or foreign affairs. As a result, any positive relationship between political engagement and attentiveness to foreign crises should weaken, over time. In effect, the least politically engaged members of society should be catching up to their more politically attentive counterparts. In contrast, Hypothesis 10 predicts that any such trend should be far weaker for other, less dramatic or more intrinsically partisan political issues, which have not been beneficiaries of increased coverage from soft news programs.[2]

While any of the individual indirect tests presented in this chapter might be dismissed as unreliable, or at least insufficiently persuasive, my hope is that by triangulating across multiple operationalizations of attentiveness and survey contexts, the preponderance of the evidence, viewed in total, will outweigh the limitations of the individual analyses. Hence, I undertake five distinct statistical investigations, ranging from a comparison of discrete U.S. military engagements, separated in time by several decades (including the Korean, Vietnam, and Persian Gulf Wars, as well as a series of smaller-scale U.S. foreign crises), to an analysis of *all* U.S. uses of military force between 1953 and 1998, to several investigations of a class of high-profile political issues that includes, but is not limited to, the realm of foreign policy. As we shall see, both hypotheses, as well as several corollaries to these hypotheses, are supported across each investigation.

ATTENDING TO WAR: KOREA, VIETNAM, AND THE PERSIAN GULF

A Few Words on the Merits and Pitfalls of Comparing Wars across Time

I begin my search for trends in public attentiveness to foreign crises by comparing public opinion pertaining to the Korean, Vietnam, and Persian Gulf Wars. I identified two survey questions asked repeatedly in nearly identical form in all three periods, as well as one question asked repeatedly during the Vietnam and Persian Gulf Wars.[3] As previously noted, these three conflicts clearly differed in numerous respects, such as the nature and extent of U.S. leadership, the international environment, average education levels among Americans during the periods in which they took place, and the duration and strategic importance of each conflict, to name only a few. And such differences almost certainly have important implications for public opinion surrounding each war. Yet, despite these many differences, given my relatively narrow purposes, and under appropriate controls, I believe that the three wars can be reasonably compared. In appendix 3 of this chapter, I discuss in somewhat greater detail various issues surrounding my comparison of the three largest-scale uses of force by the United States since World War II, and offer some justifications for my comparisons, despite the many important differences between the wars.

An additional factor complicating over-time comparisons of major political events stems from the relative scarcity of appropriate data. Few reliable indicators exist that facilitate tracking public attentiveness over time. Survey organizations ask few questions with consistent techniques and wording over long periods of time. And even fewer, if any, such items are geared toward measuring attentiveness, as opposed to, say, salience, or substantive attitudes. Yet, in order to investigate long-term trends in public attentiveness, it is necessary to find some accessible, as well as reasonably valid and reliable, indicator of attentiveness. Fortunately, several such indicators are available during both the Vietnam and Persian Gulf wars, and one is available during all three conflicts. In the former case, I revisit the NES question employed at the outset of chapter 2, which asked respondents how much attention they had paid to the two conflicts. In the latter case, I again employ opinionation, in this instance investigating trends in the percentage of survey respondents answering "don't know" or "no opinion" to identical survey questions asked on numerous occasions over an extended period of time.

Are Americans Becoming Increasingly Attentive to War?

Because of the limited availability of comparable survey questions across all three conflicts, I divide the following discussion into two parts.[4] I first compare Vietnam and the Persian Gulf War. This contrast between a war that took place in the 1960s and one taking place in the early 1990s is ideal for testing my hypothesis that the explosion of television, including the soft news media, during the decades in between these two conflicts is likely to have contributed to a significant increase in opinionation. Since there was little soft news in the 1960s, particularly on television, almost all coverage of Vietnam was located in traditional news outlets, either network newscasts or newspapers. The war did not show up unexpectedly in prime time. Nor did it appear on local TV newscasts (recall chapter 3). So if you were a person who did not seek out traditional news—as is the case with many Americans—you could have easily avoided encountering almost any coverage of Vietnam. Not so the Gulf War. As noted in chapter 2, by the 1990s, war-related information had thoroughly infiltrated prime time, across a wide array of programs. In 1991, it was simply far more difficult for a politically uninterested American to avoid encountering war-related news, even if she avoided entirely all traditional news programs and newspapers. As I have argued, a prominent element of this change was the proliferation of soft news outlets.

In the second part of this section, I expand my investigation to include public opinion during the Korean War. Though certainly controversial, the Korean War did not provoke a degree of societal unrest and discomfort comparable to that stirred by Vietnam. Hence, including the Korean conflict in my investigation helps further account for the possibility that any opinionation differential between Vietnam and the Persian Gulf might be attributable to greater ambivalence among Americans regarding Vietnam.

VIETNAM AND THE PERSIAN GULF WARS

Figure 2.1 showed that "don't know" rates during the summer and fall of 1990, *prior to the outbreak of war in the Persian Gulf*, were substantially lower than during the early years of Vietnam. Yet troop deployments to the Gulf prior to November 1990 ($\sim$ 200,000) were comparable in magnitude to the U.S. troop commitment to Vietnam in 1965 (184,000). And in late December 1990, the U.S. troop commitment to the Gulf ($\sim$ 300,000) was *lower* than U.S. troop strength in Vietnam in 1966 (389,000) (Mueller 1973, 28; Summers 1995, 21–24). Hence, in 1965 and 1966, well before Vietnam became controversial, and in the face of comparable or lower U.S. troop deployments—and, through 1965, nearly identical casualty levels (636 vs. 613, respectively)—far fewer Americans expressed an opinion about Vietnam than about the Persian Gulf, even six months prior to the latter war. Finally, these patterns emerge despite the fact that with the abolition of the draft in the 1970s, far fewer Americans had a direct personal stake in the Gulf War (i.e., the possibility of being selected involuntarily to fight in the conflict) than was the case during either Korea or Vietnam. These data suggest that something other than differences in the inherent nature of the conflicts, or the U.S. commitments to the two conflicts, most likely accounts for any observed differences in public attentiveness to the two wars.

A review of Gallup poll data from both the Vietnam and Gulf War periods revealed one survey question asked during both conflicts in which the results were partially disaggregated by education level. As discussed in chapter 4, education represents a useful, albeit far from perfect, indicator of individuals' propensity to follow politics or foreign affairs. Better-educated individuals tend, on average, to be more politically engaged and more interested in foreign affairs than are their less-educated counterparts.

This question is as follows: "Do you approve or disapprove of the way President [Johnson/Nixon/Bush] is handling the situation in [Vietnam/the Persian Gulf]?" Additionally, a series of nine CBS/*New York Times* polls conducted during the Gulf War included a nearly identical question, with the results also disaggregated by education.[5] The question wording for the latter surveys is as follows: "Do you approve of the way President Bush is handling Iraq's invasion of Kuwait?"

Comparing overall average response rates during the Gulf War surveys, at each education level, with those from the Vietnam-era survey, indicates that the level of "don't know" responses during the Gulf War was substantially lower than during Vietnam, across all levels of education. For the Vietnam era survey, "don't know" rates were 7, 10, and 17 percent for respondents with college, high-school, and grade-school level educations, respectively. The corresponding figures for the Gulf War surveys were 3, 5 and 11 percent, respectively. Consistent with Hypothesis 9, the differential between the two wars is most pronounced—albeit modestly so—among the least-educated respondents, and declines in a stepwise fashion as respondents move up the education ladder. Among respondents with less than a high school education, "don't know" rates during the Gulf War were, on average, 6 percentage points lower than during Vietnam. The corresponding differentials were 5 and 4 percentage points, respectively, among high school and college-educated respondents. This indicates that, by this one indicator, opinionation has increased by the largest amount among the *least*-educated members of the public. Additionally, also consistent with Hypothesis 9—albeit, again, only modestly so—the opinionation gap between the least- and best-educated respondents is 2 percentage points smaller in the Gulf War surveys than in the Vietnam survey (10 vs. 8 percent).

Because the surveys investigated thus far were highly limited in their scope, I looked for alternative questions asked in a broader survey context that would make it possible to account for alternative potential causal factors. One such question, employed by the NES in 1970 and 1991, and already introduced in chapter 2, asked respondents how much attention they had paid to the Vietnam and Persian Gulf wars. (For question wording and coding, see appendix 1 of this chapter, question 3.) I employ this question to again test Hypothesis 9, this time controlling for a variety of potential alternative explanations for respondents' decisions to pay attention to either war.

One excellent indicator of a respondent's propensity to follow a given issue is the relative importance of the event to the respondent.[6] Ceteris paribus, the more personally important the issue, the more attentive a typical individual is likely be to it.[7] Fortunately, the 1970 and 1991 NES surveys also asked respondents how personally important they considered the two wars.[8] For my investigation, I combine the two NES surveys into a pooled time-series cross section. To distinguish the effects of personal importance across the two wars, I interact a dummy variable—coded 1 during the Gulf War and 0 during Vietnam—with the personal importance indicator. Hypothesis 9 predicts greater overall attentiveness to Vietnam, relative to the Gulf War, and that the differences between Vietnam and the Gulf War will be most pronounced among respondents for whom the two wars were *least* personally important. If so, we should observe a larger variation in attentiveness to Vietnam, compared to the Gulf War, across respondents at different levels of personal importance. Model 1 in table 5.A2 (shown in appendix 4 of this chapter), presents the complete results of a logit analysis, intended to test Hypothesis 9.

The model also includes a series of controls, intended to account for respondents' socioeconomic status (age, education, family income, gender, race), interest in politics (interest in public affairs, attention to political campaigns), as well as internal and external political efficacy. (See appendix 1 for question wording and coding of key control variables.) The results support my hypothesis ($p < .06$ or better). At figure 5.1, the logit coefficients are transformed into probabilities of paying close attention to the two wars (with "close" defined as "a good deal," "quite a bit," or "a great deal").

During the Vietnam War (circa 1970), as the personal importance of the war for a respondent increased from its minimum to maximum values, the probability of paying close attention to the war increased by 48 percentage points ($p < .01$). The corresponding increase during the Gulf War (circa 1991) was only 17 percentage points ($p < .01$). Moreover, the 31-percentage-point difference between the two wars in the magnitude of the variations across levels of importance is itself statistically significant ($p < .01$). In other words, personal importance had a much greater influence on attentiveness during Vietnam than during the Gulf War. This supports Hypothesis 9. Finally, the differences between the two wars are largest among respondents for whom the wars were *least* personally important and smallest among respondents for whom the wars were *most* important. In other words, as Hypothesis 9 also predicts, at least in terms of influencing attentiveness, an individual's intrinsic motivation to learn about the war mattered more in 1970 than in 1991.[9] These data suggest that, at least in terms of attentiveness, individuals who do not consider a given war highly important are catching up to their more-concerned counterparts.

... AND THE KOREAN WAR

As noted, it is possible that the greater controversy surrounding the Vietnam conflict could inflate the percentage of Americans responding "don't know" due to ambivalence rather than inattentiveness. In part to account for this possibility, I now broaden my analysis to include the Korean War (1950–53). While the Korean War became quite controversial—indeed, arguably Dwight Eisenhower's most important campaign promise in the 1952 election was his pledge to "go to Korea"—it never attracted a magnitude or intensity of opposition comparable to the Vietnam War. As a result, the ambivalence versus ignorance critique makes my theoretical prediction—that opinionation during Vietnam should be

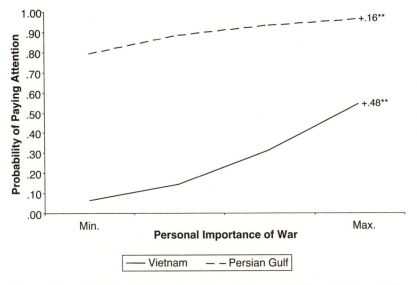

FIGURE 5.1. Probability of Paying Attention to Vietnam (1970) and Persian Gulf (1991) Wars, as Personal Importance of Wars Varies
**p < .01; SOURCE: American National Election Studies, 1970 and 1992

comparable to, or perhaps slightly stronger than, Korea—a particularly difficult test for my theory.

It is also important to bear in mind that while Vietnam arguably became the most controversial military conflict in American history (at least in the twentieth century), it did not begin that way. Through early 1966, about 60 percent of the public supported President Johnson's handling of the war.[10] It was not until July 1967—over two and a half years into the war—that popular support began to trend consistently below 50 percent (Mueller 1973, 54–56). And *opposition* to Vietnam did not surpass 50 percent until August 1968. In contrast, in thirteen surveys conducted between July 1950 and November 1952, disapproval of the Korean War reached 50 percent only once (March 1952), after which it dropped to an average of 41 percent for the remainder of the war (Mueller 1973, 45–46).[11] The war in Korea was also initially popular, with between 66 and 81 percent (depending on the question) supporting the war in the summer and fall of 1950 (Mueller 1973, 45). This suggests that Vietnam era controversy cannot account for lower "don't know" rates during the Gulf crisis, relative to Vietnam in 1965 or 1966, or to Korea in 1950.

The following survey question regarding the appropriateness of U.S. policy is available in nearly identical form during all three wars: "Do you think we did the right thing in [getting into the fighting in Vietnam or Korea/sending U.S. military forces to the Persian Gulf], or should we have stayed out?" Employing this question as the dependent variable, I conduct a series of logit analyses,

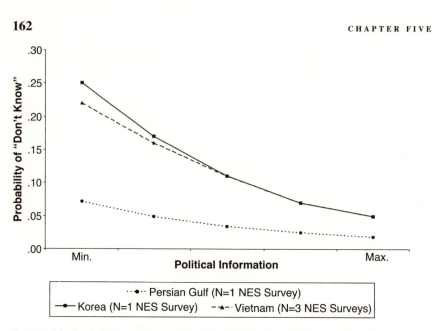

FIGURE 5.2. Probability of Responding "Don't Know" as Political Information Varies, 1952–1991

QUESTION: Do you think we did the right thing in [getting into the fighting in (Korea or Vietnam)/sending U.S. military forces to the Persian Gulf] or should we have stayed out?

including all but one NES survey conducted during the three wars—1952, 1968, 1970, 1972, and 1990–91.[12] The results indicate that political information[13] (as estimated by the interviewer)[14] strongly influences the likelihood of a "don't know" response, even when controlling for a variety of socioeconomic variables, as well as political interest, efficacy, and engagement.[15] (See appendix 1 for coding and definitions of key causal variables.) The Vietnam model pools all pertinent years (1968–72), and includes intercept dummies for 1968 and 1970. Figure 5.2 graphically illustrates the difference in opinionation as political information varies, with all controls held constant at their mean values, during each of the three wars. (The statistical results from which these figures are derived are presented in models 2–4 in table 5.A2.)

Figure 5.2 indicates that among less politically informed respondents (levels 1–2), the three wars line up precisely as the theory predicts, with the largest probability of responding "don't know" recorded during Korea, followed by Vietnam, and then the Gulf War. "Don't know" rates during Korea and Vietnam, however, differ only modestly, and the differences between these two conflicts are statistically insignificant for all groups of respondents. In contrast, "don't know" rates for the Gulf War are significantly ($p < .05$) lower than during Korea or Vietnam across all five political information groups.[16]

The overall average probabilities of responding "don't know" during the three wars, across all levels of political information, were .13, .12, and .04, for

Korea, Vietnam, and the Persian Gulf, respectively. The average level of "don't know" responses during the Gulf War was thus 9 and 8 percentage points lower, respectively, than during Korea or Vietnam. Most of the key economic and technological changes with which my theory is concerned first began to take hold in the 1970s. Hence, it is not surprising to observe a far larger differential between the 1970s and the 1990s than between the 1950s and 1960s.

Moreover, the gap between the wars diminishes as political information increases. At the lowest level of political information, the difference between the Korean and the Gulf wars is 18 percentage points. At the highest information level, the gap between the two wars drops to 3 percentage points. This supports my ninth hypothesis, which predicts that those who are relatively uninterested in politics—that is, the least politically informed—are likely to be the most profoundly affected by the changes in the mass media.[17]

Also noteworthy is the trend toward reduced variance in the public's attentiveness to the three wars across levels of political information. In 1952, during the Korean War, as respondents moved from the lowest to highest category of political information, their probability of responding "don't know" declined by 20 percentage points. During the Vietnam era, the average difference between the least and most politically informed respondents across the three NES surveys dropped to 17 percentage points. Finally, during the Gulf War, the least and most politically informed respondents differ in their probability of responding "don't know" by only 5 percentage points. This latter finding is also consistent with my ninth hypothesis, which further predicts that the attentiveness gap between the least and most politically engaged members of society should decrease, over time.[18] Finally, it is worth noting that in each of the NES surveys, respondents were *explicitly* offered the opportunity to express ambivalence—by answering "pros and cons" or "depends"—rather than "don't know," This further suggests that "don't know" answers do not indicate ambivalence.

One possible alternative explanation for changes in public attentiveness to foreign crises is increasing education levels among the American public. Between 1960 and 2000, respondents in NES surveys report a 24 percent increase in average years of schooling. As noted, few questions are available from all three wars. Even fewer also divide responses by level of education. I did, however, identify a second question (in addition to the previous NES analysis, which included education as a control) asked repeatedly during the Korean and Vietnam Wars and on several occasions during the Persian Gulf War, in which respondents were asked whether the United States had made a mistake getting into the respective conflicts, and for which the results could be disaggregated by respondents' education level (see appendix 1, question 1, which is also employed, in aggregate form, in figure 2.2).[19] Figure 5.3 presents the mean frequency of "don't know" responses for respondents at each of three education levels, across the three conflicts.

Even after accounting for rising education, opinionation during the Persian Gulf War remains stronger than during the Korean or Vietnam conflicts.[20] Moreover, consistent with Hypothesis 9, the gap in "don't know" rates across educa-

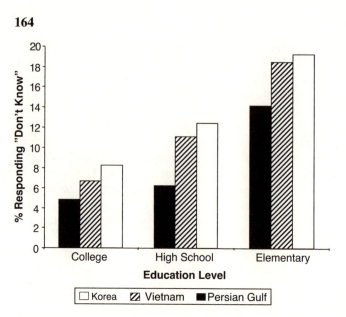

FIGURE 5.3. Mean Frequency of "Don't Know" Responses: Korea (1950–1953), Vietnam (1965–1973), and Persian Gulf (1991), by Education

QUESTIONS: (A) Do you think the United States made a mistake in going into the war in Korea, or not? (B) In view of the developments since we entered the fighting in Vietnam, do you think the U.S. made a mistake sending troops to fight in Vietnam? (C) Do you think the United States made a mistake getting involved in the war against Iraq, or not?

Korea: $N = 13$ (aggregate AIPO survey results, 1950–1953); Vietnam: $N = 23$ (aggregate AIPO survey results, 1965–1973); Persian Gulf: $N = 1,598$ individual respondents, pooled from two CBS News surveys (January 17–February 12, 1991).

tion levels is smaller—albeit modestly so—for the Gulf War than for either Korea or Vietnam. And the decline in "don't know" responses is again larger among respondents with a grade-school education than among their college-educated counterparts. Finally, it is worth reiterating that the relationships in figures 5.1 and 5.2 emerge after controlling for respondents' level of education. This suggests that rising education levels among the American people cannot adequately account for trends in opinionation to the three wars.

IS TRADITIONAL TV NEWS RESPONSIBLE FOR GREATER ATTENTIVENESS TO THE GULF WAR?

Identifying the existence of a trend toward increased attentiveness to war is not the same thing as establishing that the rise of the soft news media is responsible for the latter trend, in whole or even in part. Establishing the latter relationship is much more difficult. Unfortunately, as is so often the case in time-series analyses, data limitations preclude an unambiguous test of this latter causal relationship. Instead, I have sought to offer as compelling as possible a circumstantial case for the theory. And, as any trial lawyer will attest, a critical aspect of winning a case based on circumstantial evidence is disproving the most likely alternative explanation(s).

In this instance, bearing in mind that voluminous survey data (see chapter 3) indicate that most Americans rely heavily, and in many cases exclusively, on television for their news about politics and foreign affairs, one particularly plausible alternative explanation for differences in public attentiveness to Vietnam and the Persian Gulf wars stems from dramatic differences in the overall prevalence of television news programming available to TV viewers during the two eras. As shown in chapter 3, leaving aside the soft news media, there were far more *traditional* news outlets and a far greater overall quantity of news programming on television in 1991, as compared to the 1960s. Americans simply had far more opportunities to encounter the Gulf War in TV news programming—both local and national, on broadcast television or on cable—as compared with the Vietnam era.

Hence, my final comparison of Vietnam and the Gulf War tests this alternative hypothesis, that the rising attentiveness to war, documented above, results from greater volumes of traditional news in general, rather than the rise of the soft news media in particular. To do so, I employ the 1991 NES Gulf War Pilot Study. This survey included a question asking how many days in the past week respondents had watched the news on television. While this is not identical to asking a more general question regarding TV news consumption, there is no inherent reason to believe that the week of the NES interview should differ systematically from other weeks. Indeed, responses to this question correlate strongly with those from a second question asking respondents how much news they had watched on TV about the 1990 election campaign at .41.

Moreover, while one can imagine that respondents might consider at least *some* soft news outlets to be "news" in responding to this question, in the 2000 NES, respondents' consumption of daytime talk shows in the week prior to the NES interview is only modestly correlated with self-reported frequency of watching national network news (.06), early evening local news (.15) or late evening local news (.11) during the same time period. And in a second survey (Pew Research Center 2000), respondents' self-declared frequency of watching tabloid news shows, like *Inside Edition* or *Hard Copy*, correlated with their frequency of watching national or local newscasts at only .16 and .19, respectively. By contrast, respondents' self-reported viewing habits with respect to national and local TV news were much more closely related, correlating at .52 and .41 in the NES and Pew Research Center surveys, respectively.[21] These data suggest that the vast majority of respondents are *not* referencing the soft news media—as I have defined it in this book—when they indicate how frequently they watch the news on TV. Hence, this question appears to be a reasonable indicator of the volume of TV news, traditionally defined, typically consumed by respondents.

I converted this question into a dummy variable, coded 0 if respondents reported watching *any* TV news in the past week, and 1 if they reported watching *none*.[22] I then interacted it with respondents' level of political information,

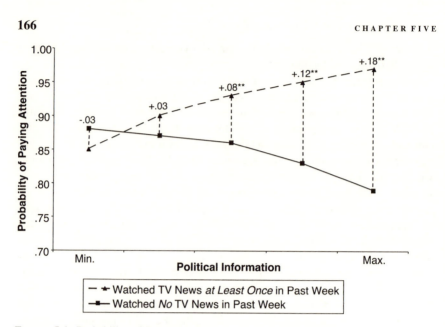

FIGURE 5.4. Probability of Paying Attention to the Persian Gulf War, as Political
Information and TV News Consumption Vary
   **p < .01

as estimated by the interviewer. If respondents, particularly those *not* interested
in politics or foreign affairs, learned about the Gulf War primarily, or even
solely, through exposure to the traditional news media, we should observe a
strong positive relationship between watching TV news and self-declared attention to the war. In contrast, if at least some respondents learned about the war
from sources *other* than TV newscasts and related programming, we would
anticipate a weaker relationship between TV news consumption and war attention. Moreover, to the extent that, consistent with my theory, politically uninterested individuals learned about the Gulf War though the soft news media, we
should observe the *weakest* relationship between TV news viewing and war
attention among the *least* politically informed respondents.

The dependent variable for this analysis is also dichotomous, coded 1 if
respondents indicated that they had paid "some," "quite a bit," or "a lot" of
attention to the war, and 0 if they paid "none" or "little" attention. I also include a range of control variables, similar to those employed in the prior analyses in this chapter (and so not repeated here). (See appendix 1 for variable
coding and definitions.) The complete statistical results are shown at model 5 in
table 5.A2 (in appendix 4). I translate the key coefficients into probabilities that
respondents were attentive to the Gulf War as their political information varies,
while I hold all other independent variables—including newspaper reading and
personal importance of the war—constant at their mean values. Figure 5.4
graphically illustrates the results.

The curves shown in figure 5.4 strongly support my hypothesis. Among the nearly one-third of all respondents at the two lowest level of political information, consuming TV news has no statistically significant impact on attentiveness to the war. As respondents' political information increases, however, TV news increasingly (and statistically significantly) influences attentiveness to the war. As one might expect, traditional news sources matter far more for politically engaged Americans, many of whom depend on such programming for their news about the nation and the world. In contrast, many politically uninterested Americans eschew traditional news programming. Hence, to the extent these latter individuals were attentive to the Gulf War, the explanation clearly lies elsewhere. My theory suggests that at least one important alternative source of war-related information for politically uninterested individuals was the soft news media.

While these data do not allow a definitive test of this claim, they do make clear that despite the massive amounts of TV news programming devoted to the war, apolitical Americans were able to find out about the Gulf War *without* tuning into the news on television (or reading newspapers, which is controlled in the logit model). This, in turn, strongly suggests that neither changes in nor the expansion of traditional TV news between the 1960s and 1990s is sufficient to account for the dramatic differences in attentiveness to the two wars documented here and in chapter 2.

SUMMARY

Taken together, my investigations into America's three largest-scale post–World War II uses of military force suggest that while the Persian Gulf War never reached the degree or depth of urgency for many Americans as that of the Vietnam War, substantially more people were at least somewhat attentive to the Gulf War than to Vietnam *at any time between 1965 and 1973*. And while, as discussed above, there were clearly many important differences between the three conflicts, the differences in attentiveness to the three wars do not appear to be attributable to the most obvious qualitative differences between the conflicts themselves, to rising educational attainment among the American people or to differences in the availability of traditional news programming on television in the different eras. Indeed, in the remainder of this chapter, I present evidence that regardless of the foreign policy crisis or other high-profile political issue one examines over the past half century, among less politically informed Americans, but *not* among their better-informed counterparts, attentiveness in the 1950s, 1960s, and 1970s was consistently and substantially lower than in the 1990s.

WAS THE GULF WAR UNIQUE? A COMPARISON OF U.S. FOREIGN CRISES FROM THE 1960s AND 1990s.

It remains possible that my comparison of Korea, Vietnam, and the Gulf War is inappropriate simply because the Persian Gulf War was unique, both in terms of its relatively rapid onset, as well as in its extremely rapid conclusion and decisive outcome. If so, comparing virtually *any* crisis or war from previous decades to the Gulf War would be suspect. Of course, to the extent this is true, one would not anticipate similar patterns emerging when comparing other crises across time that are not plagued by such unusual circumstances.

To determine whether the relationships identified above are indeed unique, and not generalizeable to other foreign policy crises, table 5.1 compares public awareness of and attentiveness to a variety of U.S. foreign crises from the 1960s and 1990s, including, for purposes of comparison, some additional data regarding the Vietnam and Persian Gulf Wars. The table presents the percentage of survey respondents at five education levels (grade school only, grade school or high school, high school diploma, some college or technical/business school after high school, college degree or better) indicating that they had "heard or read about" four U.S. military crises in the 1960s—the 1961–62 Berlin Crises, the 1962 Cuban Missile Crisis, the 1965 Dominican Republic intervention, and the Vietnam War (1964–65)—and six 1990s foreign policy crises: Panama (1989–90), the Persian Gulf crisis and war (1990–91), Somalia (1992–93), Haiti (1994), Bosnia (1995), and Kosovo (1999). Once again, I employ education level as the best available indicator of respondents' level of political engagement. The table also presents data on the percentage of respondents indicating that they had "followed," "paid attention to," or "been interested in" (as labeled in the table), the aforementioned 1990s interventions, as well as the 1948 Berlin Crisis, Vietnam, and the December 1998 U.S. and U.K. bombing campaign against Iraq, termed Operation Desert Fox.[23]

Beginning with the two wars, the data in table 5.1 essentially replicate my findings from the prior section. Americans who did not attend college were substantially more likely to report being aware of, and dramatically more likely to report being attentive to, the Gulf crisis in August 1990, compared to the Vietnam War in January and February 1965.[24] The attentiveness gap closes rapidly as respondents move up the education ladder, while the awareness gap disappears entirely among respondents with at least some college education.[25]

More importantly, the data for the other foreign crises clearly demonstrate that the relationships identified previously with respect to the three wars, and replicated here for the Gulf crisis and war and Vietnam, are not artifacts of the uniqueness of the Gulf War relative to Vietnam. Across *all* of the foreign crises shown in the table, less-educated Americans in the 1990s—but *not* highly educated members of the public—have been substantially more attentive to *every* high-profile U.S. foreign policy crises for which I was able to find pertinent survey data, relative to their counterparts in the 1960s (or in 1948). Indeed, according to these data, among Americans who did not attend college, larger percentages were attentive from the outset to the U.S. interventions in Panama, Somalia, and Kosovo than to U.S.-Cuba relations on the eve of arguably the most dramatic and high-stakes foreign policy crisis of the last half-century—the Cuban Missile Crisis.[26]

Across the eight 1960s era surveys (excluding Vietnam) shown in table 5.1, an average of 83 percent of respondents with no more than a high school education indicated that they had heard or read about U.S. foreign crises involving Cuba, Berlin, and the Dominican Republic. The corresponding figure among respondents with a college education or better is 98 percent. This represents an awareness gap of about 15 percentage points. In contrast, an average of 92 percent of respondents who did not attend any college claimed to have heard or read about the 1990s U.S. foreign crises in Panama, Somalia, Haiti, and Kosovo. The corresponding figure for respondents with a college degree or better is 97 percent. So, in the 1990s, the awareness gap between the least- and most-educated respondents fell to 5 percentage points, thereby representing a threefold decline, from the 1960s to the 1990s. Moreover, consistent with my theory, virtually all of the over-time change is located among the least-educated respondents.

Unfortunately, data on the percentage of respondents who *followed* the several 1960s crises is unavailable. I was, however, able to identify two instances of pre–soft news era surveys asking respondents whether they had been interested in the Berlin Crisis of 1948.[27] Across these two surveys, an average of 79 percent of respondents lacking any college education indicated that they were interested in the Berlin crisis. The corresponding average for respondents with a college degree was 99 percent. This represents an attentiveness gap of 20 percentage points. The corresponding averages for Panama, Somalia, Haiti, Kosovo, and Iraq (Operation Desert Fox) combined were 89 and 96 percent for respondents with no more than a high school education and those with a college degree, respectively. This represents a far smaller attentiveness gap of 7 percentage points. Once again, attentiveness to a range of foreign policy crises in the 1990s greatly exceeds that for arguably the most high-stakes foreign policy crises confronted by the United States since the end of World War II. And if the Vietnam and Persian Gulf Wars are included in these figures, the contrast between the 1960s and 1990s grows even more dramatic.

Due to differences in question wording across the two periods, these latter results should be considered merely suggestive. After all, respondents may be systematically more likely to have indicated that they *followed* an event than to express *interest* in news about a given event. Nonetheless, viewed in combination with the other results presented in this and the previous section, a clear, consistent pattern emerges—in the form of a stark attentiveness gap between the 1940s and 1960s, on the one hand, and the 1990s, on the other, primarily among relatively less educated and politically informed members of the public.

Hence, while there are almost certainly multiple factors contributing to differences in public attentiveness to the Korean, Vietnam, and the Gulf wars, these data strongly suggest that the dramatic differences presented in the prior section simply cannot be dismissed as artifacts of the different circumstances (e.g., magnitude, duration, social and political cohesion, etc.) surrounding the Gulf crisis and war, as compared to Korea and Vietnam. In other words, the Persian Gulf War does not appear to be so unique as to be inappropriate for comparison with any other U.S. military operations. Rather, the differences in

TABLE 5.1. Comparison of Public Awareness and Attentiveness regarding Select U.S. Foreign Policy Crises, by Education Level (1948–1999)

	Cuba	Dominican Republic	Berlin						Panama		Somalia			Haiti	Kosovo			
Heard or Read About Crisis	9/25/62	3/65	6/61	7/61	8/61	9/61	10/61	10/62	12/89	12/6/92	12/7/92	1/3/93	2/20/93	9/15/94	3/99	4/99	5/99	6/99
Education Level																		
Grade school	.90	.65	.67	.82	.83	.80	.85	.82	.92	.94	—	—	—	.83	.89	.86	.79	.89
Grade school or high school	.93	.72	.72	.85	.87	.84	.87	.86	.94	.94	—	—	—	.86	.94	.94	.91	.91
High school	.98	.84	.82	.93	.95	.94	.92	.94	.96	.94	—	—	—	.87	.96	.97	.94	.96
Some college/tech/business	.99	.92	.90	.93	.97	.97	.98	.98	.96	.94	—	—	—	.93	.97	.97	.94	.97
College +	1.0	.99	.95	.98	.97	.99	.99	.99	.98	.94	—	—	—	.95	.99	.98	.99	.99
Gap (grade–coll+)	.10	.34	.28	.16	.14	.19	.14	.17	.06	.00	—	—	—	.12	.10	.12	.20	.10
Gap (≤HS–coll+)	.07	.27	.23	.13	.10	.15	.12	.13	.04	.00	—	—	—	.09	.05	.04	.08	.08

	Cuba	Dominican Republic	Interest		Panama		Somalia			Haiti	Kosovo			
Followed Crisis More than "Not at All"	9/25/62	3/65	10/48	11/48	1/7/90	12/6/92	12/7/92	1/3/93	2/20/93	10/9/94	3/99	4/99	5/99	6/99
Education Level														
Grade school	—	—	.75	.70	.96	.74	.79	.91	.86	.82	.86	.83	.84	.79
Grade school or high school	—	—	.80	.77	.96	.79	.87	.96	.91	.90	.86	.92	.87	.86
High school	—	—	.93	.93	.98	.81	.90	.97	.93	.92	.86	.95	.88	.88
Some college/tech/business	—	—	.97	.91	.99	.82	.90	1.0	.94	.95	.95	.97	.91	.93

College +	—	—	.99	.98	—	—	—	—	1.0	.90	.95	.98	.95	.98	.96	.95	.97	.96
Gap (grade–coll +)	—	—	.24	.28	—	—	—	—	.04	.16	.16	.07	.09	.16	.10	.12	.13	.17
Gap (≤HS–coll +)	—	—	.19	.21	—	—	—	—	.04	.11	.08	.02	.04	.08	.10	.03	.10	.10

	Iraq (Desert Fox)	Vietnam War						Iraq (Gulf Crisis/War)			
Heard or Read about Crisis		1/12/65	2/24/65					8/29/90			
Education Level											
Grade school	—	.56	.76	—	—	—	—	.89	—	—	—
Grade school or high school	—	.63	.82	—	—	—	—	.88	—	—	—
High school	—	.78	.93	—	—	—	—	.88	—	—	—
Some college/tech/business	—	.87	.96	—	—	—	—	.96	—	—	—
College +	—	.96	.99	—	—	—	—	.98	—	—	—
Gap (grade–coll +)	—	.40	.23	—	—	—	—	.09	—	—	—
Gap (≤HS–coll +)	—	.33	.17	—	—	—	—	.10	—	—	—
	Followed	Attention							Followed		
Paid Attention to or Followed Crisis	1/99	4/29/64	6/9/64	7/28/64	8/11/64	9/1/64	11/11/64		1/7/91	1/13/91	1/17/91
Grade school	.89	.48	.49	.59	.54	.70	.50	—	.92	.97	.92
Grade school or high school	.90	.51	.56	.66	.60	.77	.59	—	.96	.99	.96
High school	.90	.58	.70	.81	.81	.91	.75	—	.98	.99	.98
Some college/tech/business	.97	.78	.78	.88	.96	.92	.78	—	.99	.99	.99
College +	.97	.84	.87	.96	.98	.95	.72	—	.99	1.0	.99
Gap (grade–coll +)	.08	.36	.38	.37	.44	.25	.22	—	.07	.03	.07
Gap (≤HS–coll +)	.07	.33	.31	.30	.38	.18	.13	—	.03	.01	.03

public attentiveness reported above reemerge across a variety of comparisons of U.S. foreign policy crises from the 1940s through the 1990s. While, as stated at the outset of this chapter, the evidence associating these trends with the rise of the soft news media is merely circumstantial, my investigations thus far *have* ruled out, or at least called into significant question, several prominent alternative potential explanations, including rising levels of education among the American public or exposure to an increased volume of traditional TV news sources. In the remainder of this chapter, I seek to further bolster the circumstantial case in support of my argument.

FILLING IN THE GAPS: PUBLIC ATTENTIVENESS TO *ALL*
U.S. USES OF FORCE, 1953–1998

The previous sections focused on periodic events, while ignoring the many years in between the various crises. To better capture long-term trends in public opinion, an ideal issue would be one that persisted in the public consciousness—and in polling data—over an extended period. Yet, few issues—particularly foreign policy crises—sustain the public's attention over long periods of time. As a result, it is difficult to identify specific issues that can be observed on a regular basis. One alternative, however, remains. The United States has employed military force abroad repeatedly throughout the entire post–World War II period. By investigating *all* U.S. major uses of military force, it is possible to offer a more complete picture of over-time trends in public attentiveness to foreign crises.

For my data set, I rely upon Oneal, Lian, and Joyner (1996), whose data update Blechman and Kaplan's (1978) widely employed data set on political uses of force. This newer data set encompasses the period 1950–88. Major uses of force from 1989 to 1995 are taken from Fordham and Sarver (2001), who further update Blechman and Kaplan (1978).[28] Finally, uses of force from 1996 to 1998 were compiled by the author.[29] (See Baum 2002a for a complete list of post-1988 uses of force employed in this study.)

The challenge for such an investigation is identifying an indicator of public attentiveness that is consistently and comparably available for all, or at least the vast majority, of U.S. uses of force. Fortunately, one such indicator exists. Previous research has found that the public evaluates presidents' performance in part as a function of their performance in foreign policy (Aldrich, Sullivan, and Borgida 1989; Hurwitz and Peffley 1987). Many studies, in turn, have shown that one consequence of the increased public attention to politics that accompanies foreign policy crises can be changes in the president's job approval ratings (Mueller 1970, 1973; Brody 1991; Baum 2002a; and many others).

A closely related change concerns the percentage of survey respondents willing to rate the president's job performance. As more people tune in to politics in a crisis situation, I anticipate that more will be willing to offer an opinion about the president. I therefore employ these changes in opinionation—which are comparably measured throughout the post–World War II era—as an indicator of the extent of public attention to foreign crises. The voluminous literature on priming effects (e.g., Iyengar and Kinder 1987) suggests that citizens ought to have an increased propensity to evaluate the president's performance based upon foreign policy in the midst of a foreign military engagement (Krosnick and Brannon 1993), and hence, opinionation on this question should disproportionately reflect the public's attentiveness to the crisis.[30] My dependent variable for this investigation is therefore opinionation in presidential approval polls conducted in close proximity to each U.S. use of force.

Throughout the post–World War II era, the Gallup organization has regularly asked Americans for their judgment concerning the president's job performance. During this period, Gallup has asked this question anywhere from nine to forty-two times per year. My data set, which is disaggregated by respondents' education level, runs from 1953 through 1998 and contains a total of 834 polls. This represents an average of 1.5 polls per month over the entire forty-six-year period. Of these, 66 took place immediately following a major use of force.[31]

In the statistical models below, I transform this indicator into a first difference. This means subtracting the "no opinion" rate in last week's or last month's approval poll (whichever was most recent) from that in the current poll (i.e., $Approve_t - Approve_{t-1}$). The resulting variable captures the change in the level of "no opinion" responses from the poll conducted immediately prior to, and the one conducted immediately following the onset of each use of force. While the level of "no opinion" responses at any given time most likely results from various factors, both individual and environmental, there is no reason to believe that such factors should produce *changes* in "no opinion" rates at the onset of foreign crises that differ systematically from changes at other times.[32]

Given that, in times of crisis, the public's response to the presidential approval question tends to represent their evaluations concerning the president's performance with respect to the crisis, my theory predicts that major political events—particularly American uses of military force—ought in recent years to generate *greater* increases in opinionation than similar events in the 1950s and 1960s. Four hypotheses follow:

$H_{5.1}$ "No opinion" rates should decline in the immediate aftermath of a use of force.

$H_{5.2}$ The *extent* of the decline, given a military engagement, should increase over time.

$H_{5.3}$ Because they are the primary consumers of soft news, the over-time decline ought to be *most* pronounced among *least* politically engaged respondents.

$H_{5.4}$ The volatility in post-use-of-force "no opinion" rates should also decline, over time, as less politically engaged Americans pay increased, and more consistent, attention to foreign crises.

As we shall see below, the data support each of these hypotheses.[33] (Note that Hypotheses 5.2 and 5.3 follow directly from Hypothesis 9, which predicts increased attentiveness to foreign crises over time, particularly among politically uninterested individuals, and a resulting trend toward a weakening relationship between political engagement and attentiveness to foreign crises.)

Hypothesis 5.1 can be substantiated by looking at the aggregate trend in average "no opinion" responses. Over the entire 1953 to 1998 period, the overall average level of "no opinion" responses for noncrisis periods is about 12.1 percent, as opposed to about 10.7 percent for polls conducted immediately following the onset of crises. This represents an approximately 1.4 point (absolute) decline (or a 13 percent change), significant at .05, in average levels of "no opinion" responses. While these results modestly support Hypothesis 5.1, of greater interest is the over-time trend in the impact of the use of military force on "no opinion" rates.

To investigate the latter, I first conduct an OLS analysis on the aggregate approval poll series. Then, to determine whether the trends identified in the aggregate analysis vary systematically across different groups of respondents, as predicted by the theory, I conduct separate OLS analyses on respondents at three education levels: less than high school, high school, or college (Krause 1997; Baum and Kernell 2001). Here again, I employ education as the best-available indicator of political engagement.

The dependent variable for this analysis is the difference in the natural logarithm of the percentage of survey respondents responding "no opinion" between polls conducted immediately prior to the initiation of uses of military force and those conducted immediately following the initiation of uses of force.[34] The key independent variables include a trend term representing the date of each poll ("Date"), a dummy variable coded "1" for presidential approval polls immediately following the onset of a U.S. military action and "0" otherwise ("Use of force"), as well as an interaction term ("Date × use of force"), intended to capture any over-time variation in the impact of uses of force. I also include the natural log of the president's approval rating ("ln%Approve") and the lagged dependent variable ("ln%No opinion$_{t-1}$"), both in level form. I add various additional controls, described in appendix 1, to account for potential alternative explanations for changes in "no opinion" rates. Table 5.A3 (shown in appendix 4 to this chapter) presents the results of the full multivariate models.[35]

The first column in table 5.A3 presents the overall aggregate results.[36] The results indicate that "no opinion" rates have indeed declined, over time ($p < .001$).[37] More importantly, the magnitude of the average decline in levels of "no opinion" responses immediately following uses of force has expanded, between 1953 and 1998, by approximately 15 percent *more* ($p < .12$) than the corresponding 42 percent over-time decline during all other periods, when the U.S. was *not* engaged in a new military activity abroad. Combining the extra post-use-of-force trend with that for non-use-of-force polls, the total change in "no opinion" rates between 1953 and 1998 predicted by the statistical model is a decline of 57 percent. Given an average level of "no opinion" responses in

1953 of 16.6 percent, this model thus predicts a decline of 7 percentage points during non-use-of-force periods, plus an additional 2.5 percentage points following uses of force. Hence the total predicted decline in post-use-of-force "no opinion" rates is about 9.5 percentage points, about one-quarter of which appears to be a result of increased public attention to the president in the immediate aftermath of a use of force.

To determine whether the declines in "no opinion" rates between 1953 and 1998, both following uses of force and, separately, for polls *not* following uses of force, are statistically significant, I again employ the King, Tomz, and Wittenberg (2000) procedure. The results (not shown) indicate that these differences are indeed significant at the .01 level for both post-use-of-force periods and for periods in which the United States did not use military force abroad. Moreover, the two trends are statistically distinguishable from one another at the .10 level.[38] This indicates that uses of force are associated with significantly *larger* declines in "no opinion" rates, over time, than can be attributed to the secular downward trend in "no opinion" rates.[39] This supports Hypothesis 5.2, as well as Hypothesis 9.

The results presented thus far, though statistically significant, are—notwithstanding the relatively large numbers of individuals represented by small percentage-point changes—arguably substantively modest. It is unclear why a relatively modest rise in the number of Americans focusing on the president following a use of force should necessarily have a meaningful effect on presidential decision making. If, however, a particular subgroup of Americans, one that may represent a not-insignificant constituency for a given president, demonstrates a far stronger effect, then this may indeed have meaningful political implications. I therefore turn to a test of Hypothesis 5.3, which represents a more critical test of the theory. Here, I investigate whether respondents at differing levels of education have been differently responsive to U.S. uses of military force, over time (as also predicted by Hypothesis 9).

To address this latter question, I turn to the partially disaggregated series and conduct three separate OLS analyses (also shown in table 5.A3) for respondents at each education level. Prior to the Clinton administration, the middle category included respondents who had completed at least some high school. During the Clinton years (1993–98), only respondents who had earned a high school diploma were placed in the middle category. This adjustment is intended to partially account for the overall increase in education levels among the general public. There were simply far fewer individuals in the 1990s than in prior decades lacking at least some high school education.[40]

The results strongly support Hypothesis 5.3 (and, hence, Hypothesis 9). Figure 5.5 presents the predicted declines in "no opinion" rates from 1953 to 1998. Several key points are discernable from figure 5.5. First, precisely as the theory predicts, drops in "no opinion" rates are far more pronounced among the least-educated respondents, and recede in a stepwise fashion as respondents move up the education ladder. Moreover, these total predicted declines track fairly closely with the actual declines, between 1953 and 1998, in post-use-of-force

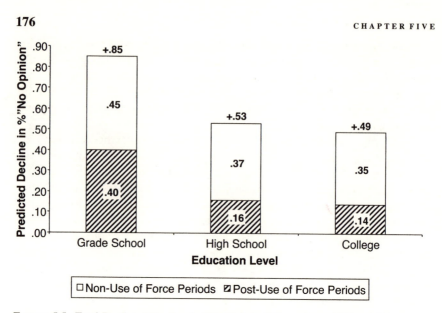

FIGURE 5.5. Total Predicted Decline in "No Opinion" Rates from 1953 to 1998, by Education Level

"no opinion" rates, of 66, 52, and 44 percent, respectively, among grade-school, high-school, and college-educated respondents.[41]

Second, variation in the magnitude of decline across the different education groups is substantially smaller during non-use-of-force periods (which represents the overall secular trend.) The predicted decline among respondents with a grade-school education during non-use-of-force periods is approximately 10 percent larger than among college-educated respondents (45 vs. 35 percent). The corresponding difference during post-use-of-force periods (40 vs. 14 percent) is far more substantial (+26 percent). More importantly, between 1953 and 1998, among respondents with a grade-school education, "no opinion" rates following U.S. uses of military force declined by 40 percent *beyond* the secular decline in "no opinion" responses. The corresponding *additional* declines among high-school and college-educated respondents are much more modest: 16 and 14 percent, respectively. At least in these data, trends in opinionation following uses of force are far more dramatic among the least-educated members of the public. This is precisely the pattern we would anticipate if increases in attentiveness were attributable to a changed television environment, in which, due to the rise of the soft news media, information about foreign crises had become "cheap" to consume, even for individuals not intrinsically interested in politics or foreign policy.

Finally, also of interest is the relative decline in the annual fluctuations in the changes in "no opinion" rates following uses of force. The overall standard deviation on changes in "no opinion" rates following nineteen uses of force during the Clinton years (1993–98, $N = 19$) was nearly 74 percent lower (3.8

vs. 6.5 percentage points) than that during the Eisenhower, Kennedy, Johnson, Nixon, Ford, and Carter administrations combined (1953–80, $N = 29$). This is consistent with Hypothesis 5.4, which anticipates that due in part to increasingly broad-based and consistently intense television coverage of U.S. uses of force, Americans ought to respond, in terms of changes in attentiveness, in a more consistent manner in the 1990s than in previous decades.

ATTENTIVENESS TO THE *END* OF WAR: CAMP DAVID (1978) VERSUS OSLO (1993) AND DAYTON (1995)

I next compare television coverage of and public attentiveness to the 1978 Camp David Accords between Egypt and Israel with TV coverage and attentiveness surrounding the 1993 Oslo Accords between Israel and the Palestinians and the 1995 Dayton Peace Accords involving Bosnia's Muslim, Serbian, and Croatian populations.

For this investigation I first review daily transcripts from the Vanderbilt Television News Archive. I compare the number of stories and minutes of network news coverage devoted to the three peace accords during the month in which the accords were signed. I find that even as coverage of these international events by the major networks declined in the 1990s, relative to the 1970s, when one factors in the explosion of nontraditional (e.g., soft) news programs on cable and on the broadcast networks, the breadth and depth of television coverage of Oslo and Dayton vastly exceeded that of Camp David in 1978. I then present some limited survey evidence suggesting that despite greater network news coverage of Camp David, the American public was more attentive to both Oslo and Dayton.

While not, strictly speaking, American foreign policy crises, Camp David, Oslo, and Dayton each involved the termination of a large-scale, long-lasting military conflict with which the United States was intimately involved. And each of the three peace agreements represented dramatic diplomatic breakthroughs of historic proportions, which were widely recognized as such. The Camp David Accords involved an agreement between Egypt's president Anwar Sadat and Israeli prime minister Menachem Begin to officially end the state of war between their two countries that had prevailed since Israel's founding in 1947. Egypt became the first Arab state to make peace with Israel, a circumstance that later cost President Sadat his life. American president Jimmy Carter played a key role in facilitating the ultimately successful peace process between Egypt and Israel.

The Oslo Accords also involved the Arab-Israeli conflict. In this instance, the issue on the table was the future of the Palestinian people living in the Gaza Strip and the West Bank, territories occupied by Israel during the 1967 Six Day War. The signatories to the agreement were Israel's prime minister Yitzhak Rabin, and Yasser Arafat, chairman of the Palestine Liberation Organization (PLO). This agreement was negotiated in Oslo, Norway, following intensive intervention by the Clinton administration, and was later signed in Washington D.C., during a high-profile ceremony on the White House lawn.

Finally, the Dayton Peace Accords, negotiated in Dayton, Ohio, under the close scrutiny of U.S. Secretary of State Madeleine Albright, officially ended a brutal four-year civil war in Bosnia, one that had the dubious distinction of introducing the term "ethnic cleansing" to the international diplomatic lexicon. As a key part of the Dayton Accord, involving Bosnia's Serbian, Muslim, and Croatian inhabitants, a multinational peacekeeping force, known as IFOR (an acronym for International Force) and led by United States troops, occupied Bosnia.

A survey of network news coverage of Camp David, Oslo, and Dayton suggests that Camp David received significantly more coverage—in terms of total number of stories and total number of minutes—by the "big three" broadcast networks than either Oslo or Dayton. According to the Vanderbilt Television News Archive, the three major networks combined presented 100 stories dealing with Camp David in September of 1978. This contrasts with 86 stories concerning Oslo during an identical time span surrounding the September 1993 accord and 73 stories on the November 1995 Dayton agreement.[42] This represents 16 and 37 percent more stories on Camp David, relative to Oslo or Dayton, respectively. The same pattern obtains for total minutes of coverage. The three major networks offered 360 minutes of Camp David coverage in September 1978, compared to 273 minutes of coverage of Oslo during a comparable period in 1993, and 204 minutes of coverage of Dayton in November 1995.[43] This represents 32 and 76 percent more minutes of coverage of Camp David, relative to Oslo and Dayton, respectively. Clearly, the major networks provided substantially greater coverage of the 1978 Camp David Accords than of either the 1993 Oslo or 1995 Dayton Accords.

Unlike 1978, by 1993 (or 1995), television coverage of a major foreign crisis extended far beyond the major networks. For instance, all-news cable channels, like CNN, which did not exist in 1978, also offered substantial coverage of politics and foreign policy. Beyond all-news cable networks, such entertainment-oriented cable networks as Comedy Central, Black Entertainment Television, MTV, and many others have increasingly offered soft news programming that emphasizes only those aspects of major news events perceived to be of interest to their audiences. Far fewer soft news programs existed in the early 1990s relative to 2002. Yet a review of program transcripts on Lexis-Nexis indicated that the vast majority of soft news programs on the air in 1993 covered the Oslo peace agreement and the signing ceremony in Washington. Among the soft programs—both cable and network—covering these events were *Inside Edition, MTV News, E! News Daily, Live with Regis and Kathie Lee, The Chevy Chase Show, The Tonight Show with Jay Leno, Late Night with David Letterman, Dateline, 20/20,* and *60 Minutes.*

For instance, Regis Philbin, in his daytime talk show *Live with Regis and Kathie Lee,* discussed the peace agreement between Israel and the Palestinians with Desert Storm hero retired general Norman Schwarzkopf. And *The Chevy Chase Show* featured a comedic monologue by *Saturday Night Live* writer Al

Franken, who lampooned the agreement between Arafat and Rabin. *E! News Daily*, in turn, discussed the fact that celebrity Casey Kasem, an Arab American, attended the signing of the Oslo Accords in Washington. And *Inside Edition* returned to the familiar soft news theme of terrorism and the dangers it posed to Americans, using the signing of the Oslo Accords as an opportunity to present a retrospective on terrorism in the United States and Israel. The reporter narrating the story overlaid video of the hand-shaking ceremony at the White House between President Clinton, Chairman Arafat, and Prime Minister Rabin with a commentary highlighting the dramatic nature of the event and emphasizing morality and justice frames, noting, in part, "the PLO-Israel peace agreement can't wipe away the blood that was shed." (Chapter 3 presented evidence that soft news programs offered substantial coverage of Bosnia, including the signing of the 1995 Dayton Accords and the resulting deployment of U.S. troops to Bosnia as part of IFOR. Hence, I do not revisit that evidence here.)

CNN primarily—though, like most news outlets, not exclusively—falls into the category of "hard," rather than "soft" news. Yet, more recent entrants to the "all news" cable market, like MSNBC and Fox, hoping to broaden their audiences, have increasingly emulated soft news programming. And, in order to avoid losing viewers to their competitors, CNN has substantially increased the percentage of its broadcasts devoted to soft-news oriented topics and formats (e.g., talk shows, roundtable debates, and audience participation programs). Despite these efforts, as noted in chapter 3, the audience for CNN and the other all-news cable networks continues to be tiny compared to that for the major networks' evening newscasts or for many soft news programs. Finally, at the times of Oslo and Dayton, in 1993 and 1995, respectively, several contemporary all-news cable networks were not yet on the air (e.g., Fox and MSNBC). Hence, it seems unlikely that the advent of CNN or other all-news cable networks could account entirely for any significant differences in overall public attentiveness to foreign policy between the 1970s and the mid-1990s.

Given the greater network news coverage of Camp David, if public attentiveness derived primarily from traditional news coverage and was not influenced by the proliferation of cable and soft news programs available by the mid-1990s, then we should expect to find greater public attentiveness to Camp David, relative to Oslo or Dayton. Yet my theory predicts the opposite relationship: an increase in the public's attentiveness to the two 1990s peace accords, relative to the 1978 Camp David Accord. Unfortunately, survey data for these three international events is far less comprehensive than for the Vietnam and Persian Gulf Wars. Hence, a systematic comparison of opinionation surrounding all three events is not possible. Some evidence from public opinion surveys is, however, available. I identified one survey question asked by CBS during the periods of Camp David and Oslo, and one asked by Gallup and Roper during the periods of Camp David and Dayton. To estimate survey respondents' attentiveness to the events, I compare levels of opinionation across the surveys. As before, my hypothesis is that higher rates of "no opinion" or "don't know" responses indicate less attentiveness to these events.

During the periods of the two Middle East accords (Camp David and Oslo) survey respondents were asked the following question: "Do you think the [recent] agreement[s] [about a future peace settlement in the Middle East/between Egypt and Israel/between Israel and the Palestine Liberation Organization] will lead to a real peace settlement in the Middle East, or do you think a peace settlement is no more likely now than it was before the [summit/agreement]?" (Brackets indicate differences in wording across the two periods.) Responses included "real peace," "no more likely," "depends," or "no opinion/don't know." A comparison of opinionation across these questions indicates that respondents in 1978 were nearly twice as likely to answer "no opinion/don't know" as their counterparts in 1993 (13.5 percent, $N = 2$ polls vs. 7.0 percent, $N = 1$ poll).

The second survey question was asked with respect to the Dayton Accords on nine separate occasions and with respect to the Camp David Accords on two occasions. For these two peace agreements, respectively, the questions were as follows: (1) "Do you approve or disapprove of the way President Carter is handling his responsibilities in the Middle East situation?" and (2) "Do you approve or disapprove of the way Bill Clinton is handling the situation in Bosnia?" In this instance, "no opinion" rates during Camp David in 1978 (19.5 percent, $N = 2$ polls) were approximately 46 percent higher than during Dayton in 1995 (13.4 percent, $N = 9$ polls). Hence, even though network news coverage of Camp David in 1978 exceeded coverage of Oslo or Dayton (in terms of numbers of stories and total minutes of coverage on nightly news broadcasts), opinionation with respect to Oslo and Dayton substantially exceeded that for Camp David.

In addition to these aggregate data, it is possible to gain some further leverage into this question by disaggregating these questions by respondents' education level. The theory predicts that changes in television coverage should have a stronger impact upon less politically engaged individuals. Because politically inattentive individuals are the primary consumers of soft news outlets, but are *not* a prime demographic for the cable all-news networks, disaggregating the data in this manner allows a partial test of whether the over-time changes described above are attributable in any significant measure to the rise of twenty-four-hour all-news cable channels.

Here, I once again employ education as an indicator of political engagement. These data are available for one survey question asked during Camp David and a similar question asked during the Dayton meetings on Bosnia. In the former case, one of the Camp David surveys employed above also asked respondents the following question: "Have you heard or read anything about the results of the Camp David summit meeting with Egypt and Israel and the United States?" In the latter case, a survey by the Associated Press, conducted between November 29 and December 3, 1995, asked respondents: "How closely have you been following news about U.S. efforts to bring peace to Bosnia?" The former question tallied only "yes" or "no" responses, while the latter included responses ranging from "very closely" to "not at all closely."

While these questions are not identical, all else equal, it should be easier for respondents to say they have *heard* of Camp David than to say they *followed* the Dayton Accords. In fact, in table 5.1 I presented evidence that across a wide range of U.S. military interventions, respondents were consistently more likely to report having heard or read about an intervention than to report having followed it. This, in turn, should make it harder to show my predicted result—that, due to the rise of soft news, more people, especially among the less educated, will report having *followed* Bosnia than having *heard or read about* Camp David. Yet, the data nonetheless firmly support my prediction.

Across all four education groups, more people claim to have followed the Dayton Accords than to have even *heard* of the Camp David Accord. Moreover, consistent with Hypothesis 9, the differences decline as respondents move up the education ladder. Among the least-educated group, 39 percent had not heard or read about Camp David, while only 31 percent claimed to have followed the situation in Bosnia "not at all closely," a difference of 8 percentage points (or a 26 percent decline from Camp David to Bosnia). Among respondents who completed high school or some college, the corresponding difference falls by half, to 4 percentage points (22 vs. 18 percent and 14 vs. 10 percent for the two education groups, respectively). And respondents with a college or graduate degree differ by only 1 percentage point across the two surveys (5 vs. 4 percent). These results suggest that explaining the greater public attentiveness to Oslo and Dayton, compared to Camp David in 1978, requires looking beyond the rise of all-news cable networks. Finally, given the difference in question wording, it seems likely that these differences would be even starker if the Bosnia respondents had been asked whether they had "heard or read anything about" Bosnia.

A comparison of fifteen public-opinion polls by no means represents definitive evidence concerning either the extent or causes of public attention to these three foreign policy events. Yet, that both Dayton and Oslo appear in these limited examples to have attracted greater public attentiveness than Camp David, especially among those at lower education levels, and in spite of greater network news coverage of Camp David, represents some additional evidence in support of my theoretical argument.

A second means of comparing opinionation across these three events involves examining "no opinion" responses to presidential approval polls surrounding each event. As above, I assume that in the midst of a foreign crisis, the public's evaluation of the president will tend to reflect their evaluation of his performance in the crisis. Hence, I argue that the difference in "no opinion" responses to Gallup's presidential approval questions, between the poll conducted immediately prior to and the one immediately following the initiation of a foreign crisis, is a reasonable indicator of public attentiveness to the crisis. As noted earlier, there is no reason to believe that shifts in "no opinion" responses at the outset of such an event ought to differ systematically from such responses at other times, unless the shifts are in response to the event itself. Hence, if attentiveness was indeed greater during the more recent events, we should observe larger declines in "no opinion" responses following the two 1990s peace agreements, compared to a peace agreement in 1978.

In fact, comparing the change in "no opinion" rates in presidential approval polls conducted immediately prior to, and averaged over the month immediately following, completion of each peace agreement yields a pattern consistent with those in the prior analyses. In the month following the signing of the Camp David Accords, "no opinion" responses in two Gallup presidential approval polls actually increased by an average of 1.5 percentage points, or 8 percent (from 15 to 16.5 percentage points, $N = 2$ polls). This suggests that the Camp David Accord had little impact on public attentiveness, despite the fact that this arguably represented President Carter's greatest foreign policy achievement. In contrast, following the Oslo and Dayton Accords, "no opinion" responses *declined* by, on average, 3 (from 11 to 8 percentage points, $N = 2$ polls) and 4 (from 9 to 5 percentage points, $N = 1$ poll) percentage points, respectively. These declines represent rates of change of 27 and 44 percent, respectively. Once again, this evidence, viewed in isolation, is far from definitive, and certainly does not establish a causal relationship between the rise of the soft news media and differences in attentiveness to these three issues. It does, however, add to the broad pattern of evidence supporting my theory.

To the extent that the public—especially its least-educated members—was indeed more attentive to Oslo and Dayton than to Camp David, the explanation clearly lies beyond traditional network news coverage of these three events by broadcast network evening newscasts, and most likely beyond the all-news cable networks as well. In fact, I presented evidence in chapter 3 suggesting that, at least with respect to Bosnia, the *broadening* of media coverage of major foreign policy events beyond the traditional network news to the soft news media has most likely contributed significantly to increased public attentiveness to the more recent peace agreements. Once again, this analysis offers some further evidence, albeit still indirect, in support of Hypothesis 9.[44]

BROADENING THE FOCAL LENS: ATTENTIVENESS TO AMERICA'S
MOST URGENT NATIONAL PROBLEMS

As I have argued, despite my emphasis in this book on foreign policy crises, my by-product theory is not limited to strictly foreign policy. Indeed, there is no theoretical reason to anticipate a different pattern for dramatic foreign policy issues than for similarly dramatic domestic policy issues, at least those amenable to cheap framing and piggybacking. In fact, I hypothesized that the theory ought to apply to any issue that comes to prominence in the soft news media. In chapter 4, I presented evidence that in addition to foreign crises, exposure to soft news was associated with increased attentiveness to the Monica Lewinsky scandal, a domestic water-cooler event possessing all of the characteristics that appeal to soft news programmers. I also presented evidence that soft news viewers—particularly those at lower education levels—were more likely than their non-soft-news-viewing or better-educated counterparts to be concerned with those types of national issues that tend to be emphasized in the soft news media (e.g., crime, scandal, terrorism, war, etc.). Consuming traditional news programming did not produce comparable effects. This suggests that soft news *does* exert a distinct priming effect (Iyengar and Kinder 1987) with respect to a particular subset of major national issues, particularly among viewers who lack alternative news sources.

In this section, in order to further test the applicability of the theory beyond foreign policy, I investigate an indicator of over-time trends in attentiveness to political issues, many of which are similar to foreign crises in their appeal to the soft news media, but which do not necessarily involve foreign policy.

For this analysis, the dependent variable is a simple additive scale, derived from a series of open-ended NES questions in which respondents are asked to name the most important problems facing the nation. My hypothesis is that those issues that grab typical individuals' attention to a sufficient extent that they name them as among the most important problems facing the nation are, almost by definition, potential—if not actual—water-cooler events. Hence, I argue that individuals who mention more "major problems" are, on average, more attentive to the major issues of the day than are their counterparts who mention fewer problems. The NES interviewers coded up to three responses by each individual. The scale, which I employ in the first two analyses in this section, thus runs from 0 to 3, with 3 representing the highest level of attentiveness to major national problems.[45] Nearly every NES survey since 1960 includes this open-ended question.[46]

While these investigations identify patterns consistent with the theory, they do not address which *types* of issues different groups of respondents tend to mention, nor whether the most commonly mentioned classes of issues have changed, over time. To address this latter issue, the final analysis in this section disaggregates the "major problems" mentioned by respondents into different categories, based on whether or not a given *class* of problem is likely to be covered by the soft news media. This latter investigation is intended to test whether, consistent with Hypotheses 9 and 10, the least politically engaged Americans, but not their more politically engaged counterparts, have grown more likely, over time, to mention those types of problems (e.g., foreign crises, crime, morality, etc.) that tend to be featured in the soft news media, but not other types of problems. If so, this would represent additional evidence that the rise of the soft news media bears at least some responsibility for the overall trends among politically inattentive Americans identified in this chapter.

Trends in Attentiveness to Major Problems Facing the Nation

Figure 5.6 presents the mean number of problems mentioned by respondents, divided into five groups, based on their level of political information, as estimated by the NES interviewer. These data indicate that across respondents in all five political information groups, the number of mentions of major problems has increased in nearly a stepwise fashion (excepting the 1970s), from the 1960s to the 1990s.[47] Consistent with Hypothesis 9, however, this increase is not evenly distributed across respondents at different levels of political infor-

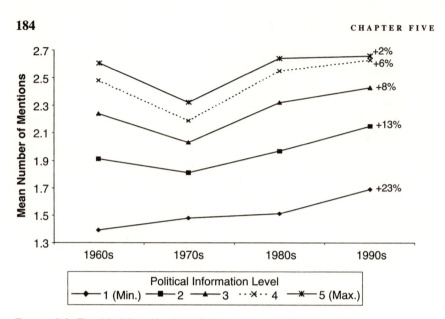

FIGURE 5.6. Trend in Mean Number of "Major Problems" Mentioned by Level of Political Information, 1960s to 1990s.

mation. From the 1960s to the 1990s, the mean number of problems mentioned by politically inattentive respondents has increased at a far more substantial rate than the corresponding increase for their highly politically attentive counterparts. While respondents at the lowest level of political information mentioned an average of 22 percent more major problems in the 1990s than in the 1960s, the corresponding increase for respondents at the highest level of political information is only 2 percent. Indeed, the rate of increase declines in a stepwise fashion as respondents move up the political information ladder.[48]

In order to determine whether these general trends are related to the changing television environment, I turn to a multivariate statistical analysis. To measure the growth and diversification of television, I employ the combined prime time audience ratings of the "big three" broadcast networks (ABC, CBS, and NBC). If the theory is correct, network ratings should predict trends in attentiveness better than a secular trend term. The most pertinent changes in the television industry, most notably the proliferation of cable, and the resulting dramatic rise in the volume and diversity of entertainment-oriented informational (and other) programming, did not emerge until after about 1980. Hence, the bulk of any TV effects on attentiveness ought to appear relatively recently. And, in fact, when I retested all of the models reported below, replacing network audience ratings with a secular trend term (not shown), the results, as predicted, were somewhat weaker.

Figure 5.7 presents the annualized trend in prime-time network audience ratings from 1960 to 1997.[49] As is clear from the figure, network ratings remained

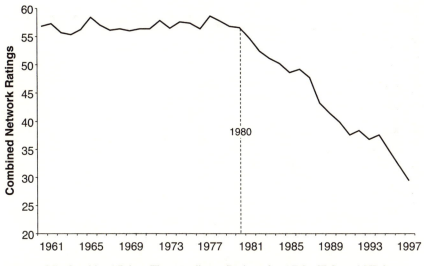

FIGURE 5.7. Combined Prime-Time Audience Ratings for ABC, CBS, and NBC, 1960–1997
SOURCE: Nielsen Media Research

fairly constant until about 1980, after which they began to fall precipitously. This decline corresponds almost perfectly with the rise of cable, which, as previously discussed, was one of the most important factors contributing to the proliferation of the soft news media. Hence, network audience ratings appear to represent an appropriate proxy for the changing television environment in the post-1980 period, including the proliferation of the soft news media.

The dependent variable for this analysis is an ordinal and symmetric scale, running from 0 to 3 (depending on the number of problems mentioned by a given respondent). (Hence, ordered logit is an appropriate estimator.) In order to capture the distinct impact of the changing television environment on different types of individuals, I interact "network ratings"—which vary only from year to year—with individual-level data on respondents' level of political information (once again, as estimated by the interviewer).

As controls, I include a series of variables addressing the respondent's socioeconomic status, interest in politics, political partisanship, media consumption habits, and political disaffection. (The key control variables are defined in appendix 1 of this chapter.) My analysis begins in 1968—the first year in which all of the key variables, including political information, were available—and includes eleven of the fifteen biennial NES surveys through 1996. I exclude the other four surveys (1970, 1974, 1986 and 1994) because they omit at least one important independent variable. The results from four ordered logit analyses employing this dependent variable are presented in models 1–4, in table 5.A4, in appendix 4.

At figure 5.8, I transform the ordered logit coefficients into probabilities of

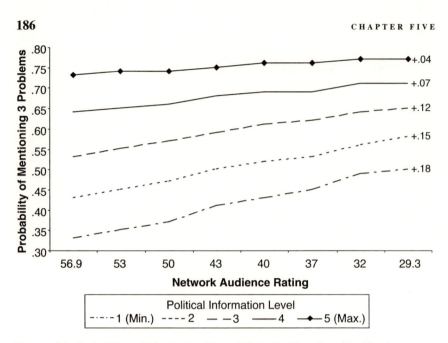

FIGURE 5.8. Probability of Mentioning Three "Major Problems" as Combined
Prime-Time Network Audience Rating Varies, 1966–1998

mentioning three major problems—the category that has changed the most over
time.[50] The probabilities are separately plotted for individuals at each level of
political information, as the major networks' combined average prime time audience rating declined from 56.9 in 1966 to 29.3 in 1998, with all other causal
variables held constant at their mean values.[51]

Several significant patterns are evident. First, not surprisingly, by comparing
the y intercepts for the various trend lines, we can see that respondents at the
highest level of political information are more likely to mention three major
problems ($p < .001$). For instance, in 1966, a respondent at the lowest level of
political information was 40 percentage points *less* likely to mention three major problems than a respondent at the highest level of political information (33
vs. 73 percent). By 1998, the corresponding difference had fallen to 26 percentage points (51 vs. 77 percent). And the over-time shrinkage in this differential
is itself significant at the .001 level.

Of greater interest are the trends in the propensity of those polled to mention
three major problems across differing categories of respondents. In fact, we can
see that the over-time decline in network audience ratings has had a substantial
effect on politically inattentive respondents. For the least politically informed
respondents, as network audience ratings fall from their highest to lowest
levels, the probability of mentioning three major problems rises from 33 to 51
percent, an 18-percentage-point increase ($p < .01$). The magnitude of the
change, in turn, declines in a stepwise fashion as political information increases
until, for respondents at the highest level of political information, falling net-

work prime-time ratings are associated with a modest and statistically insignificant increase of 4 percentage points (from 73 to 77 percent) in the probability of mentioning three major problems.[52] These results suggest that the changing television environment has had no significant impact upon the most politically informed respondents.

The explosion of television viewing options, beginning in the 1980s, appears primarily to have influenced the least politically informed individuals. Their inadvertent exposure to substantive political information—which, I argue, is attributable to the rise of the soft news media as an alternative source of information about select dramatic political issues—appears to have given them an awareness of the nation's problems they did not formerly possess.

The soft news media, in turn, are a more important source of political information for individuals who are relatively uninterested in or not knowledgeable about politics, and who thus receive such information largely as an incidental by-product of seeking entertainment. In contrast, politically knowledgeable individuals are likely to turn to more traditional sources of political information, such as newspapers, weekly newsmagazines, or network TV newscasts. Since these sources were just as available in 1998 as in 1966, it is not surprising that among politically knowledgeable respondents, attentiveness to major problems increased far more modestly than among their less-informed counterparts. Indeed, Hypothesis 9 predicts just such a pattern.

Do Individual TV Viewing Habits Influence Attentiveness to Major National Problems?

Thus far, I have measured the influence of media consumption patterns through an aggregate indicator, measuring the major networks' prime-time audience ratings. This variable is appropriate for investigating the influence of aggregate trends on individual consumers. Yet since numerous factors other than television also changed between 1966 and 1998, it is not possible to exclude a virtually infinite list of alternative potential explanations for the trends I have described. Hence, while this evidence is suggestive, it is, once again, by no means definitive. Stronger evidence would require individual-level data on media consumption habits. While the NES has not included any general media consumption variables on a regular basis throughout the time period I am investigating, one television-consumption variable is included in each survey. This question asks respondents whether they have seen any programs about the political campaigns on television. On its face, particularly given my argument that the soft news media tend to steer clear of partisan politics, this would seem a particularly poor question to employ as an indicator of exposure to politics via the *soft* news media. Indeed, it is *positively* correlated with the political information scale at .24. Yet, as we shall see, properly controlled, this variable can be rendered appropriate for testing the effects of consuming nontraditional informational programming.

For the NES television variable to be a useful indicator, it would have to be a valid measure of respondents' overall exposure to television. At first glance, this seems unlikely. In fact, as shown in model 2 at table 5.A4, in a bivariate regression, watching campaign news on TV is strongly *positively* related to education ($p < .001$). This is precisely the opposite relationship between total daily hours of television viewing and education as that found by Baum and Kernell (1999). They report that in the 1996 General Social Survey (GSS), education is strongly *inversely* related to average daily hours of television viewing; GSS respondents with less than a ninth-grade education averaged two more hours per day of television viewing than their college-educated counterparts (4.2 versus 2.2 hours per day). The relatively strong positive relationship between education and political information in the NES surveys included in my analyses ($r = .49$) suggests that the NES television variable *cannot* be reasonably employed as an indicator of general exposure to nonpolitical television.

There remains, however, a means of employing the campaign television indicator for this very purpose. When additional controls are included for interest in government and public affairs, interest in political campaigns, and whether or not the respondent read news about the campaign in a newspaper, the picture changes dramatically. With these controls included (see model 3 at table 5.A4), the coefficient on "Watch campaign on TV" flips signs, becoming negative and significant ($p < .001$). This suggests that once a viewer's intrinsic interest in watching news about politics is controlled, the NES television variable *is* a valid indicator of general frequency of watching television. This makes intuitive sense, as the more television an individual watches, the more likely she is to encounter a program about the campaign, regardless of her intent to do so.

Given that the appropriately controlled NES television variable appears to be a reasonably valid indicator of frequency of overall television viewing, I conduct a second set of analyses, interacting this new indicator with political information and network audience ratings. My hypothesis is simply that if the changing television environment is responsible for the increased number of mentions of major problems identified above, then we should observe a stronger trend toward mentioning more major problems among respondents who watch more television. Indeed, whatever portion of the overall trend that persists among individuals who claim *not* to have encountered any news about the political campaigns on television presumably represents the portion of the overall trend *not* attributable to exposure to either soft or hard news programming. (The results of these analysis are shown in model 4 of table 5.A4.)

In table 5.2, I transform the key coefficients into probabilities of mentioning three major problems among respondents who watch relatively *more* television and those who watch relatively *less* television, as political information and network prime-time audience ratings vary. Several trends are apparent in table 5.2. First, comparing the 1966 and 1998 rows for low-information respondents, we see that, in 1998, the difference between *low-frequency* TV watchers and *high-frequency* TV watchers is more than double that of 1966. This suggests that among the least politically informed respondents, watching television is more strongly associated in 1998 than in 1966 with mentioning a greater number

TABLE 5.2. Probability of Mentioning Three Major Problems, as Television Viewing, Network Prime Time Audience Rating, and Political Information Vary, 1966–1998

	Probability of Mentioning Three Problems		
Network Ratings	Non-TV Watchers	TV Watchers	Difference
Lowest Political Information			
56.9 (1966)	.28	.34	.06
29.3 (1998)	.40	.54	.14
Difference	.12*	.20*	
Highest Political Information			
56.9 (1966)	.75	.73	− .02
29.3 (1998)	.78	.76	− .02
Difference	.03	.03	

*$p < .01$

of major problems. Second, and more important for the theory, the trend among low-information respondents is nearly twice as strong among television watchers as among nonwatchers. Low-information *non*-TV watchers are 12 percentage points more likely in 1998 to mention three major problems, relative to 1966. In contrast, their frequent-TV-watching counterparts are 20 percentage points more likely to mention three problems. This represents a 67 percent differential between frequent and infrequent TV viewers.

Third, each of these relationships is far weaker, and statistically insignificant, among highly politically informed respondents. In fact, among this latter group, frequent TV watchers are slightly *less* likely to mention three problems than their less-frequent TV watching counterparts. This further suggests that, net of interest in politics and political campaigns, the NES television variable does indeed capture exposure to nonpolitical television programming. These data clearly suggest that the changing nature and role of television in American society, including nonpolitical television, have had a significant effect on politically inattentive Americans' awareness of major national problems. Indeed, a substantial portion of the overall trend toward increased attentiveness to major national problems among low-information respondents appears attributable to changes in the television environment. Once again, while this is not definitive evidence, it does represent relatively more direct evidence in support of the theory, including Hypothesis 9, than the prior, aggregate trend analysis.

Finally, recall that for several statistical investigations in chapter 4, I employed respondents' education level as an indicator of political engagement. (In that context, education was the best available indicator.) In order to retain consistency between my cross-sectional and time-series analyses, I retested *each* of the statistical models reported in this section, this time employing education in place of political information as an indicator of political engagement. The results of these latter analyses were strikingly similar to those reported above, replicating *every aspect* of my results from models employing political information as an indicator of political engagement. In order, however, to avoid further extending this already lengthy discussion, I do not report the results from these latter models. (These results are available from the author upon request.)

Deconstructing the Trend: Have the Types *of Problems Mentioned by Respondents Changed over Time?*

In chapter 4, I presented some evidence that low-education soft news consumers were relatively *more* likely to mention problems pertaining to the types of issues presented in the soft news media, both foreign and domestic, and *less* likely to mention issues pertaining to the state of the economy, compared to their better-educated or non-soft-news-consuming counterparts. My final investigation in this chapter extends that analysis by looking at over-time trends in the *types* of problems mentioned by NES respondents from 1960 to 1998, a period in which, as we have seen, the major networks' prime time audience ratings fell by nearly half. After all, while the prior analysis showed distinct trends in the *number* of major problems mentioned by NES respondents, particularly those at low levels of political information, it did not address the *substance* of those mentions. Have politically inattentive Americans grown more likely to mention *any* type of problem? Or is this trend limited to those types of issues that tend to be covered most consistently by the soft news media? If the latter were true, this would represent important additional evidence in support of the theory. In fact, the theory developed in chapter 2 holds fairly clear implications for trends in the particular *types* of problems likely to be mentioned by different groups of NES respondents. This section tests two such implications, in the form of corollaries to my ninth and tenth hypotheses:

> $H_{5.5}$ Survey respondents should be *increasingly* disproportionately likely, over time, to emphasize those political topics and themes most prevalent in the soft news media. This effect should be strongest among the least politically engaged individuals, who are least likely to seek out alternative news sources, and should weaken as political engagement increases.

> $H_{5.6}$ Survey respondents should be *less* likely, over time, to emphasize those political topics and themes that tend *not* to be covered in the soft news media. This effect should be strongest among the least politically engaged individuals, and should weaken as political engagement increases.

My data for this investigation is drawn from the NES Cumulative Data File (CDF), which includes select NES variables from 1948 to 2000. I employ the CDF, rather than the data from the prior analyses that I compiled from individual NES surveys, primarily because the present analysis requires categorization of different *types* of problems. The CDF includes information only for respondents' answers regarding the single most important problem facing the nation, which, while appropriate for assessing the different *categories* of responses, obviously cannot be employed for tallying the *number* of mentions offered by respondents. By using the CDF, rather than categorizing problems according to my own judgment, I am also able to rely on an unbiased (or at least *differently* biased) third party—the NES coders—who grouped all responses into the following ten categories: (1) agricultural; (2) economics, business, consumer issues; (3) foreign affairs and national defense; (4) government functioning, except "the economy"; (5) labor issues, except unemployment; (6) natural resources; (7) public order; (8) racial problems; (9) social welfare; and (10) other problems, including campaign-specific issues. This reduces, though it does not completely eliminate, the subjectivity of my analysis. My investigation includes every NES survey between 1960 and 1998, except 1962, when the "most important problem" question was unavailable.[53]

In order to further account for fluctuations in domestic and international circumstances that might influence respondents propensities to mention particular types of problems, in addition to a set of standard socioeconomic and political control variables, (all of which are coded identically as in the previous analyses), I also control for the state of the U.S. economy and the international security environment. For the former, I include variables measuring the annualized changes in the consumer price index (i.e., inflation) and unemployment rate, as well as the annual average score of the University of Michigan's Index of Consumer Confidence. For the latter, I include variables measuring the number of U.S. uses of military force per year, as well as whether or not the United States engaged in a militarized dispute with the Soviet Union in a given year.[54]

Finally, to determine whether, consistent with the theory, the trends differ systematically across different groups of respondents, I interact the network ratings variable with respondents' education level. I employ education, rather than political information, for the present analysis, in order to add two additional survey years (1960 and 1964) for which the latter variable was unavailable. (Recall that my results reported in the prior section are nearly perfectly replicated when education is substituted for political information.)

I employ three distinct dependent variables, each based on the different categories of problems named by respondents as the most important problem facing the nation at the time of a given NES survey. The two categories of problems that seem most likely to be covered by the soft news media are: (1) foreign affairs and national defense and (2) public order. The first category is the primary subject of this book, and so requires little explanation here. The second, according to the CDF codebook, consists of the following types of problems: "crime, drugs, civil liberties and non-racial civil rights, women's rights, abortion rights, gun control, family/social/religious/moral 'decay,' church and state, etc." While not *all* of these issues seem likely to be of interest to soft news outlets, several (e.g., crime and family/social/religious/moral "decay") are particularly suitable for cheap framing and piggybacking. Hence, for my first analysis, I combine these two categories into a dummy variable ("Soft problems"),

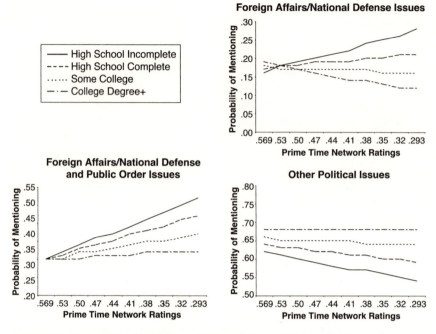

FIGURE 5.9. Probability of Mentioning Different Types of "Major Problems," as Education and Prime-Time Network Audience Ratings Vary

coded 1 if a respondent mentions problems pertaining to either foreign affairs/ national defense or public order, and 0 otherwise. The second dummy then measures the residual category, representing all problems that are relatively *less* likely to appear in the soft news media ("Hard problems"). The third dependent variable narrows my focus to foreign affairs/national defense issues, the primary topic of this book. The results from logit analyses of all three dependent variables are shown in models 5–7 in table 5.A4 (in appendix 4).

Figure 5.9 presents three graphics, in which I separately translate the key coefficients from each model into probabilities of mentioning different types of problems among respondents in four education groups, as the major networks' prime-time audience ratings drop from 56.9 in 1966 to 29.3 in 1998.[55]

The results strongly support my hypotheses. Beginning with foreign affairs/ defense and public order issues, the results in the lower-left-hand quadrant of figure 5.9 show that, consistent with Hypothesis 5.5, the least-educated NES respondents were most likely to mention these types of problems when network prime time ratings were at their lowest level (in 1998). Among this group, as network prime time audience ratings move from their highest to lowest levels, the probability that respondents will mention a problem pertaining to either foreign affairs/national defense or public order increases by 17 percentage points (from .30 to .47). This difference is significant at the .01 level. Also consistent with Hypothesis 5.5, the effects of declining network audience ratings weaken in a stepwise fashion as respondents' education level rises. Among high school graduates, those with some college education, and college graduates, the corresponding percentage point increases are 12 (from .30 to .42, $p < .01$), 7 (from .30 to .37, $p < .01$), and 2 (from .30 to .32, insig.), respectively.

The graphic in the top-right-hand quadrant of figure 5.9 narrows our focus to foreign affairs/national defense issues. Comparing this with the "soft problems" graph reveals that many, though not all, of the effects described above are attributable to respondents' attitudes regarding foreign affairs/national defense, rather than public order. This may be due to the inclusion in the public order category of several issue areas unlikely to appeal to the soft news media. Whatever the reason, among the least-educated respondents, as network prime time ratings decline, the probability they will mention a foreign affairs/national defense issue increases by 12 percentage points (from .16 to .28, $p < .01$). As before, the effects of declining network ratings weaken as respondents move up the education ladder. In this instance, among high school graduates, the corresponding increase is a far smaller 4 percentage points (from .17 to .21, $p < .01$). And among respondents with some college or a college degree, the pattern inverts, with falling network ratings associated with *decreases* in the probability they will mention a foreign affairs/national defense issue of 2 (from .18 to .16, insig.) and 7 (from .19 to .12, $p < .01$) percentage points, respectively.

These latter results are particularly striking. Politically inattentive Americans were, in these data, *most* attentive to foreign affairs problems in the 1990s, the first decade of the post–Cold War era. Recall from chapter 2 (fig. 2.3) that Americans, in the aggregate, were *less* concerned with foreign affairs in the 1990s than at any time since World War II. In fact, while it is difficult to compare these results with the annualized aggregate trend presented in figure 2.3, the data analyzed in this chapter appear to suggest that much of the aggregate decline in concern over foreign affairs since the 1950s and 1960s, when the big three networks dominated prime time, has taken place among college-educated Americans.[56] Not surprisingly, college-educated individuals—who also tend to be the most politically engaged members of the public—appear to have been more responsive than were their less-educated counterparts to the changing international environment following the end of the Cold War, and the corresponding decline in foreign affairs coverage by most traditional news outlets. Taken together, these results offer clear support for Hypothesis 5.5.

Turning, finally, to the sorts of problems that are unlikely, according to the theory, to receive much coverage in the soft news media, the results, shown in the lower-right-hand quadrant of figure 5.9, are consistent with Hypothesis 5.6. Among the least-educated respondents, as network audience shares fall from their highest to lowest levels, the probability of mentioning a traditional political issue declines by 7 percentage points (from .61 to .54, $p < .01$). Once again, this effect weakens in a stepwise fashion as respondents' education level rises. Among respondents with a high school diploma or some college education, the corresponding declines are 5 (from .64 to .59, $p < .01$) and 2 (from .66 to .64, insig.) percentage points, respectively. And, at least in these data, variations in network ratings have no effect whatsoever on respondents with a college or graduate degree. These results suggest that primarily for less-educated respondents, foreign affairs/national defense and public order issues have, to at least some extent, crowded out other types of political issues. In contrast, no such crowding out effect, or any other effect for that matter, emerges among highly educated respondents, presumably because these latter individuals possess alternative sources of news and information.

Interestingly, the different education groups have changed dramatically over time in terms of their relative propensities to mention the types of issues most likely to be covered by the soft news media. While the likelihood of mentioning these types of problems was only weakly related to education in the 1960s and 1970s, when network ratings were at their zenith, by 1998, when network ratings were at their lowest level, the *least*-educated respondents become *most* likely to mention such issues, and the *most*-educated respondents *least* likely. In the case of foreign affairs/national defense problems, when network ratings were at their highest level, the least-educated respondents were only 3 percentage points more likely their highly educated counterparts to mention a foreign affairs/national defense problem. In contrast, when network ratings reached their low point (in 1998), the gap expanded to 16 percentage points. Once again, this differential, though not definitively linked to the soft news media, is nonetheless precisely the type of pattern one would anticipate if exposure to soft news outlets was influencing the responses of the least-educated respondents, but not their better-educated counterparts. Indeed, taken together, the results presented in this section, while still somewhat circumstantial, do represent additional evidence in support of the theory.

CONCLUSION

My investigation of opinionation during three major U.S. military conflicts (Korea, Vietnam, and the Persian Gulf), as well as during a variety of other foreign crises from the 1940s through the 1990s; my analysis of presidential approval polls during U.S. major uses of force between 1953 and 1998; and my comparison of the Camp David, Oslo and Dayton Accords, all indicate that the American people have grown increasingly attentive to wars and other foreign military crises over time. Moreover, consistent with the theory, most of this increase can be traced to the least politically informed and educated segments of the population, the very individuals who are most likely to consume large amounts of soft news. This suggests that future foreign crises (and other dramatic crisis issues) will likely attract substantially broader, if not necessarily deeper, public attentiveness than similar crises in prior decades.

Moreover, my study of variations in attentiveness to major problems facing the nation between 1966 and 1998 provided additional evidence in support of the theory; a clear trend emerged toward greater attentiveness to major problems. And this trend appears directly related to individual variations in media consumption habits and aggregate changes in the television environment. Once again, the largest changes over time took place among the least politically informed respondents.

The results from my final analysis—investigating trends in the *types* of problems mentioned by NES respondents in open-ended questions—found that as network dominance of the television airwaves receded, the least-educated respondents, but not their better-educated counterparts, grew increasingly likely to mention those types of issues most likely to be covered by the soft news media, but not other issues of the type that are typically covered primarily by traditional news outlets. Since, as noted, the least politically engaged respondents are the predominant consumers of soft news, this trend is precisely what one would anticipate if the rise of the soft news media were influencing the types of issues to which politically uninterested Americans were attuned.

The theory also predicts that trends toward increased public attentiveness to foreign crises should not spill over to less dramatic, or more partisan, political issues, like the state of the economy. And in fact, the data confirmed this hypothesis (Hypothesis 10), as well as my corollaries to Hypotheses 9 and 10, in all respects. Taken together, my findings suggest the need for a new avenue of research into the relationship between changes in television coverage of foreign policy and other dramatic political issues and public opinion regarding such issues. While the American people may or may not be growing wiser, they do appear to be growing more attentive.

APPENDIX 1: DATA SOURCES AND VARIABLE DEFINITIONS

1952–2000 NES, Gallup and CBS/New York Times Variables

DATA SOURCES

The Persian Gulf War–era data are drawn from a 1990–91 American National Election Study (NES) Panel Study focused on the Gulf War, the 1992 NES survey, from on-line Lexis-Nexis retrieval of Gallup and Roper surveys and from Mueller 1994. Vietnam War–era survey data were collected through on-line Lexis-Nexis retrieval, from Mueller 1973, and from the 1966, 1968, 1970, and 1972 NES surveys. Korean War–era data are drawn from the 1952 NES survey and from Mueller 1973.

DEPENDENT VARIABLES

1. Questions: *Korean War:* "Do you think the United States made a mistake in going into the war in Korea, or not?" *Vietnam War:* "In view of the developments since we entered the fighting in Vietnam, do you think the U.S. made a mistake sending troops to fight in Vietnam?" *Persian Gulf War:* "Do you think the United States made a mistake in [getting involved in the war in/ sending troops to fight against] Iraq, or not?" Coding: 1 = "don't know" or "no opinion," 0 = all others.

2. Questions: (A) "Do you approve or disapprove of the way President [Johnson/Nixon/Bush] is handling the situation in [Vietnam/the Persian Gulf]?" and (B) "Do you think we did the right thing in [getting into the fighting in Vietnam or Korea/sending U.S. military forces to the Persian Gulf] or should we have stayed out?" Coding: 1 = "no opinion" or "don't know," 0 = all others.

3. Questions: *Vietnam War*: "How much attention have you been paying to what is going on in Vietnam: A good deal, some, or not much?" *Persian Gulf War*: "How much attention did you pay to news about the war in the Persian Gulf—a great deal, quite a bit, some, very little, or none?" Coding: 0 = some, not much, very little, or none; 1 = a great deal, quite a bit, or a good deal.

INDEPENDENT VARIABLES

(Note: standard demographic variables are not defined herein. It is necessary, however, to point out two variations in coding of NES demographic variables at different points in time. First, the 1952 *education* variable has nine categories. All other years include fifteen categories. Throughout this chapter, wherever individual years (or wars) are estimated separately, I preserve the full range of the variable. For any analysis in which 1952 and other years are pooled, I collapse the variable to its lowest common denominator across all surveys. (Varying the number of education categories has no substantive effect on the key causal variables.) Second, *family income* includes different numbers of categories in different years. Wherever the years are estimated separately, I preserve the full range of the variable. As with education, for any analysis in which multiple years are pooled, I collapse family income to its lowest common denominator across all surveys included in the model. (Like education, varying the number of income categories has virtually zero effect on the key causal variables.)

> *Importance of War*: "How important is this issue [Vietnam War/Persian Gulf War] to you personally . . . extremely important, very (important), somewhat (important), or not (important) at all? Coding: Responses of "extremely" or "very" were coded 1, while responses of "somewhat" or "not at all" were coded 0. (Note: the word *personally* was included in 1991, but not in 1970).
>
> *Follow Public Affairs*: Question: "Some people seem to follow what's going on in government and public affairs most of the time, whether there's an election going on or not. Others aren't that interested. Would you say you follow what's going on in government and public affairs most of the time, some of the time, only now and then, or hardly at all?" Coding: 1 = hardly at all, 2 = only now and then, 3 = some of the time, 4 = most of the time.
>
> *Political Information*: Interviewer's assessment of respondent's "general level of information about politics and public affairs." Coding: 1 = very low, 2 = fairly low, 3 = average, 4 = fairly high, 5 = very high. This

question was not available in 1952. A 5-point political awareness scale for 1952 was constructed from twelve NES variables. Question wording and coding for each variable employed in the 1952 scale is presented at the end of this appendix.

Attention to Political Campaigns: "Some people don't pay much attention to political campaigns. How about you? Would you say that you were very much interested, somewhat interested, or not much interested in following the political campaigns so far this year?" Coding: 0 = not much interested, 1 = somewhat interested, 2 = very much interested.

Internal Efficacy = Question: "Please tell me how much you agree or disagree with these statements. . . . Sometimes politics and government seem so complicated that a person like me can't really understand what's going on." Coding: 1 = agree, 0.5 = don't know, 0 = disagree.

External Efficacy I = Question: "Please tell me how much you agree or disagree with this statement. . . . I don't think public officials care much what people like me think." Coding: 1 = agree, 0.5 = don't know, 0 = disagree.

External Efficacy II = Question: "Please tell me how much you agree or disagree with this statement. . . . People like me don't have any say about what the government does." Coding: 1 = agree, 0.5 = don't know, 0 = disagree.

Partisanship = 4-point scale estimating the *extent* of the respondent's partisanship. Coding: 0 = apolitical, 1 = Independent, 2 = Independent, lean Democratic or Independent, lean Republican, 3 = weak Democrat or weak Republican, and 4 = strong Democrat or strong Republican.

Trust in Government = Questions: Additive scale constructed from four questions: (1) "How much of the time do you think you can trust the government in Washington to do what is right?" (coded 1 = "just about always" or "most of the time," 0 = "only some of the time" or "never"); (2) "Would you say the government is pretty much run by a few big interests looking out for themselves or that it is run for the benefit of all the people?" (coded 1 = "run for the benefit of all," 0 = "run by a few big interests"); (3) "Do you think that people in the government waste a lot of the money we pay in taxes, waste some of it, or don't waste very much of it?" (coded 1 = "waste some" or "don't waste very much," 0 = "waste a lot"); and (4) "Do you think that quite a few of the people running the government are a little crooked, not very many are, or do you think hardly any of them are crooked at all?" (coded 1 = "not very many are crooked" or "hardly any are crooked," 0 = "quite a few are crooked"). Consistent with Miller's (1974) coding conventions, respondents who answered "don't know" to one of the four questions were assigned the mean level of "trust" from the other three questions. Those responding "don't know" on more than one of the questions were excluded.

Watched Campaign on TV = Dummy variable, coded 1 if respondent saw
   any stories on TV about the election campaign.
Read about Campaign in Newspaper = Dummy variable, coded 1 if
   respondent read any stories about the election campaign in a newspaper.
Read Newspaper = Number of days per week respondent reads a
   newspaper.
Network TV News = Number of days per week respondent watches
   national network TV news.
Local TV News = Number of days per week respondent watches local TV
   news.

QUESTIONS EMPLOYED TO CONSTRUCT POLITICAL INFORMATION SCALE
FROM 1952 NES SURVEY

1. *VAR 520017* "Do you think there are any important differences between
what the Democratic and Republican parties stand for, or do you think they
are about the same." Coding: 1 = very important differences, many
differences, big differences, important differences, some differences, minor
differences or no differences; 0 = don't know.

2. *VAR 520034* "How about the candidates for vice president? Aside from
their parties, do you have any strong opinions about either of them." Coding:
1 = yes—mentions Sparkman's names, yes—mentions Nixon's name, yes—
mentions both names, no—mentions Sparkman's name, no—mentions
Nixon's name, no—mentions both names; 0 = yes—mentions neither name,
no—mentions neither name, or don't know.

3. *VAR 520041* "Generally speaking, would you say that you personally
care a good deal which party wins the presidential election this fall or that
you don't care very much which party wins." Coding: 1 = care very much,
care pretty much, pro-con/depends, or care a little/don't care very much;
0 = don't care at all or don't know.

4. *VAR 520042* "How about state and local elections. When you have state
and local elections around here would you say that you care a good deal who
wins or that you don't care very much who wins." Coding: 1 = care very
much, care pretty much, pro-con/depends or care a little/don't care very much;
0 = don't care at all or don't know. (First answer addressed *state* elections.)

5. *VAR 520043* Second answer to question #4 separately addressed *local*
elections.

6. *VAR 520046* "Now, how do you think the two parties feel about this
question [party differences on social welfare]—do you think there are any
differences between the Democratic and Republican parties on this issue, or
would you say they feel the same." Coding: 1 = Democrats will do more
than Republicans, Democrats will do a lot more than Republicans, or pro-con/
same; 0 = Democrats will do less than Republicans, Democrats will do a lot
less than Republicans, or don't know.

7. *VAR 520049* "Have you heard anything about the Taft-Hartley Law."
Coding: 1 = yes, 0 = no or don't know.

8. *VAR 520052* "Some people think that since the end of the last world war this country has gone too far in concerning itself with problems in other parts of the world. How do you feel about this? Now how do you think the two parties feel about this question—do you think there are any differences between the Democratic and Republican parties on this issue, or would you say they feel the same." Coding: 1 = Democrats will do more than Republicans, Democrats will do a lot more than Republicans, or pro-con/same; 0 = Democrats will do less than Republicans, Democrats will do a lot less than Republicans, or don't know.

9. *VAR 520097* "Now, how about working-class people—Do you think they will vote mostly Republican, mostly Democratic, or do you think they will be about evenly split." Coding: 1 = Democratic or split, 0 = Republican or don't know.

10. *VAR 520098* "Now, how about [perceived Negro vote]—Do you think they will vote mostly Republican, mostly Democratic, or do you think they will be about evenly split?" Coding: 1 = Democratic or split, 0 = Republican or don't know.

11. *VAR 520100* "Now, how about [perceived big business vote]—Do you think they will vote mostly Republican, mostly Democratic, or do you think they will be about evenly split?" Coding: 1 = Democratic or split, 0 = Republican or don't know.

12. *VAR 520101* "Now, how about [perceived labor union vote]—Do you think they will vote mostly Republican, mostly Democratic, or do you think they will be about evenly split?" Coding: 1 = Democratic or split, 0 = Republican or don't know.

(Responses were collapsed into a 5-point scale, as follows: 0–1 correct response = 1; 2–4 correct responses = 2; 5–8 correct responses = 3; 9–10 correct responses = 4; 11–12 correct responses = 5. The alpha reliability score for the twelve variables employed in the scale is .74, indicating that this is a fairly reliable scale.)

Control Variables for Analysis of Major U.S. Uses of Force, 1953–1998

Cold War: Dummy variable coded 1 prior to 1989 and 0 from 1989 to 1998.[57]

Vietnam Syndrome: Dummy variable coded 1 between 1974 and 1990.[58]

Divided Government: Following Ostrom and Simon (1985), this variable is coded 0 during periods of unified government, 1 when a single house of Congress is controlled by the opposition party, and 2 when both houses of Congress are controlled by the opposition.

New President: Dummy variable, coded 1 for the first three months after a new president assumes office.

Second Administration: Dummy variable coded 1 during a president's second term in office, when the president cannot run for reelection.

Lame Duck: Dummy variable coded 1 during a president's final two years in office in a second administration, following the final midterm election of the president's tenure.

Months to Next Election: counts the number of months until the next presidential election, during election years.[59]

Scandal: Dummy variable, coded 1 during the primary periods of the Watergate (1974), Iran-Contra (1987), and Monica Lewinsky (1998) scandals.

Polls per Year: Counts the number of presidential approval polls conducted by Gallup each year.[60]

Misery Index: Following Ostrom and Simon (1985), I combine the U.S. unemployment and inflation rates into an index of economic misery.[61]

Republican President: Dummy variable, coded 1 when a Republican occupies the White House.[62]

Prominence of Foreign Policy: Change in the annualized average percentage of the public mentioning a foreign policy issue when asked by Gallup to name the most important problem facing the nation between the last poll conducted prior to a given use of force and the first poll conducted following the use of force.[63]

APPENDIX 2: TESTING FOR FLOOR AND CEILING EFFECTS

To determine whether the relationships identified in figure 5.1 might be an artifact of a ceiling effect, as the probability of paying attention to the Gulf War approached 100 percent, I conducted two tests. The first is a likelihood ratio test, intended to determine whether an interaction term—interacting "Importance of war" and a war dummy (coded $0 =$ Vietnam and $1 =$ Persian Gulf)—contributes to the model. The results indicate that the interaction term is indeed significant ($p < .05$). And the likelihood ratio test confirmed that the interaction was a statistically significant contributor to the model ($p < .01$). Second, as shown in figure 5.A1, the linear link functions, based on the logit coefficients, indicate that the curves for the two wars are not parallel (that is, they converge). If, in contrast, the relationships were entirely an artifact of a ceiling effect, the two curves should be parallel.

The relationships in figure 5.2, in turn, suggest the possibility that the opposite problem, a floor effect, might be present in that analysis, as the probability of answering "don't know" to the Gulf War question approaches zero. I therefore conducted the same two tests as described above. I first interacted political information with a categorical variable, coded $0 =$ Korea, $1 =$ Vietnam, and $2 =$ Persian Gulf. I then ran a logit model, including all surveys from all three wars, including all controls plus the interaction term. The results indicate, once again, that the interaction term is statistically significant ($p < .01$). And, as before, the likelihood ratio test confirmed that the interaction was a significant

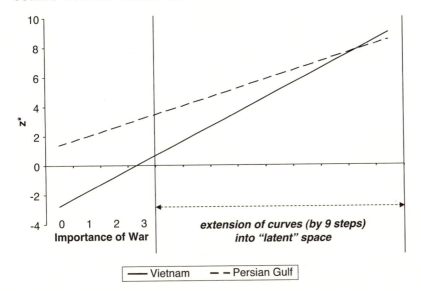

FIGURE 5.A1. Linear Link Function Test of Interaction between Personal Importance of War and the Two Wars

NOTE: Intersecting lines indicate relationships are *not* artifact of ceiling effect.

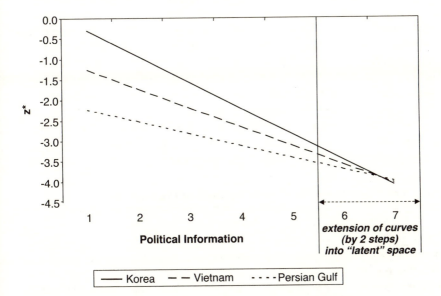

FIGURE 5.A2. Linear Link Function Test of Interaction between Political Information and the Three Wars

NOTE: intersecting lines indicate relationships are *not* artifact of floor effect.

contributor to the model ($p < .01$). Moreover, as shown in figure 5.A2, the linear link functions, based on the logit coefficients, indicate that the curves for the rthree wars are not parallel (as before, they converge). Combined, these results suggest that it is unlikely that the differences shown in figures 5.1 and 5.2 are artifacts of either floor or ceiling effects.

APPENDIX 3. COMPARING KOREA, VIETNAM, AND THE PERSIAN GULF WAR

Survey response rates can be sensitive to variations in question wording, survey organization, and technique. In chapter 2, I noted that across a large number of nearly identical surveys, many more Americans were willing to express an opinion about the Persian Gulf War than about Vietnam. In figure 2.1, of the eighty-six Vietnam-era polls, twenty-six were conducted by telephone for the Nixon administration by the Opinion Research Group (ORG). The others were conducted in person by Gallup. In contrast, all Persian Gulf Crisis/War polls were Gallup telephone surveys.

Typically, response rates are higher for in-person surveys (Groves and Kahn 1979). Hence, while such differences could account for some of the variation across the wars, it seems improbable that they could account for the consistently *lower* "don't know" rates throughout the Persian Gulf polls. Also, a series of tests (not shown) revealed no statistically significant difference in "don't know" rates between the Nixon era Gallup and ORG surveys. At the same time, a statistically significant ($p < .001$) secular *downward* trend in "don't know" rates between 1965 and 1973 (totaling about 12 percentage points), even as Vietnam grew increasingly controversial, suggests that *lower* "don't know" rates during the Gulf Crisis cannot be attributed to Vietnam-era controversy.[64] The secular downward trend also suggests that Americans did not "tune out" from Vietnam as it became increasingly controversial (and as television coverage intensified, particularly in the aftermath of the Tet Offensive, which began in late January 1968). With respect to the Gulf Crisis, table 5.A1 strongly sug-

TABLE 5.A1. "Don't Know" Rates during Persian Gulf Crisis and War

Survey Organization	Average % "Don't Know"	# of Polls	Period
Gallup (see fig. 1.1)	7.5	39	8/90–9/91
CBS/*New York Times*, CBS	7.5	16	8/90–2/91
ABC/*Washington Post*, ABC	5.5	15	9/90–1/91
Time/CNN	8.3	8	9/90–11/90
Los Angeles Times	4.0	7	8/90–2/91
Black	8.5	4	8/90–12/90
ABC	3.0	4	3/91–9/91

Source: Mueller 1994, 193–97.

gests that the gap in "don't know" rates shown in figure 2.1 is not an artifact of differences in survey organizations. Across all Persian Gulf surveys, and survey organizations, "don't know" rates are never more than 1 percentage point higher than the overall Gallup average. Indeed, the only outliers, the *Los Angeles Times* and ABC polls, registered *lower* average "don't know" rates than Gallup.[65]

APPENDIX 4. STATISTICAL TABLES

TABLE 5.A2. Logit Analyses of Public Attentiveness to Korea, Vietnam, and Persian Gulf Wars

	Coef. (Std. Err.)				
	Vietnam vs. Gulf Model 1	Korea (1952)[a] Model 2	Vietnam (1968–72) Model 3	Iraq (1990–91) Model 4	Iraq (1990–91) Model 5
Media Consumption					
No TV news	—	—	—	—	.437 (.639)
Read newspaper (days per week)	—	—	—	—	.031 (.035)*
SES/Demographics					
Age	.015 (.003)***	.006 (.006)	.012 (.003)***	.014 (.007)*	.064 (.033)*
Age^2	—	—	—	—	-.0008 (.0003)*
Education	-.026 (.024)	-.008 (.055)	.020 (.018)	-.044 (.045)	-.097 (.049)*
Family income	.031 (.016)^	-.097 (.065)	.045 (.044)	-.029 (.018)	.051 (.020)*
Male	.052 (.104)	-.415 (.203)*	-.463 (.092)***	-.313 (.258)	-.607 (.221)**
White	-.196 (.149)	—	—	—	.090 (.295)
Political Knowledge & Attitudes					
Importance of war	.983 (.116)***	—	—	—	.507 (.139)***
Political information[a]	—	-.466 (.136)***	-.413 (.045)***	-.350 (.139)**	.453 (.134)***
Follow public affairs	.457 (.054)***	—	—	—	-.559 (.121)***
Interest in campaigns	-.071 (.060)	—	—	—	—
Party identification	-.017 (.025)	-.048 (.048)	.006 (.021)	.000 (.073)	.057 (.054)
Partisanship	.045 (.042)	-.085 (.105)	.041 (.045)	-.302 (.136)*	-.113 (.110)

Political Efficacy									
Internal efficacy	−.158	(.120)	−.133	(.258)	.273	(.112)*	−.326	(.322)	.229	(.302)
External efficacy I	.223	(.112)*	—		—		—		−.264	(.245)
External efficacy II	−.001	(.113)	−.045	(.212)	.078	(.090)	.056	(.288)	.273	(.278)
Period Dummies										
1968 dummy	—		—		.765	(.106)***	—		—	
1970 dummy	—		—		.867	(.101)***	—		—	
Persian Gulf War	4.157	(.463)***	—		—		—		—	
Interaction Terms										
Persian Gulf War × importance of war	−.387	(.208)^	—		—		—		—	
Political information × no TV news	—		—		—		—		−.632	(.315)*
Constant	−4.243	(.506)***	.035	(.525)	−2.368	(.338)***	−.808	(.886)	1.523	(1.104)
Pseudo R^2	.25		.06		.07		.06		.15	
	(N = 2,496)		(N = 1,276)		(N = 5,432)		(N = 1,736)		(N = 1,247)	

Note: All models employ heteroscedasticity-consistent ("robust") standard errors.

a1952 political information variable is a 5-point scale derived from twelve political knowledge questions (see appendix 1 to this chapter).

^$p < .10$, *$p < .05$, **$p < .01$, ***$p < .001$

TABLE 5.A3. OLS Analysis of Effect of Using Military Force on Change in (logged) "No Opinion" Responses to Gallup's Presidential Approval Polls, 1953–1998

| | Coef. (Std. Err.) | | | |
	Total	Grade School	High School	College
Trend				
Date (in years)	−.0091 (.0015)***	−.0099 (.0024)***	−.0080 (.0017)***	−.0077 (.0024)***
Domestic Politics				
ln%Approve	−.178 (.041)***	−.342 (.062)***	−.262 (.049)***	−.173 (.058)***
ln%No opinion$_{t-1}$	−.546 (.041)***	−.831 (.048)***	−.703 (.043)***	−.765 (.044)***
Scandal	−.248 (.041)***	−.429 (.058)***	−.322 (.048)***	−.344 (.059)***
Months to next election	.016 (.004)***	.024 (.005)***	.018 (.004)***	.020 (.005)***
Second administration	−.078 (.026)**	−.090 (.041)*	−.082 (.029)**	−.140 (.040)**
Lame duck	.085 (.036)*	.108 (.058)^	.093 (.039)*	.099 (.058)*
Divided government	.059 (.016)***	.067 (.023)**	.063 (.018)***	.063 (.020)***
New president	.279 (.064)***	.274 (.065)***	.354 (.064)***	.482 (.091)***
Republican president	−.078 (.028)**	−.030 (.042)	−.065 (.033)*	−.143 (.040)*
Polls per year	−.000 (.002)	.007 (.002)**	−.001 (.002)	−.001 (.003)

Domestic Economy				
Misery index	−.020 (.006)**	−.047 (.010)***	−.035 (.008)***	−.026 (.011)***
Foreign Policy				
Use of force	.052 (.039)	.145 (.052)**	.035 (.041)	.058 (.071)
Prominence of foreign policy	−.002 (.001)^	−.002 (.002)	−.002 (.001)^	−.003 (.002)^
Cold War	.036 (.050)	.100 (.084)	.044 (.056)	.016 (.072)
Vietnam syndrome	.155 (.028)***	.205 (.047)***	.229 (.034)***	.252 (.043)***
Interaction Term				
Date × use of force	−.0033 (.0021)	−.0088 (.0032)**	−.0034 (.0026)	−.0031 (.0032)
Constant	2.052 (.241)***	1.923 (.171)***	1.605 (.133)***	1.456 (.155)***
R^2	.30	.33	.38	.32
	(N = 825)	(N = 820)	(N = 823)	(N = 824)

Note: All models employ heteroscedasticity-consistent ("robust") standard errors.

^$p < .10$, *$p < .05$, **$p < .01$, ***$p < .001$

TABLE 5.A4. Logit and Ordered Logit Analyses of Likelihood of Mentioning Major Problems as Education Level, Political Information, Television Viewing, and Network Audience Ratings Vary, 1960s–1990s

	Coef. (Std. Err.)						
	Major Problems Model 1	Education		Major Problems Model 4	"Soft" Problems Model 5	"Hard" Problems Model 6	Foreign Policy Problems Model 7
		Model 2	Model 3				
Network ratings	3.127 (.797)***	—	—	2.309 (.882)**	-3.330 (.504)***	1.463 (.495)**	-3.877 (.658)***
Political Knowledge & Attitudes							
Political information	.636 (.123)***	—	—	.675 (.126)***	—	—	—
Attention to public affairs	.166 (.023)***	—	.357 (.015)***	.165 (.023)***	.033 (.015)*	.085 (.015)***	.061 (.018)***
Interest in political campaigns	.079 (.031)**	—	.240 (.021)***	.080 (.031)**	—	—	—
Party identification	-.013 (.010)	—	—	-.012 (.010)	.048 (.007)***	-.045 (.007)***	.016 (.008)*
Partisanship	-.044 (.021)*	—	—	-.046 (.021)*	.021 (.015)	.012 (.014)	.003 (.017)
Political Trust & Efficacy							
External efficacy I	-.034 (.044)	—	—	-.034 (.044)	—	—	—

	(1)	(2)	(3)	(4)	(5)	(6)	(7)
External efficacy II	.121	—	—	.121	—	—	−.002
	(.044)**			(.044)**			(.001)*
Internal efficacy	−.032	—	—	−.030	—	—	−.788
	(.045)			(.045)			(.118)***
Trust in government	−.099	—	—	−.101	—	—	.033
	(.020)***			(.020)***			(.016)*
Media Consumption Habits							
Read campaign stories in newspaper	.141	—	.674	.139	—	—	−.034
	(.045)**		(.029)***	(.046)**			(.034)
Watch campaign news on TV	.166	.517	−.307	−.185	—	—	
	(.051)***	(.027)***	(.034)***	(.321)			
SES/Demographics							
Age	−.009	—	—	−.009	−.0009	−.001	61.691
	(.001)***			(.001)***	(.0009)	(.0009)	(1.965)***
Education	.141	—	—	.141	−.414	.305	60.582
	(.019)***			(.019)***	(.087)***	(.086)***	(11.061)***
Family income	.091	—	—	.091	.010	.039	
	(.019)***			(.019)***	(.014)	(.013)**	
Male	−.163	—	—	−.164	−.100	.138	
	(.038)***			(.038)***	(.028)***	(.028)***	
U.S. Economy							
Unemployment	—	—	—	—	24.392	−26.254	
					(1.461)***	(1.466)***	
Inflation	—	—	—	—	−10.346	28.071	
					(8.924)	(8.857)**	

TABLE 5.A4. *Continued*

	Coef. (Std. Err.)						
	Major Problems Model 1	Education		Major Problems Model 4	"Soft" Problems Model 5	"Hard" Problems Model 6	Foreign Policy Problems Model 7
		Model 2	Model 3				
Consumer confidence	—	—	—	—	.042 (.002)***	−.043 (.002)***	.064 (.003)***
International Environment							
Number of U.S. uses of force per year	—	—	—	—	.014 (.020)	−.101 (.020)***	.222 (.023)***
Dispute with USSR	—	—	—	—	.668 (.056)***	−.704 (.055)***	1.816 (.074)***
Interaction Terms							
Political information × network ratings	−.475 (.244)*	—	—	−.358 (.256)	—	—	—
Network ratings × watch campaign news on TV	—	—	—	1.342 (.703)*	—	—	—

	(1)	(2)	(3)	(4)	(5)	(6)	(7)
Political information × network ratings × watch campaign news on TV	—	—	—	−.242 (.099)**	—	—	—
Education × network ratings	—	—	—	—	.723 (.171)***	−.379 (.169)*	1.479 (.224)***
Constant 1	−.641 (.428)	−2.259 (.032)	−1.543 (.051)	−.818 (.465)	−3.179 (.313)***	3.483 (.308)***	−6.813 (.414)***
Constant 2	1.816 (.422)	−1.217 (.026)	−.332 (.043)	1.643 (.459)	—	—	—
Constant 3	3.276 (.424)	−.364 (.024)	.613 (.042)	3.105 (.460)	—	—	—
Constant 4	—	1.029 (.025)	2.177 (.045)	—	—	—	—
Constant 5	—	2.035 (.027)	3.266 (.047)	—	—	—	—
Pseudo R^2	.07	.01	.03	.07	.05	.06	.13
	(N = 12,085)	(N = 28,597)	(N = 21,452)	(N = 12,085)	(N = 25,330)	(N = 25,330)	(N = 25,330)

Note: All models employ heteroscedasticity-consistent ("robust") standard errors.
*$p < .05$, **$p < .01$, ***$p < .001$

Rallying Round the Water Cooler

IN DECEMBER 1998, as he had done repeatedly since the end of the Persian Gulf War, Saddam Hussein ceased cooperating with United Nations weapons inspectors. At the time, the U.S. House of Representatives was poised to impeach President Clinton for his conduct in the Monica Lewinsky scandal. Despite his domestic political problems, the president responded to Hussein's defiance by threatening to use military force if Iraq did not reverse course. Unlike the many prior postwar crises with Iraq, however, this time Saddam did not blink, and, on December 16, the United States and Great Britain launched a four-day aerial bombing campaign, termed Operation Desert Fox.

Despite accusations from some political opponents and media commentators that, like the Afghanistan-Sudan cruise missile strikes of the previous August, this was another "wag the dog" scenario (i.e., an attempt to distract the nation from the president's impending impeachment trial in the Senate), many political leaders, including Republicans, supported the president. For instance, John Kasich, Republican chairman of the House Budget Committee, stated: "He [President Clinton] has the message now that he'll have total support in order to take firm action" (quoted in Kahn 1998). And a series of polls conducted by Gallup found that the public also rallied behind the president.[1] In a survey conducted the day before the initiation of Desert Fox (on December 15) President Clinton's approval rating stood at 63 percent. Within four days, on December 19—the final day of Operation Desert Fox—the president's approval rating had spiked an impressive 10 percentage points, to 73 percent.[2]

More recently, a pair of Gallup polls conducted immediately prior to and in the aftermath of 9/11 showed public approval of President Bush's job performance spiking by fully 35 percentage points, from 51 to 86 percent, the largest "rally-round-the-flag" effect ever recorded.[3] These anecdotes suggest that even in an era of heightened public cynicism about politics (Nye, Zelikow, and King 1997; Dionne 1991; Rosenstone and Hansen 1993; A. Miller 1974) and increasingly critical coverage of presidents and their policies by the traditional news media (Groeling and Kernell 1998; Grossman and Kumar 1981; Patterson 1996; Brody 1991), the American public remains willing to rally around the flag in times of crisis.

This book is about the effects of a changed media environment on public opinion regarding foreign policy. The previous chapters have focused primarily on the influence of these changes on public attention to foreign crises. Yet these changes in the mass media, and resulting increases in public attentiveness, also seem likely to affect the propensity of the public to rally behind the president in times of crisis. Research has shown that the magnitude and duration of rallies depends in significant measure on the nature (i.e., projection of either biparti-sanship or elite criticism of the president) and extent (i.e., volume) of media coverage (Brody 1991, 1994; Lian and Oneal 1993; Oneal, Lian, and Joyner 1996; Zaller and Chiu 1999). If the rally phenomenon is indeed indexed, even in part, to the content of media coverage, then changes in the latter ought to produce observable effects on the former. Indeed, because the soft news media are causing more politically inattentive individuals to pay attention to news about foreign crises than in the past, it ought to cause them to be more attuned to potential rally events. This, I shall argue, ought, all else equal, to enhance their propensity to rally when such events arise. The present chapter explores the nature and extent of such effects.

DECONSTRUCTING THE RALLY PHENOMENON

Ever since Mueller (1970, 1973) introduced the phrase "rally round the flag" to the political science lexicon, it has remained a fixture in the literature on public opinion and foreign policy. Indeed, scholars have repeatedly confirmed the exis-tence of relatively short-lived spikes in presidential approval ratings that fre-quently accompany sudden, high-profile foreign policy events (Mueller 1970, 1973; Parker 1995; Brody and Shapiro 1989; Oneal, Lian, and Joyner 1996; Jordan and Page 1992; Lian and Oneal 1993; Brody 1991).

Despite the substantial body of research devoted to the rally phenomenon, relatively little attention has been paid to its constituent elements. That is, the vast majority of such studies aggregate public opinion into a single monolithic entity, which either does or does not rally.[4] Yet recent research has found that different constituencies typically respond differently to presidents' activities ac-cording to their own interests and attentiveness (Krause 1997; Sniderman, Brody, and Tetlock 1991; Fornier 1998; Baum and Kernell 2001). In previous chapters, I presented evidence that different segments of the public, with differ-ent degrees of intrinsic interest in politics or foreign affairs, tend to expose themselves to qualitatively distinct sources of news and information about poli-tics and foreign policy. As a result, while political sophisticates have always managed to learn about politics and foreign policy from whatever news sources were available (radio, newspaper, magazines, or television), their less politically engaged counterparts, many of whom previously remained largely aloof from politics, are now able to learn about at least some major political events through the soft news media. This suggests that, like the other phenomena I have inves-tigated, any effects of the changing television environment on the rally phenom-enon are likely to vary across different types of individuals. Hence, I disaggre-gate public opinion along two dimensions—one individual and the other environmental—that have proven fruitful in previous studies of heterogeneous public opinion: political sophistication and the president's partisan affiliation. As in their responses to most other presidential activities, I anticipate that dif-ferent groups of Americans most likely weigh various individual, contextual and situational factors differently in evaluating a presidential foreign policy initiative. In particular, I argue that environmental and personal circumstances, refracted through differences in media consumption, will weigh heavily in influencing whether and to what extent different types of individuals will rally. (See Baum 2002a for a more complete explication of the heterogeneous rally effect model, as well as derivation and testing of additional hypotheses.)

In order to understand why we should expect to find a heterogeneous rally effect, I employ two models of public opinion change, each suggesting a distinct set of hypotheses, based on either environmental (i.e., political) or personal (i.e., political sophistication) factors. The first, which emphasizes situational factors, focuses on the size of the population available to rally under differing political circumstances. This model, proposed by Kernell and Hibbs (1981), addresses the importance of threshold effects in explaining opinion change (on threshold effects, see also Edwards and Swenson 1997). That is, individuals who are closest to the point of ambivalence between approval and disapproval, for whatever reason, are most likely to change their opinion in response to external circumstances.

The second model, which emphasizes the influence of individual characteristics, focuses on the proportion of the public likely to be responsive to a candidate rally event. Numerous studies have found that individuals differ in their responses to information in the political environment, depending on their political sophistication (Iyengar 1993; J. Miller and Krosnick 1996; Sniderman, Brody, and Tetlock 1991). This latter model emphasizes both the propensity of different types of individuals to encounter political messages in the environment and their susceptibility to having their opinion influenced by such information (Zaller 1992; McGuire 1969, 1973).

An appropriate means of detecting the presence of heterogeneity in time-series relationships, such as that anticipated by the latter model and also employed in chapter 5, involves separately performing an econometric analysis for each subgroup that might differ in the way they assess the environment (Krause 1997). I employ this strategy here as well.

HYPOTHESES

Zaller (1992) develops a two-step reception-acceptance model of public opinion change (see also McGuire 1969 and 1973). Zaller's model anticipates heterogeneous responses to political stimuli, depending on individuals' political awareness. He argues that individuals at different levels of political awareness tend to react differently to information to which they are exposed (step two), as well as to have varying propensities to encounter political information available in the environment (step one). Highly unaware individuals, Zaller argues, tend not to *expose* themselves to political information. As a result, their opinions tend to be stable, even in a fairly information-intensive environment, like that surrounding a high-profile foreign policy activity. Since they are relatively less likely to *receive* new information, they have no basis upon which to alter their opinions. Highly politically aware individuals are also relatively immune to having their opinions swayed by new information, but for a different reason. Political sophisticates have well-formed belief systems, or ideologies, through which they are able to filter any new information. This filtering process allows these individuals to, in effect, resist *accepting* dissonant messages, even if they *receive* them.[5] Moderately politically aware individuals are thus most susceptible to having their opinions altered by new information, as they typically pay enough attention to receive the information, but lack sufficiently well formed belief systems to screen out, or counterargue, dissonant messages.

Applying Zaller's model to the rally phenomenon, a picture emerges of the types of individuals most likely to respond favorably when the president engages in a foreign policy activity. These individuals are unlikely to consist of either the least or the most politically aware members of the population. The former group will tend to be largely oblivious to all but the most dramatic and highest profile political events. Hence, ceteris paribus, their approval or disapproval of the president will most likely vary only modestly, even in the face of a presidential foreign policy success or failure. The latter, highly politically aware group is also relatively unlikely to rally. These are political ideologues, who tend to approve or disapprove of a president with relatively high resolve. Like their less politically aware counterparts, albeit for different reasons, their approval or disapproval of a president is unlikely to be swayed by external events.

This leaves the middle group, best characterized as moderately politically aware, as most likely to be both sufficiently attentive to receive news about a foreign policy engagement and potentially willing to respond by upgrading their evaluation of the president. Zaller's model suggests it is these latter individuals who will account for the majority of any rally effect enjoyed by a president. This, in turn, suggests a hypothesis:

$H_{6.1}$ In the aftermath of a rally event, the largest rally will be among moderately politically aware individuals.

It seems possible, however, that at least some of the assumptions underlying Zaller's model—especially those concerning differing exposure to information by different types of individuals—might become less applicable as the information environment itself changes, over time. To assess this possibility, it is necessary to break down this general pattern even further, by recognizing that individuals at the top and bottom of the political awareness scale have, in all likelihood, responded differently to the changing media environment over the past five decades. And this is where changes in television broadcasting, particularly the rise of the soft news media, enter our story. In chapter 2, I argued that in the face of rising competition, television broadcasters have sought to repackage political information into formats that would appeal to politically uninterested individuals. Chapters 4 and 5 then presented evidence that the least politically attentive members of society are, as a consequence, increasingly attentive to high-profile political issues, including foreign policy crises. This suggests that the propensity of low-awareness individuals to be *exposed* to information about a given political issue has increased. In contrast, highly politically aware individuals have remained fairly consistent in their attentiveness to politics; they have always successfully sought out information from whatever sources were available. Hence, in terms of attentiveness to foreign crises, the least politically aware members of society are, in effect, catching up to their highly politically aware counterparts.

Moreover, to the extent that a relatively large proportion of the political information that low-awareness individuals consume comes from the soft news media, those factors that previous scholars (e.g., Brody 1991; Brody and Shapiro 1989; Oneal, Lian, and Joyner 1996) associate with *mitigating* the rally phenomenon—that is, critical media coverage, indexed to partisan criticism of the president's policies—should be less influential for these individuals, at least in the earliest stages of a crisis. After all, as previously discussed, soft news tends to eschew divisive partisan political rhetoric in favor of dramatic, sensational story lines, such as the heroism of American soldiers under adverse circumstances. And this is the very type of coverage most likely to fuel a patriotic rally—again, at least in the short run. (In the next chapter, I explain why—given the ex ante availability and propensity to rally of low-awareness individuals—this is the case despite the tendency, discussed in chapter 3, of soft news outlets to emphasize negative, critical coverage of U.S. overseas military engagements.)[6] Hence, since, as we have seen, the least politically aware members of society have become, over time, relatively more likely to attend to foreign crises via the soft news media, we might expect to see a reduction in the discrepancy between the least politically aware individuals and their moderately aware counterparts. In other words, we might anticipate a trend toward larger rallies in the early stages of crises among less politically aware individuals. In contrast, highly politically aware individuals are as likely as ever to successfully counterargue any dissonant information, even in an environment characterized by increasing partisanship in foreign policy, so they are less likely to have changed. This suggests two additional hypotheses:

$H_{6.2}$ Averaging across the entire post–World War II period, the *least* politically aware individuals should rally more, on average, than the *most* politically aware individuals.

$H_{6.3}$ The least politically aware individuals should exhibit the strongest trend toward larger rally effects, over time, while highly politically aware individuals should exhibit no such trend.

While variations in political awareness can help account for differences in rally effects, this one dimension is insufficient to provide a complete picture of the rally phenomenon. For instance, the two major political parties are composed of, and responsive to, quite different constituencies. Lower socioeconomic status (SES) groups tend to identify with the Democratic Party, while higher SES groups are more likely to identify with the Republican Party. This suggests that individuals at different levels of political awareness—which is *strongly* positively correlated with SES—are likely to differ in their responsiveness to policy initiatives of presidents from different political parties.

In an effort to explain how different groups of Americans respond to variations in economic performance, Kernell and Hibbs (1981) propose a "threshold" model of presidential approval.[7] They argue that in determining which economic policies to pursue, presidents must respond strategically to the preferences of different constituencies. A president's support will typically be drawn from both members of his own party and, to a lesser extent, members of the opposition party and Independents. The president's fellow partisans, they argue, typically support a president strongly and in large numbers. Opposition party and Independent approvers, however, will tend to approve more weakly than the president's fellow partisans. In other words, opposition and Independent approvers lie closer to the threshold of approval. By the same logic, larger numbers of opposition and Independent disapprovers will also tend to lie near the threshold. And, due to their relatively weakly held preferences, these are the constituencies who are most likely to alter their evaluation of the president in response to changing economic circumstances, such as higher unemployment or inflation. Hence, a strategic president will treat his fellow partisans as more or less "locked in" in their support (Baum and Kernell 2001) and focus his efforts on appealing to these marginal constituencies. Kernell and Hibbs (1981) find in their empirical tests that opposition party members and Independents are indeed most likely to change their evaluation of a president in response to changing economic circumstances.

Unless politics truly does stop at the water's edge—a dubious hypothesis at best—there is no intrinsic reason to believe that the heterogeneity Kernell and Hibbs (1981) found among different partisan groups in their responses to changing external circumstances should be limited to changes in the economy. For instance, it seems likely that different groups of Americans will be differentially willing to reassess their evaluation of a president following a high-profile foreign policy event, depending on their location relative to the threshold of approval. Strong disapprovers and approvers are unlikely to reevaluate the president in the face of a potential rally event, regardless of the circumstances or outcome. These individuals typically possess sufficiently intense ideologically driven preferences that they will be able to counterargue any signals from political elites suggesting that they should alter their evaluation of the president (Zaller 1992).

At the same time, as the partisan threshold model suggests, the larger the number of approvers among identifiers of a given segment of the population, the smaller the number available to upgrade their evaluation of the president. And individuals at differing levels of political sophistication are likely to differ ex ante in their propensity to approve of presidents from different parties. Just such a pattern becomes apparent when one breaks out the average levels of approval of Republican and Democratic presidents, from 1953 to 1998, by respondents' level of education (grade school, high school, or college). As before, throughout this chapter I employ education as an indicator of political awareness.

Respondents with a grade school education are, on average, nearly 9 percentage points more likely to approve Democratic presidents (55.5 vs. 46.8 percent), while college-educated respondents are nearly 11 percentage points more likely to approve Republican presidents (64.0 vs. 53.3 percent). High-school-educated respondents, in turn, are almost equally likely to approve presidents of either party (54.5 vs. 55.8 percent, for Democratic and Republican presidents, respectively). Moreover, during Democratic administrations, the three education groups differ hardly at all in their evaluations of the president (varying only from 55.5 to 53.3 percent). In contrast, during Republican administrations, college-educated respondents' average approval rate exceeds that of their grade-school-educated counterparts by over 17 percentage points (ranging from 46.8 to 64.0 percent). This suggests that during a Republican administration, there are more low-education individuals available to upgrade their evaluation of the president in response to a high-profile foreign policy event.

And, during Republican, but not Democratic, administrations, this gap has increased, over time. Table 6.1 separately presents the approval ratings of each education group, by administration and party, in chronological order. The table also presents the difference between the least- and most-educated respondents during each administration.

These data indicate that not only are low-education Americans far less likely to approve of Republican presidents than their better-educated counterparts, but that this gap has expanded since the mid-1970s. Prior to the Ford administration—perhaps not coincidentally the first post-Watergate Republican presidency—the average difference between the least- and most-educated Americans' evaluations of Republican presidents (Eisenhower and Nixon) was 10.1 percentage points. In the post-Watergate era (Ford, Reagan, and G.H.W. Bush), the average discrepancy has expanded to over 17 percentage points. This suggests that the availability of low-education Americans to rally behind Republican presidents has increased over time. Comparable patterns do not emerge in these data for Democratic presidents.[8]

If, as suggested by Hypothesis 6.3, the least politically engaged Americans are increasingly among the most likely segments of the population to rally, this would, at first glance, appear to advantage Democratic presidents, who are traditionally more dependent than their Republican counterparts on this politically uninterested constituency. Yet these individuals are far more likely than their high-awareness counterparts to approve of a Democratic president ex ante. Hence, there are likely to be fewer low-awareness individuals available to rally when a Democratic president engages in a high-profile foreign policy activity. In other words, during a Democratic presidency, there are likely to be fewer low-awareness individuals located near the threshold of approval. Since an individual who *already* approves of the president cannot reevaluate upward in the aftermath of a potential rally event, this suggests, seemingly paradoxically, that

TABLE 6.1. Presidential Approval by Administration and Education, 1953–1998, as Percentage

Administration	Grade School	High School	College	Difference (College % − Grade %)
Education Level				
Democratic Presidents				
Kennedy	69.5	72.9	66.8	−2.7
Johnson	55.9	56.5	53.8	−2.1
Carter	48.2	46.2	47.2	−1.0
Clinton	56.0	53.7	53.1	−2.9
Republican Presidents				
Eisenhower	59.6	66.1	71.4	11.8
Nixon	44.0	48.8	52.4	8.4
Ford	36.5	44.5	52.2	15.7
Reagan	38.7	50.8	58.6	19.9
Bush	48.8	61.4	64.0	15.2

Republican presidents are more likely to benefit from rallies among politically uninterested members of the public. After all, during Republican administrations, there will be more disapproving low-awareness individuals available to upgrade their evaluation of the president when a rally event arises. This suggests two final hypotheses.

$H_{6.4}$ The largest over-time increase in the magnitude of rallies will occur among the least politically engaged individuals during Republican administrations.

$H_{6.5}$ There will be no significant trend towards larger rallies, over time, during Democratic administrations.

DATA AND METHODOLOGY

Mueller (1970, 1973) lists six categories of rally events: sudden military interventions, major military developments in ongoing wars, major diplomatic developments, dramatic technological developments, meetings between the U.S. president and leaders of other major powers, and the start of each presidential term. He argues that for an event to be classified as a potential rally event, it should satisfy three criteria: (1) be international, (2) directly involve the United States in general and the president in particular, and (3) be "specific, dramatic and sharply focused" (1973, 209). Oneal, Lian, and Joyner (1996, 265) further restrict their definition of rally events to "major uses of force during a crisis." This, they argue, ensures that they are "considering only cases that were truly consequential for the U.S. and salient to the public, necessary conditions for a rally." Following Oneal and his colleagues (1996), I restrict my analysis to major uses of force during a foreign policy crisis. For my data set, in turn, I rely upon the identical data concerning major U.S. uses and deployments of military force (henceforth referred to as "uses of force") employed in chapter 5, where I investigated trends in public attentiveness to U.S. uses of force between 1953 and 1998.

Coding a rally event is not as straightforward as it might seem. It is unclear, for instance, whether the appropriate rally variable would be a simple dummy variable, coded 1 for the period immediately following the initiation of a potential rally event, or a time-indexed variable, which recognizes the gradual erosion of the rally effect (Kernell 1975). Because I am primarily concerned with short-term spikes in presidential approval following the initiation of a use of force, a dummy variable specification arguably seems more appropriate than a time-indexed variable. This is particularly true because, unlike the latter type of variable, a dummy specification does not impose the assumption that all rallies erode similarly, in a linear fashion. Rather, it merely captures the initial spike in approval, which is, after all, what the original definition of the rally effect emphasized. Indeed, preliminary testing indicated that a rally dummy ("Rally") performs as well or better than time-indexed variables that assume a gradual erosion of the rally effect over the course of anywhere from three to six months. Hence, I employ the dummy specification throughout my statistical testing. As noted in chapter 5, my data includes a total of 834 Gallup polls, of which 66 take place immediately following the initiation of a potential rally event.[9]

My other key causal variable is simply the date on which a given survey was conducted. In order to account for trends in rally events, I interact this variable with the rally dummy. For my dependent variables, in turn, in order to account for extreme differences in the *levels* of approval across different partisan groups, I employ the difference in the natural logarithms of the presidential approval ratings between the current (t) and immediately preceding ($t - 1$) Gallup polls. To capture any heterogeneity in the influence of the various causal variables, I employ separate equations for respondents with grade school, high school, and college educations. I then separately test these models for Republican and Democratic administrations.[10]

In testing my several hypotheses, I employ a variety of control variables, intended to account for alternative domestic and international political and economic factors that might influence variations in presidential approval. Among the controls, to account for any unique characteristics of a given president, I include in all models either a series of administration dummies or a Cold War dummy.[11] For those models investigating over-time trends, I employ the latter, Cold War dummy, coded 1 from 1953 to 1988 and 0 from 1989 to 1998. This is intended to account for the possibility that fundamental changes in public perceptions of foreign policy following the end of the Cold War could produce trends in rally effects having little to do with the phenomena under consideration. Those models that do not investigate over-time trends employ the administration dummies. (All other control variables are described and defined in appendix 1 of this chapter.)

Consistent with a majority of the presidential approval literature, I assume an AR(1) autoregressive error structure and include the lagged value of the logged approval rating as an additional control variable.[12] Where evidence of serial autocorrelation persists even after including the lag of approval, I include additional autoregressive (AR) terms, as necessary.[13] Throughout my analyses, I employ Ordinary Least Squares with heteroscedasticity-consistent standard errors. I vary the model specification as necessary to test each of the hypotheses introduced in the prior section.

STATISTICAL TESTS

Table 6.A1, shown in appendix 2 to this chapter, presents the results from six models, intended to test Hypotheses 6.1, 6.2, and 6.3. Hypothesis 6.1 predicts that rallies should be largest among *moderately* politically aware individuals. Hypothesis 6.2 then predicts that the *least* politically aware individuals should rally more than their counterparts at the highest levels of awareness, while Hypothesis 6.3 predicts that the least politically aware individuals will exhibit the strongest trend toward larger rallies, over time.

The first three analyses offer clear support for Hypotheses 6.1 and 6.2. Beginning with the former, among respondents with a grade-school education, presidents receive about a 4 percent rally in the immediate aftermath of using force abroad ($p < .05$). The corresponding rallies are 4.3 ($p < .01$) and 2.9 percent ($p < .05$), respectively, among respondents with a high-school or college education. Hence, the three groups line up precisely as the reception-acceptance model predicts, with the strongest rally effect among high-school-educated respondents. Moreover, the rally effect is larger among grade-school respondents than among their college-educated counterparts, thereby supporting Hypothesis 6.2.[14]

Turning to my tests of Hypothesis 6.3, among respondents with a grade-school education, the predicted magnitude of rallies increased between 1953 and 1998 by nearly 6.4 percent ($p < .05$). This contrasts sharply with a 5.5 percent *decline* in average presidential approval rates among grade-school respondents during nonrally periods over the same period of time. The corresponding effects among high-school- and college-educated respondents during rally periods were statistically insignificant increases of 2.3 and 1.6 percent, respectively.[15]

Hypotheses 6.4 and 6.5 predict the biggest trend toward larger rallies over time among low-awareness individuals during Republican administrations, and no such trend during Democratic administrations. Table 6.A2, also in appendix 2, presents the results from six additional models, intended to test these two hypotheses. Beginning with the former hypothesis, my results indicate that among respondents with a grade-school education, the average magnitude of rallies during Republican administrations increased between the Eisenhower and G.H.W. Bush presidencies by nearly 22 percent ($p < .001$). This compares to increases of about 15.3 percent among respondents with a high-school education ($p < .01$) and 14.5 percent among college-educated respondents ($p < .01$).[16] These results clearly support Hypothesis 6.4.

Turning to the latter hypothesis, my results indicate that among respondents with a grade-school education, during Democratic presidencies (from the Kennedy to the Clinton administration), the magnitude of a typical rally has *declined* by about 28 percent. Yet, among low-education respondents, the difference between the overall secular decline in approval of Democratic presidents and postrally event declines in approval rates is *not* statistically significant. This suggests that rally events have had little impact on the evaluations of Democratic presidents among relatively uneducated Americans. The corresponding trends for high-school and college-educated respondents are declines of 12 and 18 percent, respectively. As before, however, in both instances, the differences between the overall secular declines and postrally event changes in approval rates are statistically insignificant. Moreover, across all three groups of respondents, neither the *secular* decline in approval of Democratic presidents nor that in the immediate aftermath of potential rally events is statistically significant. Taken together, these results offer clear support for Hypothesis 6.5.

CONCLUSION

The rally-round-the-flag phenomenon remains only partially understood. Beyond general agreement that presidents do indeed enjoy sudden, and usually brief, spikes in their popularity in the immediate aftermath of high-profile foreign policy activities, scholars have been unable to definitely determine either the sources or the substantive implications of the rally effect.

Yet this phenomenon holds potentially critical implications for our understanding of the linkage between domestic politics and foreign policy. The rally effect is central to the debate in the scholarly literature and the popular press regarding whether political leaders ever use military force for domestic political reasons—the so-called wag-the-dog scenario, or diversionary use of force. The potential political value to a president of using military force as a distraction from domestic difficulties depends on the willingness of the public to rally. If, as some scholars (e.g., Meernik and Waterman 1996; Brody 1991) maintain, rally effects are ephemeral and politically insignificant, then the logic behind a diversionary use of force quickly collapses.

Indeed, these results suggest a potentially useful avenue for future research into the relationship between public opinion and foreign policy decision making. By disaggregating public opinion into its constituent elements, and thereby determining which segments of the population are most responsive, or resistant, to presidential efforts to use foreign policy for domestic purposes, it should be possible to improve our understanding of this controversial phenomenon and its political implications.

While this chapter has not directly addressed the political significance of the rally effect, it has clarified several closely related issues. For instance, I found that rallies are increasingly driven by the least politically sophisticated segments of the public. This suggests that the constituent elements of the rally phenomenon have changed over time. And my results from prior chapters suggest that this is in all likelihood attributable, at least in part, to the changing television environment, most notably the rise of the soft news media. This further suggests that the political importance of rallies depends in some measure on the centrality of this low-awareness group within a president's support coalition. If these individuals are an important constituency for a president, then such rallies, however brief, may be politically meaningful, especially if they take place during critical periods, like election campaigns. Otherwise, they may, as Meernik and Waterman (1996) and Brody (1991) have suggested, be politically inconsequential.

A trend toward rallies increasingly located among the least politically aware segments of the population—the primary consumers of soft news outlets—would, at first glance, appear to advantage Democratic presidents, who are relatively more dependent on lower-SES groups for their political support. Yet just the opposite pattern emerged; the evidence, at least in these data, indicates that Republican presidents were more likely to benefit from rallies among politically unsophisticated members of the public. This is because low-SES individuals are far more likely to approve of a Democratic president ex ante, leaving fewer low-awareness individuals available to rally when a potential rally event arises during a Democratic administration. Hence, in at least this one sense, the rise of the soft news media appears likely to disproportionately benefit Republican presidents.

Taken together, the results presented in this chapter suggest that by increasing the attentiveness to foreign crises of segments of the population who might otherwise tune out foreign affairs entirely, the soft news media may have important, albeit sometimes nonobvious, implications for the future of the rally phenomenon and for its political significance. In particular, future presidents appear likely to be increasingly dependent on the least politically attentive segments of the population for post-use-of-force rallies. In the final two chapters of the book, I turn from assessing a single, albeit potentially important, implication of the changing television environment to a broader investigation of a series of implications of increased public attentiveness to high-profile political issues, including foreign crises.

APPENDIX 1: VARIABLE DEFINITIONS

Divided Government. Dummy variable, coded 0 in times of unified government and 1 if the opposition party controls at least one house of Congress.
Economy. I employ two common indicators of economic performance, *Inflation* and *Unemployment* (Ostrom and Simon 1985; Baum and Kernell 2001; Kernell 1975).[17] The first measures the monthly change in the consumer

price index and the second measures the monthly change in the national unemployment rate. Both are averaged over the period of two to four months prior to the current period.[18]

Presidential Honeymoon. Dummy variable, coded 1 during the first three months of each new administration's term in office, and 0 otherwise. Following Kernell (1975), I treat the first three months of both terms for two-term presidents as a "new" administration (but see Brody 1991).[19]

Presidential Election Year. Dummy variable, coded 1 during presidential election years and 0 for all other years.[20]

Immigration to United States. This variable tallies the annual percent change in the number of legal immigrants to the United States.[21]

Lame Duck President. Dummy variable, coded 1 during a president's second elected term in office, and 0 otherwise.[22]

Foreign Policy Salience. Annualized average percentage of the public mentioning a foreign policy issue when asked by Gallup to name the most important problem facing the nation.[23]

APPENDIX 2: STATISTICAL TABLES

TABLE 6.A1. OLS Analyses of Rally Event Trends, 1953–1998, by Education (Dependent Variable: $lnApprove_t - lnApprove_{t-1}$)

Coef. (Std. Err.)

	Overall Average Rally Size (1953–1998 Pooled)			Rally Trend		
	Grade School	High School	College	Grade School	High School	College
Trend						
Date (in years)	—	—	—	−.0012 (.0005)*	−.0004 (.0005)	−.0002 (.0005)
Domestic Politics						
Presidential election year	.0006 (.009)	−.006 (.006)	−.017 (.007)*	.003 (.009)	−.005 (.007)	−.014 (.007)^
Lame duck	.008 (.009)	−.003 (.008)	−.012 (.008)	.014 (.007)^	.003 (.007)	−.004 (.007)
Divided government	.021 (.013)^	.027 (.011)*	.035 (.013)**	−.011 (.006)^	.010 (.007)	.026 (.009)**
New administration	.032 (.013)**	.039 (.012)**	.056 (.017)***	.026 (.012)*	.037 (.013)**	.052 (.016)***
$lnApprove_{t-1}$	−.129 (.022)***	−.108 (.020)***	−.128 (.027)***	−.094 (.018)***	−.110 (.023)***	−.113 (.028)***
Domestic Economy						
$Inflation_{(t-2\ldots t-4)/3}$	−4.524 (1.868)*	−4.547 (1.307)***	−4.845 (1.379)***	−2.665 (1.478)^	−3.913 (1.192)***	−4.139 (1.235)***
$Unemployment_{(t-2\ldots t-4)/3}$	−.117 (.107)	−.036 (.087)	−.020 (.100)	−.171 (.099)^	−.053 (.089)	−.021 (.096)
Foreign Policy						
Rally[a]	.040 (.018)*	.043 (.015)**	.029 (.015)*	−.158 (.073)*	−.029 (.063)	−.013 (.064)
%ΔImmigration	.046 (.030)	.036 (.019)^	.030 (.019)	.033 (.023)	.044 (.018)*	.036 (.018)*
lnForeign policy salience	.011 (.009)	.010 (.008)	.013 (.010)	−.0004 (.006)	.007 (.006)	.007 (.007)
Cold War	—	—	—	−.027 (.016)^	−.013 (.011)	−.0009 (.009)

TABLE 6.A1. Continued

	Coef. (Std. Err.)					
	Overall Average Rally Size (1953–1998 Pooled)			Rally Trend		
	Grade School	High School	College	Grade School	High School	College
Administration Dummies						
Kennedy	.034 (.014)**	.021 (.013)	−.003 (.016)	—	—	—
Johnson	.007 (.013)	−.0001 (.013)	−.016 (.016)	—	—	—
Nixon	−.010 (.012)	−.012 (.011)	−.022 (.014)	—	—	—
Ford	−.017 (.024)	−.006 (.021)	−.008 (.026)	—	—	—
Carter	.039 (.024)	.024 (.022)	.012 (.026)	—	—	—
Reagan	−.033 (.014)*	−.006 (.012)	−.0002 (.013)	—	—	—
Bush	−.005 (.021)	.007 (.016)	−.0005 (.017)	—	—	—
Clinton	.027 (.021)	.008 (.019)	−.005 (.022)	—	—	—
Interaction Term						
Date × rally	—	—	—	.0025 (.0009)***	.0009 (.0008)	.0005 (.0008)
Constant	−.082 (.018)***	−.057 (.016)***	−.053 (.016)***	.044 (.035)	−.015 (.030)	−.044 (.028)
AR(1)	−.421 (.066)***	−.274 (.059)***	−.249 (.053)***	−.442 (.064)***	−.249 (.051)***	−.256 (.052)***
AR(2)	−.278 (.059)***	−.077 (.046)^	—	−.304 (.057)***	—	—
AR(3)	−.123 (.058)*	—	—	−.147 (.056)**	—	—
AR(4)	−.099 (.047)*	—	—	−.114 (.046)**	—	—
Adjusted R^2	.23	.14	.14	.23	.13	.14
F-Statistic	11.968***	7.337***	7.926***	14.941***	9.929***	10.267***
Durbin-Watson Statistic	2.007	2.002	2.008	2.009	2.038	2.011
	(N = 804)	(N = 812)	(N = 817)	(N = 804)	(N = 817)	(N = 817)

Note: All models employ heteroscedasticity-consistent ("robust") standard errors.

^"Rally" variable in this analysis is identical to "Use of force" variable employed in chapter 5 (see table 5.A3).

$^p < .10$, $^*p < .05$, $^{**}p < .01$, $^{***}p < .001$

TABLE 6.A2. OLS Analyses of Rally Event Trends, 1953–98, by Education and President's Party (Dependent Variable: $lnApprove_t - lnApprove_{t-1}$)

	Coef. (Std. Err.)					
	Democratic Administrations			Republican Administrations		
	Grade School	High School	College	Grade School	High School	College
Trend						
Date (in years)	−.004 (.003)	−.002 (.003)	−.002 (.004)	−.002 (.0005)**	−.0003 (.0004)	.0001 (.0004)
Domestic Politics						
Presidential election year	.008 (.011)	−.002 (.012)	−.009 (.016)	.008 (.010)	.005 (.007)	−.001 (.008)
Lame duck	.046 (.025)^	.023 (.025)	.017 (.029)	.004 (.008)	−.002 (.007)	−.007 (.008)
Divided government	.019 (.019)	.017 (.018)	.017 (.021)	−.020 (.021)	−.020 (.019)	−.014 (.018)
New administration	.045 (.019)*	.038 (.014)**	.050 (.015)***	.017 (.019)	.044 (.020)*	.067 (.029)*
$lnApprove_{t-1}$	−.163 (.030)***	−.122 (.027)***	−.121 (.032)***	−.144 (.032)***	−.012 (.035)***	−.171 (.053)***
Economy						
Inflation$_{(t-2 \ldots t-4)/3}$	−4.179 (3.188)	−6.032 (2.527)*	−5.961 (3.295)^	−.544 (2.547)	−1.445 (1.652)	−1.906 (1.716)
Unemployment$_{(t-2 \ldots t-4)/3}$	−.285 (.248)	.009 (.225)	−.129 (.232)	−.132 (.125)	−.077 (.099)	.006 (.115)

Table 6.A2. *Continued*

	Coef. (Std. Err.)					
	Democratic Administrations			Republican Administrations		
	Grade School	High School	College	Grade School	High School	College
Foreign Policy						
Rally[a]	.176 (.114)	.094 (.121)	.152 (.161)	−.418 (.122)***	−.213 (.093)*	−.190 (.072)**
%ΔImmigration	.031 (.041)	.019 (.037)	.004 (.046)	.063 (.037)^	.058 (.023)**	.076 (.028)**
lnForeign policy salience	−.023 (.014)	−.015 (.013)	−.021 (.017)	.022 (.010)*	.020 (.008)**	.031 (.011)**
Cold War	−.033 (.065)	−.001 (.058)	−.004 (.077)	−.036 (.021)^	−.020 (.015)	−.013 (.013)
Interaction Term						
Date × rally	−.002 (.001)	−.0007 (.001)	−.002 (.002)	.006 (.002)***	.004 (.001)**	.003 (.001)**
Constant	.139 (.223)	.051 (.204)	.051 (.272)	.087 (.040)*	.016 (.030)	−.020 (.029)
AR(1)	−.403 (.064)***	−.310 (.053)***	−.263 (.057)***	−.441 (.083)***	−.259 (.084)**	−.239 (.086)**
AR(2)	−.200 (.061)***	—	—	−.329 (.077)***	−.159 (.062)**	—
AR(3)	—	—	—	−.180 (.072)**	—	—
AR(4)	—	—	—	−.137 (.059)*	—	—
Adjusted R^2	.23	.15	.13	.25	.15	.17
F-Statistic	8.006***	5.531***	4.646***	10.240***	6.661***	7.783***
Durbin-Watson Statistic	2.018	2.014	2.052	2.011	1.946	1.943
	(N = 345)	(N = 348)	(N = 348)	(N = 462)	(N = 466)	(N = 468)

Notes: All models employ heteroscedasticity-consistent ("robust") standard errors.

[a]"Rally" variable in this analysis is identical to "Use of force" variable employed in chapter 5 (see table 5.A2).

^$p < .10$, *$p < .05$, **$p < .01$, ***$p < .001$

Soft News and World Views: Foreign Policy Attitudes of the Inattentive Public

DOES COVERAGE of foreign policy crises in the soft news media matter? Or is it just a curious novelty, devoid of any real political significance? I began chapter 3 with the story of an anonymous e-mail petition condemning the plight of women in Afghanistan. The petition was circulated by a concerned individual who claimed to have learned about the oppressive policies of the Taliban regime toward women from *The Oprah Winfrey Show*. While politicians are not always responsive to e-mail petitions, the attention Oprah Winfrey focused on the plight of women in Afghanistan appears not to have gone unnoticed by the Bush administration. In March 2002, President Bush asked Winfrey to participate in a U.S. delegation to Afghanistan—an offer she declined—intended to highlight the improved educational opportunities for girls in the post-Taliban environment (*New York Times*, March 30, 2002, sec. A). This anecdote suggests that soft news coverage of foreign policy issues can influence public attitudes about world events. Indeed, even the president of the United States appears to have recognized the potential influence of the soft news media—in this instance *The Oprah Winfrey Show*—in his efforts to showcase what he considered to be a U.S. foreign policy success.

In chapter 4, I presented evidence that consumers of soft news outlets, particularly those who are relatively uneducated or uninterested in politics, tend to view the issues and themes most prevalent in the soft news media (e.g., crime, morality, scandal, or foreign crises), relative to other policy areas, as the nation's most urgent problems. Consuming hard news, in contrast, had a much weaker effect on respondents' propensities to mention these popular soft news topics. Indeed, the evidence in chapter 5 suggests that these patterns may help account for a trend toward an increased propensity among politically inattentive Americans to emphasize soft-news-friendly issues, when asked about the most urgent problems facing the nation. And in the last chapter, I found that increased attentiveness to foreign policy among politically uninterested Americans appears to have altered the constituent elements of the rally-round-the-flag phenomenon. These findings suggest the rise of the soft news media has potentially important implications for public attitudes about politics and foreign policy.

In this chapter, I further explore the questions of *whether* and *how* greater attentiveness among the least politically informed segments of the public matters. Specifically, I investigate the effects on public attitudes—particularly among the least politically engaged segments of the public—of learning about politics and foreign policy via the soft news media. After all, there are many possible sources of information about a given issue, and attending to information in one context, such as a soft news program, may hold quite different implications from attentiveness in other contexts, like a traditional news outlet. Indeed, the content analysis investigations reported in chapter 3 indicate that the soft news media cover foreign policy events in very different ways than traditional news outlets, placing far greater emphasis on dramatic, human-interest themes (e.g., violence, heroism, tragedy, etc.) and episodic frames.

Unfortunately, assessing the qualitative effects of soft news consumption on public opinion regarding foreign policy is extremely difficult for the simple reason that public opinion surveys rarely ask the types of questions necessary for assessing the latter in tandem with questions concerning the former. I conducted an exhaustive search for such surveys in a variety of public opinion poll archives. In the end, I was able to identify only five polls that include *both* a battery of media consumption questions—including questions regarding soft news outlets—and at least one question concerning respondents' opinions regarding a high-profile foreign policy issue or event. These five surveys allow me to investigate the effects of soft news consumption on public attitudes toward the following issues: (1) U.S. policy regarding the civil war in Bosnia, including military intervention, (2) NATO enlargement, (3) U.S.-Japanese relations, (4) President Clinton's overall management of foreign policy, and (5) the appropriate U.S. role in the world.[1]

My goal is to determine whether the opinions of people who get their news about foreign policy from the soft news media differ from those who do not. It certainly seems plausible that the sorts of differences between soft and hard news coverage of foreign crises identified in chapter 3 could influence the opinions of soft news consumers in ways different from exposure to hard news, or exposure to *any* type of news by politically attentive individuals. Such influence seems particularly likely if an individual lacks alternative sources of news and information or sufficient knowledge about politics to place any information gleaned from a soft news outlet into a broader context. And, as we shall see, evidence of such differences emerges in each of my investigations. In every instance, the least educated or politically engaged members of the public who consume a great deal of soft news are more likely than their better educated, more politically engaged, or non-soft-news-consuming counterparts to express skepticism regarding U.S. military interventions and other multilateral engagements, as well as distrust of an important U.S. ally.

In order to determine whether any over-time trends have emerged consistent with these individual-level patterns, I also investigate trends in popular support for *reducing* the U.S. role in the world, employing NES surveys from 1960 to 2000. Before turning to my statistical investigations, however, I first develop a general conceptual framework intended to help explain how and why soft news consumption might cause politically inattentive individuals to express distrust of an activist or multilateral American foreign policy. From this discussion, I derive a series of hypotheses, which I test in subsequent sections of the chapter.

Why Might Soft News Consumers Be More Distrustful of Internationalism?

How might exposure to soft news coverage of foreign policy issues influence consumers' opinions? To help answer this question, I develop a theoretical framework based on the interaction between information suppliers (the soft news media) and consumers (individuals with differing personal characteristics). Beginning with the latter, to understand the likely responses of different types of individuals to soft news coverage of foreign policy, I revisit the two-step reception-acceptance model described in the last chapter (McGuire 1969, 1973; Zaller 1992). Recall that, according to the reception-acceptance model, the *least* politically aware individuals are—except when exceptionally high-profile events arise—relatively impervious to being persuaded or otherwise influenced by political stimuli. This is simply because they tend not to be *exposed* to most political messages in the first instance. In contrast, while highly politically aware individuals are far more likely to be *exposed* to political information, they will tend to reject or counterargue any messages that contradict their preexisting attitudes.

I refer to this latter propensity to reject information inconsistent with preexisting attitudes, given exposure, as *selective acceptance*. The two-step reception-acceptance model suggests that because they possess a broad range of attitudes regarding political issues, highly aware individuals are better equipped to employ selective acceptance, given message reception, than their-less aware counterparts, who possess a far narrower range of preexisting political attitudes upon which to draw.

Turning to the information suppliers, I consider here whether differences in the *types* of foreign policy coverage offered by soft and hard news outlets are likely to produce differing effects on consumers. Specifically, I assess the distinct effects of episodic versus thematic frames in the media (Iyengar 1991), differences in the susceptibility of different types of individuals to being manipulated by frames (Druckman 2001b), and how these differences influence the likelihood that a given individual will support or oppose governmental intervention in order to resolve a problem (Iyengar 1991).

As we shall see, one central general predication emerges from my theoretical framework. That is, politically inattentive individuals who consume soft news are likely to be more suspicious of a proactive, internationalist U.S. foreign policy, more distrustful of U.S. allies, less likely to support policies perceived as expanding U.S. foreign entanglements, and less likely to consider it America's responsibility to act to resolve the problems of other nations or regions, as compared to their counterparts who are either interested in politics or who do not consume soft news. In short, in at least some circumstances and for some individuals, greater soft news consumption seems likely to be associated with reduced support for an activist U.S. foreign policy.

Selective Acceptance

In recent decades, research in cognitive psychology has found a great deal of evidence that individuals find it easier to accept information that "fits" with their preexisting (either in memory or "on-line") attitudes, values, or affects (Tetlock 1984, 1985, 1986, 1989; Popkin 1994; Lodge and McGraw 1995; Lodge, Steenbergen, and Brau 1995; Sniderman 1993; Sniderman, Brody, and Tetlock 1991; Aldrich, Sullivan, and Borgida 1989; and many others). This is because reconciling contradictory pieces of information requires expending a great deal of cognitive energy. As noted in chapter 2, Popkin (1994) refers to this psychological propensity as a "goodness-of-fit test," whereby individuals, in deciding whether or not to accept a given piece of new information, evaluate the extent to which it is consistent or inconsistent with their preexisting causal narratives. The less consistent the information, Popkin argues, the less likely the individual is to accept it or be influenced by it.

In an interesting wrinkle to the reception-acceptance model, also noted in the prior chapter, because soft news employs cheap framing and piggybacking, low-awareness individuals would appear more likely to be *exposed* to political information in the first instance, and hence to accept it, if it is presented in the soft news media. After all, politically inattentive individuals tend to prefer soft over hard news. And a soft news story about foreign policy will typically be far more accessible than a story on the same subject presented by a traditional news outlet, particularly for individuals not intrinsically interested in politics or foreign affairs. As noted, according to the reception-acceptance model, the politically uninterested are unlikely to tune in to political news coverage by the traditional news media, and so are unlikely to be *exposed* to stories about foreign affairs in that context. And even if they do watch a traditional news program, they are relatively less likely to pay attention to or understand the relatively more complex information about foreign affairs they might encounter.[2] It therefore follows that the opinions of low-information individuals, to the extent they are influenced by media exposure at all, are more likely to be influenced by exposure to politics in the soft news media, relative to traditional news outlets.

My content analysis investigations (see chapter 3), in turn, offer some insight into the nature of any such influence. I found that in their coverage of foreign affairs, the soft news media emphasize such easily understandable, and largely negative, themes as danger and injustice in considerably greater proportion than do the traditional news media. The soft news media are also more likely to draw analogies to past U.S. foreign policy failures and less likely to feature commentary from credible sources. Research in social psychology (Skowronski and Carlston 1987, 1989; Reeder and Spores 1983), in turn, has shown that negative information tends to outweigh positive information in influencing people's evaluations of individuals or objects, particularly those involving moral judgment (e.g., "right vs. wrong," "good vs. evil," etc.). This is because negative information is more useful in reaching a judgment about an individual or object. For instance, typical individuals tend to consider *bad* behavior as characteristic primarily of bad people, while *good* behavior is more likely to be viewed as potentially characteristic of either good or bad people (i.e., good people sometimes do bad things, but bad people usually do not do good things). Hence, all else equal, negative information is less ambiguous. And, as discussed in chapter 2, America's leaders routinely frame the nation's adversaries as the embodiment of evil (e.g., G.H.W. Bush likening Saddam Hussein to Hitler, or G. W. Bush branding Al Qaeda and its supporters as "evildoers"). Hence, in evaluating U.S. foreign policy initiatives, the American people are strongly encouraged by their leaders to base their opinions on moral judgment, thereby reinforcing the centrality of negative information.

Most importantly, politically uninterested individuals are relatively unlikely to possess sufficient contextual knowledge to place such dramatic or pessimistic themes into a broader context. In other words, these are the very individuals who, once they decide to pay attention to a highly accessible story about foreign policy, are *least* likely to be capable of successfully counterarguing a message that, unchecked, might tend to induce suspicion of U.S. engagement in the world.

By the same token, politically uninformed Americans are typically far more likely than their more highly aware counterparts to support isolationism (Kull and Destler 1999; Holsti 1996). For instance, nearly half of the least politically informed respondents in the 2000 NES agreed with the proposition that the United States "would be better off if we just stayed home and did not concern ourselves with problems in other parts of the world."[3] Given their isolationist leanings, many politically uninterested soft news consumers, find little incentive to *try* to counterargue messages that are, after all, generally consistent with their preexisting sensibilities. Hence, according to the selective acceptance hypothesis, inattentive individuals who are sympathetic, ex ante, to isolationism and are exposed to pro-isolationist messages in a highly accessible format, are relatively likely to accept, and be influenced (or at least reinforced) by, such messages. And, given their limited range of accessible political attitudes, politically inattentive individuals who are *not* prone, ex ante, to support isolationism are likely to be *less effective* at counterarguing isolationist messages than their more politically attentive, pro-internationalist counterparts. Hence, despite their internationalist sensibilities, they may nonetheless be influenced by any pro-isolationist messages to which they are exposed, albeit presumably somewhat less strongly so than politically inattentive isolationists.

Of course, it is possible that politically uninterested individuals, because they tend to be sympathetic to isolationist messages and themes, might seek out media outlets that they consider likely to present news about the world that would tend to confirm their predispositions. In other words, politically uninterested individuals might seek out soft news outlets because they anticipate finding support for their pro-isolationist worldviews. Similarly, it is also possible that soft news outlets, in seeking to appeal to an audience that tends to be suspicious of U.S. overseas engagements, might self-consciously bias their coverage of foreign policy in a pro-isolationist direction. Indeed, Hamilton (2003) has found that ratings-driven news broadcasters tend to tailor the content of their news reporting to the ideological preferences of their marginal viewers (i.e., those viewers who are relatively less likely to stay tuned if the program presents information which they find distasteful). If soft news outlets do, in fact, deliberately slant their coverage of foreign crises in a pro-isolationist direction, this would tend to produce effects comparable to those I describe in this chapter.

Yet, the evidence presented in chapter 4 suggests that neither of these possibilities is likely. Recall that soft news consumers appear to watch, listen to, and read soft news primarily for purposes of entertainment, *not* in order to learn about the nation or the world. As previously noted, this strongly suggests that to the extent they are learning about the world through the soft news media, consumers of these media outlets are doing so primarily as an incidental by-product of seeking entertainment. This, in turn, suggests that viewers of soft news outlets do not typically tune in to these media outlets for their occasional coverage of foreign policy in times of crisis. Hence, it seems highly unlikely that low-interest individuals are self-selecting into pro-isolationist media environments in order to reinforce their predispositions. Indeed, it seems unlikely that politically inattentive individuals would self-consciously seek out *any* news—soft or hard—in order to reinforce their political views, whatever they may be. Rather, any exposure to the types of themes that induce pro-isolationist reactions seems likely to be largely incidental. Given this, in turn, it seems relatively unlikely that soft news programmers would bother tailoring the content of foreign affairs coverage to suit the pro-isolationist sensibilities of marginal audience members who are, after all, tuning in for entertainment, not politics.

Highly politically engaged individuals, in contrast, tend to be overwhelmingly internationalist in their predispositions (Kull and Destler 1999; Holsti 1996). Indeed, only about 10 percent of the most highly politically informed respondents agreed with the aforementioned pro-isolationist position in the 2000 NES. These individuals are, according to the reception-acceptance model, capable of counterarguing the vast majority of messages inconsistent with their preexisting attitudes. And, given their overwhelming internationalist sensibilities, *most* highly politically informed individuals, unlike many of their less-informed counterparts, are motivated to counterargue any isolationist messages they might encounter.

The Differing Effects of Episodic versus Thematic Frames

An additional factor that seems likely to influence the opinions of at least politically uninterested soft news consumers is the overwhelming propensity of the soft news media to employ episodic framing, while eschewing thematic frames. Most news outlets, soft and hard, tend to make liberal use of episodic frames (Iyengar 1991). Yet my content analysis, reported in chapter 3, found that the soft news media rely almost *exclusively* on episodic framing, doing so in 95 percent of the reports I investigated. In contrast, while, in covering U.S. foreign crises, traditional news outlets employed thematic frames with about the same frequency as episodic frames (69 percent of all hard news reports for both types of frames), the soft news media reports employed thematic frames in only 16 percent of the reports I investigated.

Research in social psychology has found that episodic frames are more likely than thematic frames to capture people's attention, particularly if they are relatively uninvolved, ex ante, with the object of the frame (Fiske and Taylor 1991; Chaiken and Eagly 1976). Additional research has shown that people are more likely to *remember* episodic frames, because they are more vivid (Lynn, Shavitt, and Ostrom 1985), and that vivid information—because it is emotionally involving and concrete—disproportionately influences people's judgments and causal explanations (Nisbett and Ross 1980; Larson 1985). Iyengar (1991), in turn, found that thematic frames—which place stories into a broader social, economic, political, or geopolitical context—are more likely than episodic frames to cause people to turn to government for a solution to whatever problem is at issue. Thematic frames tend to engender a sense of social responsibility, and hence a motivation to see society take action to address a given problem. In contrast, episodic frames focus on individual stories of hardship or disaster. While such stories may tug at people's heartstrings and evoke sympathy, Iyengar found that they tended to cause people to see the problem being discussed at an individual level, attributing responsibility for the problem, and for the solution, to the individuals involved, rather than to society as a whole. Hence, episodic frames, while they make good television drama, tend not to engender support for a governmental or societal response.

Given the overwhelming soft news emphasis on episodic frames, it is not surprising that politically uninterested individuals—the very individuals *most* likely to be influenced by framing (Druckman 2001b; Stanovich and West 1998; Levin, Schneider and Gaeth 1998)—would tend not to favor an activist U.S. foreign policy. After all, the almost exclusively episodic and predominantly negative information about foreign crises they receive via the soft news media, tends to reinforce a belief that whatever the problem at issue, the United States should not be responsible for fixing it.

Hypotheses

Taken together, the soft news media's emphasis on highly accessible themes and episodic frames—centered on human drama, violence, and danger abroad—combined with the propensity of low-awareness individuals to ignore, or fail to be exposed to, all but the most highly accessible political messages, as well as the psychological tendency for human beings to selectively accept information consistent with their preexisting beliefs appear to point in a single direction, toward a negative relationship between consuming soft news and sympathy for a proactive or internationalist U.S. foreign policy. These factors also suggest that this relationship is likely to be most pronounced among the least politically engaged members of the public. A number of hypotheses, six of which I test in the next section, follow from this discussion. These are as follows:

$H_{7.1}$ Among politically inattentive individuals, increased soft news consumption will be associated with greater opposition to U.S. military interventions and support for isolationist positions and themes.

$H_{7.2}$ The pro-isolationist effect of soft news exposure will be stronger among politically inattentive individuals who *are* sympathetic, ex ante, to isolationism, than among inattentive individuals who are *not* sympathetic, ex ante, to isolationism.

$H_{7.3}$ As respondents' political attentiveness increases, the pattern described in $H_{7.1}$ will weaken, and may reverse among the most highly politically engaged respondents.

$H_{7.4}$ Traditional news consumption will influence politically inattentive individuals' attitudes regarding isolationism or support for U.S. military interventions less than soft news consumption. The effects on politically attentive individuals will be modest, but may or may not be weaker than the effects of soft news.

$H_{7.5}$ Due to the proliferation of soft news over the past two decades, the least politically engaged segments of the population will have grown increasingly sympathetic to isolationism, over time.

$H_{7.6}$ As respondents' political attentiveness increases, the pattern described in $H_{7.5}$ will weaken.

A Caveat and a Clarification

Before turning to hypothesis testing, it is important to recognize that there are doubtless exceptions to the general patterns predicted above, most notably foreign crises that enjoy broad bipartisan support at both the mass and elite levels. The post-9/11 U.S. attack against the Taliban regime in Afghanistan, and the War on Terrorism in general, appear to be cases in point. In this instance, it seems unlikely that politically inattentive soft news consumers would have been particularly less likely to support the war effort, at least initially, than their counterparts who relied on traditional news sources. In an environment of overwhelming, bipartisan, and broad-based popular and elite support, such as that surrounding the War on Terrorism, I would anticipate coverage in the soft news media, though placing different degrees of emphasis on different aspects of the story than traditional news coverage, would nonetheless *reinforce*, rather than *undermine*, the public consensus, at least in the short term. Zaller (1994) refers to this as the "mainstreaming effect," which arises when a president's policy enjoys broad elite support, behind which the news media typically fall into line in lockstep.

Most likely reinforcing this effect is the unique *nature* of the War on Terrorism, which differs from virtually all of the foreign crises investigated in this study in that it involves a direct attack on U.S. territory. Whereas many politically inattentive individuals are generally suspicious of a proactive U.S. foreign policy, it does not necessarily follow that they will oppose a forceful U.S. response to a direct attack against America. Indeed, due to the unambiguous and highly accessible "us versus them" and "good versus evil" frames associated with the War on Terrorism, such individuals would seem likely to support military action with at least as much enthusiasm as political sophisticates.

In fact, some suggestive, albeit indirect, evidence exists in support of this conjecture concerning the War on Terrorism. In one survey conducted by the Pew Research Center (2001), respondents who did not graduate from high school—among the heaviest consumers of soft news—were slightly *more* likely than college graduates to express confidence that the U.S. military would win the War on Terrorism (77 vs. 71 percent). And a second survey (Pew Research Center 2002a) found that respondents with less than a high-school education differed only modestly from college-educated respondents in their support for direct U.S. military action to fight terrorism in Iraq—with (.59 vs. .60) or without (.76 vs. .70) the added assumption that the conflict would produce thousands of U.S. casualties. Differently educated individuals also differed only modestly in their support for using U.S. military force to fight terrorism (post-9/11) in Somalia (.74 vs. .76) and Sudan (.80 vs. .74), and in their support for keeping U.S. troops in Afghanistan to maintain civil order (.67 vs. .70).[4]

Of course, few, if any, U.S. foreign policy activities, even uses of force, have ever enjoyed widespread bipartisan support on a scale comparable to the post-9/11 War on Terrorism. Indeed, none of the foreign crises examined in this study—including the Persian Gulf crisis, prior to the outbreak of war—have enjoyed broad or sustained public and elite support. And as we shall see, the patterns for the foreign policy issues and events investigated in this chapter across groups of Americans at different levels of education and political engagement differ dramatically from those noted above with respect to the War on Terrorism. Hence, notwithstanding this arguably unique circumstance, the general predictions outlined above appear most likely to be the rule, rather than the exception.

I conclude this section by briefly addressing what might appear to be, at first glance, an inconsistency between the general predictions outlined above and my finding from the previous chapter that the least politically informed Americans are increasingly prone to rally round the flag in times of crisis. After all, if exposure to soft news outlets causes low-information consumers to recoil from foreign entanglements, why would it simultaneously induce larger postcrisis initiation rallies? The answer, foreshadowed above, is that it is important to take into account the effects of soft news exposure on the propensity of politically inattentive individuals to receive *any* information about foreign crises, as well as their *availability* to rally.

Prior to the rise of the soft news media, the least politically informed segments of the public remained largely oblivious to many U.S. foreign policy activities, including uses of military force (recall table 5.1). I have shown that the proliferation of soft news outlets has increased the propensity of these individuals to *pay attention* when the United States employs or deploys force abroad. Even if one assumes that soft news coverage tends to be less prone than that of the traditional news media to induce a patriotic rally response, the fact that previously inattentive Americans—many of whom sympathize with isolationism—are exposed to *any* coverage of a crisis, even in the soft news media, most likely increases their propensity to rally. After all, absent *any* exposure, this propensity is presumably zero. Hence, the net effect of an increased number of politically uninformed individuals becoming aware of foreign crises, even via the soft news media, is likely to be a trend toward larger rallies among this segment of the population. This overall pattern will hold even if only a relatively small percentage of formerly unaware individuals—who, by definition, *could not* previously have rallied—react positively upon encountering soft news coverage of a foreign crisis.

It is, of course, possible that exposure to soft news coverage could produce *anti-rallies* among formerly unaware individuals, particularly those with isolationist leanings. Yet, according to the 2000 NES, the least politically informed isolationists (those who advocate staying out of the world's problems) are 17 percentage points *less* likely to approve of the president's job performance, compared to their internationalist counterparts (those who *oppose* reducing the U.S. role in the world). This gap persists even after accounting for respondents' party identification.[5] Hence, the very respondents who are *most* prone to react negatively upon learning of an American use of force abroad are disproportionately likely to *already* disapprove of the president's job performance. And if they *already* disapprove, prior to a given foreign policy engagement, such individuals obviously cannot re-evaluate the president downwards.

Additionally, also in the 2000 NES, the least politically informed internationalists are three times more likely than their isolationist counterparts to respond "no opinion" to the presidential approval question. Once again, the gap persists even after accounting for respondents' partisan preferences.[6] There are therefore far more politically inattentive internationalists available to reevaluate the president *upward* in the aftermath of a use of force abroad than there are inattentive isolationists available to reevaluate *downward*. Combined with the aforementioned approval gap, this suggests that, in the net, *anti-rallies* among previously unaware individuals, though not impossible, are relatively improbable. It further suggests that my prior finding of a trend toward larger rallies, over time, among politically unengaged Americans is not necessarily inconsistent with the prediction that exposure to soft news coverage tends to induce greater suspicion of U.S. involvement in world affairs among politically inattentive consumers. I now turn to a series of statistical tests of my hypotheses.

Soft News and Support for U.S. Military Involvement in Bosnia

My first test of Hypotheses 7.1, 7.3, and 7.4 focuses on U.S. involvement in the Bosnian Civil War in the early 1990s. I employ two surveys: a May 1994 North Carolina statewide telephone poll, conducted by the *News and Observer* newspaper, and a May 1993 Harris telephone poll (henceforth, the Carolina and Harris polls, respectively). The fortuitous coincidence that these surveys happen to include questions concerning a U.S. foreign crisis (Bosnia) addressed in previous chapters allows me to maintain a close link between this analysis and my prior investigations into the correlates of attentiveness.

Prior to the Dayton Peace Accords of November 1995, the mid-1990s were characterized by a gradual escalation of U.S. and NATO military and diplomatic involvement in Bosnia. In mid-1993, the Clinton administration sought— with little success—to convince its allies to support exempting anti-Serbian forces from a United Nations–imposed embargo on weapons sales to Bosnia. This proposal was aimed at helping Bosnia's Muslim population, which, due in large measure to the Serbian ethnic cleansing campaign, was perceived by the international community as a victim of aggression. At the same time, the United States was engaged in diplomatic negotiations and public hand-wringing regarding the proper U.S. role in ending the civil war. Later that year, the UN Security Council endorsed a U.S.-initiated NATO plan to enforce a no-fly zone over Bosnia, intended to protect the Muslim population from Serbian aerial bombardment.

By the time of the May 1994 survey, in response to the bombing of a civilian marketplace in Sarajevo by Serbian forces, America and its NATO allies were in the midst of an extended air strike campaign against Serbian targets. And President Clinton was promising more, and more intense, air strikes if the Serbs did not agree to talk peace. Indeed, the U.S. military engagement in Bosnia was gradually escalating, causing alarm in some circles in Washington, who feared a Vietnam-like quagmire. Hence, both surveys took place at times when Bosnia was a regular topic of news broadcasts—both hard and soft—and, hence, of fairly substantial interest to many Americans.

For my dependent variables in the 1994 Carolina poll, I focus on two questions asking respondents whether and how strongly they supported or opposed "U.S. military action in Bosnia" and "the national health care plan proposed by President Clinton." For each question, responses were coded as follows: 1 = strongly oppose, 2 = somewhat oppose, 3 = somewhat favor, and 4 = strongly favor. Because the response categories form a reasonably symmetric, ordinal scale, ordered logit is an appropriate estimator for this analysis.

I include the latter question in order to test an extension of my seventh hypothesis, which holds that public attentiveness to the types of issues *not* typically covered in the soft news media will not be influenced by soft news consumption. If so, it follows in a fairly straightforward manner that if the soft news media does not cover an issue, then peoples' opinions about that issue ought not to be influenced by exposure to the soft news media, regardless of their intrinsic interest in the issue or in politics in general. An issue as complex and partisan as reforming the U.S. health care system is not the type of issue one would anticipate encountering in the soft news media. Hence, I do not expect exposure to soft news outlets to be significantly related to respondents' opinions about this issue.

My key causal variable in the Carolina poll is based on a series of questions asking respondents how frequently they watch a variety of soft and hard news TV programs. As in prior analyses, I combined these questions into two scales, one measuring soft news consumption and the other hard news consumption. The soft news scale is based on respondents' self reported viewing of the following four types of programs: (1) "Talk shows like *Oprah, Donahue*, or *Geraldo*," (2) MTV, (3) "Shows about celebrities, like *Entertainment Tonight*," and (4) "Real-life drama shows, like *A Current Affair, Hard Copy*, or *Rescue-911*."[7] The hard news scale, in turn, is based on respondents' self-reported viewing habits with respect to the following three program formats: (1) "National and international news on NBC, ABC, CBS, or CNN," (2) "Discussions of news and business on public television," and (3) "Local evening news at 6:00 or 11:00." Responses to each question ranged from 1 ("never") to 4 ("often").[8]

Turning to the 1993 Harris poll, for my dependent variables I focus on four questions asking respondents (1) whether they supported or opposed "allowing the Bosnians to buy weapons to defend themselves against the Serbs," (2) how they would "rate President Clinton's handling of events in the former Yugoslavia, including Serbia and Bosnia,"[9] (3) whether they supported or opposed "eliminating Medicare and having most Americans choose their health insurance through the same program," and (4) whether they "feel that government policy tends to favor jobs too much, favor the environment too much, or has . . . the balance about right?" I transformed the responses from the first three questions into dichotomous variables, suitable for a logit estimator, coded 1 if respondents supported the item and 0 otherwise. The final question, which allows three possible responses—0 = favors jobs too much, 0.5 = about right, 1 = favors the environment too much—is suitable for an ordered logit estimator. As before, I include the final two questions in order to test the aforementioned extension of my seventh hypothesis. Once again, if this hypothesis is valid, it follows that if people do *not* encounter news about Medicare or environmental policy in the soft news media, then their opinions about those issues should not be affected by consuming soft news. Like President Clinton's health care reform proposal, neither Medicare nor environmental policy is the type of dramatic, human-interest-oriented issue amenable to cheap framing and piggybacking. Hence, I do not expect exposure to soft news outlets to be significantly related to respondents' opinions about either issue.

My key causal variable in the Harris survey is based on a series of questions asking respondents whether or not they watch the television talk shows hosted by Phil Donahue, Arsenio Hall, Sally Jesse Raphael, Jay Leno, David Letterman, Regis Philbin and Kathie Lee Gifford, Joan Rivers, Geraldo Rivera, Montel Williams, and Oprah Winfrey. I coded each question 1 if a respondent indicated that he or she watches a given talk show, and 0 otherwise. I then combined these questions into a ten-item scale measuring respondents' talk show viewing habits.[10] Unfortunately, no suitable questions were included in this survey for estimating respondents' exposure to traditional news sources. Hence, I could not construct an analogous hard news index for this analysis.

The control variables, which differ slightly across the two surveys (depending on availability and performance in the models), fall into four primary categories: socioeconomic status; political partisanship; salience of U.S. policy toward Bosnia (operationalized as whether the respondent mentioned Bosnia as the nation's "most important problem" in an open-ended question); and attitudes toward the key U.S. allies with troops on the ground in Bosnia (Britain and France), and toward the United Nations.[11] To determine whether any effects of watching soft news differ across different types of respondents, I interact the soft news and talk show indexes with the level of the respondents' education. As before, I employ education as a rough indicator of respondents' degree of political engagement. The complete statistical results from my investigations of the Carolina and Harris polls are reported in models 1–2 and 3–6, respectively, of table 7.A1, in the appendix of this chapter.[12]

To begin with, the results appear to support my extension of Hypothesis 7. Soft news appears, in these data, to have only a modest influence, if any, on respondents' opinions regarding health care reform, Medicare, and environmental policy. In sharp contrast, in both surveys, soft news consumption appears to have a much larger influence on respondents' views of the U.S. intervention in Bosnia. Figures 7.1 and 7.2 present three graphics in which I have transformed the logit coefficients from the several Bosnia models into probabilities of supporting U.S. policy in Bosnia, among respondents at different levels of education.[13] Figure 7.1 presents the probabilities of *strongly approving* a U.S. military role in Bosnia—the category with the largest soft news effects—from the Carolina poll. The top and bottom graphics in figure 7.2, respectively, adapted from the Harris poll, track respondents' probabilities of supporting lifting the arms embargo on Bosnia's Muslim population and supporting President Clinton's handling of U.S. policy toward Bosnia.

Figure 7.1 indicates that as soft news exposure increases among all respondents, except those with a postgraduate education, support for a U.S. military role in Bosnia declines. Moreover, the declines are statistically significant ($p <$ .05 or $p <$ .10) for the 55 percent of respondents who did not attend college.[14] As has been the case throughout the book, the strongest effects emerge among the least educated respondents. Among respondents who did not complete high school, as soft news exposure increases from its minimum to maximum values, the probability of *strongly approving* a U.S. military role in Bosnia declines by 39 percentage points ($p <$ .05). Among these same respondents, the corresponding effects on the probabilities of *strongly opposing* a U.S. military role in Bosnia or opposing it somewhat increase by 13 and 23 percentage points, respectively ($p <$ .05). These patterns weaken in a stepwise fashion as respondents move up the education ladder, though, as noted, the effects remain statistically significant and substantial in magnitude among all respondents who did not attend college. Finally, consistent with Hypothesis 7.4, no comparable interaction emerges between hard news consumption and respondents' education level (see model 1 at table 7.A3, in the appendix to this chapter).

Turning to the results of the Harris poll, figure 7.2 indicates that among the

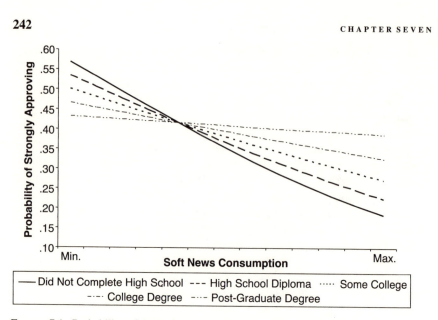

FIGURE 7.1. Probability of Strongly Approving U.S. Military Role in Bosnia, as Soft News Consumption and Education Vary

40 percent of respondents who did not attend college, increased talk show exposure is again associated with reduced support for U.S. policy with respect to Bosnia.[15] Among the least-educated respondents—who did not complete high school—as talk show consumption increases from its minimum to maximum values, the probability of supporting the lifting of the arms embargo on Bosnia declines by 24 percentage points. Among these same respondents, as talk show consumption increases from its minimum to maximum values, the probability of approving President Clinton's handling of the situation in Bosnia declines by 20 percentage points. The relationships once again weaken in a stepwise fashion as respondents move up the education ladder.

Interestingly, in both cases, college-educated respondents move in the opposite direction from their less-educated counterparts. Among the *most* highly educated respondents (those with a postgraduate degree), as talk show consumption increases from its lowest to highest values, the probability of favoring lifting the arms embargo and approving of President Clinton's policies toward Bosnia increase by 36 and 30 percentage points, respectively. Each of these results supports Hypotheses 7.1 and 7.3.

These latter increases raise the possibility that among at least some political sophisticates, who presumably possess a context for understanding information about U.S. policy toward Bosnia, increased exposure to such information, even in the soft news media, is less likely to induce fear of or opposition to a proactive U.S. policy. Indeed, one can imagine that, placed into a broader informa-

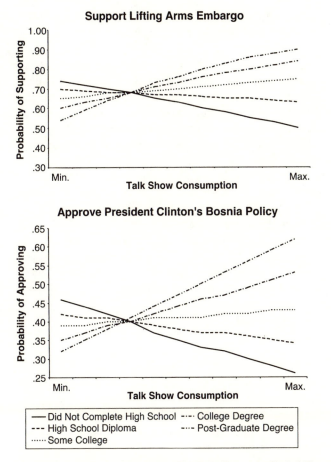

FIGURE 7.2. Effects of Watching TV Talk Shows on Probability of
Supporting U.S. Policy toward Bosnia, as Talk Show Consumption and
Education Vary

tional context, exposure to potential dangers in the world via soft news may
even prompt politically sophisticated individuals to support a *more* assertive
U.S. foreign policy, such as that advocated by President Clinton with respect to
Bosnia, and including the lifting of the UN arms embargo on Bosnia's Muslims.

The debate surrounding the pros and cons of lifting the Bosnia arms embargo
illustrates why this might be the case. Less politically sophisticated individuals,
lacking a broad context for understanding U.S. policy toward Bosnia, may have
focused primarily on the short-term possibility of an increased level of violence
if the embargo were lifted. Absent a broader perspective, these individuals may
have seen lifting of the arms embargo as, in effect, adding fuel to the fire. After
all, they may have encountered a fair amount of information in the soft news

media detailing the brutality of the civil war in Bosnia. Such individuals might not wish to pursue any policy that seemed likely to exacerbate the level of violence.

In contrast, politically informed individuals may be relatively more likely to focus on the longer-term effects of lifting the embargo. Such individuals might reasonably conclude that, even if it resulted in a short-term escalation of the civil war, enhancing the Bosnian Muslims' capacity to defend themselves would presumably reduce the likelihood that the United States would need to contemplate a larger-scale and far more dangerous intervention at a later date. Hence, political sophisticates might look at the identical information yet draw the conclusion opposite from politically unengaged individuals, who lack a broader context for understanding the likely longer-term implications of lifting the arms embargo.

Regardless of the explanation for the latter reversal, the results from these two surveys taken together suggest that—net of a variety of potentially mitigating factors, such as political partisanship and exposure to traditional news— among respondents lacking a college education, but not among their better-educated counterparts, consuming soft news programming, but not hard news, is associated with greater opposition to a proactive U.S. policy with respect to Bosnia.

Soft News and the Merits of NATO Enlargement

I turn next to a second test of Hypotheses 7.1, 7.3, and 7.4, this time employing a March 1998 Gallup poll (telephone survey, $N = 1,009$) which queried respondents regarding their media consumption habits, as well as their views regarding the expansion of NATO into Eastern Europe. As my dependent variable, I focus on the following question: "How in your view does the NATO military alliance affect U.S.-Russian relations these days? Does it make U.S.-Russian relations: 1. much better, 2. somewhat better, 3. somewhat worse, 4. much worse, 5. no effect, or 6. don't know/refused?"

I collapsed the responses into two categories, where 0 = much worse, somewhat worse, or no effect and 1 = somewhat or much better.[16] Once again, the independent variables fall into three categories: (1) socioeconomic status, (2) political engagement and partisanship, and (3) media consumption habits (hard and soft news indexes, and respondents' trust of hard and soft news).[17] The hard and soft news indexes consist of eleven and four items, respectively, concerning respondents' interest in and attention to news and entertainment programming on television, on the radio, in magazines, and in the newspaper.[18]

Most of the control variables are identical to those employed in chapter 4, in my investigation of public attentiveness to the Northern Ireland peace process. Hence, I do not redefine them here, but instead refer the interested reader to appendix 2 in chapter 4, where they are defined. The two media trust indexes, in turn, allow me to account for the differing degrees of credibility that respondents may attribute to soft versus hard news sources. After all, not surprisingly, roughly twice as many respondents indicated that they considered the hard news media trustworthy as trusted the soft news media. This suggests, ceteris paribus, that a respondent is more likely to be influenced by a story presented in a hard news context.

As in the previous analyses, there are no questions included in the survey suitable for estimating respondents' overall degree of interest in international affairs. Hence, I once again employ respondents' education level as an indicator of overall political engagement. As in prior investigations, to determine the differing effects of soft news consumption on respondents at differing levels of education, I interact the soft news index with education.[19] The results from a logit analysis of the effects of soft news consumption on attitudes toward NATO enlargement among respondents at differing education levels are presented in model 7 in table 7.A1.

The results indicate that increased soft news consumption is associated with the view that NATO enlargement is bad for U.S-Russian relations ($p < .05$). This effect, however, weakens as respondents' education level increases. At figure 7.3, I have converted the key coefficients into probabilities of holding a positive view of NATO enlargement, vis-à-vis U.S.-Russian relations, as soft news consumption and education vary, with all other independent variables held constant at their mean values.[20]

The curves shown in figure 7.3 clearly indicate that respondents who consume a great deal of soft news differ materially in their views of NATO enlargement from their counterparts who do not. And this relationship is strongest among the least-educated respondents. Among those who did not attend high school, as soft news consumption increases from its minimum to maximum values, the probability of viewing NATO enlargement as positive for U.S.-Russian relations drops precipitously, by 71 percentage points. Among respondents who attended but did not complete high school and those with a high school diploma, the corresponding declines are 48 and 20 percentage points, respectively. In fact, among all respondents who did not attend college (about 40 percent of the total), soft news consumption is associated with a decreasing likelihood of viewing NATO enlargement as good for U.S.-Russian relations. The relationships, in turn, weaken in a stepwise fashion as respondents move up the education ladder.

Similar to the case of Bosnia, among respondents at the two highest education levels, the relationships invert, with heavy soft news consumption associated with an increase in the propensity to view NATO enlargement as positive for U.S.-Russian relations. While these increases are smaller in magnitude than the corresponding decline among respondents at the two lowest education levels, they nonetheless once again raise the possibility that, at least among some political sophisticates, increased exposure to information about NATO expansion, even in the soft news media, is unlikely to induce greater suspicion of a proactive U.S. foreign policy. As discussed above, such individuals are more likely than their less politically engaged counterparts to possess the necessary tools for counterarguing any information that might conflict with their

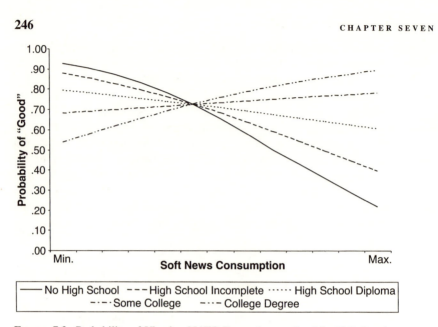

FIGURE 7.3. Probability of Viewing NATO Expansion as *Good* for U.S.-Russian Relations, as Soft News Consumption and Education Vary

political predispositions (Zaller 1992). Again, regardless of the reasons for the reversal among highly educated respondents, consistent with Hypotheses 7.1 and 7.3, the results presented in this investigation point toward a clear positive relationship among low-education respondents between consuming soft news and a propensity to worry about the potential negative consequences of NATO enlargement.

Turning to Hypothesis 7.4, in this instance the effects of consuming hard news appear similar to those of soft news consumption (see model 2 at table 7.A3). Once again, however, consistent with my hypothesis, the effects are uniformly weaker than the corresponding effects of consuming soft news. Among respondents who did not attend high school, who attended *some* high school, or who graduated from high school, a maximum increase in hard news consumption is associated with declines in the probability of viewing NATO enlargement as "good" for U.S.-Russian relations of 57 (from .93 to .36), 28 (from .89 to .61) and 19 (from .81 to .62) percentage points, respectively. Among respondents who attended some college, variations in hard news consumption have no effect whatsoever on attitudes toward NATO enlargement. Finally, among respondents with a college degree, the relationship reverses and greater hard news consumption is associated with a relatively modest 13-percentage-point *increase* in the probability of viewing NATO enlargement as positive for U.S.-Russian relations (from .57 to .80).

Given the previously described volatility in the opinions expressed by politically inattentive individuals in responding to public opinion surveys (Zaller and Feldman 1992; Asher 1998), the question arises as to whether the least-educated respondents possess any meaningful attitudes at all with respect to the implications—pro or con—of NATO enlargement. At first glance, it seems entirely possible that many of the least-educated respondents are essentially expressing nonattitudes (Asher 1998). And, indeed, it would probably be something of a stretch to interpret these results as suggesting that a typical respondent with less than a high school education has thought at length about, or understands, the implications of NATO enlargement for U.S.-Russian relations.

The previously described effects of soft news consumption, however, do not require that respondents understand the nuances of this issue. Due to the extraordinary salience of the Cold War for nearly five decades, the vast majority of Americans—even those lacking a great deal of education or interest in politics—are aware that NATO is an alliance between the United States and Europe, or at least that it involves a U.S. overseas commitment. It is not necessary to understand the implications of NATO enlargement to recognize that it most likely entails expanding U.S. commitments abroad. And if one recognizes that a policy involves an expanded U.S. role in the world, and one prefers that the U.S. *reduce* its overseas commitments, then it is possible to express opposition to such an expansion by asserting that it would be "bad" for the United States, without truly understanding the nuances of the policy, or even without having previously thought about it. Hence, while the least-educated respondents may not have carefully reasoned opinions about NATO or U.S.-Russian relations, it does not necessarily follow that the effects described in this section are artifacts of nonattitudes.

Daytime Talk Shows and Attitudes toward Japan

In early 1994, the United States became embroiled in another in a long string of trade disputes with Japan, this time concerning telecommunications equipment and medical products, culminating in a threat by the Clinton administration to impose trade sanctions (Associated Press 1994). In the midst of the controversy (in June 1994), the emperor of Japan, along with his wife, embarked on a visit to the United States, including a controversial stop at Pearl Harbor. The confluence of these events briefly returned Japan to the forefront of U.S. foreign policy. In this section, I further test Hypotheses 7.1 and 7.3, employing a May 1994 Harris poll which included a series of questions on U.S.-Japanese relations in general, and on the emperor's visit in particular. For my dependent variable in this analysis, I focus on one such question: "Tell me what your attitude is toward Japan and the Japanese people—generally warm and friendly, not particularly warm and friendly, or unfriendly and hostile?" I recoded the responses into a dichotomous indicator, suitable for a logit estimator, where 0 = not particularly warm and friendly or unfriendly and hostile, and 1 = generally warm and friendly.

My key causal variable is based on a similar series of questions as those employed in the previously discussed 1993 Harris poll, which in this instance asks respondents whether or not they watch the television talk shows hosted by Phil Donahue, Arsenio Hall, Sally Jesse Raphael, Jay Leno, David Letterman, Regis Philbin and Kathie Lee Gifford, Joan Rivers, Geraldo Rivera, Montel Williams, Oprah Winfrey, Ricki Lake, Rolonda Watts, and Bertice Berry.[21] As above, I coded each question 1 if a respondent indicated that he or she watches a given talk show, and 0 otherwise. I combined these questions into a thirteen-item scale measuring respondents' talk show viewing habits.[22] Unfortunately, as in the 1993 Harris poll, no suitable questions were included for estimating respondents' consumption of traditional news. Indeed, the closest approximation to such a question concerned respondents' propensity to watch another talk show host, Ted Koppel, whose program *Nightline* is heavily oriented toward hard news. I therefore included this latter question as a best available, albeit admittedly *far* from ideal, proxy for respondents' interest in traditional news.

The control variables fall into four distinct groups: (1) socioeconomic status, (2) political partisanship, (3) propensity to watch Ted Koppel's *Nightline*, and (4) respondents' estimate of the state of U.S.-Japanese relations.[23] To determine whether the effects of watching talk shows differ across different types of respondents, I once again interact the talk show index with respondents' education level. The results from a logit analysis of this dependent variable are reported in model 8 in Table 7.A1.

The results indicate, as has been the case throughout this chapter, that TV talk show consumption appears to influence respondents' attitudes, and that the valence and extent of this influence varies with education. At figure 7.4, I transform the logit coefficients into probabilities of expressing warm feelings toward Japan among respondents at different levels of education and talk show consumption.

Figure 7.4 indicates that among the two-thirds of respondents lacking a four-year college degree, as talk show exposure increases, the probability they will express warm feelings toward Japan declines.[24] Among the least-educated respondents, who did not complete high school, as talk show consumption increases from its minimum to maximum values, the probability of having warm feelings toward Japan declines by 37 percentage points. As has so often been the case throughout this book, these patterns weaken in a stepwise fashion as respondents move up the education ladder.

Interestingly, as in the prior investigations, college-educated respondents move modestly in the opposite direction from their less-educated counterparts. Among the *most* highly educated respondents (those with a postgraduate degree), as talk show consumption increases from its lowest to highest values, the probability of having warm feelings toward Japan increases by 15 percentage points. Though, due to probability weighting, I cannot readily evaluate the statistical significance of this increase, it does, once again, raise the possibility, consistent with the selective acceptance hypothesis, that political sophisticates are less apt to be persuaded by negative coverage of Japan in the soft news media. Once again, these results support Hypotheses 7.1 and 7.3.

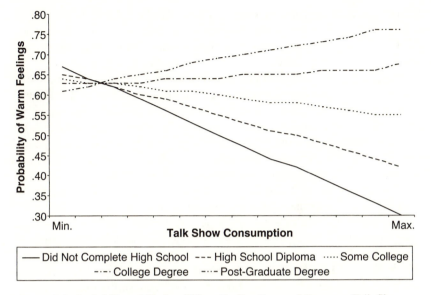

FIGURE 7.4. Probability of Having "Warm Feelings" toward Japan, as Talk Show Consumption and Education Vary

Daytime Talk Shows and Foreign Policy Attitudes

The 2000 NES survey differed from all previous NES surveys in asking respondents a considerably broader range of questions regarding their media consumption habits, including a question concerning whether and how much they watch daytime talk shows, like those hosted by Oprah Winfrey and Rosie O'Donnell. This makes it possible to explore the effects of watching these programs on respondents' attitudes regarding foreign policy, thereby further testing Hypotheses 7.1, 7.3, and 7.4, as well as testing Hypothesis 7.2. For my dependent variables, I focus on the following three questions: (1) "Do you agree or disagree with this statement: This country would be better off if we just stayed home and did not concern ourselves with problems in other parts of the world"; (2) "Do you approve or disapprove of the way Bill Clinton is handling our relations with foreign countries?"; and (3) "Do you approve or disapprove of the way Bill Clinton is handling the economy?"[25] The latter question allows me to conduct an additional test of my aforementioned extension of Hypothesis 7, which predicts no soft news effects for traditional (partisan or non-dramatic) political issues. (Recall from chapter 4 that soft news consumption did not appear to influence respondents' self-reported attentiveness to news about the U.S. economy, even during a recession.)

The key causal variable ("Watch daytime talk shows"), in turn, is based on the following question: "How many times in the last week have you watched daytime television talk shows such as *Oprah Winfrey, Rosie O'Donnell,* or *Jerry Springer?"* I collapsed the responses into four categories: $0 =$ never, $1 = 1$–2 times, $2 = 3$–5 times, $3 = 6 +$ times or every day. As with my other analyses of NES data, the control variables fall into four categories: (1) socioeconomic status, (2) political interest and knowledge, (3) political trust and efficacy, and (4) media consumption habits. Once again, I also include interaction terms (e.g., "Watch daytime talk shows $\times$ political information") to investigate whether, consistent with Hypothesis 7.3, consuming talk shows has a stronger effect on the attitudes of respondents who are *not* intrinsically interested in politics, as well as to determine whether, consistent with Hypothesis 7.2, any such effects vary with respondents' ex ante support for isolationism. This also allows me to investigate the effects of hard news consumption on different types of respondents, thereby testing Hypothesis 7.4.

As in chapter 5, I employ respondents' levels of political information—based on the interviewer's assessment of each respondent's political knowledge—as my indicator of political engagement. Most of the control variables are identical to those employed in the NES "major problems facing the nation" analysis in chapter 5, and so are not redefined here. The only noteworthy exceptions are a set of TV news consumption variables, which in this instance code the number of days in the past week (0–7) the respondent reported watching national network news, early evening local news, or late evening local news.

Beginning with the effects of consuming soft news, models 1–7 in table 7.A2 (in the appendix), present the results of seven logit analyses, employing each dependent variable described above. Because the NES models employ a much broader range of control variables than do the others in this chapter, in order to insure that my results are in no way artifacts of model specifications, I begin my first analysis of each dependent variable by presenting a "basic" model, excluding all control variables. The basic models are in each instance broadly consistent with the full multivariate models. This suggests that the relationships are not artifacts of a particular model specification. Hence, I focus on the fully specified models.

The results clearly support Hypotheses 7.1 through 7.3, as well as my extension of Hypothesis 7. In these data, watching daytime talk shows influences public attitudes regarding foreign policy, but *not* regarding the economy. Beginning with the latter test, for which the dependent variable measures approval of President Clinton's handling of the economy, neither the coefficient on "Watch daytime talk shows" nor that on the interaction term is statistically significant. The state of the economy is not a frequent topic on daytime talk shows (or other soft news outlets). Hence, it is unsurprising that watching talk shows would not influence respondents' attitudes regarding the president's handling of the economy.[26] In contrast, watching daytime talk shows *does* appear to influence respondents' attitudes toward foreign policy. For convenience, I refer to those who agreed with the proposition that "this country would be better off if we just stayed home" as isolationists, and those who disagreed with this proposition as internationalists. Once again, I translate the logit coefficients into probabilities of supporting an isolationist foreign policy or approving of President Clinton's foreign policy, as respondents' exposure to daytime talk shows and political information vary from their lowest to highest values.

Consistent with Hypothesis 7.1, among the least politically informed respondents, a maximum increase in talk show viewing is associated with a 36 percentage point increase in isolationist sentiment (from .34 to .70, $p < .05$) and a 28 percentage point decrease in support for President Clinton's handling of foreign policy (from .73 to .46, $p < .05$). In contrast, consistent with Hypothesis 7.3, among highly politically informed respondents, the corresponding increase in talk show consumption is associated with a statistically insignificant 4 percentage point *decline* in isolationism (from .15 to .11) and a 16 percentage point *increase* (from .74 to .90, $p < .05$) in support for the president's handling of foreign policy.

These latter results are consistent with my findings from the prior investigations into public attitudes regarding Bosnia, Japan, and NATO expansion, and with the theoretical argument developed at the outset of this chapter. In the prior analyses, highly educated respondents were somewhat *more* likely to view NATO enlargement and Japan favorably, and to support a proactive U.S. policy toward Bosnia, as their soft news or talk show consumption increased. Once again, it is not too surprising that political sophisticates might draw quite different lessons than their less politically attuned counterparts from exposure to foreign policy information in a soft news context. For one thing, such information would presumably enhance these individuals' overall knowledge about foreign affairs by only a very small degree, if at all. And, perhaps more importantly, for the reasons discussed earlier in the chapter, such information seems more likely to reinforce their relatively strong predispositions—which for 90 percent of respondents at the highest level of political information (in the 2000 NES) means *opposition* to isolationism—rather than change them.

I next briefly turn to the effects of consuming hard news. Models 3 and 4 in Table 7.A3 retest Hypothesis 7.4—which predicts weaker hard news effects—against both dependent variables. These results indicate, once again consistent with my hypothesis, that consuming hard news has no statistically significant effect on respondents' attitudes toward either President Clinton's foreign policy management or isolationism, regardless of their level of political information.

What remains, however, is to explicitly test whether, as Hypothesis 7.2 predicts, the effects of consuming talk shows on attitudes toward isolationism expressed in the 2000 NES vary with respondents' preexisting isolationist propensities. To address this question, I employ the previously described isolationism question as an explanatory variable, interacting it with talk show consumption and political information. As my dependent variable, I employ the aforementioned question asking respondents whether they approve of President Clinton's management of foreign policy. Given President Clinton's avowed support for a proactive, multilateral approach to U.S. foreign policy, it seems highly probable (indeed virtually certain) that most isolationists would be less likely than their internationalist counterparts to approve of President Clinton's handling of foreign policy. And, in fact, in the 2000 NES, 71 percent of internationalists approved of President Clinton's foreign policy management, compared to just 57 percent of isolationists.

Unfortunately, because only 10 percent of highly politically informed respondents adopted the isolationist position, it is difficult to draw meaningful inferences concerning the effects of variations in talk show consumption on isolationism among political sophisticates. This problem is exacerbated by the fact that the isolationism question was asked of only half of the respondents in the 2000 NES, thereby substantially reducing the number of available observations. In order to mitigate somewhat the problem of "empty boxes" that can result from dividing a relatively small number of respondents into a large number of subgroups, I collapse the political information scale into three categories.[27] Even with this adjustment, however, there remain an inadequate number of highly informed isolationists (nearly 50 percent fewer than any of the other categories) to allow a meaningful estimate of the substantive effects of talk show consumption on this subgroup. For instance, only *one* highly informed isolationist received the highest score on the talk show consumption scale. Hence, I do not report the effects of talk show consumption for this latter group. (The results from this analysis are presented in model 7 in table 7.A2.)

Beginning with the least politically informed isolationists, as daytime talk show consumption increases from its lowest to highest levels, the probability of approving of President Clinton's handling of foreign policy *declines* by 51 percentage points (from .64 to .14, $p < .05$). Among the least-informed internationalists, in turn, a maximum increase in talk show consumption is associated with a statistically insignificant 21 percentage point decline (from .76 to .55) in the probability of approving of President Clinton's handling of U.S. foreign policy. This represents less than half as large an effect as among low-information isolationists. Finally, among *highly* politically informed internationalists, a maximum increase in talk show consumption is associated with an 18 percentage point *increase* in support for President Clinton's foreign policy management (from .75 to .93, $p < .05$).

Given the nature of soft news coverage of foreign crises, as described in chapter 3, these results are precisely what the reception-acceptance model, including the selective-acceptance hypothesis, would predict. The attitudes of politically uninformed isolationists are strongly reinforced by exposure to daytime talk shows. Their more internationally oriented, yet also relatively uninformed, counterparts appear in these data to have been able to resist *some* of the pro-isolationist effects of consuming daytime talk shows; such effects among this group are far smaller and statistically insignificant. They do not, however, appear able to be able to resist such messages entirely. After all, the *direction* of the effect of talk show consumption on low-information internationalist respondents is the same as for low-information isolationists. At least in these data, talk show exposure is clearly associated with increased isolationism among low-information respondents, regardless of their views regarding the appropriate U.S. role in the world, albeit far more strongly so for respondents predisposed to support isolationism. Additionally, as the reception-acceptance model antici-pates, highly informed respondents who oppose isolationism are able to coun-terargue any pro-isolationist messages in daytime talk shows, while finding re-inforcement for their internationalist predispositions. Taken together, these results strongly support Hypothesis 7.2.

Turning, finally, to the effects of hard news coverage on support for President Clinton's foreign policy, the results from this analysis (shown in model 5 at table 7.A3) indicate that, as one might anticipate given the results of my content analysis (see chapter 3), exposure to hard news increases support for President Clinton's foreign policy regardless of respondents' isolationist leanings, albeit predictably more strongly so for internationalists. Among the least-informed internationalists, as the frequency of watching national network news increases from 0 to 7 days per week, the probability of supporting President Clinton's management of foreign policy increases by 25 percentage points (from .63 to .88, $p < .05$). The corresponding increase among highly informed internationalists is 13 percentage points (from .71 to .84, $p < .10$). Among the least politically informed isolationists, in turn, a maximum increase in national news watching is associated with a statistically insignificant 10-percentage point increase in the probability of supporting President Clinton's foreign policy (from .60 to .70).

In this instance, given the more pro-internationalist tenor of hard news, rela-tive to soft news, any reinforcement effect should be more likely to apply to internationalists than to isolationists. Hence, it is not surprising that the stron-gest effects emerge among internationalists, whose attitudes are significantly reinforced by exposure to hard news, regardless of their level of political infor-mation. In order to evaluate these results against the Hypothesis 7.4, the appro-priate comparison therefore involves the reinforcement effect of soft news con-sumption on low-information isolationists, relative to the corresponding effect of hard news consumption on low-information internationalists. And in fact, the reinforcement effect of exposure to national network news by low-information internationalists is less than half as large as that associated with exposure to soft news by low-information isolationists. Similarly, the effects of hard news expo-sure on low-information isolationists are considerably weaker than the effects of soft news exposure on their internationalist counterparts. Once again, each of these results is consistent with my Hypothesis 7.4.

ISOLATIONISM TRENDS, 1960–2000

The patterns identified in the five surveys investigated thus far each suggest that at least among the less-educated or politically inattentive segments of the public, soft news consumption is associated with increased skepticism of a proactive or multilateral approach to U.S. foreign policy. Given the dramatic proliferation of soft news outlets over the past decade, it seems likely, though by no means certain, that this pattern would be associated with an aggregate trend toward rising isolationism, particularly among the least-educated or least–politically attentive Americans, for whom the soft news media are an important sources of information about the world. Indeed, Hypotheses 7.5 and 7.6 predict just such a pattern.

To test these latter hypotheses, I again turn to the NES Cumulative Data File (CDF), which, as previously discussed, includes data from 1948 to 2000. For most of this period, the NES has regularly included the aforementioned isolationism question.[28] My data include fourteen of the twenty-one election-year NES surveys between 1960 and 2000. The other seven surveys—1962, 1964, 1966, 1970, 1974, 1978, and 1982—did not include the isolationism question.

To investigate over-time trends, I created dummy variables for each decade from the 1960s to the 1990s, and also for 2000. I then interacted respondents' education level with each dummy variable.[29] This allows me to separately determine the propensity of differently educated respondents to support isolationism in each decade. To the extent that the rise of soft news has influenced these relationships, one would anticipate, consistent with Hypothesis 7.5, a general trend toward increased support for isolationism among the least-educated respondents—the heaviest consumers of soft news—but, consistent with Hypothesis 7.6, not among highly educated respondents.

Because in this instance I am investigating long-term trends with respect to a single issue area (isolationism), it is important to correct for the extreme fluctuations in public attitudes that may result from short-term events. In other words, in any single year the influence of soft news foreign affairs coverage on attitudes toward isolationism may well be overwhelmed by individuals' reactions to real-world events at the time of the NES survey. For instance, a failed military intervention might temporarily inflate the tendency of respondents to express distrust of foreign entanglements for reasons not necessarily having anything to do with the soft news media. Unfortunately, there is no perfect way to eliminate entirely this potential problem. It can, however, be mitigated somewhat by averaging across multiple NES surveys, conducted in different years. I have elected to aggregate the data at the level of decades. While the ideal level of aggregation is certainly subject to debate, I believe that by aggregating in this way I am able to capture long-term, systematic trends, independent of the effects of specific, short-term international events.

Additionally, because my data on network audience ratings, along with several other controls employed in my prior analysis of the NES CDF (investigating "major problems facing the nation"), does not extend to 2000, I instead employ the secular passage of time as my indicator of the growth and diversification of television. While, as discussed in chapter 5, network audience ratings are in some respects a superior indicator, in this analysis, for reasons that shall become apparent below, it is particularly important to retain an observation for 2000. Hence, I sacrifice some degree of validity in my indicator of the over-time diversification of television in exchange for retaining a particularly important set of observations in my data set.[30]

I also include several control variables to account for respondents' socio-economic status, political engagement, and partisanship. Each of these controls

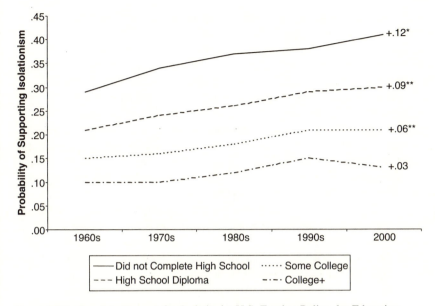

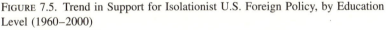

FIGURE 7.5. Trend in Support for Isolationist U.S. Foreign Policy, by Education
Level (1960–2000)
    **$p < .01$, *$p < .05$

is employed in various prior NES investigations throughout the book, and is
defined in earlier chapters, so I do not redefine them here. Instead, I turn directly to the results of my investigation, in the form of a logit analysis (shown
in model 8 in table 7.A2). In Figure 7.5, I transform the key coefficients into
probabilities of supporting isolationism among respondents at each of four education levels.

The curves in Figure 7.5 support my hypotheses. Among respondents who
did not attend high school, between the 1960s and 2000, the probability of
supporting isolationism increased by 12 percentage points (from .29 to .41,
$p < .05$). This represents clear support for Hypothesis 7.5. Moreover, the corresponding trend weakens in a stepwise fashion as respondents move up the education ladder, until among respondents with a college or postgraduate degree,
no statistically significant trend emerges from the 1960s to 2000. These latter
results support Hypothesis 7.6

These data by no means establish a causal linkage between the individual-
level analyses presented above and the aggregate trends shown in figure 7.5.
Indeed, given that the beginning of the trend shown in the figure predates the
widespread proliferation of soft news, the latter is clearly not the sole explanation for the former. Nevertheless, the overall patterns in these relationships are,
in most key respects, consistent with what one would anticipate finding *if* the
proliferation of soft news outlets were indeed influencing those Americans most
prone to watch soft news programs to become increasingly sympathetic to iso-

lationist positions and themes. Similarly, if the soft news media were at least partly responsible for rising isolationism, we would also anticipate weaker relationships among highly educated respondents, who are least likely to consume or be influenced by soft news outlets. And this pattern also emerges in the data. Nevertheless, given the many potential problems inherent in any analysis of long-term trends, these results should be interpreted as merely suggestive.

While it is not possible to address all possible alternative explanations for the patterns in figure 7.5, including the 2000 NES in this analysis makes it possible to discount one relatively obvious alternative. That is, it is possible that the end of the Cold War—which removed for many Americans the primary rationale for an outwardly focused American foreign policy—rather than the proliferation of the soft news media, might be responsible for rising isolationism. If so, however, one would not anticipate any meaningful variation from the 1990s to 2000. After all, the Cold War was just as "over" in 2000 as in the 1990s. In fact, from the 1990s to 2000, the data reveal a 3 percentage point *rise* in isolationism among the least-educated respondents, a 1 percentage point increase among those with a high school diploma, and no change whatsoever among respondents who attended some college. And among college-educated respondents, isolationism *declined* by 2 percentage points from the 1990s to 2000, after rising by 3 percentage points from the 1980s to the 1990s. In fact, isolationism among all four education groups increased from the 1980s to 1990s.

In 2000, in turn, among the *least*-educated respondents, support for isolationism reached its highest level (.63) since the NES began asking the question in 1956, while pro-isolationist sentiments among the other three education groups remained similar, or declined, from the 1990s to 2000. While the end of the Cold War could potentially account for rising isolationism from the 1980s to the 1990s, it cannot explain why isolationism *increased* from the 1990s to 2000 among respondents who did not attend college, while simultaneously *decreasing* among respondents with a college degree. Overall, while these patterns do not rule out the end of the Cold War as an influential factor, they do appear more consistent with my alternative hypothesis, that the rise of the soft news media has influenced—largely, though not necessarily exclusively, in a pro-isolationist direction—the foreign policy attitudes of the less-educated segments of the public.

CONCLUSION

Each of the statistical investigations presented in this chapter appears to point in a single direction, toward a clear association between consuming soft news and opposition to, or distrust of, a proactive, multilateral, or interventionist U.S. foreign policy. This general suspicion of internationalism extended to disapproval of the foreign policy management of President Clinton—who, during his tenure in office, was widely associated with a multilateral and activist foreign policy agenda—and to negative feelings toward a principal U.S. ally in Asia.

Yet the seeming association between soft news consumption and isolationism—or at least suspicion of a multilateral and proactive U.S. approach to foreign policy—does not affect all Americans equally. As has been the case throughout the book, the strongest effects of soft news consumption appear mostly limited to the less educated and politically inattentive segments of the population, who are also the primary consumers of soft news programs.

My analysis of over-time trends in support for isolationism produced patterns consistent with the individual-level findings: low-education NES respondents, but not their better-educated counterparts, have grown increasingly supportive of isolationism, over time. Indeed, among highly educated and politically engaged individuals, exposure to soft news, to the extent it has any effect at all, appears in these data to essentially *reinforce* a predominant internationalist predisposition. These patterns are consistent with the two-step reception-acceptance model, including the selective acceptance hypothesis. And, for low-information respondents, they are precisely what one would anticipate arising from exposure to overwhelmingly episodic framing of foreign policy issues and events, combined with an emphasis on violence, tragedy, and other forms of human drama, such as prevails in the soft news media.

Interestingly, in at least some instances, highly educated or politically engaged individuals appear also to have been influenced by exposure to soft news, albeit in different ways than their less-informed or educated counterparts. For political sophisticates, consuming soft news appears in these data to have *reinforced* support for several major U.S. foreign policy initiatives, including U.S. intervention in Bosnia and NATO enlargement, as well as for a key U.S. ally (Japan), and more generally for an outwardly focused approach to U.S. foreign policy. Once again, this appears consistent with the reception-acceptance model, including the selective-acceptance hypothesis.

When I replicated my statistical models, substituting hard news in place of soft news, I found, as anticipated, that the interactions that arose between education and political information, on the one hand, and soft news consumption, on the other, were either substantially weaker or absent altogether. In other words, in every instance, consuming hard news programming—which typically presents information in less accessible formats than do the soft news media—had far less impact on politically inattentive or uneducated individuals than consuming soft news shows. And here, consistent with the reception-acceptance model, highly educated or politically informed respondents mirror their less educated and informed counterparts; they also appear relatively immune to having their opinions influenced by hard news, again presumably due to their previously described capacity to counterargue dissonant information. The exception concerns the hypothesized reinforcement effect. In these data, internationalists at all levels of political information did find *some* measure of reinforcement for their attitudes through consuming hard news. Nevertheless, also consistent with my fourth hypothesis, these effects were small among low-information respondents, compared to the reinforcement effect of soft news on isolationists.

I began this chapter by introducing a general theoretical framework, from which I derived a series of hypotheses based on logical extensions of the hypotheses developed in chapter 2. Statistical testing revealed a clear and persistent pattern—one consistent with this theoretical framework, and with my hypotheses. That is, among individuals who are not highly educated or politically engaged, but not among their more highly educated or engaged counterparts, increased exposure to soft news tends to be associated with reduced support for a variety of U.S. foreign policy initiatives, as well as, more generally, for a proactive or internationalist approach to foreign policy. Moreover, the results from my final analysis of the NES CDF suggest that this seemingly pro-isolationist effect among the less-educated segments of the public has strengthened in recent years, as the soft news media has proliferated.

In hindsight, this pattern, though not explicitly predicted by the general theoretical argument delineated in chapter 2, is not surprising. After all, as we saw in chapter 3, the soft news media self-consciously package information about foreign crises in ways designed to appeal to apolitical consumers. One presumably unintended by-product of this packaging is that the same episodic framing of human drama in a violent context that makes a story compelling may also produce a repellent effect, particularly among viewers who lack sufficient knowledge about an issue to place such information into a broader context. After all, while millions of people enjoy watching Arnold Schwarzenegger and Bruce Willis vanquish terrorists and other evildoers from the safety of their movie theater seats or living room couches, how many would actually choose to confront real-world dangers comparable to those of their celluloid heroes? Indeed, taken together, the results from these several analyses represent considerable evidence that the soft news media do influence public attitudes regarding foreign policy—particularly among relatively apolitical individuals—and do so in seemingly predictable ways.

APPENDIX: Statistical Tables

Table 7.A1. Logit and Ordered Logit Analyses of Effects of Consuming Soft News on Attitudes toward Bosnia, NATO Expansion, Japan, Healthcare Reform, Medicare, and the Jobs vs. Environment Trade-off, as Education Varies

	Coef. (Std. Err.)							
	U.S. in Bosnia Model 1	Healthcare Reform Model 2	Bosnia Gun Ban Model 3	Clinton on Bosnia Model 4	Medicare Model 5	Jobs vs. Environment Model 6	NATO Enlargement Model 7	Japan Feelings[a] Model 8
Media Consumption Habits								
Soft news index	−.181	−.110	—	—	—	—	−.442	—
	(.090)*	(.092)					(.166)**	
TV talk shows	—	—	−.182	.141	−.052	−.047	—	−.159
			(.092)*	(.082)^	(.099)	(.071)		(.067)*
Hard news index	−.033	−.009	—	—	—	—	−.134	.112
	(.058)	(.052)					(.347)	(.148)
Soft news trust index	—	—	—	—	—	—	.144	—
							(.102)	
Hard news trust index	—	—	—	—	—	—	.020	—
							(.027)	
SES/Demographics								
Age	−.061	.0002	−.022	−.054	.005	−.087	.039	—
	(.035)^	(.035)	(.032)	(.030)^	(.033)	(.020)***	(.034)	
Age²	.0008	−.0001	.0003	.0004	−.0003	.0007	−.0005	—
	(.0004)*	(.0004)	(.0003)	(.0003)	(.0003)	(.0002)***	(.0004)	
Education	−.267	−.361	−.223	.148	−.174	.067	−.605	−.062
	(.261)	(.263)	(.129)^	(.121)	(.138)	(.094)	(.185)***	(.102)
Family income	−.090	−.029	.103	.117	.155	.043	.153	−.039
	(.064)	(.064)	(.053)*	(.052)*	(.060)**	(.037)	(.070)*	(.041)

TABLE 7.A1. Continued

	Coef. (Std. Err.)							
	U.S. in Bosnia Model 1	Healthcare Reform Model 2	Bosnia Gun Ban Model 3	Clinton on Bosnia Model 4	Medicare Model 5	Jobs vs. Environment Model 6	NATO Enlargement Model 7	Japan Feelings[a] Model 8
Male	-.031 (.183)	-.093 (.200)	.325 (.164)*	-.202 (.171)	.009 (.179)	-.204 (.122)^	-.070 (.198)	-.169 (.145)
Married	.310 (.210)	.110 (.219)	—	—	—	—	—	—
White	.613 (.364)^	-.103 (.709)	.468 (.461)	.540 (.471)	-.512 (.777)	.096 (.378)	.120 (.312)	-.033 (.247)
Black	1.280 (.410)**	-.910 (.738)	.017 (.528)	.403 (.531)	-.969 (.832)	-.311 (.426)	-.735 (.388)^	-.367 (.405)
Hispanic	—	—	-.407 (.380)	-1.184 (.423)**	-.616 (.442)	.266 (.313)	—	—
Political Attitudes								
Party identification	-.042 (.065)	-.294 (.060)***	.088 (.105)	.007 (.107)	.361 (.109)***	.492 (.074)***	.112 (.071)	.042 (.084)
Partisanship	—	—	—	—	—	—	-.001 (.169)	—
Liberal-conservative scale	—	—	—	—	—	—	-.190 (.115)^	.006 (.100)
Voted in 1992	-.180 (.215)	.119 (.238)	—	—	—	—	—	—
Approve of president	—	—	-.124 (.066)^	-.765 (.070)***	.276 (.081)***	.006 (.052)	.904 (.242)***	-.013 (.109)

	(N = 465)	(N = 466)	(N = 964)	(N = 990)	(N = 646)	(N = 1,031)	(N = 716)	(N = 1,051)
Bosnia as important national problem	—	—	.510 (.420)	-.153 (.383)	—	—	—	—
Affect toward UK	—	—	-.271 (.120)*	-.034 (.123)	—	—	—	—
Affect toward France	—	—	.187 (.082)*	.068 (.082)	—	—	—	—
Attitude toward UN	—	—	.120 (.091)	-.377 (.100)***	—	—	—	—
State of U.S.-Japan Relations	—	—	—	—	—	—	—	.383 (.063)***
Interaction Terms								
Soft news index × education	.033 (.030)	.025 (.030)	—	—	—	—	.122 (.041)**	—
TV talk shows × education	—	—	.077 (.030)**	-.053 (.027)*	.029 (.031)	.021 (.022)	—	.043 (.021)*
Constant 1	-4.769 (1.235)	-4.709 (1.522)	-.185 (.986)	-1.093 (.951)	1.639 (1.215)	-2.099 (.676)	1.260 (1.081)	-.139 (.504)
Constant 2	-3.052 (1.222)	-3.018 (1.516)	—	—	—	-.303 (.676)	—	—
Constant 3	-1.640 (1.213)	-2.185 (1.514)	—	—	—	—	—	—
Pseudo R^2	.03	.06	.06	.20	.07	.05	.07	.04

Note: All models employ heteroscedasticity-consistent ("robust") standard errors and probability weighting ("pweight" in Stata).

[a]For the "Japan Feelings" model: (1) the "Hard news index" item is based on a single question, asking whether respondents watch Ted Koppel (host of the program *Nightline*), and (2) I was unable to retrieve the "age" variable from the original data file.

[p]p < .10, *p < .05, **p < .01, ***p < .001

TABLE 7.A2. Logit Analyses of Effects of Watching Daytime Talk Shows on Attitudes toward Foreign and Domestic Politics, and Isolationism Trends, as Political Information or Education Vary

	Coef. (Std. Err.)							
	Isolationism Model 1	Clinton Foreign Policy Model 2	Clinton Economic Policy Model 3	Isolationism Model 4	Clinton Foreign Policy Model 5	Clinton Economic Policy Model 6	Clinton Foreign Policy Model 7	Isolationism Trend (1960–2000) Model 8
Media Consumption Habits								
Watch daytime talk shows	.515 (.318)^	−.381 (.227)^	−.031 (.242)	.711 (.356)*	−.628 (.282)*	−.163 (.323)	−.729 (.573)	—
Watch network news (days per week)	—	—	—	−.032 (.043)	.048 (.035)	.040 (.038)	.084 (.056)	—
Watch early local news (days per week)	—	—	—	.011 (.041)	−.073 (.032)*	−.012 (.034)	−.063 (.051)	—
Watch late local news (days per week)	—	—	—	.002 (.040)	.046 (.030)	.032 (.034)	.110 (.047)*	—
Read newspaper (days per week)	—	—	—	−.075 (.036)*	−.013 (.027)	.055 (.032)^	−.049 (.045)	—
How often listen to political talk radio	—	—	—	−.041 (.093)	−.039 (.065)	.004 (.070)	−.092 (.107)	—
Internet access	—	—	—	−.356 (.223)	−.203 (.178)	.008 (.204)	.011 (.270)	—
SES/Demographics								
Education	—	—	—	−.129 (.044)**	.040 (.033)	.112 (.036)**	.044 (.056)	—
Age	—	—	—	−.024 (.028)	−.024 (.025)	−.039 (.028)	−.019 (.040)	−.020 (.006)***

Age²	—	—	—	.0002 (.0003)	.0002 (.0002)	.0003 (.0003)	.0001 (.0004)	.0003 (.0001)***
Family income	—	—	—	-.001 (.003)	.002 (.003)	.002 (.003)	-.013 (.032)	-.189 (.020)***
Male	—	—	—	-.042 (.210)	-.151 (.154)	.152 (.170)	.221 (.250)	-.091 (.040)*
Married	—	—	—	.236 (.202)	-.081 (.155)	.071 (.179)	-.068 (.268)	—
Black	—	—	—	-.410 (.322)	-.306 (.293)	.002 (.362)	-.198 (.463)	.192 (.059)***
Political Knowledge & Attitudes								
Political information	-.464 (.092)***	-.130 (.060)*	.027 (.065)	-.254 (.120)*	.010 (.091)	-.008 (.102)	-.035 (.193)	—
Approve of president	—	—	—	-.127 (.227)	2.074 (.163)***	2.509 (.195)***	2.218 (.256)***	—
Party identification	—	—	—	-.020 (.054)	-.264 (.042)***	-.291 (.053)***	-.250 (.064)***	-.036 (.010)***
Attention to public affairs	—	—	—	-.013 (.127)	-.114 (.101)	.017 (.107)	-.198 (.148)	-.288 (.020)***
Partisanship	—	—	—	.102 (.102)	.150 (.075)*	.211 (.086)**	.265 (.114)*	-.080 (.020)***
Isolationism	—	—	—	—	—	—	-.563 (.309)^	—
Political Trust & Efficacy								
External efficacy I	—	—	—	-.110 (.250)	.260 (.180)	.235 (.209)	.371 (.292)	—
External efficacy II	—	—	—	-.497 (.226)*	.123 (.176)	.159 (.196)	-.350 (.286)	—

TABLE 7.A2. Continued

	Coef. (Std. Err.)							
	Isolationism Model 1	Clinton Foreign Policy Model 2	Clinton Economic Policy Model 3	Isolationism Model 4	Clinton Foreign Policy Model 5	Clinton Economic Policy Model 6	Clinton Foreign Policy Model 7	Isolationism Trend (1960–2000) Model 8
Internal efficacy	—	—	—	.111 (.231)	-.355 (.170)*	.137 (.188)	-.010 (.271)	—
Trust in government	—	—	—	-.407 (.119)***	.444 (.088)***	.214 (.101)*	.509 (.151)***	—
Decade Dummies								
1970s								.296 (.185)
1980s								.349 (.185)^
1990s								.354 (.172)*
2000								.605 (.370)^
Interaction Terms								
Political information × watch daytime talk shows	-.108 (.096)	.202 (.072)**	.079 (.076)	-.174 (.107)^	.209 (.084)**	.076 (.098)	.425 (.244)^	—

Isolationism × watch daytime talk shows	—	—	—	—	—	—	.923 (.795)	—
Isolationism × political information × watch daytime talk shows	—	—	—	—	—	—	.296 (.390)	—
1960s × education	—	—	—	—	—	—	—	-.440 (.072)***
1970s × education	—	—	—	—	—	—	—	-.521 (.057)***
1980s × education	—	—	—	—	—	—	—	-.476 (.050)***
1990s × education	—	—	—	—	—	—	—	-.410 (.038)***
2000 × education	—	—	—	—	—	—	—	-.503 (.119)***
Constant	.370 (.308)	1.069 (.218)***	.960 (.234)***	4.282 (1.013)***	-1.135 (.797)	-1.520 (.817)^	-1.658 (1.373)	1.544 (.207)***
Pseudo R^2	.06	.01	.01	.13	.30	.32	.33	.08
	(N = 745)	(N = 1,427)	(N = 1,419)	(N = 714)	(N = 1,380)	(N = 1,376)	(N = 607)	(N = 16,306)

Note: All models employ White's heteroscedasticity-consistent ("robust") standard errors.

^p < .10, *p < .05, **p < .01, ***p < .001

TABLE 7.A3. Logit and Ordered Logit Analyses of Effects of Consuming Hard News on Attitudes toward U.S. Foreign Policy, as Political Information or Education Varies

	Coef. (Std. Err.)				
	Bosnia Model 1	NATO Enlargement Model 2	Isolationism Model 3	Clinton Foreign Policy Model 4	Clinton Foreign Policy Model 5
Media Consumption Habits					
Watch daytime TV talk shows	—	—	.180 (.115)	.021 (.099)	.011 (.175)
Soft news index	−.097 (.038)**	.009 (.052)	—	—	—
Hard news index	.023 (.166)	-1.482 (.757)*	—	—	—
Watch network news (days per week)	—	—	−.059 (.109)	−.032 (.090)	.272 (.149)^
Watch early local news (days per week)	—	—	.006 (.041)	−.071 (.032)*	−.061 (.050)
Watch late local news (days per week)	—	—	.001 (.040)	.045 (.030)	.106 (.047)*
Read newspaper (days per week)	—	—	−.073 (.036)*	−.015 (.027)	−.051 (.044)
How often listen to political talk radio	—	—	−.047 (.094)	−.037 (.064)	−.079 (.110)
Internet access	—	—	−.322 (.221)	−.203 (.179)	.015 (.273)
Soft news trust index	—	.141 (.102)	—	—	—
Hard news trust index	—	.014 (.027)	—	—	—
SES/Demographics					
Education	.224 (.561)	−.628 (.245)**	−.133 (.043)**	.039 (.033)	.031 (.061)
Age	−.064 (.036)^	.036 (.034)	−.021 (.028)	−.024 (.024)	−.015 (.039)
Age^2	.0008 (.0004)*	.000 (.000)	.0002 (.0003)	.0002 (.0002)	.00004 (.0004)
Family income	−.081 (.065)	.134 (.067)*	−.0003 (.0033)	.002 (.003)	−.021 (.031)

TABLE 7.A3. *Continued*

	Coef. (Std. Err.)				
	Bosnia Model 1	NATO Enlargement Model 2	Isolationism Model 3	Clinton Foreign Policy Model 4	Clinton Foreign Policy Model 5
Male	−.018 (.183)	−.050 (.199)	−.027 (.211)	−.162 (.153)	.242 (.255)
Married	.292 (.208)	—	.222 (.201)	−.073 (.155)	−.019 (.262)
Black	1.383 (.400)***	−.728 (.384)^	−.351 (.315)	−.391 (.281)	−.339 (.434)
White	.702 (.348)*	.167 (.298)	—	—	—
Political Interest/ Knowledge					
Political information	—	—	−.370 (.149)**	.021 (.112)	.167 (.230)
Approve of president	—	.819 (.237)***	−.144 (.228)	2.070 (.163)***	2.225 (.255)***
Party identification	−.031 (.063)	.116 (.072)	−.016 (.054)	−.273 (.041)***	−.279 (.065)***
Attention to public affairs	—	—	−.009 (.128)	−.117 (.100)	−.219 (.150)
Partisanship	—	.040 (.167)	.108 (.103)	.167 (.075)*	.295 (.117)**
Voted in 1992	−.173 (.214)	—	—	—	—
Liberal-conservative scale	—	−.153 (.119)	—	—	—
Political Trust & Efficacy					
External efficacy I	—	—	−.084 (.250)	.272 (.180)	.289 (.295)
External efficacy II	—	—	−.507 (.227)*	.123 (.175)	−.294 (.283)
Internal efficacy	—	—	.097 (.229)	−.340 (.169)*	.025 (.270)
Trust in government	—	—	−.389 (.118)***	.428 (.088)***	.507 (.150)***

TABLE 7.A3. *Continued*

	Bosnia Model 1	NATO Enlargement Model 2	Isolationism Model 3	Clinton Foreign Policy Model 4	Clinton Foreign Policy Model 5
			Coef. (Std. Err.)		
Interaction Terms					
Political information × watch network news	—	—	.010 (.032)	.023 (.024)	−.051 (.059)
Isolationism × watch network news	—	—	—	—	−.620 (.216)**
Isolationism × political information × watch network news	—	—	—	—	.177 (.089)*
Hard news index × education	−.023 (.058)	.372 (.171)*	—	—	—
Constant 1	−3.438 (1.696)	1.277 (1.253)	4.535 (1.014)***	−1.122 (.830)	−2.087 (1.408)
Constant 2	−1.719 (1.675)	—	—	—	—
Constant 3	−.309 (1.673)	—	—	—	—
Pseudo R^2	.03 ($N = 465$)	.06 ($N = 716$)	.13 ($N = 714$)	.29 ($N = 1380$)	.33 ($N = 607$)

Note: All models employ heteroscedasticity-consistent ("robust") standard errors.
$\hat{p} < .10$, *$p < .05$, **$p < .01$, ***$p < .001$

Soft News, Public Opinion, and American Foreign Policy: The Good, the Bad, and the Merely Entertaining

A GREAT MANY individuals are not particularly interested in politics. And, since the end of the Cold War, notwithstanding an apparently relatively brief post–9/11 spike, many Americans claim to have largely lost interest in foreign affairs. Yet, in the post–Cold War era, when the United States employs military force abroad, Americans appear to be paying closer attention than ever before. To resolve this apparent paradox, I developed an incidental by-product model of information consumption. My theoretical model identified a prime suspect: the rise of the soft news media.

My argument centered on the interaction between individual human cognitive processes and the strategic behavior of television broadcasters adapting to changing market circumstances. According to the model, an implicit, if not explicit, recognition of individual-level decision-making processes has influenced in important ways television broadcasters' strategic responses to a changing media marketplace.

Beginning in the 1980s, news broadcasters, facing unprecedented competitive pressures, came to recognize that real-life human drama could attract a large audience, and could be produced at far lower cost than fictional drama. Broadcasters thus sought to make information about a select few political issues, including foreign crises, accessible to even politically uninterested segments of the audience. And in this they appear to have succeeded. Through cheap framing, the soft news media have successfully piggybacked information about foreign crises to entertainment-oriented informational programming. Soft news consumers thereby gain information about such crises (or other highly accessible issues) as an incidental by-product of seeking entertainment.

Indeed, I have documented both the dramatic and rapid proliferation of the soft news media, as well as their surprisingly substantial coverage of foreign policy crises. My individual-level analyses then demonstrated that people *do* attend to these types of issues—but not other, less dramatic or salacious issues—in the soft news media, without necessarily seeking to do so. I also offered evidence that this process has contributed to the aggregate trend toward greater attentiveness to foreign crises introduced at the outset of this study and elaborated in chapter 5—a trend that appears to be driven largely by the least politically engaged members of the public, who also happen to be the heaviest consumers of soft news programming.

The difficulty in establishing clear causal chains in aggregate trend analyses makes this latter evidence less definitive. After all, there are typically numerous causes of any long-term behavioral trend, and it is exceedingly difficult to determine the magnitude of the effect of any single causal factor. In essence, I have sought to make the most convincing circumstantial case possible, given the rather severe limitations in the available data. Despite these shortcomings, my investigations of America's three major post–World War II military conflicts and, indeed, *all* major uses of force by the United States since 1953 do indicate that different groups of Americans have responded to America's military crises in manners consistent with the theory's predictions and with my individual-level findings.

That these patterns arise for unprompted mentions of major national problems pertaining to foreign affairs and social order—precisely the types of political issues most likely to be covered by soft news outlets—but *not* for other types of issues, and that they are mostly limited to the least politically attentive segments of the population, represents further evidence that more than a mere secular trend, attributable to myriad causes, is at work. Rather, taken together, my individual-level and aggregate time-series statistical investigations clearly support my core theoretical argument, which holds that strategic media practices, undertaken in response to changing economic, regulatory, and technological circumstances, have altered many Americans' propensity to pay attention to select high-profile political issues, including foreign policy crises. My findings demonstrate that this effect is most pronounced for individuals who are neither intrinsically interested in such issues nor actively seeking such information.

After all, even in a trial court, a purely circumstantial case can, at times, exceed the threshold for a conviction "beyond a reasonable doubt." I leave it to the reader to decide whether I have met this lofty standard, particularly with respect to the over-time trends described in chapter 5. My hope, however, is that most readers will conclude that, when the evidence is viewed as a whole, my case becomes fairly strong, and more so than most potential alternative explanations for these trends.

What remains is to consider what, if anything, this all means for politics and democracy in America. In chapters 6 and 7, I considered several possible implications of the theory for public opinion. I found that the changing media environment has altered the constituent elements of the rally-round-the-flag phenomenon, by influencing the types of individuals who are likely to respond to a use of force by rallying behind the president. I then explored the effects of soft news consumption on public attitudes toward foreign affairs. Here I found that the same factors that can make a foreign crisis entertaining to follow—most prominently violence and human drama—also tend to induce suspicion of a proactive or multilateral approach to U.S. foreign policy among politically inattentive individuals, but not among their more-attentive counterparts. I devote the bulk of this chapter to further addressing the implications of the theory for public opinion in America, as well as for politics and foreign policy, and, ultimately, for America's democracy. Before turning to these issues, however, I first briefly assess the past and possible future role of the Internet in contributing to the developments described in this book.

What about the Internet?

In this study, I have largely relegated the Internet to the inauspicious role of control variable in various regression models. Many analysts and pundits, particularly those studying the "new media," argue, overtly or implicitly, that the Internet is revolutionizing (or has already revolutionized) American politics. The ability of consumers to choose both the format and content of the information that crosses their desktops gives individuals unprecedented power to shape their own interactions with the political world. Indeed, due to its undeniable impact on the news cycle, the Internet has clearly contributed, albeit perhaps primarily indirectly, to the proliferation of the soft news media. The Internet, after all, represents a new source of competitive pressure confronting television broadcasters. For instance, a Web site—the "Drudge Report"—has been credited with first breaking the Monica Lewinsky scandal. In fact, the Internet could, in principle, be readily integrated into my theoretical argument. Internet users who log on to their favorite entertainment-oriented sites frequently encounter numerous links to traditional news items. By bringing news to the net surfer, an entertainment-oriented Web site may reduce the opportunity costs of attending to a news item (though perhaps not to the same extent as an entertainment news program on television).

Nevertheless, I elected to focus on television, which, as of 2003, remains by far the predominant medium for political communication in America. Proponents of the "Internet revolution" perspective cite surveys showing that anywhere from 40 to 60 percent of Americans now use the Internet. Yet when one probes such survey evidence a little more deeply, it becomes apparent that, as yet, only a relatively small minority of the public uses the Internet as a regular source of information about politics or international affairs. For instance, according to a June 1998 survey (Pew Research Center 1998b), among the 75 percent of Americans who reported either reading, watching, or listening to the news during the course of a typical day, only 4 percent cited the Internet as their "main" source for news. And, according to a second survey, in December 1998 (Pew Research Center 1998d), just over 40 percent of respondents claimed to use the Internet for *any* purpose, including e-mail. Of that group, 44 percent reported using the Internet to find news about politics, while half reported going online for international news. So, overall, only about 18 and 22 percent of respondents in this latter survey, respectively, used the Internet as a source of political or international news. Moreover, of this group, the mean frequency of going online for news of *any* type was once every few weeks. Hence, at the end of 1998, only about one-fifth of the public used the Internet to access political or international news. And these Americans did so, on average, only once every few weeks. By comparison, two-thirds of these same respondents claimed to have watched an average of fifteen to thirty minutes of television news on the day of the Pew Center interview!

A more recent survey (Pew Research Center 2000), found 54 percent of respondents claiming to use the Internet, a substantial increase from December 1998. Of this group, 61 percent used the Internet as a source for news of any type at least once a week. This represents about one-third of all respondents— clearly a significant percentage. Still, according to the same survey, only 39 percent of self-declared *Internet users* used the net as a source of political news, while 45 percent of this group used the net as a source of international news. This compares to 44 percent who used the net to find entertainment news and 66 percent who used it for accessing weather reports. And the mean frequency of using the Internet for *any* type of news fell between "once every few weeks" and "1–2 days per week." By comparison, in this survey, similar to the December 1998 poll, over 60 percent of all respondents claimed to have watched an average of fifteen to thirty minutes of television news on the day before the interview. Finally, an April 2002 survey (Pew Research Center 2002b) found only a slight increase from 2000 in respondents' frequency of using the Internet as a news source.

While, according to these data, the Internet is growing in importance, television remains the predominant source of news for most Americans. Indeed, the typical American's occasional use of the Internet as a source of political or international news seems insufficient to justify the frequent claims by journalists and pundits that the Internet is "revolutionizing" American politics. We may well be in the early stages of such a revolution. But, as of today, at least as a source of political and international news, the Internet remains something of a novelty medium, used *occasionally* for this purpose by many Americans, but primarily so by individuals who are *already* interested in learning about politics before they go online.[1]

Finally, and perhaps most importantly, my theory concerns the ability of politically uninterested individuals to attend to politics, including foreign policy, without necessarily seeking to do so. And the Internet is fundamentally an interactive, rather than a passive, medium, in which users have a great deal of control over the content they consume. In other words, with some exceptions, the World Wide Web does not typically take users where they don't want to go. While, as noted above, aspects of my argument may apply to the Internet, perhaps increasingly so in the future, most people who use the Internet as an entertainment medium are relatively less likely than TV viewers to inadvertently encounter, or consume, political information disguised as entertainment. Hence, while the Internet has clearly contributed to the changing media environment, as of this writing it is far less important than television as a source of news about politics and foreign policy for the politically uninterested.

Looking Beyond Foreign Policy: Soft News and Presidential Politics

This book has focused on foreign policy. Yet, I have argued that my theory is general, and so not strictly limited to the realm of foreign crises. In fact, perhaps the best places to look for future trends in the intersection between entertainment and politics underlying the theory are the "borderline" issues that have some, though not necessarily all, of the characteristics that have traditionally appeal to the soft news media. Perhaps the quintessential examples of such issues are presidential elections and scandals. In this section I consider both, beginning with the former.

The 2000 Presidential Election

During the 1960 presidential campaign, Richard Nixon sought to "humanize" himself by playing piano on *The Tonight Show* (Rosenberg 2000). And in 1992, Bill Clinton courted young voters by playing his saxophone on the *Arsenio Hall Show* and appearing on MTV. Scholars have treated these and other candidate appearances on entertainment-oriented media outlets largely as curiosities; interesting fodder for journalists, but of only marginal political consequence. The 2000 election cycle suggests the need to rethink this conventional wisdom. Politicking in the entertainment media moved from occasional oddity to political center stage, as the candidates competed aggressively for the millions of voters who consider Oprah Winfrey and Regis Philbin trusted friends, or who depend on Jay Leno's late-night monologues for their daily dose of "news" about public affairs.

In chapter 2, I argued that most water-cooler events constitute or involve, or share characteristics similar to, *dramatic crises*. Though not a "crisis" in the usual sense, a close presidential race in its latter stages does involve high drama and a clear beginning, middle, and end. Hence, it may share many of the characteristics of a crisis (as discussed in chapter 2). Indeed, Alexis de Tocqueville (2000), in *Democracy in America*, described U.S. presidential elections as short-term national crises.

And here a clear trend is emerging. In an effort to show themselves as "regular guys," the 2000 presidential election found presidential and vice-presidential aspirants bantering with Oprah Winfrey, Rosie O'Donnell, Queen Latifah, and Regis Philbin, trading one-liners with Jay Leno, David Letterman, and Jon Stewart (of Comedy Central's *Daily Show*), discussing rap music with MTV's youthful viewers and even courting the kid (or perhaps parent) vote on Nickelodeon. During the presidential primaries, candidates for the Reform Party nomination depended almost entirely on the talk-show circuit to get their message to the public (Bennett 1999).

Yet, such programs are clearly not in the business of educating the public about presidential politics. As one publicist for the *Tonight Show* commented regarding appearances by presidential candidates in 2000: "Of course ratings are a top priority. . . . We are not sending a political message one way or another. . . . If people get anything out of it, that's fine, but that's not why we're here. We're not 'Hardball'" (Niemberg 2001). Along these same lines, Oprah Winfrey describes her program's priorities as follows: "Originally, our goal was to uplift, enlighten, encourage and entertain through the medium of television. Now our mission statement for 'The Oprah Winfrey Show' is to use television to transform people's lives, to make viewers see themselves differently and to bring happiness and a sense of fulfillment into every home" (Feder 2000).

Given this decidedly apolitical orientation, it is not too surprising that Oprah Winfrey's interviews with Al Gore and George W. Bush were the first political interviews of her fifteen-year career as a talk-show host (LaGanga 2000). In explaining her reluctance to bring political candidates onto her show, Winfrey commented: "I've tried to stay out of politics for my entire tenure on the air. Basically, it's a no-win situation. Over the years, I have not found that interviewing politicians about the issues worked for my viewing audience. I try to bring issues that people understand through their hearts and their feelings so they can make decisions" (Feder 2000).

So, why would Oprah Winfrey, Jay Leno, Queen Latifah, Rosie O'Donnell, David Letterman, Regis Philbin, MTV, and the *Daily Show* interview presidential and vice-presidential candidates? The answer, simply stated, is that over the past decade, TV talk-show producers have learned that if they focus on candidates' personal qualities rather than "arcane" policy debates, their audiences will respond. In other words, entertainment-oriented TV talk shows have learned to tailor coverage of presidential politics to fit the interests of their audience. And the ratings suggest they have done their homework. For instance, Al Gore's September 11, 2000, appearance on *The Oprah Winfrey Show*—the show's 2000–2001 season premier—was watched by 8.7 million households, well above the program's average of 7.5 million households during the prior season (Getlin 2000) and up fully 27 percent from Oprah's 1999–2000 premier episode (Lowry 2000). And George W. Bush's appearance on the program eight days later earned even higher ratings (Getlin 2000).

Presidential aspirants, in turn, travel the TV talk-show circuit with good reason. While talk-show viewers are not among the most politically engaged Americans, low-interest individuals do vote in substantial numbers. According to the 2000 NES, 60 percent of respondents who indicated that they follow what's going on in government and public affairs "hardly at all" or "only now and then" claimed to have voted.[2] And two-thirds of respondents who watched more than one standard deviation above the mean quantity of daytime TV talk shows indicated that they had done so. While self-declared voting rates in surveys are typically inflated (by about 10 percent, according to Kelly and Mirer 1974), the difference between these respondents and the self-declared voting rates for frequent network news viewers is less than 16 percentage points. And recent research (Bernstein, Chada, and Montjoy 2001) suggests that the *least* politically engaged individuals are *least* likely to falsely report having voted.

Clearly, many talk-show viewers and politically inattentive individuals vote. One-on-one interviews on *Meet the Press* or *The News Hour with Jim Lehrer* are unlikely to reach these potential voters. In today's increasingly personality-driven political environment, appearances on TV talk shows afford candidates perhaps their best opportunity to communicate with a substantial niche of the electorate. As James Bennett (1999) notes, "If a candidate wants to excite people who normally do not vote, reaching past 'Meet the Press' is probably not a bad way to start."

And in 2000, this strategy appears to have produced tangible results. For instance, CNN initiated daily tracking polls of the public's support for Al Gore and George W. Bush on September 7, 2000. That same month (on the eleventh and nineteenth, respectively), the two candidates appeared on *The Oprah Winfrey Show*. In the four tracking polls conducted prior to Gore's September 11, 2000, appearance on *Oprah*, Gore led Bush by an average of 2 percentage points, well within the polls' margins of error. In the week following his appearance, Gore's lead more than tripled, to an average of 6.6 percentage points ($p < .17$).[3] But this spike was short-lived. In the week following Governor George W. Bush's September 19 appearance on *Oprah*, Gore's lead fell back to 3 percentage points, on average ($p < .05$). These trends, though far from definitive, do suggest that substantial numbers of voters may have been influenced by candidate appearances on this decidedly apolitical talk show. Indeed, focus groups during the campaign found that candidate appearances on talk shows like *The Tonight Show with Jay Leno* and *The Oprah Winfrey Show* weighed heavily in many voters' minds as they contemplated their vote choice (Decker 2000)

Moreover, for the first time in recent history, the aftermath of the election attracted even greater media and public attention than the election itself. The postelection ballot counting controversy in Florida—and, to a lesser extent, in several other states—attracted saturation coverage by both the traditional and soft news media. This clearly indicates that under at least some, albeit perhaps not all, circumstances, presidential elections *can* become water-cooler events. The postelection controversy, attributable to the almost unprecedented parity in the vote totals for the two major party candidates in 2000, appears to constitute a "dramatic crisis," as defined in chapter 2. In fact, rightly or wrongly, numerous journalists, pundits, and politicians, as well as the Chief Justice of the Supreme Court, William Rehnquist, worried aloud that the controversy surrounding the election could have provoked a constitutional crisis.

To determine whether and how talk-show coverage of the 2000 presidential election influenced voters, I revisit the 2000 NES survey. Specifically, I seek to determine whether individuals who consume daytime talk shows are more likely than their counterparts who do not—net of a variety of other factors—to indicate that they paid attention to the presidential campaign or cared about its outcome. The specific questions are as follows: (1) "Some people don't pay much attention to political campaigns. How about you? Would you say that you have been very much interested, somewhat interested or not much interested in the political campaigns so far this year?" (Responses were coded as follows: 0 = not much interested, 1 = somewhat interested, 2 = very much interested.); and (2) "Generally speaking, would you say that you personally care a good deal who wins the presidential election this fall, or that you don't care very much who wins?" (Responses were coded as follows: 0 = don't care very much, and 1 = care a good deal.)

The independent variables are virtually identical to those employed in prior NES investigations throughout this book, and so are not redefined here. The only noteworthy exceptions are the indicator of respondents' level of intrinsic interest in politics, as well as two dummy variables measuring respondents' self-declared intent to vote for either George W. Bush or Al Gore. The latter variables are included because individuals who express an intent to vote for one or the other candidate are presumably much more likely than their counterparts who do not intend to vote to indicate that they care about the outcome of the election. With regard to the former variable, rather than employ the interviewer's assessment of the respondents' levels of political information, I instead rely on two questions measuring respondents' self-described interest in national politics. The first concerns respondents' self-reported propensity to follow government and public affairs in general, and the latter, defined above, concerns the extent to which respondents report having followed the 2000 election campaign. For the model in which respondents' attention to the 2000 campaign is the dependent variable, I employ only the former question; when the dependent variable is the degree to which the respondent cares about the outcome of the election, I combine both questions into a 6-point "political interest" scale (where 6 represents maximum interest).[4] Since the present investigation specifically concerns a national election, these indicators capture respondents' ex ante propensity to pay attention to information about the campaign more directly than the interviewer's estimate of their overall level of political information.

The results of two ordered logit and two logit analyses—with and without the full battery of control variables—(shown in the appendix to this chapter, at table 8.A1) are, once again, consistent with my fifth and sixth hypotheses. In both cases, the coefficients in the basic models, though somewhat smaller in magnitude, are broadly consistent with those in the fully specified models. Hence, I focus on the latter models. I begin by assessing the effects of talk-show viewing on attention to the campaign. Translating the key coefficients into probabilities reveals that among respondents who report following government and public affairs "hardly at all," as talk-show viewing increases from zero to six or more times per week, the probability of being "not much interested" in the campaign declines by 19 percentage points (from .29 to .10, $p < .01$). The probability of being "very much interested," in turn, increases by 20 percentage points (from .10 to .30, $p < .01$). Finally, the probability of being "somewhat interested" changes hardly at all (from .61 to .59, insig.) In sharp contrast, among respondents who report following government and public affairs "most of the time," the corresponding effects of increased talk-show viewing are substantively smaller and statistically insignificant. These results support my fifth and sixth hypotheses.

Turning to the effects of talk-show viewing on respondents' propensity to care about the outcome of the election, among respondents who report being uninterested in the 2000 election campaigns, as talk-show viewing increases from zero to six or more times per week, the probability of caring about the outcome of the presidential election increases by 29 percentage points (from .42 to .71, $p < .05$). Though my theory does not directly address salience, this finding is nonetheless broadly consistent with my fifth hypothesis. In sharp contrast, among respondents who report being highly interested in politics, the corresponding effect of increased talk-show viewing is a substantively modest 5 percentage point *decline* in the probability of caring about the outcome of the election (from .98 to .93, $p < .05$).

Consistent with my sixth hypothesis, the effect among politically engaged individuals is far smaller than among their less-engaged counterparts. Interestingly, while also not directly predicted by the theory, the inverse relationship between talk-show viewing and concern over the election outcome among political sophisticates is consistent with my earlier conjecture that for these latter individuals, spending time consuming entertainment-oriented programming may represent something of a distraction from the more information-intensive campaign information presented in the traditional news media. This suggests that highly politically engaged individuals who watch large numbers of talk shows may lose some of their otherwise exceedingly high degree of engagement with the campaign. (And, indeed, the probabilities of being concerned with the election are extremely high for political sophisticates, ranging from .89 to .98, as talk show or network news consumption varies.)[5]

Most importantly for my purposes, these results clearly suggest that entertainment-oriented TV talk-show coverage of campaign 2000 had important effects on the likelihood that usually politically inattentive Americans would both attend to the campaign and perceive themselves as having a personal stake in its outcome. Finally, in a separate study, reported elsewhere (Baum 2002b), I find that, as in their coverage of foreign crises, TV talk-show coverage of presidential politics differs in important ways from campaign coverage by the traditional news media, and that these differences have important consequences for politics. Most notably, I find evidence that watching entertainment-oriented TV talk shows influenced many politically inattentive individuals' vote choice in 2000—increasing their likelihood of voting for the opposition party candidate—while, for these same individuals, consuming traditional news programming did not.

Chapters 3 through 5 presented evidence that soft news outlets typically ignore most political issues, including presidential primaries (except when celebrities, like Donald Trump or Warren Beatty, are involved) and off-year elections, and that, as a result, exposure to soft news programming is not associated with enhanced attentiveness to either presidential primaries or off-year elections. These findings may appear at least somewhat surprising in light of the preceding discussion. Yet, as I argued in chapter 5, primaries and off-year elections are not the same as general presidential elections. Primary elections usually involve a large number of candidates, many of whom are not well known nationally, competing mostly for the support of party activists. Hence, primaries tend to be highly partisan affairs and thus unappealing to many Americans who are not ideological purists or party activists. A great many Americans view primaries as relatively uninteresting sideshows, or previews to the main event in the fall. Off-year elections, in turn, lack the high drama of a presidential campaign. The stakes are typically seen as lower, and the campaigns usually focus to a far greater extent on local, particularistic issues. Hence, again, off-year elections seem less likely than presidential elections to appeal to soft news programmers.

Whether or not coverage of presidential politics by the soft news media will extend to primaries or off-year elections in the future is unclear. The evidence from 2000 does suggest, however, that for better or worse, presidential elections—particularly given a close race—are likely to become a routine topic for at least some soft news shows. If so, coverage by soft news outlets will most likely continue to emphasize relatively nonpartisan, personality-oriented topics and themes. One can imagine, in turn, that such coverage could enhance a trend, decried by many political observers (and to which it may already have contributed), toward personality-centric presidential campaigns. If so, in the future we should anticipate presidential campaigns in which, to an even greater degree than today, policy positions and party loyalties matter less than the mass marketing skills of candidates and their handlers.

The Monica Lewinsky Scandal

I have argued that for many individuals, information about a select few political issues can be received as an incidental by-product of paying attention to entertainment-oriented programming. The Monica Lewinsky scandal, once again, offers a quintessential case in point. Coverage of the Lewinsky scandal by soft news programs represents just the entertainment-oriented "slant" on a political issue that, I have argued, is more likely to catch many individuals' attention than traditional news coverage of the issue. Moreover, in watching the more salacious presentation of the scandal offered by soft news outlets, viewers were almost certainly exposed to some substantive information about public policy that was piggybacked to the entertainment-oriented information that dominates such programs.

For instance, on February 21, 1998, many soft news programs, reporting on secret testimony by Deputy White House Counsel Bruce Lindsey before Independent Counsel Kenneth Starr's grand jury, also noted and covered at some length President Clinton's United Nations speech that same day concerning international cooperation on terrorism. Courtroom dramas involving high-profile individuals are a favored topic of the soft news media, even absent the context of a presidential sex scandal. Hence, Lindsey's testimony was an ideal soft news topic. Any information a soft news viewer may have received concerning the state of global cooperation on terrorism would most likely have been primarily an incidental by-product of paying attention to the more titillating scandal story.

Having paid attention to a soft news program, my Gateway Hypothesis predicts that individuals subsequently become more likely to tune in when additional news and information about the issues discussed on the soft news program are reported, albeit in somewhat less-salacious terms, on more-traditional news programs. Along these lines, ratings for President Clinton's 1998 State of the Union Address were up over 30 percent from his 1997 Address. This suggests that, having had a taste of exposure to President Clinton's difficulties in the soft news media, many people began to seek additional information.

For many viewers, it was doubtless not the substance of the State of the

Union Address that attracted their attention. Yet, by tuning in for whatever reason, viewers found themselves exposed to substantial information about public policy. Such exposure for many individuals was an incidental by-product of their search for entertainment (i.e., more information about the scandal; in this instance, comments by the president). And some evidence suggests the sensationalistic coverage of the scandal did, in fact, raise the public's awareness of public policy issues. In the days following the 1998 State of the Union Address, President Clinton's job approval ratings rose by as many as 21 percentage points, from about 58 percent prior to the address to anywhere from 68 to 79 percent in the days following the address. This represented a much larger than normal spike, which numerous surveys indicated was primarily attributable to favorable reactions to the president's policy proposals.

Of course, part of this spike may have been due to sympathy for a president under siege or to a perception that Clinton's performance, under great pressure, exceeded popular expectations. Yet most polls showed strong public approval of the policies outlined in the president's address, suggesting that the polls in fact represented the public's evaluation of *policies*, more than the state of the scandal. Zaller (1998) makes just this argument in explaining the persistence of President Clinton's high approval ratings throughout the duration of the Lewinsky scandal, in spite of the seemingly endless stream of scandal-related revelations. In this instance, cheap framing and piggybacking appear to have played important roles in contributing to the sharp rise in President Clinton's post-speech approval ratings.

THE SOFT NEWS MEDIA AND FACTUAL KNOWLEDGE ABOUT FOREIGN CRISES

Throughout this book, I have drawn a sharp distinction between attentiveness or learning (broadly defined) and factual knowledge about politics. Following a large literature in cognitive psychology and political behavior (for a review of this literature, see Sniderman 1993), I argued that by relying on informational shortcuts and heuristic cues, many individuals who know and care little about politics are nonetheless able to make reasoned judgments about a wide range of topics, including politics. Hence, attentiveness to soft news coverage of select political issues may facilitate "learning," in this relatively narrow sense, without significantly increasing the volume of factual political knowledge that individuals uninterested in politics store in memory. Yet, it does not necessarily follow that exposure to information about a given political issue, such as a foreign crisis, via the soft news media, will have no effect whatsoever on viewers' knowledge about the crisis, at least in the relative short-term.

Unfortunately, the vast majority of the surveys I have employed in this book do not include appropriate questions for identifying any factual-knowledge-enhancing effects associated with exposure to soft news coverage of foreign crises. One survey (*Times Mirror* 1990), however, does include such a question. Recall from chapter 4 that exposure to soft news outlets was associated with substantially increased attentiveness to Operation Just Cause in Panama. In addition to asking respondents whether they had followed the events in Panama, the survey—conducted while the invasion was still underway (January 4–7, 1990)—also asked respondents the following question: "Do you happen to know where General Manuel Noriega took refuge to escape capture by American troops?"

I employ this question—coded 1 for correct responses ("Vatican Sanctuary" or "Catholic Church") and 0 otherwise—as my dependent variable. I thus investigate whether soft news consumption influenced respondents'—particularly those least likely to be intrinsically interested in foreign policy—propensity to correctly identify the location where General Noriega sought refuge. Since the hunt for Noriega was the most prominent aspect of the Panama invasion, and was covered intensely by the media—including the soft news media—this seems an appropriate place to search for any knowledge-enhancing effects associated with consuming soft news.

To test whether the effects of soft news exposure vary among respondents with differing intrinsic levels of interest in politics or foreign affairs, I interact a soft news consumption scale (identical to that employed in my prior investigation of attentiveness to Operation Just Cause in chapter 4) with respondents' education level. The control variables, including a hard news consumption scale, are also identical to those employed in chapter 4 (see table 4.3). Hence, I do not revisit them here. Instead, I turn straight to the results of a logit analysis employing this dependent variable (shown in the final column of table 8.A1, in the appendix to this chapter). At figure 8.1, I translate the key coefficients into probabilities of offering a correct response, as respondents' education level varies, and with all controls held constant at their mean values.

The curves shown in figure 8.1 indicate that among the roughly 15 percent of respondents lacking a high school diploma, exposure to soft news, net of exposure to hard news (among other controls), was positively associated with knowing where General Noriega sought refuge. Among those who did not attend high school, as soft news consumption varies from its lowest to highest levels, the probability of offering the correct answer increases by 32 percentage points (from .56 to .88). The corresponding increase among respondents who attended "some" high school is 11 percentage points (from .75 to .86). Soft news consumption had virtually no effect on high school graduates (about one-third of all respondents).

Interestingly, consistent with many of my statistical investigations in this book, among college-educated respondents (roughly half of the survey sample), the effects reverse, with greater soft news exposure associated with a *reduced* propensity to offer the correct response. Among those who completed "some" college, a maximum increase in soft news exposure is associated with a 12-percentage-point decline (from .94 to .82) in the probability of knowing where General Noriega took refuge. The corresponding decline for college graduates is 17 percentage points (from .97 to .80).[6] Once again, these data suggest that

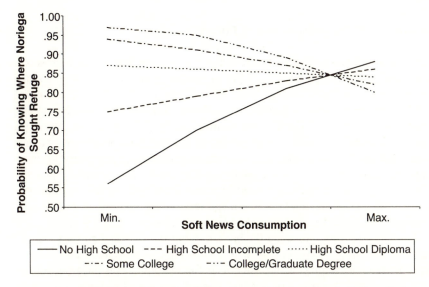

FIGURE 8.1. Probability of Knowing Where General Noriega Sought Refuge during U.S. Invasion of Panama, as Soft News Consumption and Education Vary

for highly educated individuals, consuming soft news represents more of a distraction from a given foreign policy crisis than a source of information about it.

These results address only one question, concerning only one foreign policy crisis. It is therefore difficult to generalize beyond this particular survey or event. After all, as we have seen, Operation Just Cause was one of the highest-profile foreign policy events of the past two decades. And, as noted, the search for General Noriega was by far the highest-profile aspect of the invasion. Hence, it is not terribly surprising that the knowledge effects of soft news exposure would, in this instance, be limited to a relatively small percentage of respondents. Most Americans probably found it difficult to *avoid* information about Panama. Indeed, somewhat paradoxically, the extraordinarily high profile of Operation Just Cause makes finding distinct soft news effects of any kind—with respect to either attentiveness or factual knowledge—all the more impressive.

My findings in this limited investigation clearly demonstrate that exposure to soft news outlets can have at least *some* effect on factual political knowledge, at least with respect to those high-profile issues, like foreign crises, that attract substantial soft news coverage, and at least in the short run. Unfortunately, these data do not allow a test of the extent or duration of such knowledge-enhancing effects. I therefore leave the important question of whether such effects are substantial and durable, or merely shallow and fleeting, for future research.

BROADER IMPLICATIONS FOR PUBLIC POLICY

Substantial scholarly research has found that public opinion can, at least some-times, influence foreign policy making in general (Powlick 1995; Powlick and Katz 1998a, 1998b; Hinckley 1992; Risse-Kappen 1991; Page and Shapiro 1983), and crisis decision making in particular (Bartels 1991; Gaubatz 1999; Zaller 1994; James and Oneal 1991; Ostrom and Job 1986). This suggests that changes in how television covers foreign policy may have important practical consequences for American politics. Additional research is necessary to deter-mine the actual effects of rising public scrutiny on the policy making process. Yet, in a democratic political system in which leaders are directly accountable to the public, it seems unlikely that heightened public scrutiny of policy deci-sion making would be entirely without consequence.

Scholars have long pondered the barriers to information and political partici-pation confronting democratic citizens. I have presented evidence that some of these barriers are falling. Where America's foreign policy was once the domain of a fairly small "foreign policy elite," the soft news media appear to have, to some extent, "democratized" foreign policy. Many Americans used to go about their lives largely oblivious to the foreign policy decisions of their leaders, despite the potentially profound effects of those decisions on their lives. While, according to recent survey data, even after 9/11 (Kurtz 2002) contemporary Americans care no more, and perhaps even less, about foreign policy than their parents and grandparents did, they are *more* likely to be exposed to the nation's major overseas activities, at least those involving the actual or potential use of military force.

A number of potentially significant implications follow from these devel-opments. First, the increasing importance of soft news outlets as sources of po-litical information will force political leaders to adapt to this new media en-vironment. For instance, no longer can presidents rely on nationally televised prime-time speeches to communicate to a majority of the American public. Cable and satellite television—including the soft news media—have robbed presidents of much of their audience (Baum and Kernell 1999; Hess 1998). And, for better or worse, millions of voters make their voting decisions based more on candidates' personal characteristics—the predominant emphasis of soft news outlets—than their policy positions, the latter of which receive relatively greater emphasis in traditional news outlets.

These developments suggest the need for substantial changes in the commu-nication strategies employed by America's political leaders. As the television marketplace increasingly segments, and as viewers are better able to identify programming tailored to their personal tastes and preferences, political leaders confront a fundamental paradigm shift. No longer can they merely send out a broadcast signal and, in effect, wait for the audience to come to them, as exem-plified by the traditional presidential prime-time speech or press conference.

Rather, political leaders must increasingly seek out the audience. This means heeding the lesson of the parable of the Drunkard's Search (Popkin 1994). This story concerns a man who drops his car keys while attempting to enter his car after a night of heavy drinking. Rather than looking near his car, where it is dark, he crosses the street to look for his keys under the nearest streetlight. When a nearby police officer inquires why the drunkard is looking for his keys across the street from where he dropped them, the drunkard responds that it's easier to see under the light. The drunkard reasons that even though the keys are unlikely to be found under the streetlight, across the street, he has a better chance of finding them there, in the light, than near the car, in the dark.

Popkin employs this story to emphasize that if a political candidate's goal is to get an audience to pay attention to him or her, the most effective strategy is to locate his or her campaign message where the intended audience is most likely to look for it. For my purposes, the implication, simply stated, is that if America's political leaders wish to communicate with the public, they will have to learn to put the information where the public is likely to notice it. One element in such a strategy clearly involves tailoring their messages to the sensibilities of the soft news audience. The previously noted appearances by the major presidential candidates on a variety of soft news programs, particularly talk shows, suggests that these candidates, at least, have begun to learn this lesson. As a result of candidate appearances during the 2000 campaign on programs like *The Oprah Winfrey Show* and *The Daily Show*, many Americans who might otherwise have largely ignored the presidential campaign were exposed to at least *some* information about the candidates prior to election day.[7] And, given the gateway effect described in chapters 2 and 4, some of these viewers may have subsequently sought out additional information from more traditional news sources.

Perhaps most importantly, the relatively apolitical audiences of most soft news programs, including talk shows, represent an exceptionally large pool of unusually persuadable potential voters. As previously discussed, political sophisticates and ideologues—the primary audience for many hard news outlets—tend to counterargue any information inconsistent with their preexisting preferences. This implies that appeals by presidential candidates are unlikely to change the minds of most hard news enthusiasts. In sharp contrast, even though they are somewhat less likely to vote, those soft news viewers who do vote are far more prone to be persuaded by candidate appeals, if properly tailored to their sensibilities (Baum 2002b). Hence, future presidential candidates would be wise to devote a greater proportion of their campaign efforts to appealing to this hitherto largely ignored portion of the electorate.

Beyond presidential elections, this phenomenon is also likely to affect public communications regarding foreign policy. The bully pulpit is, arguably, the president's most important source of political influence. Whenever presidents wish to undertake major foreign policy initiatives, they typically seek to explain their policies to the American people in the hopes of gaining the public's support, or at least its acquiescence. For the past four decades, presidents have relied primarily on prime-time, nationally televised speeches and press conferences for this purpose. They have also dispatched their senior foreign policy advisers to conduct interviews on the political TV talk-show circuit (e.g., *Meet the Press, This Week,* and *Face the Nation*). For future presidents, the new media environment represents both a challenge and an opportunity. It represents a challenge because presidents cannot count on communicating effectively with the American people solely through speeches or press conferences broadcast on the major networks or all-news cable channels, or even through appearances by their lieutenants on Sunday morning political talk shows. Failure to reach out to the less politically engaged segments of the public through the many soft news media outlets may result in reduced support for presidential policy initiatives, both foreign and domestic.

One important example is the long-standing debate concerning America's role in the world. Prior to 9/11, America's multilaterally-oriented, internationalist foreign policy had come under intense criticism from proponents of isolationism and unilateralism. Advocates of unilateralist and isolationist themes, like perennial presidential candidate and pundit Patrick Buchanan, took full advantage of the soft news media, appearing regularly, for instance, on cable talk shows. Though less embracing of multilateralism than his predecessor, President George W. Bush is an avowed internationalist. Yet, even in the post-9/11 political environment, if he fails to succeed in framing his internationalist arguments in terms appealing to the soft news media, in order to communicate to the millions of Americans who do not watch, read, or listen to traditional news sources, his isolationist political opponents may, over the longer term, gain a tactical advantage in this important political debate. In effect, large numbers of Americans may hear only one side of the story.

And given the general appeal of isolationist themes for politically inattentive individuals and the propensity of the soft news media to reinforce the isolationist propensities of its mostly politically inattentive audience, the evidence presented in the last chapter suggests that, unless properly countered, isolationist arguments may find a sympathetic audience among soft news consumers. For better or worse, by controlling the "spin," or framing, of the issue, and as the immediacy of 9/11 fades, those who would scale back America's role in the world may win the debate, essentially by default.

Nevertheless, the rise of the soft news media also offers an opportunity, because, to the extent they are able to adapt their messages accordingly, soft news outlets open up a previously nonexistent window for presidents to communicate with segments of the population that have traditionally tuned out entirely politics and foreign affairs. This may allow future presidents to expand their support coalitions beyond the traditionally politically engaged segments of the population. Broader support coalitions, in turn, may translate into more effective leadership, particularly in difficult times. Whether the soft news media ultimately help or hinder future presidential leadership efforts depends in no small measure in how presidents respond to this relatively new media phenomenon.

IMPLICATIONS FOR FOREIGN CRISIS DECISION MAKING

Another implication of my findings concerns the effect of a more-attentive public on foreign crisis decision-making. Elsewhere (Baum 2000a, 2000b; Baum, Hiscox, and O'Mahony 2001), I develop and test a theory of how public scrutiny can constrain presidential decision making. Below, I present a brief sketch of the central argument.

Research has found that public support is a valuable resource for presidents in pursuing their policy agendas (Kernell 1997; Page, Shapiro, and Dempsey 1987; Ostrom and Simon 1985; Neustadt 1990), as well as in enhancing their international credibility (Fearon 1994; Smith 1998; Schultz 1998; Putnam 1988). After all, once a president issues a public threat against a foreign nation, he is likely to pay a domestic political price—a domestic audience cost—if he backs down. According to the theoretical logic of domestic audience costs (Fearon 1994; Smith 1998; Schultz 1998; and others), this vulnerability should enhance a president's credibility to an adversary, thereby increasing the likelihood that the adversary will back down without a fight.

Yet, an attentive public can be a double-edged sword. As President G.H.W. Bush's failure to win reelection in the aftermath of the Persian Gulf War decisively demonstrated, public opinion can be fickle. Today's supporters may become tomorrow's opponents, should a policy initiative be perceived as failing. In deciding whether to use force, presidents must consider both the potential political and strategic upside, should a policy turn out well, and the potential downside should the policy fail. The more attentive the public, the greater the domestic political benefit from success or the cost of failure. Politically, however, due in part to increasingly hostile and negative media coverage of the presidency (Groeling and Kernell 1998; Grossman and Kumar 1981; Patterson 1996; Brody 1991), the potential political downside usually outweighs the potential upside.[8] As a result, all else equal, presidents will prefer to conduct their foreign policies free from excessive public scrutiny.

Of course, all else is frequently not equal, and hence there are limitations to this calculus. When a crisis involves fundamental national security interests, strategic calculations will often trump domestic political considerations, and presidents will most likely prefer to rally the public in order to maximize their credibility with the adversary abroad as well as enhance public and congressional support at home. In other words, when the stakes are high, the *strategic* benefit of generating domestic audience costs by attracting public scrutiny, in terms of enhanced credibility, seems likely to outweigh the potential *political* costs. Arguably a case in point is the G. W. Bush administration's intensive efforts to rally domestic and international support for ousting the regime of Saddam Hussein in Iraq. When, however, such interests are *not* at stake, domestic political considerations will loom large. Presidents will be more likely to use force or take other aggressive foreign policy actions if the public is inattentive, because the political costs of failure are limited by public disinterest.

According to this logic, a trend toward increased public attentiveness to foreign crises should result in a reduced willingness of U.S. presidents to employ military force, and more risk-averse behavior when they nonetheless do so, in low-stakes crisis situations. With respect to the latter prediction, Feaver and Gelpi (1999) argue that America's political leaders have indeed become highly risk-averse with respect to the use of military force. For instance, they report the results from a survey they conducted, which found, in part, that ". . . overwhelmingly, both civilian and military leaders agreed with the statement, 'The American public will rarely tolerate large numbers of U.S. casualties in military operations.'"

Elsewhere (Baum 2000b), I report some evidence substantiating both of the above-predicted trends. For instance, a logit analysis of trends in major U.S. foreign crises from 1946 to 1994, using the *International Crisis Behavior* (ICB) data set (Brecher and Wilkenfeld 1998), indicated that, during that period, the probability of American intervention in international crisis situations involving limited strategic stakes for the United States declined by about 25 percent ($p < .10$).[9] And in an OLS analysis, employing the Jones, Bremer, and Singer (1996) *Militarized Interstate Dispute* (MID) data set, I found that, between 1946 and 1992, the predicted number of fatalities associated with relatively low-stakes MIDs declined from an average of between 25 and 100 fatalities per MID to nearly zero ($p < .05$).[10] And if the MID data are limited to instances where the United States is coded as having used military force, the pattern becomes even starker. In this case, the average number of U.S. fatalities in low-stakes MIDs involving a U.S. use of force fell from between 100 and 250 in 1946 to, again, just above zero in 1992 ($p < .05$).

In both data sets, these trends emerged only for militarized disputes or foreign policy crises involving relatively *low* strategic stakes—the trends for *high*-stakes disputes and crises were substantively small and statistically insignificant—suggesting that when important U.S. national security interests are at stake, America's leaders remain willing to intervene and to risk the lives of U.S. soldiers in order to defend America's vital interests. But when the strategic stakes involved are modest, domestic political concerns appear to have increasingly pressured presidents to pursue risk-averse strategies designed to minimize casualties (at least over the periods covered by the two data sets).[11] (See Baum 2000a and 2000b for a more thorough treatment of this argument and evidence.)

Some anecdotal evidence suggests the trend toward increased risk aversion among America's political leaders may have accelerated over the past decade. Beginning most notably with the Persian Gulf War, the United States has increasingly relied on high-tech air power to fight its battles. Indeed, minimizing casualties was arguably among the highest priorities for U.S. forces during America's post–Cold War military interventions in Somalia, Bosnia, Kosovo, and Haiti. For instance, Daalder and O'Hanlon (2000) assert, with respect to the 1999 NATO air war in Kosovo, that the desire to minimize casualties in order to avoid a domestic public backlash was foremost in the minds of senior Clinton administration officials. Daalder and O'Hanlon argue that this presumed public casualty aversion profoundly influenced the strategic and tactical operations, and thus the effectiveness, of the air war. Similarly, Feaver and Gelpi (1999) argue, with respect to U.S.-led peacekeeping operations in Bosnia, that "casualty aversion reached an unprecedented level. 'Force protection,' meaning the prevention of U.S. casualties, became an explicit mission goal, on par with, if not superseding, the primary mission of restoring peace to Bosnia." And in 2001, in Afghanistan—certainly a "high stakes" military engagement if ever there was one—the United States again opted to rely primarily on air power in its war against Al Qaeda and the Taliban. Rightly or wrongly, critics of the Bush administration have attributed the sparse use of U.S. ground forces in Afghanistan to concern over the American public's intolerance for casualties.

Taken together, the aforementioned statistical results, combined with anecdotal evidence from the past decade, suggest that a trend has emerged toward both a reduced propensity to intervene in low-stakes crises and more risk-averse behavior once the United States becomes involved in such situations. Indeed, the manner in which the United States prosecuted its war in Afghanistan suggests that in the past several years—recall that the MID and ICB data sets extend to only 1992 and 1994, respectively—this pattern of heightened risk aversion in U.S. military operations may even have extended to circumstances involving vital U.S. national security interests.

The conceptual framework presented in the last chapter sought to explain why different groups of Americans might have developed, over time, substantively different perspectives with respect to the costs and benefits of using U.S. military force abroad. As we have seen, over the past two decades, politically unengaged Americans have grown increasingly attentive to news about foreign crises via the soft news media. And, as we have also seen, soft news outlets tend to emphasize the dangers and risks, and the likelihood of failure, associated with U.S. foreign policy initiatives. The net effect, documented in chapter 7, is an inverse relationship between exposure to soft news programming and support for a proactive or multilateral approach to U.S. foreign policy among the least politically attentive or educated segments of the population, but not among their more-attentive or better-educated counterparts. Chapter 7 also documented a trend toward reduced support for U.S. engagement in the world among politically inattentive Americans who consume lots of soft news, but, again, not among their more attentive counterparts.

For the same reasons, those Americans whose window onto the world is limited to the soft news media—again, typically the least educated or politically engaged members of the public—seem likely to be the most sensitive to the potential for large-scale casualties in U.S. military operations. After all, it stands to reason that individuals who oppose a particular military intervention, or a proactive U.S. foreign policy in general, will also oppose risking the lives of U.S. troops for "foreign adventures" that they consider unwise in the first instance. In fact, in a series of statistical analyses of the impact of expected casualties during the Persian Gulf and Kosovo wars (not shown), I found that the least educated and politically engaged members of the public were indeed significantly more sensitive to the fear or expectation of substantial U.S. casualties than were their better-educated or more-attentive counterparts, Among the former group, as the fear or expectation of casualties increased, the probability of supporting the U.S. policy with respect to the Persian Gulf crisis and war or the Kosovo air war declined precipitously. The corresponding effects on highly educated or politically attentive individuals were far smaller and in most cases statistically insignificant. These results (available from the author upon request) once again suggest, albeit in this latter instance only indirectly, that the rise of the soft news media may indeed hold fairly wide-ranging implications for the future conduct of American foreign policy.

AND FINALLY . . . IMPLICATIONS FOR AMERICA'S DEMOCRACY

It is tempting to take heart from the apparent leveling off of attentiveness to foreign policy across differing sectors of American society. After all, a more broadly attentive public might yield more broad-based participation in the political process. Indeed, previous research (Iyengar 1990) has found that individuals who know more about a given issue when they encounter news about it on television tend to learn more than individuals encountering the issue for the first time. This suggests even inadvertent initial attention to an issue, say in the context of a soft news program, may result in, or at least pave the way for, a better-informed public. For instance, as a consequence of encountering a political issue in the soft news media, more citizens may subsequently pay closer attention to news about that issue in *traditional* contexts (e.g., network newscasts or newspapers). Indeed, in chapter 4, I presented some evidence suggesting that such gateway effects do indeed occur.

More attentive citizens are arguably better situated to evaluate the effectiveness of their leaders in protecting America's vital international interests. Many democratic theorists, who have lamented widespread citizen ignorance and the decline in civic participation (e.g., Barber 1984; Putnam 2000), would likely consider this a desirable outcome. Moreover, recent research (Zaller 2002) suggests that politically unengaged individuals, to the extent they pay any attention to political events at all, are more likely than their more ideologically oriented counterparts to adapt their attitudes to changing circumstances. For instance, politically unengaged individuals are more likely to cross party lines to vote out of office a president perceived as ineffective. Political ideologues, in contrast, typically stick with their party's standard bearer in all but the most dire of circumstances. Are the latter, political sophisticates necessarily doing their country a better service than the former, less politically engaged individuals by sticking with their party's leader almost regardless of his or her performance in office?

By the same token, it is unclear whether more information necessarily makes better citizens, particularly if the quality of that information is suspect. Students of foreign policy have a long history of disdain for participation in foreign affairs by a largely ignorant public (e.g., Almond 1950; Lippman 1934). According to this "Almond-Lippman Consensus" (Holsti 1992) among America's political elites, the public is profoundly ignorant regarding foreign affairs, and as such ill equipped to understand, let alone participate in, America's foreign policy making process. Even today, in editorial pages and television talk shows, foreign policy "experts" regularly lament the rise of what they view as a public-opinion-driven foreign policy. Though these commentators rarely consider the implications of their comments, the clear logical implication is that political leaders ought to discount the views of the mass public in formulating the nation's foreign policy.

This view, at least in public declarations, appears to remain prevalent in Washington as well. For instance, when asked by reporters about the implications of dissent within the Republican Party concerning his administration's professed intention of toppling the regime of Saddam Hussein in Iraq, by force if necessary, President George W. Bush responded: "People should be allowed to express their opinion. But America needs to know, I'll be making up my mind based upon the latest intelligence and how best to protect our own country plus our friends and allies" (Bumiller 2002). President Bush's comment could hardly illustrate more clearly the view that presidential foreign policy decisions should be based upon dispassionate considerations of national security, and not public preferences.

The object of the most recent wave of hand-wringing on this topic—one which may well have given President Bush an added incentive to deny being influenced by public opinion in his Iraq policy—is former President Clinton, who was regularly accused by his detractors of allowing public passions to influence his major decisions regarding the use of American military force in such diverse locales as Somalia and Kosovo, with presumably negative consequences. It remains unclear to what extent President Clinton or his predecessors really allowed popular pressures to influence their major foreign policy decisions, or, for that matter, to what extent they *should* have done so. The leader of any democracy, including the president of the United States, is elected both to lead the people and to follow their will. To be effective, a president must be both responsive to the electorate and capable of leading it where he believes America's foreign policy should go, even if his position is unpopular. The line between these two competing responsibilities has always been murky. Indeed, scholars and pundits regularly debate, without resolution, where this line ought to be drawn. Still, whether or not this particular accusation against President Clinton is justified, it remains unclear whether the soft news media are good or bad for democracy, or the extent to which the views of an increasingly attentive public should be heeded by America's political decision-makers.

Media critics frequently complain that the rise of "scandal-driven" soft news (or tabloid journalism, as it is frequently termed) has turned America into a nation of voyeurs, where fame is celebrated for its own sake (e.g., Kelly 2001; Sabato, Stencel, and Lichter 2000). Others counter that by making political discourse more accessible, entertainment-oriented news may have, perhaps inadvertently, elevated politics and brought more Americans into the political process (e.g., Zaller 1999).[12] Those taking the former view correctly point out that the types of coverage of political issues featured in the soft news media are by no means limited to that venue. Indeed, virtually all news outlets offer at least *some* "soft" coverage of political stories; many offer a great deal indeed. In some instances, and regarding some stories, the line between the soft and hard news media has been difficult to discern. Noteworthy cases in point include the Monica Lewinsky scandal, the death of Princess Diana, the O. J. Simpson trial and the Gary Condit affair. In all four instances, notwithstanding familiarity with specific reporters or anchors, if an individual tuned in to a random news broadcast, that individual would have had a very difficult time determining, from substance alone, whether he or she was watching *World News Tonight* or *Entertainment Tonight*. More recently, in the immediate aftermath of 9/11, at least *some* of the coverage of 9/11-related issues by entertainment newsmagazine programs was almost entirely indistinguishable from that found in traditional news venues.

Still, advocates of the latter perspective might counter that such instances are relatively few and far between, and that even relatively salacious coverage does impart serious information. Indeed, if, as argued by advocates of low-information rationality, politically inattentive individuals are able, with a reasonable degree of accuracy, to differentiate between candidates and policies that do or do not best represent their political self-interest, and make reasoned decisions through reliance on heuristic cues and cognitive shortcuts, then the repackaging of political information as entertainment might not be such a bad thing after all.

Regardless of one's views on this question, it seems likely that the changing media environment described in this book will influence, at least to some extent, directly or indirectly, the responsiveness of America's political leaders to the electorate. Certainly it will bring at least some major policy issues to the attention of a broader segment of the public than was the case with comparable issues in previous decades. And in doing so, the soft news media may, for better or worse, enhance the democratic responsiveness of elected officials, by, in effect, increasing the pressure on America's political leaders to bring their policies more closely in line with public preferences.

Zaller (2002) argues that politicians are well advised to avoid taking politically inattentive members of the populace for granted. While these individuals usually support policies that enjoy widespread popular and elite support—due to the so-called mainstreaming effect (Zaller 1994)—they also tend to be less deeply wedded to society's dominant political ideologies and institutions. Hence, under some circumstances, they may swing strongly against the prevailing political mainstream. This suggests that the least politically informed members of the public can, under some circumstances, be a primary instrument of political change. In a particularly extreme example of this phenomenon, Converse (1969) attributes the rise of the Nazi party in Germany in the 1930s to the willingness of young voters who lacked strong ideological or emotional political attachments to abandon the mainstream parties. Frustrated by economic depression and with little hope for improvement, the youngest and least ideologically partisan members of the population were thus largely responsible for sweeping an antidemocratic government into power. This suggests, contrary to the Almond-Lippman Consensus, that politicians ignore the politically inattentive segments of the public at their peril.

Nevertheless, even if one holds that a president's primary duty is to follow the will of the people, one cannot help but wonder about the implications of a citizenry increasingly learning about the world through the relatively narrow lens of the entertainment-oriented soft news media. After all, as we saw in the last chapter, though the soft news media are clearly not responsible for the prevalent suspicion of internationalism among the least politically engaged segments of the American public, they do tend to cover foreign crises in ways that cause politically inattentive individuals to further recoil from foreign entanglements. Taken to an extreme, this could potentially lead to a substantial increase in public support for an isolationist American foreign policy.

Since this is a book about the entertainment media, it seems appropriate to end with several references from that genre. In the 1991 film *Grand Canyon*, Steve Martin's character, a successful movie producer, proudly proclaims to a friend "all of life's riddles are answered in the movies." Following Martin's suggestion, I look to the movies for a concluding thought on the softening of news about politics and foreign affairs. In the 1987 film, *Broadcast News*, William Hurt's character, a high-profile network TV news anchor, is accused by a colleague of advancing his career by crossing the line between news and entertainment. Hurt responds: "It's hard *not* to cross it. They keep *moving* the little sucker, don't they?" Seventeen years later, one is tempted to conclude that any "line" that may once have existed between news and entertainment, however malleable, may be a relic of twentieth-century journalism. At some point in the nearly two decades since William Hurt spoke these words, for better or worse, "they" appear to have given up on moving the line in favor of abandoning it altogether. Only the passage of time will reveal whether this ultimately benefits or hinders America's democracy.

APPENDIX: STATISTICAL TABLES

TABLE 8.A1. Logit and Ordered Logit Analyses of Effects of Watching Daytime Talk Shows/Soft News Shows on Likelihood of Following or Caring about Outcome of 2000 Presidential Election or Knowing Where General Noriega Sought Refuge during Operation Just Cause

Coef. (Std. Err.)

| | Interest in Campaign | | Care about Election Outcome | | Know about Noriega |
	Model 1	Model 2	Model 3	Model 4	Model 5
Media Consumption Habits					
Watch daytime talk shows	.286 (.121)*	.438 (.176)**	.207 (.145)	.429 (.221)*	—
Soft news index	—	—	—	—	.923 (.509)^
Hard news index	—	—	—	—	.809 (.229)***
Watch network news (days per week)	—	.128 (.030)***	—	−.054 (.047)	—
Watch early local news (days per week)	—	.001 (.028)	—	−.032 (.046)	—
Watch late local news (days per week)	—	.032 (.027)	—	.034 (.042)	—
Read newspaper (days per week)	—	−.012 (.025)	—	−.090 (.040)*	—
Listen to talk radio	—	.193 (.063)**	—	.103 (.104)	—
Cable access	—	.043 (.165)	—	.632 (.247)**	—
Internet access	—	.171 (.156)	—	−.121 (.243)	—
SES/Demographics					
Education	—	.037 (.032)	—	−.006 (.052)	1.181 (.345)***

Age	—	.0001 (.005)	—	.006 (.007)	.024 (.007)***
Family income	—	.004 (.019)	—	.027 (.032)	.214 (.095)*
Male	—	-.169 (.139)	—	-.168 (.207)	.642 (.220)**
White	—	-.175 (.174)	—	-.069 (.263)	-.536 (.623)
Black	—	—	—	—	-2.011 (.676)**
Unemployed	—	—	—	—	-.071 (.264)
Political Engagement					
Political interest scale	—	—	.852 (.069)***	.896 (.104)***	—
Follow government/public affairs	1.322 (.077)***	1.075 (.104)***	—	—	—
Partisanship	.390 (.054)***	.319 (.074)***	.570 (.071)***	.492 (.103)***	-.056 (.278)
Party identification	.049 (.071)	.079 (.119)	.014 (.108)	.299 (.186)	—
Plan to vote Democratic	—	.318 (.269)	—	.661 (.339)*	—
Plan to vote Republican	—	.269 (.273)	—	.327 (.327)	—
Personal importance of Panama invasion	—	—	—	—	.565 (.209)**
Political Trust & Efficacy					
External efficacy I	—	.126 (.156)	—	-.001 (.258)	—
External efficacy II	—	.092 (.161)	—	.224 (.252)	—
Internal efficacy	—	.268 (.150)^	—	-.052 (.228)	—
Trust in government	—	-.055 (.077)	—	.118 (.134)	—

TABLE 8.A1. Continued

	Coef. (Std. Err.)				
	Interest in Campaign		Care about Election Outcome		Know about Noriega
	Model 1	Model 2	Model 3	Model 4	Model 5
Interaction Terms					
Political interest × watch daytime talk shows	—	—	−.120 (.058)*	−.185 (.075)**	—
Follow government/public affairs × watch daytime talk shows	−.158 (.070)*	−.227 (.095)*	—	—	—
Soft news index × education	—	—	—	—	−.336 (.144)*
Constant 1	.615 (.169)	1.146 (.641)	−1.547 (.208)***	−2.752 (.938)**	−4.535 (1.404)***
Constant 2	3.463 (.203)	4.253 (.652)	—	—	—
Pseudo R^2	.18	.18	.24	.21	.19
	(N = 1,506)	(N = 1,086)	(N = 1,500)	(N = 1,082)	(N = 1,080)

Note: All models employ heteroscedasticity-consistent ("robust") standard errors.
[†]p < .10, *p < .05, **p < .01, ***p < .001

NOTES

CHAPTER ONE: WAR AND ENTERTAINMENT

1. J. Scott 1998.
2. CBS/*New York Times* poll, August 20, 1998.
3. Pew Research Center for the People and the Press, August 21, 1998.
4. Entertainment-oriented informational television programming is sometimes referred to as "infotainment." For purposes of this study, however, I employ the term "soft news," which arguably carries with it less normative baggage.
5. As of November 2002, a combined average of about 3.275 million households at any given point in time tuned in to the five major all-news cable networks (Fox, CNN, MSNBC, CNBC, and HLN). This figure, however, does not account for possible viewer overlap. In other words, one viewer may tune in to multiple cable networks on any given day. Hence, it almost certainly overstates the daily average number of unique cable news viewers.
6. Nielsen ratings are for various periods in 2002. (See chapter 3 for details.)
7. In interviews, the author of the book on which the film was based indicated that the book was written with Bill Clinton in mind.
8. The programs I reviewed included: *Entertainment Tonight, Access Hollywood, Extra, The Daily Show, E! News Daily, The Tonight Show with Jay Leno, Late Night with Conan O'Brien, Politically Incorrect, Howard Stern, 60 Minutes, 20/20*, and *Dateline*. In those cases where I could not determine from the soft news program abstracts whether the *Wag the Dog* theme was addressed in a given story, I counted the story as *non–Wag the Dog*–related coverage of the missile strikes. Hence, the figures reported below are conservative.
9. Newsweek poll, August 20–21, 1998.
10. For instance, according to the 2000 American National Election Study, respondents with less than a twelfth-grade education watch nearly three times as many daytime talk shows as their counterparts possessing a college or postgraduate degree.
11. Another survey (Pew Research Center 1998c) conducted in the aftermath of the attack on Afghanistan and Sudan found that respondents with a primary-school education were twice as likely as their counterparts with a postgraduate degree (54 percent vs. 27 percent) to believe that the president's motivation was primarily to "turn attention away from [the Lewinsky] affair." As noted, less-educated individuals are among the primary consumers of soft news.
12. Throughout the book, I employ the terms "foreign crisis" and "foreign policy crisis" interchangeably. For my purposes, both refer to *American* foreign policy activities.
13. Because the dividing lines between the soft and hard news media are not in every instance entirely clear, in my statistical analyses in subsequent chapters, I rely on empirical testing to determine the appropriate placement of several relatively ambiguous cases, like local TV news.
14. There have only been three such high-profile scandals since World War II (Watergate in 1974, Iran-Contra in 1987, and the Monica Lewinsky affair in 1998).

15. This suggests that foreign crises represent a specific *domain* of politics (Iyengar 1990) that, for reasons to be discussed in chapter 2, are most likely to attract greater public attentiveness. Moreover, as I shall later describe in detail, the theory offers different behavioral predictions for different types of individuals.

16. Whether or not politics truly "stops at the water's edge," or if it ever did so, remains a subject of much controversy. It seems clear, however, that partisan political preferences are a less-reliable predictor of support for U.S. military operations than for attitudes regarding most domestic political issues. For instance, presumably due to this distinction, during the 2000 presidential debates, the two candidates disagreed hardly at all on matters of foreign policy, instead reserving their harshest mutual criticism for purely domestic political issues.

17. According to a content analysis by the Center for Media and Public Affairs (*Media Monitor* 2000), the percentage of stories on the evening newscasts of the major networks devoted to foreign news coverage fell from 50 percent in 1990 and 1991 to less than 23 percent between 1996 and 1998. Excluding coverage of the Persian Gulf crisis and war during the 1990–91 period and the Kosovo air war during the 1996–99 period foreign coverage fell from about one-third of network news stories in 1990–91 to an average of 21 percent of network news stories in the 1996–99 period. Similarly, a study by the Joan Shorenstein Center found that the percentage of network airtime devoted to foreign news fell from 45 percent in the 1970s to 13.5 percent in 1995 (Hoge 1997, 48). Indeed, the total minutes of coverage originating from the network foreign bureaus of ABC, NBC and CBS, combined, fell by 65 percent between 1989 and 2000 (Shaw 2001). And one 1998 study by the University of California at San Diego found that between 1983 and 1998 total newspaper coverage focusing on foreign affairs fell from 10 percent to 2 percent. Other indicators of the decline in foreign news coverage include the shrinking foreign affairs staffing of major media outlets. According to Shaw (2001), between 1989 and 2001, *Time* magazine reduced its foreign correspondents corps from thirty-three to twenty-four, while, in the last fifteen years, the number of ABC News foreign bureaus fell from seventeen to seven.

18. Excerpted from Kinchla 1980.

CHAPTER TWO: SOFT NEWS AND THE ACCIDENTALLY ATTENTIVE PUBLIC

1. Comments made during CNN's *Reliable Sources* program, June 19, 1999.

2. Throughout the book, I frequently describe certain segments of the public as "learning" about politics or foreign affairs from the soft news media. By this I do not refer to acquiring and retaining substantial factual knowledge about politics. A great deal of research in cognitive psychology, some of which is cited in this chapter, demonstrates that "learning" does not necessarily require storing in memory lots of facts. In other words, learning comes in many forms, and due to people's capacity to employ informational shortcuts, or heuristic cues, it is not necessarily the case that one must acquire and retain in memory substantial volumes of factual knowledge about an issue in order to form a reasoned opinion or make a reasoned decision about it. Hence, my use of the term "learning" refers primarily to enhancing one's degree of awareness of a given issue and improving one's ability to form a reasoned (albeit not necessarily "reasonable") opinion about it. Nevertheless, in the concluding chapter, I present some evidence that exposure to foreign crises via soft news coverage *can* be associated with enhanced factual knowledge about such events, at least among individuals who do not typically consume traditional sources of news.

3. The argument I develop below also applies, to a lesser extent, to the radio and print media, which have responded to similar market forces with similar strategic innovations. Because, however, of television's clear predominance as the primary source of news and information about political issues for a vast majority of the public, I focus my discussion primarily on television.

4. For a similar application of the standard expected utility model, see Hamilton 2003.

5. In my model, the P term differs from the more common usage familiar to students of voting and elections, where P typically represents the probability that an individual's vote will affect the outcome of an election. Not surprisingly, in these models P tends to be vanishingly small, usually approaching zero. In my model, in contrast, P represents the probability of receiving "useful" information from paying attention to political issues—with "useful" meaning any information that gives the individual pleasure, for whatever reason (Lupia and McCubbins 1998). Given this definition, it is easy to see why in my variant of the traditional expected utility model, P tends to be quite large. For instance, most individuals predisposed to watching a given entertainment program on television can be reasonably confident that they will receive the type of pleasurable (i.e., entertaining or titillating) stimulation they seek. Similarly, one can count on most local news broadcasts and network newsmagazines (e.g., *20/20*) to offer large doses of human drama, relative to coverage of more "mundane" political issues. Viewers of these programs are not necessarily seeking information about politics. A high P term, however, does not require a high probability of receiving information about politics. Rather, it merely requires that the individual have an expectation of receiving whatever sort of information a program promises to deliver and which she is seeking. Any information about politics transmitted as an incidental by-product of watching such programs will not necessarily factor into the individual's decision calculus. This suggests that for many individuals, in this context, the P term is indeed quite large, even approaching 100 percent. Hence, I assume that P's value is 100 percent. By doing so, I effectively hold P constant, thereby reducing the model to benefits minus costs, or $B - C$.

6. The total number of American fatalities attributed to the Vietnam War is just over 58,000.

7. The American National Election Study (NES), which originated in 1948, is the nation's most extensive and long-running election-related public opinion survey. The NES is conducted biennially—in every U.S. election year—by the University of Michigan, Center for Political Studies and the Inter-university Consortium for Political and Social Research. The survey is based entirely on lengthy in-person interviews of a random sample of the electorate, both prior to and immediately following the election. The identical question, asked by the NES in 1968, found 56 percent of respondents paying "a good deal" of attention to Vietnam. A nearly identical number (55 percent) claimed the war issue would be very important in deciding how they would vote in the 1968 presidential election. Though only 8 percent claimed not to be following the war, nearly twice that number (15 percent) claimed that the war in Vietnam would not affect their vote, identical to the percentage who in 1970 considered the Vietnam War unimportant.

8. The corresponding difference between 1968 and 1991 is a nearly identical 8 percentage points.

9. See chapter 4 for a discussion of the validity of employing "no opinion" and "don't know" responses as indicators of inattentiveness.

10. It is worth noting that, as figure 2.2 clearly shows, "don't know" rates during the Vietnam War trend downward, over time. In other words, as the controversy surrounding the war increased, "don't know" rates receded. This suggests it is unlikely that respond-

ing "don't know" was primarily an indicator of ambivalence or uncertainty regarding the appropriate response.

11. The Gulf crisis period includes the latter half of 1991, when the only prominent U.S. activity in the Persian Gulf was protecting the Kurds in Northern Iraq.

12. On January 26, 1973, a Gallup poll, conducted for the Nixon administration, produced a "don't know" rate of 6 percent, the only instance of such a rate below 8 percent in the entire 1965–73 period.

13. Note that the Vietnam War garnered, on average, 3.3 percent fewer "don't know" responses than the Korean War had, suggesting that the greater controversy of the Vietnam War, relative to the Gulf War, cannot fully account for this difference.

14. Gallup/CBS Poll, January 16–19, 1991.

15. By comparison, in two Gallup polls conducted on March 27 and June 15, 1952, only 19 percent of respondents specifically mentioned the Korean War as the nation's most important problem.

16. The GSS Surveys have been conducted every year since 1972. However, the question used in constructing this figure was asked only for a consistent set of countries between 1974 and 1994. During that twenty-year period, the particular question shown in the figure was asked, regarding these six countries, on 13 occasions.

17. For substantial additional evidence that Americans interest in foreign affairs has not increased over the past several decades, see Rielly 1999. Rielly reports the results of the 1998 Chicago Council on Foreign Relations survey on American public opinion regarding foreign policy. Among other results, Rielly notes that when asked to name the "two or three biggest foreign policy problems facing the United States today," the most common answer among the general public was "don't know," which was mentioned by 21 percent of respondents. The second most common answer, terrorism, was mentioned by only 12 percent of "general public" respondents. The latter figure would doubtless have been higher in the aftermath of 9/11. Yet previously cited survey data (Kurtz 2002) suggests that the post-9/11 spike in public interest in foreign affairs was fairly short-lived. Of course, future major overseas events, such as the war in Iraq, are likely to again heighten the public's concern with foreign affairs, at least temporarily.

18. The incorporation of real-world events into the plots of fictional TV programs reemerged in the aftermath of September 11, 2001. Indeed, since 9/11, the Pentagon coined a term—"militainment"—for fictional television programming that features real-world military-related issues or events

19. "Useful" is, of course, a relative term. For knowledge to be useful, it need only satisfy, in some manner, whatever purpose an individual may have for acquiring it, ranging from distraction to entertainment to enlightenment.

20. Throughout this discussion, I assume that a typical individual is more likely to consume television, most of the time, for purposes of *entertainment*, rather than for enlightenment. Individuals certainly differ in their reasons for watching television. I believe, however, it is reasonable to assume that for most individuals, most of the time— with the exception of a relatively small minority who use the media primarily to gather information about the world—television is more frequently employed for entertainment purposes than for education or enlightenment.

21. Passive learning is possible because individuals are more likely to accept information presented in a nonconflictual manner, which does not arouse excitement (Krugman and Hartley 1970). Individuals learn passively by first *choosing* to expose themselves to a particular type of information (e.g., political news), say by watching the network news, but then surrendering control of the *specific* information to which they are exposed

(Zukin with Snyder 1984). For instance, individuals unwilling to *read* about a political issue in the newspaper may be willing to *watch* a news story about the issue, even if they are not particularly interested in the subject matter, simply because watching television requires less effort (Eveland and Scheufele 2000). Incidental learning is merely an extreme form of passive learning, whereby the individual actively seeks one variety of information—say, entertainment—and is unwittingly exposed to and accepts information of another sort entirely (e.g., political news). (For a related argument, see Popkin 1994.)

22. In fact, my argument could be restated in terms of the public's demand for entertainment. Prior to the "information revolution," there may have existed an excess demand for entertainment among the public that went unmet and is currently better satisfied by more diverse programming.

23. It is not necessarily the case, however, that the distinction between traditional and soft news has disappeared or that politically apathetic individuals have come to anticipate heightened benefits from consuming political news. Along these lines, Lutz (1975) points out an important distinction between first- and second-order cognitive effects in influencing attitude change. The former concerns information that directly addresses a given attitude object, such as an advertisement intended to convince a viewer to buy a particular brand of toothpaste. The latter concerns the effects of such new information, or attributes, on attitudes that are *not* the overt object of the information. In other words, the effects of information on attitudes tend to diffuse beyond the immediate object of attention, through a sort of cognitive branching process. So the toothpaste commercial may inadvertently trigger a change in a viewer's attitudes about other, seemingly unrelated objects. This suggests that information attended to by a viewer due to its entertainment value may have the unintended effect of influencing that individual's attitudes toward other things, like, say, a foreign policy crisis.

24. Though broadcasters have sought to make traditional news more accessible, continued falling ratings for network newscasts, and more recently for local TV news (Patterson 2000), suggest the audience for *traditional* news has not broadened.

25. Krugman and Hartley (1970) note that as an ideal vehicle for passive learning, television has allowed many people to develop opinions on serious issues about which they would previously have replied "don't know" if queried (because they would have avoided learning about such issues).

26. Iyengar (1990, 168) identifies an "accessibility bias," which he defines as "the general tendency of individuals to attach greater weight to considerations that are, for whatever reason, momentarily prominent or salient."

27. Gamson and Modigliani (1987, 143) offer the following operational definition of a frame: "a central organizing idea or story line that provides meaning to an unfolding strip of events, weaving a connection among them. The frame suggests what the controversy is about, the essence of the issue." This definition adequately captures my use of the term in this study (but see Druckman 2002 for a discussion of differing definitions and uses of the term).

28. Lisa Gregorish, interview with author, Los Angeles, Calif., June 20, 2000. Gregorish is also a former executive producer for the tabloid television magazine program *Hard Copy*. She also previously served as vice president of news and news director at Fox's New York, Dallas, and Salt Lake City stations.

29. This refers to the media's tendency to divide protagonists involved in a story into two groups, those whom the audience should identify with, and those who are the "other" or "outsider."

30. This refers to the "perception of control by powerful others" (Neuman, Just, and Crigler 1992, 62).

31. These findings complement a large literature on individual media uses and gratification. This literature (e.g., Katz and Foulkes 1962; Katz, Blumler, and Gurevitch 1973–74; Rosengren, Wenner, and Palmgreen 1985; Swanson 1987; and many others) argues that individuals "use" the media to fulfill various social and psychological needs, including diversion, easing of social tension and conflict, establishing substitute personal relationships, reinforcing personal identity (e.g., value reinforcement), gaining comfort through familiarity, learning about social problems, and surveillance. For instance, one study (Katzman 1972) found that television soap operas tend to reinforce dominant social values. It is unsurprising that the frames most frequently employed by typical individuals are directly linked to several of the predominant uses of the mass media identified by social psychologists.

32. Along these lines, Hill (1985) found that TV news is better able to influence the agenda of viewers (i.e., induce them to focus on a given issue) who possess a *prior* awareness of a given news topic.

33. The idea of causal narratives is similar to the concept of a *schema* from cognitive psychology (e.g., Conover and Feldman 1984; Tetlock 1985, 1986, 1989). Conover and Feldman (1984) define a schema as "a cognitive structure of 'organized prior knowledge, abstracted from experience with specific instances' that guides 'the processing of new information and the retrieval of stored information' "

34. It is important to point out that the degree of cognitive conflict evoked by mutually incompatible causal narratives, or schemas, is likely to vary widely for different individuals at differing levels of cognitive sophistication (Tetlock 1985, 1986; Iyengar 1993; Zaller 1992; Ottati and Wyer 1990).

35. In the latter case, the past decade has witnessed the emergence of numerous niche-targeted newsmagazines.

36. The Internet has also influenced traditional news media outlets. I reserve consideration of the Internet, however, for the concluding chapter.

37. This account was substantiated, in an interview with the author, by Mark L. Berlin, attorney adviser, Office of Political Programming, Mass Media Bureau, Federal Communications Commission (FCC), Washington, D.C. (June 29, 2000).

38. Interview with Berlin.

39. According to Berlin, broadcasters who failed to meet the minimum requirements for news and public affairs content faced greater scrutiny by the FCC when their broadcast licenses came up for renewal. Stations that met these requirements could be renewed at the FCC staff level, while violators had to be approved at more senior levels (interview with author). Moreover, in 1948, the National Association of Broadcasters replaced its voluntary code of programming standards with a more stringent code, consistent with the FCC's 1946 *Blue Book*, which established standards for several types of programs, including public affairs programming (FCC 1998). Corvo notes (Committee for Concerned Journalists [CCJ] 1998b) that in the early years of television, broadcasters used news, in part, as a public relations tool intended to preempt additional government mandates by convincing Congress that the networks were devoted to public service.

40. Berlin commented that changes in American society over the same time period, such as increased diversity, provided additional impetus for changes in the television marketplace.

41. Several additional technological innovations have also contributed to the changing economics of news. In 1968, "video" was a rare commodity. Television news footage was filmed using two-inch film, which had to be developed before being broadcast,

usually necessitating a delay of at least one day. The widespread adoption first of analog and later of digital video technology completely eliminated this delay. In addition, the rise of independent news organizations, which provide local television affiliates and independent stations with an alternative to their prior dependence upon the networks for national and international news, allows these stations to dramatically increase their coverage of national and international issues. The proliferation of independent "expert" consultants—commonly referred to as "talking heads"—represents another important innovation. These "experts" broadcast commentaries regarding major issues via satellite, which can be inexpensively purchased ("downlinked") for live broadcast by any interested station, without the investment of going to that individual for an interview. Along with cable, the advent of satellite broadcasting, making possible live coverage of issues around the globe, is one of the most significant innovations in television news in the past forty years. In recent years, the audience has received information in real time, without the one- or two-day film transport and development delays of the 1960s. Thanks to these and other technological innovations, television in general, and television news in particular, now presents vastly more information on far more diverse topics, from around the world, and at far less cost, than was technically possible in the 1960s.

43. Even with the addition of two new broadcast networks in the 1990s (Fox and WB), there has been some consolidation among major broadcasters in recent years. Nevertheless, programming content has continued to expand and diversify.

44. Webster and Lichty (1991) refer to this strategy as "counter-programming." Berlin corroborated this account in an interview with the author.

45. Niche programming, per se, is not entirely new. After all, television viewers have always had the opportunity to choose between, say, sports, news, or children's cartoons. Yet, by and large, the primary marketing strategy of the major networks prior to the 1980s was to try to capture the largest possible share of the viewing audience at any given point in time, and with any given program (Webster and Lichty 1991). And niche marketing in news programming is almost entirely a post-1980 phenomenon.

45. Deregulation of the radio industry began several years earlier, in 1979. It was not until the pro-deregulation Reagan administration assumed office that deregulation was extended to the television industry.

46. Http://www.ultimatetv.com/news/nielsen.

47. Similarly, the average cost for one hour of a network "sitcom" is about $1.8 million, or over 3.5 times the cost of a one-hour episode of *Dateline* (Davis and Owen 1998, 100).

48. These data do not take into account potential revenues from reruns or syndication, which might advantage *ER* relative to *Dateline*. Still, while episodes of an original drama series are presumably easier to reuse than episodes of a news-oriented program, NBC has nonetheless found ways to reuse material from *Dateline*, in the form of "historical" programs, like MSNBC's *Time and Again*. Hence, the implications of reruns and syndication are somewhat unclear. (I thank James Hamilton for pointing out this issue to me.)

49. In recent years, local news broadcasts have routinely covered national and international stories, along with regular doses of celebrity gossip, scandal, police car chases, and other crime dramas. Yet, local news programs did not always cover even the most high-profile political issues. For instance, during the height of the Vietnam War, local news was much more locally oriented than it is today. As we shall see in chapter 3, local television news offered very little coverage of Vietnam, even at its most high-profile moments (e.g., the 1968 Tet Offensive, which corresponded with the height of television coverage of the war).

50. For a discussion of episodic and thematic framing in TV news, see Iyengar 1991.

51. This discussion does suggest one manner by which expected benefits might be *indirectly* increased by soft news. Piaget argued that emotions provide the primary motivation for intellectual activity, such as learning (Ginsburg and Opper 1969, 15). This suggests individuals are more likely to pay attention to information that gives them emotional gratification. Hence, when information is offered by someone with whom an individual enjoys an emotionally gratifying relationship, such as a celebrity, she is more likely to associate it with pleasurable stimulation, and thus perceive it as personally "beneficial." Psychoanalytic theory refers to this latter process as *object relations*. In the context of soft news, media personalities with a high degree of credibility for their fans (e.g., Oprah Winfrey, Rosie O'Donnell, Howard Stern, or perhaps a teen idol on MTV) are signaling, merely by discussing an issue, that the issue warrants their fans' attention (Popkin 1994; Page, Shapiro, and Dempsey 1987; see also Bovitz, Druckman, and Lupia 1997 on the conditions for persuasion). Having been alerted to an issue by, say, their favorite talk show host, fans of these soft news celebrities are more likely to be willing to pay attention the next time they encounter news about the issue in the course of channel surfing. In fact, according to one survey (Pew Research Center 2000), Oprah Winfrey and Rosie O'Donnell are about as important in influencing respondents' choices for president as the opinions of Bill Gates, Ted Turner, Elizabeth Dole, Nancy Reagan, Ted Kennedy, Jesse Ventura, local newspapers, and ministers, priests, or rabbis.

52. Gregorish interview.

53. While these shows tend to be largely apolitical, part of the mix for many of them is talk about whatever story—whether it involves sports, celebrities or politics—is dominating the headlines at the moment.

54. I employ the term "tabloid" in a broad context, referring to programs that *look* like traditional newscasts but emphasize entertainment-oriented issues, rather than traditional news topics. This reference is not meant to carry any implications regarding journalistic standards, which vary across different entertainment-oriented news programs.

55. Hamilton (1998) tells a similar story with respect to local TV news coverage of war. He argues that these programs cover wars primarily because the key audience demographic for local TV news prefers stories involving violence, and, of course, wars involve large-scale violence. Whether the source of violence is crime or war is thus, according to Hamilton, of secondary importance to local news broadcasters. Hamilton (2003), in turn, finds that news outlets, including the soft news media, attempt to match their programming content to the preferences of their marginal viewers (those least loyal to a program and hence most willing to turn the channels if they don't like what they see).

56. Gregorish interview.

57. Gregorish interview.

58. Barry Berk, interview with author, Los Angeles, Calif., June 20, 2000.

59. Gregorish interview.

60. Berk interview.

61. Gregorish interview.

62. Gregorish interview.

63. Gregorish interview.

64. Berk interview.

65. For instance, NBC's *Today* show earned its largest rating since the 1989 Loma Prieta earthquake for a broadcast featuring scandal coverage during the first week of the scandal.

66. According to Graber (1997, 106–8), journalists will prefer to cover a story if it:

(1) will likely have a strong impact on the lives of audience members; (2) involves violence, conflict, disaster, or scandal; (3) is familiar; (4) has proximity to the audience; and (5) is timely and novel. Graber adds that conflict, proximity, and timeliness are most important. Each of these conditions clearly affects the extent to which a story can be framed in widely accessible and compelling terms (i.e., cheap framing).

67. The contrast between war coverage on *The Oprah Winfrey Show* and the emphasis of traditional news programming on military tactics and precision bombing campaigns also illustrates the increasing niche orientation of the traditional and soft news media. The former orientation may be intended, in part, to have a greater appeal for the largely female audience that typically watches *The Oprah Winfrey Show*, while the latter type of coverage has traditionally held greater appeal for a male audience.

68. Berk interview.

69. I do, however, present some evidence in the concluding chapter that exposure to soft news outlets can enhance some individuals' knowledge about particular foreign crisis events.

70. Throughout the book, whenever I introduce a new hypothesis, beyond those listed above, I number it based on its location within a given chapter. For instance, the first "new" hypothesis to appear in chapter 4 is numbered $H_{4.1}$.

71. Borrowing from Edelman's (1989) notion of symbolic politics, Neuman (1990, 169) terms the latter two types of issues *symbolic crises*. These are issues that are, in a sense, manufactured by political entrepreneurs, and that are unlikely to be fundamentally resolved in the short run. Nonetheless, they may be redefined by political elites and the media, for a limited period of time, as national crises.

72. Neuman (1990) defines the audience attention cycle in the form of as S-shaped logistic curve. This, however, represents cumulative, rather than marginal, changes. The curves presented in figure 2.A1, in contrast, represent marginal, rather than cumulative, changes. Hence, for my purposes, the logistic curve is inappropriate.

CHAPTER THREE: "I HEARD IT ON *OPRAH*"

1. Some evidence of the increasing dominance of television as a source of news is available from a series of polls conducted during the 1992 and 1996 presidential election campaigns by the *Times Mirror* Center and the Pew Research Center for the People and the Press ("Pew Center"). On six occasions (two in 1996 and four in 1992), respondents were asked from where they got their news about the presidential campaign. Overall, across the six surveys, 84 percent named television as their primary source of campaign news. Additionally, in a May 1997 survey conducted by Roper Starch Worldwide, 69 percent of respondents claimed to get most of their news from television, compared to 37 percent from newspapers, 14 percent from radio, 7 percent from "other people," and 5 percent from magazines. The poll also found that over half of the public (53 percent) considered television the most reliable news source, more than double the next-most-reliable source, newspapers (23 percent). Commenting on the poll's results, Bradford Fay, senior vice president at Roper Starch, noted "In the nearly four decades of this ongoing poll, television's lead as a news source is the second largest ever" (Roper Center Online 1998)

2. The figures add up to more than 100 percent because respondents were allowed to mention multiple sources.

3. These figures represent the percentage of respondents who reported watching a program "sometimes" or "regularly."

4. Gregorish interview.

5. Each item was rated by respondents on a five-point scale, running from not important (1) to extremely important (5). The percentages reported in the text refer to items receiving a score of 3 or better (representing moderately to extremely important).

6. Similar media consumption patterns (for both hard and soft news shows) emerge in Pew Center surveys conducted in 1996 and 2000 (not shown).

7. Nielsen Media Research, "NTI NAD Report," July 2002. All percentages are for adults over age eighteen, and are based on the education level for heads of households. Unfortunately, disaggregated Nielsen ratings (e.g., by education level) are considered proprietary by television broadcasters, and hence are not generally available to the public. Thanks, however, to the generous assistance of Barbara Osborn, at the University of California, San Diego, I was able to obtain the partially disaggregated data reported herein. Osborn provided much of the Nielsen ratings data presented in this section. I obtained additional ratings data through searches of news reports on Lexis-Nexis.

8. Wherever possible in table 3.1, I present relatively long-term averages (i.e., 3–6 months). Where such data were inaccessible, however, I employ the most recent period for which I was able to acquire the appropriate ratings data.

9. As recently as the early 1980s, the three networks' evening news programs, combined, captured about three quarters of America's TV-watching households. By 2002, the corresponding share had fallen to 43 (Pennington 2002; Smith 2001). In 2002, the three network newscasts, combined, attracted an average of about 30 million viewers per evening.

10. To determine airtimes for *ET, Extra,* and *Access Hollywood,* I reviewed the schedules for each show from a random sample of local markets nationwide, as listed on the programs' respective Web sites.

11. During the first quarter of 2002, the top twelve cable news programs, in order, were *Larry King Live* (CNN), *The Fox Report with Shephard Smith* (Fox), *The O'Reilly Factor* (Fox), *Newsnight with Aaron Brown* (CNN), *Hannity and Colmes* (Fox), *Crossfire* (CNN), *The Point* (CNN), *On the Record with Greta Van Susteren* (Fox), *Wolf Blitzer Reports* (CNN), *The News with Brian Williams* (MSNBC), *Hardball with Chris Matthews* (MSBNC), and *Alan Keyes, Making Sense* (MSNBC). Ratings for these programs ranged from 0.2 to 1.0, with a mean of about 0.5. In the fourth quarter of 2002, *The O'Reilly Factor* replaced *Larry King Live* as the top-rated cable news show.

12. For instance, the newspaper with the largest circulation in America is not the *Wall Street Journal,* but the *National Enquirer.*

13. Throughout this section, I frequently indicate that a given program offered "at least" a given number of programs or stories addressing a given issue or event. I do so because these data were derived from incomplete sources, such as program listings in *TV Guide,* which offer only sporadic listings of program topics. Hence, in these instances, the cited figures are in all likelihood incomplete.

14. In addition, the program frequently addresses issues concerning international terrorism, including an entire program devoted to such incidents as the World Trade Center bombing and the bombing of the Oklahoma City Federal Building.

15. *Access Hollywood*'s network debut in September 1996 postdates the other high-profile U.S. foreign crises in the 1990s that I investigate in this chapter (except for Kosovo, which was featured in at least one episode of the program). The program has covered each major U.S. foreign crisis that has emerged since its debut. For instance, as of September 1999, it had covered U.S. crises with Iraq in eight separate broadcasts and

Bosnia, where the U.S. intervention took place almost eight months prior to the program's debut, on three separate occasions.

16. The TV talk show figures represent the sum of between seven and nine programs (depending on the year).

17. ABC's *World News Tonight* presented 215 stories on Somalia between 1992 and 1995, and 241 stories on Haiti during that same period. The corresponding figures for Bosnia and Kosovo were 304 and 197 stories, respectively, between June 1995 and June 1999 (Vanderbilt Television News Archive).

18. The exceptions were late-night TV talk shows (e.g., *The Tonight Show with Jay Leno* and *The Late Show with David Letterman*) and MTV. The former programs, for whom the frequency-of-watching question is not included in the 1996 Pew Center survey, have a long tradition of political humor, which continued in 1996. And in 1996, MTV continued its "Rock the Vote" campaign, intended to bring young voters into the political process. These figures cover the period January through April 1996. I chose the April 1996 cut-off point for two reasons. First, by May the primary season was all but concluded and the nomination wrapped up. Hence, as expected, adding May and June— technically the final primary months—to the figures in table 3.1 changes the overall tallies only marginally. Second, in the next chapter, I investigate the influence of soft news consumption on attentiveness to the 1996 Republican primaries. The survey I employ was concluded in early May. Hence, in order to draw linkages between the content analysis in this chapter and the statistical analysis in the next chapter, it is useful to limit the content analysis to a time period that the survey respondents could potentially reference in their responses. (Keywords employed in this search included: "Bob Dole," "Steve Forbes," "Lamar Alexander," "Phil Gramm," "Pat Buchanan," "Alan Keyes," "primary," "campaign," "candidate," "election," "caucus," "republican." All hits mentioned at least one candidate, plus at least one of the other key words.)

19. The Lewinsky scandal first broke in January 1998. I end my content analysis of the Lewinsky scandal in April in order to facilitate linkages between this analysis and a related statistical analysis in the next chapter, which investigates the influence of soft news exposure on attentiveness to the Lewinsky scandal. The latter analysis employs a Pew Center survey, conducted in early May 1998. As was the case with the 1996 Republican primaries, in order to draw such linkages, it is useful to content analyze a time period that the Pew Center respondents could potentially reference in responding to the survey.

20. Keywords for the latter analysis included "NAFTA," "World Trade Organization," or "WTO," and "Monica Lewinsky." Keywords for the 1998 elections included: "election" or "campaign" and "Congress" or "governor" or "legislature." Keywords for the tobacco debate included: "Congress" and "tobacco" (all hits included both terms).

21. All WTO coverage focused on the rioting at a December 1999 WTO meeting in Seattle. Perhaps due to the absence of serious injuries or fatalities, even the riots failed to attract substantial soft news coverage of the WTO. Not surprisingly, coverage of NAFTA and the WTO was far greater in network newscasts. For instance, the *CBS Evening News* covered NAFTA and the WTO in 67 and 23 separate broadcasts, respectively, and the figures for the other major networks are comparable.

22. By all accounts, soft news coverage of the Lewinsky scandal was even more intense in the summer of 1998, a period not covered by table 3.2.

23. The average hard news report was 591 words in length. Unfortunately, many of

these written transcripts did not include information on the report's duration. It is, however, possible to estimate the duration by calculating the number of words per second in those instances where both word counts and duration information are available, and then applying the words-per-second algorithm to the other reports, for whom only the word counts are available. Seven of the 55 national news reports included information on their duration. Across these seven reports, the average number of words per second was 3.37. Dividing the word count from all 55 reports by this figure yields an estimated average duration of hard news reports of 2:56.

24. Calculating Cohen's Kappa score (R. Cook 1998, Banerjee et al. 1999) indicates that this degree of intercoder agreement is highly unlikely to be attributable to chance.

25. All significance levels reported in this section are based on two-tailed t tests of the null hypothesis that coverage by the soft and hard news media are statistically indistinguishable on whatever dimension is being investigated by a given question.

26. Only fairly unambiguous failures are coded as such. Military operations involving less certain outcomes, like the U.S. bombing of Afghanistan and Sudan in 1998, are not counted as either "failures" or "successes." The index of agreement score on this question (across coders) was approximately 93 percent.

27. The programs I reviewed included: *Extra, Dateline, The Tonight Show with Jay Leno, The Late Show with David Letterman, Late Night with Conan O'Brien, A Current Affair, Live with Regis and Kathie Lee, Entertainment Tonight, Howard Stern, E! News Daily, The E! Gossip Show,* and *The Geraldo Rivera Show.*

28. For the ABC News trend, I searched the following keywords in the Vanderbilt Television News Archives: "World Trade Center," "Bin Laden," "9/11," "September 11," "Anthrax," "Al Qaeda," or any word starting with "terror" or "Afghan."

29. Http://extratv.warnerbros.com/dailynews/index.html.

30. Http://www.insideedition.com/archives.htm.

31. In chapter 5, I discuss various issues surrounding my limited comparison of these conflicts.

32. Nineteen sixty-eight was a leap year, and so there were twenty-nine days in February.

33. I conducted Lexis-Nexis searches using "Vietnam" and "Iraq" as search terms.

34. Another alternative would be to turn to the printed copy of the 1968 *New York Times Index.* The difficulty is that, in all likelihood, on-line searches would yield quite different results from searches based on a printed text. The reason is simply that there are most likely numerous passages on any given topic that will not be cross-referenced in the printed index, because, for instance, the primary theme of the article may not be directly related to the item being searched (at least not in the appropriate context). Hence, comparing an electronic index, which is capable of essentially universal cross-referencing, with a printed index, seems inappropriate.

35. These figures exclude all unscheduled broadcasts, such as live "breaking news," dealing with the two crises, which, during the Persian Gulf War, seemingly monopolized the television day. My estimates must therefore be considered extremely conservative.

36. Interestingly, in 1998, when I contacted the Sally Jesse Raphael show by e-mail, to see if they had covered any foreign crises in the 1990s, I received a reply directly from the host herself (or at least someone claiming to be her), thanking me for my interest, but indicating emphatically that the show simply *does not* cover politics or foreign policy. Apparently, she did not recall having addressed the Gulf War in 1991.

37. These figures are based on "topic lists" provided by Burrelle's Transcripts, in

Livingston, N.J. The keyword for the January–March 1991 topic list was "Gulf War"; that for the August–December 1990 list was "Iraq."

38. Topic Lists on CBS and NBC programming were acquired from Burrelle's Transcripts. LaMay (1991) reports that network television news broadcasts devoted 2,658 minutes of airtime to the Persian Gulf crisis and war between December 1990 and March 1991 (figures cited in Brody 1994).

39. I was able to acquire the film registers only from the first eighteen days of each period. In all likelihood, a review of the entire month would have raised the overall 1991 average somewhat, as the period covered in my review did not extend to the beginning of the ground war on February 24, 1991.

40. WABI News Film Registers were provided by Heather White of the Northeast Historic Film Society.

CHAPTER FOUR: BRINGING WAR TO THE MASSES

1. The previously cited CMPA study (*Media Monitor* 1997a) indicated that the first three items are the primary topics of soft news. Five types of soft news are included in this scale, including entertainment newsmagazines, network newsmagazines, daytime television talk shows, MTV, and tabloid newspapers.

2. Lisa Gregorish, interview with author, Los Angeles, Calif., June 20, 2000.

3. Barry Berk, interview with author, Los Angeles, Calif., June 20, 2000.

4. I include domestic terrorism because it has long, even before 9/11, been closely linked in the minds of most Americans to international terrorism.

5. In part in order to enhance scale reliability, I include print media and radio sources in each index. As previously discussed, these media have, in many respects, undergone similar changes as television. The results are not materially affected when the nontelevision media variables are excluded.

6. The two exceptions in the hard news index are daily newspapers and radio news, which are dichotomous variables, coded 1 if the respondent reads newspapers or listens to news on the radio, and 0 otherwise. In each case, several variables are included that measure respondents' self-declared frequency of following a particular type of news, such as news about entertainment. While these do not, strictly speaking, measure exposure, they are closely related. Moreover, including these variables improves the alpha reliability scores of the indexes, while excluding them does not significantly weaken the results.

7. It is nonetheless worth noting here that, somewhat surprisingly, several of the political interest and participation variables are insignificant in some or all of the models reported in table 4.2. In most cases, this is at least in part attributable to multicollinearity among the control variables. For example, approval of President Clinton and party identification are correlated at .43. Nonetheless, for three reasons, this is not a major concern for my analyses. First, multicollinearity *weakens*, rather than strengthens, coefficients on collinear variables. Second, all of the suspect variables are included in my models only as controls, and, hence, their substantive interpretations are not important for testing my hypotheses. Third, and most important, additional testing revealed that including or excluding these controls does not materially affect the coefficients or significance levels for the key causal variables.

8. While these interaction terms approach or achieve statistical significance, is important to bear in mind that an interaction term need not be statistically significant itself for

statistically significant interactive effects to arise. It is frequently the case that a statistically insignificant interaction term is nonetheless associated with highly significant effects in at least some regions of the two variables included in the interaction. This is the case in many of the models I present throughout the book.

9. King, Tomz, and Wittenberg (2000) (see also Tomz, Wittenberg, and King 1998) developed a technique—based on conducting repeated simulations of a given model to derive predicted values for each β—for producing confidence intervals surrounding probabilities derived from transformed logit coefficients. By reviewing the confidence intervals, it is possible to determine whether the predicted probabilities are statistically distinguishable from one another. I employ this technique repeatedly throughout the book. The procedure developed by King and his colleagues, however, does not allow probability weighting ("pweight" in Stata). This is arguably an important element in analyzing public opinion surveys, particularly those that unlike, say, the NES surveys, do not attempt to ensure that the respondents are representative of the national population. Hence, wherever probability weighting appears appropriate (as in the current models), I instead translate coefficients into probabilities using the standard logit equation ("exp(z)/ [1 + exp(z)]" in Stata). Unfortunately, unlike the King, Tomz, and Wittenberg methodology, this procedure does not produce confidence intervals surrounding the predicted probabilities.

10. Among the highest soft news consumers, those *most* interested in international affairs are modestly *less* likely to have followed the terrorism debate than their less intrinsically interested counterparts. This suggests that for politically engaged individuals, soft news represents something of a distraction. These differences, however, are extremely small and thus are most likely substantively meaningless.

11. Variations in soft news consumption produce somewhat weaker, though not insubstantial, effects on the probabilities of following the three issues "not too closely" or "very closely" (not shown). Overall, the magnitude of the effects of increased soft news consumption decline as respondents' self-reported interest in news about international affairs increases.

12. One potential problem with my approach concerns the possibility of reverse causality between interest in international affairs and interest in the three foreign crisis issues. It is possible that respondents interested in these issues report systematically greater interest in international affairs *because* of their interest in those issues. (Indeed, the "interest in news about international affairs" question was asked *after* the foreign crisis questions, thereby perhaps increasing the possibility that the former may have influenced responses to the latter.) To investigate this, I constructed a system of two equations (not shown) simultaneously estimating the influence of attentiveness to a foreign crisis on interest in news about international affairs and the influence of the latter on the former. I then estimated the system, employing three-stage least squares ("reg3" in Stata). I repeated this process for each of the three crisis attention variables. In each case, the results—which were robust across numerous specifications of the exogenous variables—indicated that interest in international affairs increased the likelihood of being attentive to foreign crises, while being attentive had no effect on interest in international affairs. Such results are, of course, only as good as the instruments created for the endogenous variables. In this case, the R^2 values for the various models suggest that the instruments for interest in international affairs (.40 for Bosnia, .29 for Lebanon, and .38 for terrorism) were superior to those for attentiveness to the three crisis issues (.23, .26, and .20, respectively). Hence, these results must be interpreted with caution. (Results of these tests are available from the author.)

13. The relationships in figure 4.1 are strongest for the antiterrorism debate (which is unambiguously linked by the public to the issue of international terrorism). This is most likely due, in large measure, to the national trauma produced by attacks on the World Trade Center and the Oklahoma City bombing. Millions of Americans perceived themselves as holding a personal stake in the terrorism debate—indeed, the United States suffered significant casualties from the aforementioned terrorist attacks, while the other two crises produced nearly zero U.S. casualties—and so it was a more immediate concern (and thus more accessible) than Bosnia or the Israel-Lebanon conflict.

14. Primary elections involving major scandals or celebrities may not follow this general pattern. Examples here include Gary Hart's affair with Donna Rice, which derailed his campaign in 1988; Bill Clinton's various scandals during the 1992 primary (e.g., Gennifer Flowers and marijuana use.); and the involvement of Warren Beatty and Donald Trump in the 2000 primaries (Bauder 1999). Each of these candidates attracted some soft news coverage, due either to their personal foibles or their personal notoriety.

15. All variables except newspaper reading (see appendix 2) are coded identically to the 1996 Pew survey.

16. The probabilities are "approximate" because several missing values on the high end of soft news consumption were interpolated to produce the extreme boundary probabilities.

17. Unfortunately, due to the inclusion of probability weighting, in this instance I was unable to employ the King, Tomz, and Wittenberg (2000) technique to estimate the statistical significance of the interactive effects of soft news consumption and political engagement.

18. For this analysis, I drop the elements of the original hard and soft news indexes that measure respondents' *interest* in various types of news (e.g., news about politics, business, entertainment, celebrities, etc.), as distinct from their self-declared *exposure* to various news outlets. Since the former are almost certainly *causes* of the latter (indeed, that is why they were included in the original indexes), they are more appropriately employed as exogenous causal variables in this analysis, intended to identify the correlates of consuming soft and hard news.

19. The two equations that make up the system are as follows: (1) Hard news consumption $= \alpha + \beta_1$ (Soft news consumption) $+ \beta_2$ (Interest in business news) $+ \beta_3$ (Interest in political news) $+ \beta_4$ (Interest in science news) $+ \beta_5$ (Interest in international news) $+ \beta_6$ (Age) $+ \beta_7$ (Education) $+ \beta_8$ (Family income) $+ \beta_9$ (Gender) $+ \beta_{10}$ (White) $+ \beta_{11}$ (Voted in 1992) $+ \beta_{12}$ (Partisanship) $+ \beta_{13}$ (Approve of president) $+ \beta_{14}$ (Party identification) $+ \beta_{15}$ (Married) $+ \beta_{15}$ (Political knowledge) $+ \varepsilon_i$; and (2) Soft news consumption $= \theta + \phi_1$ (Hard news consumption) $+ \phi_2$ (Interest in entertainment news) $+ \phi_3$ (Interest in celebrity news) $+ \phi_4$ (Interest in crime news) $+ \phi_5$ (Age) $+ \phi_6$ (Education) $+ \phi_7$ (Family income) $+ \phi_8$ (Gender) $+ \phi_9$ (White) $+ \phi_{10}$ (Voted in 1992) $+ \phi_1{}^t$ (Partisanship) $+ \phi_{12}$ (Approve of president) $+ \phi_{13}$ (Party identification) $+ \phi_{14}$ (Married) $+ \phi_{16}$ (Political knowledge) $+ \varepsilon_j$.

In a 3SLS model, each endogenous variable is "caused" by either causally prior endogenous variables or by exogenous variables, and the errors are assumed to be independent across equations. This type of model is appropriate when all equations in a model are just- or overidentified. To meet this requirement, each equation must satisfy the Order Condition, which entails excluding at least $G - 1$ variables, where G equals the total number of equations in the system. In this two-equation system, each equation must therefore exclude at least one variable. While the two models share a number of common exogenous variables, they each exclude a minimum of three variables. Hence, the system satisfies the Order Condition and is overidentified.

20. It is important to point out that system identification is purely theoretical, as I have chosen to include and exclude exogenous variables on the basis of theory. For instance, I have excluded interest in international affairs news from the soft news consumption model because I previously found that people do not watch soft news with the intention of learning about world affairs. If, however, the theory is flawed, then the system may in fact be underidentified. If so, the standard errors may be biased. In this case, however, this seems relatively unlikely, as the results are highly robust to variations in the exogenous variables included in each equation.

21. The utility of this test also depends on the quality of the instruments for hard and soft news produced as part of the 3SLS process. The R^2 values for the two models of .37 and .28, for the hard and soft news models, respectively, suggest that the instruments, though not ideal, are nonetheless reasonably valid.

22. The wording and coding for all questions from the 2000 Pew Center survey, including the components of the soft and hard news indexes, are identical to the 1996 Pew Center survey (see appendix 2). In this instance, the soft news index includes the following seven items: network TV newsmagazines, TV talk shows like *Jerry Springer*, TV talk shows like *The Oprah Winfrey Show*, Court TV, *People Magazine*, entertainment/tabloid TV newsmagazine shows (like *Entertainment Tonight* and *Inside Edition*), and tabloid newspapers (like the *National Enquirer*). The hard news index, in turn, includes the following twelve items: national network TV news, *The News Hour with Jim Lehrer*, CNN, C-SPAN, Fox News Network, CNBC, MSNBC, weekly newsmagazines, weekly business magazines, National Public Radio, magazines such as *Atlantic* and *Harper's*, and whether or not the respondent regularly reads a daily newspaper (dummy variable). The alpha reliability scores for the soft and hard news indexes are .70 and .73, respectively. The only differences among the controls in the 1996 and 2000 hard news models are the addition in the 2000 model of variables measuring whether or not respondents follow national or international news regularly or only when major events arise and how closely the respondents follow local news. Two controls from the 1996 3SLS models—presidential approval and political knowledge—were unavailable in this survey. Finally, for the soft news model, the 2000 survey, unlike the 1996 survey, did not include a question measuring the extent to which respondents follow news about celebrities.

23. For the 1990 survey, the alpha reliability scores for the hard and soft news indexes are .62 and .58, respectively. The corresponding alpha reliability scores for the 1993 survey are .44 and .58, respectively. For the 1993 survey, the low alpha score for the hard news index is attributable to the availability of only two hard news items in the survey: national network TV news and local TV news.

24. The question asks respondents to name the most important issue of the past month. I recoded the responses into a dummy variable, coded 1 if he or she mentions the Panama invasion and 0 otherwise.

25. In the Panama survey, probability weighting had only a modest effect on the key coefficients and standard errors. Hence, I employed the King, Tomz, and Wittenberg (2000) procedure, absent probability weighting, to compute predicted significance levels for the Panama results. The predicted probabilities are virtually identical to those derived from the standard logit transformation ("exp(z) / [1 + exp(z)]" in Stata), based on a logit model with probability weighting included. (The only appreciable difference is a slightly smaller coefficient on the soft news index when the weight is dropped, which

works *against* my hypotheses.) Nonetheless, because there were minor differences, the curves shown in the top graphic in figure 4.3 are based on probabilities derived from the standard logit transformation. Unfortunately, the King, Tomz, and Wittenberg (2000) methodology did not produce comparable results for the Bosnia model. Hence, in the latter case, I am unable to report reliable significance levels for the differences in the effects of soft news on respondents at different levels of education. Because, however, the coefficient on the soft news index is statistically significant, we can be confident that the differences in attentiveness to Bosnia associated with changes in soft news consumption are *at minimum* statistically significant among the *least*-educated respondents.

26. This placed the Gulf War in the top 1 percent of all news stories since 1986. By June 2002, however, due to the events of 9/11 and its aftermath, the Panama invasion fell to 24th on this list, while Gulf War fell to 11th place.

27. This latter indicator places the Gulf War in a five-way tie for sixth place on the list, along with the Rodney King Case (May 1992), Midwestern floods (August 1993), the high school shooting in Littleton, Colorado (April 1999), and the Crash of TWA Flight 800 (July 1996). The Panama invasion places 11th on the revised list, while the Bosnia intervention places 60th (based on the percentage of respondents who report following the issues "very" or "fairly" closely).

28. I focus on the first fifteen days of each conflict because Operation Just Cause was effectively over following the surrender of General Noriega on January 3, 1990. Hence, the first two weeks of each conflict, when active hostilities were underway in both cases, is the most appropriate time frame for comparison.

29. The alpha reliability scores for the hard and soft news indexes are .60 and .59, respectively.

30. Once again, each element in the hard news and soft news indexes consists of a four-point scale, with four representing the maximum frequency of receiving news from a given source.

31. The coefficients reported in table 4.A2 (at appendix 3) are based upon logit models with a probability weight included ("pweight" in Stata). While, as previously noted, the King, Tomz, and Wittenberg (2000) methodology does not allow probability weighting, in this instance, I was again able to produce virtually identical results to those reported in table 4.A2 by employing the "svyset" command in Stata, and then rerunning the logit models *without* the probability weight. This suggests that the Gallup survey was *not* heavily biased by the nature of the sample. Hence, I employed this latter model to compute predicted probabilities and confidence intervals.

32. Significance levels were calculated using the King, Tomz, and Wittenberg (2000) procedure. As in the previous analyses, when probability weighting is excluded, the coefficients on the key causal variables decline somewhat in magnitude and significance. Hence, the confidence intervals produced by this procedure understate the actual significance levels of the key variables, as shown in table 4.A4, which include probability weighting.

33. Indeed, the more specific the answer (e.g., mentioning a particular issue as opposed to a "class" of issues), the greater the extent to which the response most likely also reflects salience, or personal importance, as opposed to mere attentiveness.

34. Each element in the hard news and soft news indexes once again consists of a four-point scale, with four representing the maximum frequency receiving news from a given source. The alpha reliability scores for the hard and soft news indexes are .72 and .59, respectively.

35. As in the previous analysis, the coefficients reported in table 4.A4 are based upon logit models with a probability weight included. As before, I was able to produce nearly identical results to those reported in table 4.A4 by employing the "svyset" command in Stata, and then rerunning the logit models *without* the probability weight. Hence, I employed this latter model to compute predicted probabilities and confidence intervals. These probabilities are, as before, nearly identical to those derived from the standard logit transformation, based on a logit model with probability weighting included. In fact, the coefficient on soft news consumption is modestly weaker when probability weighting is removed. Hence, these predicted probabilities once again modestly understate the true magnitude of the effects of soft news consumption.

36. For this survey, I was able to construct a crude index of respondents' awareness of major political figures from a series of questions asking respondents to evaluate various high-profile public- and private-sector individuals (see appendix 2). The resulting scale, however, performed relatively poorly in a variety of tests and model specifications. Hence, I elected to employ it only as a control variable.

37. Significance levels were calculated using the King, Tomz, and Wittenberg (2000) procedure. Once again, when probability weighting is excluded, the coefficients on the key causal variables decline somewhat in magnitude and significance. Hence, the confidence intervals produced by this procedure understate the actual significance levels of the key variables, as shown in table 4.A4, which include probability weighting.

38. Interestingly, many of the control variables perform better in these latter models, suggesting that foreign aid is most likely qualitatively different from the other foreign affairs issues mentioned by respondents. This reinforces my decision to emphasize a form of the dependent variable in which foreign aid is treated as a non-foreign-affairs issue.

39. The respective questions are as follows: (1) "Now, a few questions about the allegation that President Clinton lied under oath about a sexual relationship with Monica Lewinsky. Thinking specifically about this allegation, how important an issue do you think this whole situation is to the nation—of great importance, of some importance, or of very little importance?" Coding: 1 = None, 2 = Very little importance, 3 = Some importance, 4 = Great importance; and (2) "Do you think President Clinton ordered the attack on sites in Afghanistan and Sudan mainly to fight terrorism or mainly because he wanted to turn public attention away from the Monica Lewinsky affair?" Coding: 0 = fight terrorism, 1 = turn attention away from affair. (Answers of "don't know" and "refused" were recoded as missing data.).

40. I code "don't know/refused" responses as missing. The results are similar, though somewhat weaker, when the fully specified four-category dependent variable is employed. In this instance, I prefer a dichotomous specification for purely instrumental reasons: the overall explained variance in the model increases by 227 percent when the dependent variable is dichotomized.

41. It is also possible that respondents tuned in to the Lewinsky scandal as a result of their exposure to information about the missile strikes, rather than the other way around. This possibility, however, seems fairly improbable on its face, except perhaps for a tiny minority of individuals. After all, by August 20, 1998, the Lewinsky scandal had been dominating the national headlines—including the soft news media—for over seven months.

42. I replicated the results reported in this section using a second poll (a Minnesota state telephone survey, conducted by the Market Solutions Group between August 19 and

21, 1998). The results from this second analysis, available from the author upon request, largely mirror those reported here.

43. This, of course, assumes that the survey questions being investigated are similar in both form and substance.

44. Similarly, Zaller (1991) found a strong relationship between "no opinion" and "don't know" responses and political awareness (measured by several scales that he constructed) during the Vietnam War. As individuals moved up the scale toward greater political awareness, their propensity to respond "don't know" declined monotonically.

45. In 1996, feeling-thermometer questions were asked for the following individuals: Bill Clinton, Bob Dole, Elizabeth Dole, Ross Perot, Al Gore, Pat Choate, James Campbell, the Democratic candidate for House of Representatives in the respondent's district, the Republican House candidate, Hillary Clinton, Pat Buchanan, Jesse Jackson, Newt Gingrich, Colin Powell, Steve Forbes, Phil Gramm, Louis Farrakahn, Lamar Alexandar, and Pat Robertson. Due to the absence of "don't know" responses, Bill Clinton is excluded from this calculation (his exclusion has no effect on the results).

46. In 1998, feeling-thermometer questions were asked for the following individuals: Bill Clinton, Hillary Clinton, Elizabeth Dole, Al Gore, the Democratic candidate for House of Representatives in the respondent's district, the Republican House candidate, the Democratic Senate candidate, the Republican Senate candidate, Pat Buchanan, Newt Gingrich, Steve Forbes, George Bush Jr., Dan Quayle, Ken Starr, Dick Gephardt, Paul Wellstone, John McCain, Bill Bradley, Bob Kerrey, John Kerry, Gary Bauer, and John Ashcroft. Due to the near or total absence of "don't know" responses, Bill and Hillary Clinton are excluded from these calculations (their exclusion has only a marginal effect on the results).

47. The 1966 NES Survey included the identical question, but it was asked only of respondents who claimed to be paying attention to the Vietnam War. Hence, it is inappropriate for this analysis.

48. One implication of the theory, developed in chapter 2, is that we should expect to find a weakened relationship, over time, between the causal variables in tables 4.A7 and "don't know" rates. Yet the coefficients are, in many instances, largest during the Gulf War. This is deceiving, however, as logit coefficients are not interpreted in a linear fashion, like OLS coefficients. In fact, consistent with the theory, when the coefficients are translated into probabilities, the variation in probability of responding "don't know" during the Gulf War is far smaller across levels of political information, mentions of foreign policy problems, education, and interest in the political campaigns than during the prior wars. I explore these data in greater detail in chapter 5.

49. The "most important problems" question was not included in the 1952 NES study.

50. Responses to the former question were coded as follows: 1 = Very closely, 2 = Somewhat closely, 3 = Not too closely, 4 = Not at all closely, and 5 = don't know/refused. The latter question was worded as follows: "Do you think there will or will not come a time when Israel and the Arab nations will be able to settle their differences and live in peace?" 1 = Yes, 2 = No, 3 = Don't know/refused.

51. The factor loadings are as follows: .39 (for the first opinionation question), .40 (for education), .57 (for the second opinionation question), and .61 (for extent of following the Middle East situation).

52. The precise question wording for the three questions is as follows: (1) "Do you think the agreements will lead to a real peace settlement in the Middle East, or do you think a peace settlement is no more likely now than it was before the summit?" 1 =

Real peace, 2 = No more likely, 3 = Depends, 4 = Don't know/No answer; (2) "Who do you think is most responsible for those agreements—President Carter, President Sadat of Egypt, or Prime Minister Begin of Israel?" 1 = Carter, 2 = Sadat, 3 = Begin, 4 = Sadat and Begin, not Carter, 5 = Other two or all three, 9 = Don't know/ No answer; and (3) "Did Jimmy Carter accomplish more than you expected him to at the summit, less than you expected, or did he accomplish just about what you expected?" 1 = More, 2 = Less, 3 = About what expected, 4 = Don't know/No answer.

53. The factor loadings are as follows: .52 (for the first opinionation question), .46 (for the second opinionation question), .49 (for the third opinionation question), and .40 (for education).

54. For instance, in one survey (Pew Research Center 1998), the most highly educated respondents were about 54 percent and 50 percent more likely than the least-educated respondents, respectively, to follow international and national news on a regular basis.

55. Due to multicollinearity across the several indicators of political interest and knowledge, I tested these latter variables separately from those included in the upper half of table 4.A7.

56. Except where otherwise indicated, responses of "don't know," "no answer," or "refused" are coded as missing.

CHAPTER FIVE: TUNING OUT THE WORLD ISN'T AS EASY AS IT USED TO BE

1. This is known as the problem of ecological inference (King 1997).

2. As we shall see, however, in relatively rare instances, exceptional drama sometimes outweighs the aversion of the soft news media to covering potentially divisive, partisan political issues.

3. I am mindful of the striking difference in survey responses that sometimes results from relatively minor variations in question wording. Because such variations are unavoidable in the present study, wherever possible I attempt to replicate my findings across multiple dependent variables and survey contexts.

4. Few poll questions were repeated during all three major post–World War II conflicts. The two that I was able to identify, which were asked on multiple occasions by the Gallup organization and the NES, are shown in appendix 1 to this chapter, questions 1 and 2B.

5. The Vietnam figures are drawn from a single Gallup poll, while the Persian Gulf data are based on nine CBS/*New York Times* surveys, plus two Gallup polls. The Gallup polls are from February 15, 1968, December 16, 1990, and January 19, 1991. The CBS/*New York Times* surveys are from January and February 1991. Additionally, because the CBS/*New York Times* polls grouped "don't know" and "no answer/not applicable" into a single category, the results for January and February 1991 almost certainly *overstate* the true percentage of "don't know" responses.

6. Recall that I treat personal importance as essentially analogous to salience. Here, I employ it as an indicator of the propensity to pay attention. I subsequently replicate this analysis using a second indicator of attentiveness, based on opinionation regarding the several wars.

7. Self-declared personal importance of the Vietnam and Persian Gulf wars correlates moderately well with education, interest in public affairs, and interest in political campaigns at .10, .22, and .19, respectively.

8. The 1991 NES Gulf War Pilot Study is a special extension of the 1990 survey devoted to public reactions to the Persian Gulf War.

9. It is possible that some, or all, of the convergence at higher levels of personal importance may be due to a ceiling effect (Wright 1993), as the probability that a respondent will pay close attention to the Gulf War approaches 100 percent. I consider this possibility in appendix 2 to this chapter and conclude that these relationships are not an artifact of a ceiling effect.

10. This figure is based on the question employed in figure 2.1.

11. These figures are based on a nearly identical question to that presented in figure 2.1.

12. The identical question was also asked in 1966. As noted in chapter 4, however, in that year the question was asked only of respondents who claimed to have been paying attention to Vietnam. Hence, it is inappropriate for this analysis.

13. While personal importance arguably represents a superior indicator of one's propensity to seek out information about a war, it is available in only two NES surveys (1970 and 1991) Hence, I employ political information, which is available in all pertinent NES surveys, as, in effect, a second-best indicator.

14. Zaller (1992, 338) thoroughly evaluates the issues associated with using this subjective rating. He found that the interviewer's assessment performed as well as most scales constructed from ten to fifteen direct-knowledge questions. He also (Zaller 1985) looked for, but failed to find, any evidence of a systematic bias in favor of higher-status individuals, such a white males. The interviewer's assessment was unavailable in 1952. I therefore constructed a scale from twelve direct factual knowledge questions (see appendix 1).

15. Other SES variables, such as race and employment status, proved insignificant and are thus excluded. Multicollinearity suppresses the significance levels on several of the independent variables. This, however, is of limited concern, since these are included primarily as controls, and muticollinearity tends to weaken, rather than strengthen, the coefficients on collinear variables. Several other variables tested as controls are excluded here (e.g., interest in public affairs and attention to political campaigns), either because they were highly insignificant in all models or because they were not available in all NES surveys included in this analysis (or both).

16. The difference between Korea and Vietnam may be somewhat understated due to a subtle yet significant change in question wording, beginning in 1964, which Kinder (1983) describes as a shift "from a gentle to a somewhat more insistent invitation to admit to no opinion at all."

17. Though the rate of decline in "don't know" rates drops off as respondents move up the political information ladder, the negative slopes in the three curves persist even at the higher information levels. This is most likely because even highly politically informed individuals are influenced by changes in media coverage of war, albeit to a lesser extent than their less-informed counterparts. After all, even highly informed individuals today may encounter more news about a given water-cooler event in the course of watching traditional news programs than would have been the case in prior decades.

18. As before, it is possible that some of the convergence in figure 5.2 at the highest information levels may be due to a floor effect (Wright 1993), as the probability of responding "don't know" approaches zero. I consider this possibility in appendix 2 and present evidence that these relationships are not an artifact of a floor effect.

19. The question concerns whether the United States did the right thing, or made a mistake, in becoming involved in each conflict.

20. The Korea and Vietnam means are derived from multiple AIPO surveys, while the Gulf War average is drawn from two polls conducted by CBS News on January 17, and February 12, 1991.

21. For the latter NES correlation test, I focus on *early evening* local newscasts, which appear in closer proximity to network national newscasts. As one might expect, *late evening* local newscasts correlated somewhat less strongly with national news watching, at .35.

22. About 10 percent of respondents reported watching *no* TV news in the prior week.

23. Unfortunately, the latter questions were not asked by survey organizations with respect to the 1960s foreign crises included in table 5.1.

24. The Gulf Crisis "awareness" question is as follows: "Generally speaking, do you approve or disapprove of the decision to send American military troops to the Persian Gulf or not—or haven't you heard enough about that yet to say?" The percentages shown in the figure represent those offering a response *other* than "haven't heard enough about that to say." It is possible that this framing of the question could induce higher response rates than the standard "Have you heard or read about . . ." question employed for the other foreign crises, including Vietnam. Yet, it is worth noting that the percentages are strikingly similar across the two wars for respondents at the two highest education levels. Moreover, the responses mirror most other polls that queried respondents' attentiveness to, and interest in, the Gulf crisis/war.

25. For the Gulf crisis, the question asked respondents how closely they were "following the situation in the Gulf." Responses of "not at all closely" were coded 0, and all other responses representing *more* than "not at all closely" were coded 1. The Vietnam polls, in turn, asked respondents whether or not they had "given any attention to developments in South Vietnam." Responses were coded as follows: 0 = no and 1 = yes or very little.

26. I emphasize the "high school diploma or less" category in these comparisons because the percentage of Americans in this group has declined less, over time, than that for the lowest education group, representing only those *lacking* a high school diploma.

27. The precise question wording was: "Do you take a great deal of interest, some interest, or practically none at all in news about the Berlin question?" Responses were recoded 0 = none and 1 = some or a great deal (NORC Foreign Affairs survey, October 1948).

28. Following Oneal, Lian, and Joyner (1996), I code all uses of force-measuring levels 1–3 on Blechman and Kaplan's (1978) scale as "major uses of force." Of these, I exclude several events that appeared inconsistent with the aforementioned definitions, either because they represented long-scheduled military exercises (e.g., "Team Spirit" in Korea in March 1990), or a cancellation of a previously scheduled withdrawal of forces, rather than a proactive and unscheduled force deployment (e.g., November 1991 in Korea), or because they clearly did not constitute major uses of force during a U.S. foreign policy crisis (e.g., U.S. support for withdrawal of UN forces from Somalia in January–March 1995, which took place long after the United States withdrew its forces from that nation). Recoding some or all of the excluded events as major uses of force, however, had only a marginal effect on the reported results.

29. I identified "uses of force" through searches of a variety of Internet-based timelines of U.S. foreign policy. All such instances were then confirmed through newspaper reports accessed via Lexis-Nexis.

30. I allowed a lag of no more than one month between the onset of a crisis and the

next Gallup poll. If the first Gallup poll following the onset of a crisis was conducted more than a month following the event's onset, that event was excluded.

31. The actual number of observations in the several models varies from 823 to 825, depending on availability of several variables included in the various models. All data prior to the George H. W. Bush Administration is from Edwards 1990. Data from the first Bush administration was provided to the author (in electronic form) by George Edwards, for which I am extremely grateful. Finally, data from the Clinton administration was assembled by the author through searches of Gallup polls in Lexis-Nexis.

32. To test this, I compared changes in "no opinion" rates across a series of randomly selected Militarized Interstate Disputes (Jones, Bremer, and Singer 1996) in which the United States was *not* involved with those in which the United States *was* involved. The results indicated that the average change in "no opinion" rates following initiation of a MID was well over 200 percent larger if the United States was involved. In additional tests, I investigated several surveys conducted in the immediate aftermath of the August 20, 1998, U.S. cruise missile strikes against suspected terrorist sites in Afghanistan and Sudan (*Star Tribune*, Minnesota Poll #98008B, "Clinton, Lewinsky, Scandal/Morality," August 19–21, 1998, and Pew Research Center, "News Interest Index," August 1998). In these surveys respondents' propensity to answer "don't know" when asked whether they approved of President Clinton's job performance was highly significantly related ($p <$ .001) to their propensity to indicate that they followed the missile strikes and to offer an opinion (as opposed to responding "don't know") when asked if they approved of the strikes.

33. Interestingly, it seems that in the days before the twenty-four-hour news cycle, the typical rally-round-the-flag effect—defined as an increase in presidential approval following a use of force or other sudden, dramatic political event (Mueller 1970, 1973)—was somewhat longer in duration than in the post-1980 period. According to data provided by Hugick and Gallup (1991), the average duration of rallies remained relatively constant prior to the 1980s. Broken down approximately by decade, the average rally-effect duration for Presidents Roosevelt, Truman, and Eisenhower was 11.3 weeks, compared to 11.5 weeks for Presidents Kennedy and Johnson and 10.5 weeks for Presidents Nixon, Ford, and Carter. This contrasts sharply with the average duration of 4.6 weeks for Presidents Reagan and G.H.W. Bush. According to data compiled by the author, the average duration of rallies during the Clinton administration was even shorter, about 1.4 weeks. This phenomenon may be attributable, at least in part, to increased media and public scrutiny when foreign crises arise.

34. I employ a logarithmic transformation to smooth the approval series, the values of which are bounded between zero and one and include occasional extreme outliers. Nevertheless, the results are robust when the dependent variable is employed either as an untransformed first difference or in level form.

35. I reran the fully specified models with an additional control variable measuring the annual number of immigrants to the United States. This variable was intended to account for the possibility that increased opinionation surrounding U.S. uses of force abroad might be attributable to increases in the foreign-born population of the United States (Iyengar 1990). It proved insignificant and had no material effect on the key coefficients. Hence, it is omitted from the reported results. I also retested the models with an additional variable included to account for the number of uses of military force per year by the United States. Since this variable also proved insignificant across all model specifications, it too was dropped from the reported results.

36. Lagrange Multiplier tests did not detect the presence of serial autocorrelation in any of the models.

37. The secular trend is most likely due in part to the dramatic increase in presidential public communication over the past four decades, which Kernell (1997) refers to as the leadership strategy of "going public."

38. While this substantive effect may appear modest, when one considers that there were approximately 270 million people living in the United States in 1998, this difference represents almost 26 million more Americans willing to offer an opinion in 1998 than in 1953. Of the 270 million U.S. residents in 1998, approximately 200 million were over age 18 (http://www.census.gov/population/www/estimates/popest.html). This compares to approximately 150 million total U.S. residents in 1953, which would translate, in 1953 figures, to about 14.3 million more individuals with opinions in 1998, relative to 1953.

39. Interestingly, disapproval ratings (not shown) are far more strongly inversely related to "no opinion" rates than are approval ratings. This suggests that if they do form an opinion in the future, individuals currently responding "no opinion" are more likely to move into the disapproval category. This could help explain why presidents might be concerned with "no opinion" rates. An attentive public appears to represent a more potentially disapproving public. (Note that excluding the approval variable from the right-hand side does not materially affect the key relationships.)

40. By collapsing the two lower-education categories into one, it is possible to test whether the relationships presented below are significantly influenced by this category change. In fact, when the categories are collapsed and the models retested (not shown), the results remain comparable to those reported below (though, as would be expected, modestly weakened for the lower groups). This suggests that these results are not an artifact of any arbitrary categorization of respondents.

41. These figures represent the percentage difference between the *actual* 1953–54 and 1997–98 post-use-of-force "no opinion" rates.

42. Because the Oslo Agreement was completed on September 13, 1993, while Camp David was announced on the eighteenth, I began my survey of network news coverage of Oslo five days earlier than for Camp David. The Dayton Accord was reached on November 21, 1995. I thus shifted my investigation of network news coverage of Dayton by three days, relative to Camp David. Overall, I investigated one month's worth of coverage for each event.

43. The Vanderbilt Television News Archive's coverage of *weekend* news broadcasts during each period is incomplete, and thus the actual numbers may differ slightly from those reported.

44. Some limited additional evidence that the public has become increasingly opinionated concerning U.S. uses of force is provided by Kohut and Toth (1995, 138–39), who present the results of a series of public opinion polls conducted in the early stages of a series of major U.S. military conflicts from 1950 to 1992, including Korea, Vietnam, Grenada, Panama, Iraq, and Somalia. While the pattern in the percentages shown below is not perfectly consistent, the overtime downward trend in "don't know" responses in these "early" crisis surveys, which were intended to gauge American's initial reactions to the various conflicts, is unmistakable:

Korea	Vietnam			Grenada	Panama	Iraq		Somalia
(8/50)	(1/65)	(5/65)	(11/65)	(11/83)	(1/90)	(8/90)	(1/91)	(12/92)
15%	22%	22%	15%	8%	10%	8%	8%	5%

45. In pre-1968 NES surveys, the question asked respondents to name "the most im-

portant issue that the government in Washington should respond to." After 1968, the question was always: "What is the most important problem facing the nation?"

46. The sole exception is 1962. Additionally, in 1970 and 1996, four responses were coded. In order to maintain consistency, I recorded only the first three possible responses in constructing my indexes for 1970 and 1996.

47. The exception is the 1970s, when the average number of major problems mentioned declined for respondents at four of the five levels of political information. Even in this instance, however, the least politically informed respondents mentioned more problems than did their counterparts in the 1960s.

48. One potential concern with this dependent variable is the possibility that mentioning more "major problems" merely reflects well-documented trends toward increasing cynicism about politics among the American public (Nye, Zelikow, and King 1997; Dionne 1991; Rosenstone and Hansen 1993; Miller 1974). If so, this scale should correlate reasonably well with other indicators of cynicism, such as trust in government or internal and external political efficacy. In fact, the major-problems scale correlates at less than .10 with all of these alternative indicators. Moreover, a factor analysis revealed that these other three indicators of political disaffection and the major-problems scale load on a common underlying factor at only about .10. This strongly suggests that these several indicators are not capturing a single underlying factor. Hence, we can be reasonably confident that the major-problems scale is not merely a proxy for political cynicism. Nevertheless, I include a series of alternative indicators of cynicism and efficacy as controls in the models reported below.

49. In all of my time-series analyses of NES data that employ network audience ratings, in order to avoid dropping all 1998 observations, I apply the 1997 network rating to the 1998 NES survey.

50. In interpreting the coefficients, the King, Tomz, and Wittenberg (2000) simulation procedure makes it possible to extend the analysis to years not explicitly covered by the data. In order to avoid straying too far from the actual data, however, I have chosen to extrapolate simulated probabilities only for 1966 and 1998, thereby extending my analysis by two elections, or four years. The former observation is included because the networks received their lowest election-year audience rating of the decade, by a small amount, in 1966, and the latter year is included because the networks earned their lowest audience rating to date in 1998. (Recall that the "real" data included in this analysis extends from 1968 to 1996. Nevertheless, the differences in the reported results produced by this extrapolation proved to be modest.)

51. Network ratings were slightly higher than 56.9 in several years during the 1960s and 1970s. I employ 56.9, however, because it was the highest network rating during the earliest decade in my data set (the 1960s), and in the same year, data was available for the other variables in the models. (Employing the absolute highest audience rating from the 1960–98 period produces nearly identical results to those based on the 56.9 rating of 1966.)

52. Variations in the probability of mentioning one major problem, as network audience ratings and political information vary, follow an inverse pattern, while the probabilities of mentioning zero or two major problems vary far more modestly (not shown).

53. Data for several independent variables, including network ratings, were unavailable for 2000. Hence, the 2000 NES is excluded from this analysis.

54. Data on U.S. uses of force are drawn from the identical data set employed in my investigation earlier in this chapter of all major uses of force by the United States from 1953 to 1998 (Oneal, Lian, and Joyner 1996; Fordham and Sarver 2001). Data on U.S.

militarized disputes with the Soviet Union are taken from the Militarized Interstate Dispute dataset (Jones, Bremer, and Singer 1996). I also tested dummy variables for the Vietnam War and Persian Gulf crisis, but neither dummy materially affected the results, and so they were excluded.

55. The NES CDF collapses education into four categories: (1) did not complete high school, (2) high school diploma, (3) some college, and (4) college or postgraduate degree.

56. At first glance, my results may seem at odds with figure 2.3. When, however, one takes into account the different numbers of respondents in the several education groups, combined with the differing *magnitudes* of predicted increases or decreases in the propensity to mention foreign affairs/national defense issues, these data do not appear inconsistent with the aggregate trend shown in figure 2.3. Indeed, the annualized aggregate trend in the probability of mentioning a foreign affairs problem, based on the NES CDF data, largely mirrors that shown in figure 2.3, the latter of which is based on a much larger number of polls.

57. The results are largely unaffected by dating the end of the Cold War at 1989, 1990, or 1991.

58. I code 1990 as the last year of the Vietnam Syndrome because many analysts have credited the 1991 Persian Gulf War as effectively restoring America's self-confidence in its status as a military superpower.

59. This variable runs from 12 to 1, as a presidential election approaches, with all off-year observations coded 12.

60. There are two reasons for including this variable. First, the greater the number of polls per year, the closer the likely average proximity of a given poll to the actual start date of a military operation. This could potentially bias the results in favor of more recent crises, simply because Gallup has increased the frequency of its polling in recent years. And second, by accounting for the frequency of polling, I am able to address a potential criticism of using "no opinion" rates to measure attentiveness. Specifically, it is possible that secular declines in "no opinion" responses may merely reflect the increasing prevalence of polling in the United States and the public's resulting increased comfort in answering survey questions.

61. Also following Ostrom and Simon (1985), I use the current period, rather than the lagged misery index or a first difference.

62. This variable accounts for the possibility that Republicans might engender systematically greater or lesser confidence among the public in their management of foreign policy. Though this may change in the post–Cold War period, Republican presidents historically have enjoyed greater public confidence in their management of foreign policy than have their Democratic counterparts.

63. Because the "most important problems" question is asked by Gallup with far less frequency than the presidential approval question, responses to the former question are far less likely to fluctuate with most individual uses of force. Hence, in most instances—albeit, presumably, with some exceptions—this latter variable most likely captures the general public opinion environment with respect to foreign policy, rather than public reactions to any specific events. Still, though I am employing this variable, in aggregate form, in a manner distinct from other portions of the book (where I employ individual level data), it most likely still taps, at least in part, the same underlying concept—attentiveness—as "no opinion" rates. Indeed, in level form, this variable correlates with "no opinion" rates at nearly .31. Yet, any multicollinearity between this variable and the transformed "no opinion" rate indicator should weaken my results, thereby biasing the models *against* my hypotheses. And, in any event, the transformed dependent variable

correlates far more modestly (at about .02) with the first difference form of the "most important problems" variable.

64. Test results are available from the author upon request.

65. These data are based on the same question employed in figure 2.1, with minor variations in question wording. The precise wording, by survey organization, is as follows: (1) Gallup: (*a*) "Do you approve or disapprove of the way George Bush is handling this current situation in the Middle East involving Iraq and Kuwait?" and (*b*) (after January 15, 1991) "Do you approve or disapprove of the way George Bush is handling the situation in the Persian Gulf region? (2) CBS/*New York Times*, CBS: "Do you approve or disapprove of the way George Bush is handling Iraq's invasion of Kuwait? Would you say you approve/disapprove strongly or somewhat?" (3) ABC/*Washington Post*, ABC: "Do you approve or disapprove of the way George Bush is handling the situation caused by Iraq's invasion of Kuwait? Is that approve/disapprove strongly or approve/disapprove not strongly?" (4) *Time*/CNN: "Do you think President Bush is doing a good or poor job handling this (the) crisis with Iraq?" (5) *Los Angeles Times*: "Do you approve or disapprove of the way George Bush is handling the Iraq situation in the Middle East?" (6) Black: "Do you approve or disapprove of the way George Bush is handling the Iraq situation?" (7) ABC: "Do you approve or disapprove of the way George Bush is handling the situation in the Persian Gulf?" (Mueller 1994, 193–97).

CHAPTER SIX: RALLYING ROUND THE WATER COOLER

1. Gallup, ABC, CBS, NBC/*Wall Street Journal*, and CNN/*USA Today* polls; November 13, 15, 16 and 20, 1998; December 3, 16, and 19, 1998.

2. Still, it is worth noting that this particular rally was short-lived. By December 28, just nine days after recording a 73 percent approval rating, the president's approval rating had fallen back to 64 percent. A series of ABC News/*Washington Post* surveys found a similar pattern A poll completed on December 13, three days before the initiation of Operation Desert Fox, found 64 percent of respondents approving of the president's job performance. One week later, in a survey conducted on December 19 and 20, the president's approval rating rose to 67 percent. Yet, in their very next survey, conducted on January 8–11, President Clinton's approval rating fell to 62 percent, 2 percentage points below his pre–Desert Fox rating.

3. Gallup Polls, September 7–10 and 14–15, 2001. Other major polling organizations recorded similar post attack approval ratings (e.g., 86 percent in a September 13, 2001 ABC News/*Washington Post* poll, and 84 percent in a September 13–14, 2001 CBS News/*New York Times* poll).

4. One exception is Hristoulas, James, and Rioux (2000), who divide approval data into four groups: overall, partisan (i.e., Democrats and Republicans), opposition identifiers, and Independents. They find some differences in rally effects, but they do not offer theoretical explanations for those differences. A second exception is Edwards and Swenson (1997), who investigate, at the individual level, the correlates of a rally following a single U.S. use of force early in the Clinton administration. Though it is difficult to compare my over-time results with results derived from a single event, Edwards and Swenson's argument that, ceteris paribus, those with the greatest propensity to approve of the president are most likely to rally, appears consistent with my theoretical framework.

5. This process is similar to the social-psychological concept of *selective attention* (Campbell et al. 1960).

6. It does not necessarily follow, however, that any such rallies will be sustained or that they will spill over to enhanced public support for a president's policies. Indeed, one can imagine that the same episodic coverage of a foreign crisis by soft news outlets that induces a short-term patriotic rally response may also, albeit perhaps not immediately, induce greater suspicion of the merits of a policy. For instance, many Americans may respond enthusiastically to an episodic story of a wounded American soldier overcoming the odds to survive behind enemy lines (like the previously discussed story of Scott O'Grady). And this enthusiasm may be reflected in a short-term spike in support for the president. Yet, this story may have no lasting effect on public evaluations of the merits of the policy. Indeed, an episodic story focusing on the dangers faced by American soldiers may ultimately enhance public *opposition* to the policy.

7. Kernell and Hibbs (1981) test several variants of the threshold model, but find the strongest support for the partisan variant.

8. The reasons for the discrepancy between Republican and Democratic administrations are complex. One likely contributing factor is the relatively higher level of political sophistication—and hence ideological orientation—of Republican identifiers. As noted, ideologues tend to resist contrary information in the media. Hence, all else equal, Republican identifiers are less likely to evaluate a Democratic president positively than Democratic identifiers are to evaluate a Republican president positively.

9. The actual number of observations in the several models varies from 804 to 817, depending on availability of control variables and inclusion of autoregressive terms to correct for serial autocorrelation.

10. Following Hristoulas et al. (2000), I also tested my models with two additional variants of the dependent variable, based on including only partisan identifiers and opposition party members. These models were tested against the full series. Neither specification, however, outperformed those reported below. Hence, I do not report results based on these variants of the dependent variable.

11. Collinearity prohibits including both the administration and Cold War dummies in the same models. For my trend analyses, I concluded that the possibility of a Cold War effect was of greater theoretical concern than that of any administration-specific effects. The results, however, are comparable regardless of the model specification.

12. One implication of this specification is that the coefficients on the independent variables represent their immediate, or impact, effect on the dependent variable, rather than a cumulative effect. Rao and Miller (1972, 44–46) discuss the importance of distinguishing between the immediate, or "impact," effect of a causal variable, and its cumulative (long-term) effect, absorbed through the lagged dependent variable.

13. These procedures alleviate the problem of serial autocorrelation in nearly all of the reported models. In several instances, however, some evidence of serial autocorrelation persisted despite my best efforts. In each case, additional *AR* terms had little effect on the magnitude or significance of the coefficients, suggesting that the results are not significantly biased by any remaining autocorrelation.

14. A Wald Coefficient Test (henceforth "Wald Test") indicated that we may reject the null hypotheses that the coefficients on *Rally* for the three education groups are statistically indistinguishable from one another at the .07 level. It is important to point out, however, that the Wald Test does not allow the inclusion of *AR* terms. In the presence of serial autocorrelation, this may produce biased coefficients, thereby reducing the accuracy of the test. In this instance, however, the inability to account for serial autocorrelation *reduces* the magnitude of the differences across groups, suggesting that this particular Wald Test most likely understates the true significance of the differences.

15. A Wald Test indicated that the null hypothesis could, in this instance, be rejected at the .001 level.

16. A Wald Test, however, indicated that the null hypothesis could not be rejected. As before, the inability to account for serial autocorrelation reduces the magnitude and significance of the differences across groups, suggesting that the Wald Test results, once again, most likely understate the true significance of the differences.

17. I retested my series, employing the University of Michigan's Index of Consumer Sentiment—which correlates with its Index of Consumer Expectations at .97—in place of inflation and unemployment. The results were comparable to those from the original models. Hence, I report only the models using the traditional macroeconomic indicators.

18. Varying the number of months included in this average from two to six months did not materially affect the results. Hence, I report only the three-month lag structure, which modestly outperformed the others. I also tested the monthly change in aggregate national income, but found that it was consistently outperformed by the other indicators.

19. Limiting this variable to the first three months of a president's first term in office had no material effect on the key relationships.

20. Previous research (Gaubatz 1999; A. Smith 1996) has found that that the United States is less likely to employ military force in presidential election years. Proximity to a presidential election may also influence a president's approval rating.

21. As noted in chapter 5, Iyengar (1990) found that immigrants tend to be more internationally oriented than native-born Americans, due to continued ties to their home countries. This suggests that as the percentage of Americans born abroad has risen over the past several decades, the salience of foreign policy crises for the American people may also, in the aggregate, have increased. A larger foreign-born population may simply be more interested in major events outside the United States.

22. Previous research (Brody 1991; Stimson 1976; Mueller 1973; Kernell 1978) has found that presidents grow less popular over time. Additional studies (J. Cohen 1995) have also found that presidents tend to devote greater attention to foreign policy in their second terms, as the Congress becomes less inclined to follow a lame duck president's lead on domestic affairs. I also tested an alternative specification of the Lame duck dummy, coded 1 only during the final two years of a president's second term. This variable, however, was consistently outperformed by the four-year version of the dummy. Hence, I include only the latter version in the reported results.

23. This variable accounts for any effects on approval ratings of variations in the salience of foreign policy to the American public. An additional variable tallying the number of disputes with Russia (as identified by the Militarized Interstate Dispute data set) in which the United States was engaged at the time of a use of force proved statistically insignificant in several variants of the model and hence was not included in the reported results. This variable was intended to capture the level of tensions between the United States and Russia at the time of a given use of force. Finally, additional controls for the three major post–World War II U.S. wars (Korea, Vietnam, and the Persian Gulf) and for Soviet involvement in a potential rally event had little or no effect on the key conceptual variables, so they were also omitted from the reported results.

CHAPTER SEVEN: SOFT NEWS AND WORLD VIEWS

1. The five surveys are as follows: (1) a March 1998 Gallup poll (poll #9803011, "The Media: Source and Accuracy"), (2) the 2000 NES survey, (3) a May 1993 Harris

Poll (poll #931103), (4) a May 1994 *North Carolina News and Observer* statewide poll, and (5) a May 1994 Harris Poll (poll #941103).

2. Hamilton (2003), for instance, found in a content analysis that relative to soft news programs, hard news outlets systematically employ more complex terminology in their reporting.

3. This figure is based on the previously described five-point interviewer assessment of the respondent's level of political information.

4. Interestingly, the only hypothetical use-of-force scenario included in the survey in which differently educated respondents differed significantly involved the Philippines and Indonesia (asked in tandem in a single question). In this instance, college-educated respondents were 17 percentage points more likely than their counterparts without a high school diploma to support the use of military force (.61 vs. .78). This difference may be attributable to either the relative lack of publicity of the role of these nations in the War on Terrorism, or simply to the fact that two countries, rather than one, were included in the question. Regardless, the relatively wide gap in this instance was clearly the exception rather than the rule. Lastly, it is worth noting that this sole exception to the general pattern with respect to the War on Terrorism conforms to my overall prediction of less support for an activist U.S. foreign policy among the least-educated segments of the public.

5. For instance, among low-information Democratic identifiers, the corresponding gap is nearly 20 percentage points. And Democratic disapprovers are presumably located closer to the threshold of approval, with respect to President Clinton, than any other group of disapproving respondents (see chapter 6; see also Edwards and Swenson 1997). Across all 15 NES surveys for which the presidential approval question is available in the NES CDF (1972–2000), isolationists are, on average, over 10 percentage points *less* likely to approve a president's job performance. This gap persists even after accounting for respondents' partisan preferences.

6. Low-information Republican isolationists are *less than half* as likely as their fellow partisan internationalists to respond "don't know" to the presidential approval question. Low-information Democratic isolationists, in turn, are *just over one-third* as likely as their internationalist counterparts to fail to offer an opinion regarding the president's job performance. And, among those lacking an opinion regarding President Clinton, Democratic internationalists are, in all likelihood, closest to the threshold of approval (see chapter 6; see also Edwards and Swenson 1997). As before, the patterns remain similar if one pools all fifteen NES surveys during the 1972–2000 period.

7. The precise question wording is as follows: "How often do you watch ———? Would you say often, sometimes, rarely, or never?"

8. The alpha reliability scores for the hard and soft news scales are .57 and .54, respectively.

9. Responses were coded 0 = only fair or poor; 1 = excellent or pretty good.

10. The alpha reliability score for the talk show scale is .74.

11. The questions regarding Britain and France asked respondents to rate each country on a four-point scale, coded 1 = close ally, 2 = friendly [but] not ally, 3 = not friendly, and 4 = enemy. The UN question, in turn, is based on the following three questions: (1) "Overall, how would you rate the job the United Nations is doing in working for peace in the world—excellent, pretty good, only fair, or poor?" (coded 0 = poor or only fair and 1 = pretty good or excellent); (2) Do you feel that the UN is an effective organization for peace or not?" (coded 0 = no, 1 = yes); and (3) All things considered, do you think the UN is worthwhile or not worthwhile?" (coded 0 = not

worthwhile, 1 = worthwhile). The three questions were added together to form a scale, which I recoded to a 0–1 interval, where 1 = maximum support for the United Nations. These questions are included to account for the possibility that a respondents' views toward the key U.S. allies involved on the ground in Bosnia or toward the United Nations might influence their views of U.S. policy toward Bosnia.

12. For every statistical investigation in this chapter, as a robustness check, before running the full multivariate models, I ran basic models, including only the key causal variables. In each instance, the results were largely consistent with those from the fully specified models. Hence, with the exception of my NES models, which include a much larger range of control variables, I report only the latter models in the text. (Results from the basic models are available from the author.)

13. The precise education categories vary slightly across the different models in this chapter. The primary reason is that the various surveys sometimes differ in their available response categories.

14. In this instance, probability weighting had only a minimal effect on the coefficients and standard errors. Hence, I was able to employ the King, Tomz, and Wittenberg (2000) technique to derive confidence intervals and standard errors.

15. Unfortunately, in this instance, probability weighting produced fairly substantial effects. Hence, I am unable to employ the King, Tomz, and Wittenberg (2000) procedure to estimate the statistical significance of the several curves. Nonetheless, given that the base category for talk shows is significant at the .01 level, we can be confident that, *at minimum*, the relationships shown in figure 7.2 are statistically significant among the least-educated respondents.

16. Responses of "don't know/refused" are coded as missing.

17. The two trust indexes are based on the following question: "Now, apart from how FREQUENTLY you use them as sources of news, we'd like to know whether or not you can trust the accuracy of the news and information you get from each of the following news sources. First, do you feel you can trust the accuracy of the news and information you get from ———? How about ———?: 1 = Yes, can trust, 2 = No, cannot trust, 3 = Mixed, 4 = Don't know/Refused." Responses were recoded as follows: 0 = no, cannot trust, 0.5 = mixed or don't know/refused, 1 = yes, can trust. Both hard and soft news trust indexes were constructed from identical items as the corresponding media consumption indexes.

18. The hard news index includes the following 11 items: nightly network news programs, local TV news programs, CNN, C-SPAN, public TV news, cable news other than CNN, Sunday morning TV news shows, National Public Radio, national network news on the radio, weekly newsmagazines and daily newspapers. The soft news index, in turn, includes the following 4 items: TV entertainment news shows (e.g., *Hard Copy* or *Access Hollywood*), TV talk shows (e.g., *The Oprah Winfrey Show* or *The Rosie O'Donnell Show*), radio talk shows, and TV newsmagazine shows (e.g., *20/20* or *Dateline*). In this instance, the alpha reliability scores for the hard and soft news indexes are .65 and .52, respectively.

19. Education is coded as follows: 1 = eighth-grade education or less, 2 = high school incomplete, 3 = high school complete, 4 = some college or business/technical school after high school, 5 = college or postgraduate degree. This coding differs slightly from that employed in the prior section due to differences in the available response items.

20. The probabilities reported in figure 7.3 are based upon the standard logit transformation, which does not produce confidence intervals surrounding the estimated proba-

bilities. As previously noted, the King, Tomz, and Wittenberg (2000) methodology does not allow probability weighting. In this instance, perhaps due in part to the relatively low N of 715 in the logit model, weighting had an important effect on the magnitude of the coefficients. Hence, it was inappropriate to employ this procedure, absent weighting. Since, however, the coefficient on the soft news index is statistically significant ($p < .01$), we can be confident that, *at minimum*, the curve shown in figure 7.3 for the *least*-educated respondents is statistically significant.

21. I excluded several other talk show hosts, such as Ted Koppel and Charlie Rose, whose programs are not oriented primarily toward soft new topics and themes.

22. The alpha reliability score for the talk show scale is .79.

23. The latter question is worded as follows: "How would you rate the current state of relations between the United States and Japan—excellent, pretty good, only fair, or poor." Including this question as a control allows me to tap into respondents' affect toward Japan, independent of their perceptions of contemporaneous official governmental relations.

24. Unfortunately, as in the prior analysis, probability weighting produced fairly substantial effects. Hence, I am once again unable to employ the King, Tomz, and Wittenberg (2000) procedure to estimate the statistical significance of the curves shown in figure 7.4. Nonetheless, as before, given that the base category for talk show consumption is significant at the .05 level, we can be confident that, *at minimum*, the relationships shown in figure 7.4 are statistically significant among the *least*-educated respondents.

25. For the first question, responses were coded 0 = disagree, 1 = agree; for the second and third questions, responses were coded 0 = disapprove, 1 = approve. Since all three recoded variables are dichotomous, I employ logit estimators in each instance.

26. It is possible that including the presidential approval question as a control variable could disproportionately influence the economic policy approval model, relative to the foreign policy approval model, if the president's approval ratings were significantly more closely related to the former. Yet, in the 2000 NES, respondents' overall approval of President Clinton's job performance correlates with the economic and foreign policy approval variables at quite similar rates: .58 and .52, respectively. Moreover, models 1–3 in table 7.A2 indicate that my results are in no way an artifact of any particular model specification.

27. Following Baum and Kernell (1999), I collapse the five-point scale as follows: political information levels 1–2 are coded as "low" (1), level 3 is coded as "medium" (2), and levels 4–5 are coded as "high" (3).

28. While the substantive isolationism question has remained constant, the preface to the question has varied somewhat over the years, as follows: In 1960: "Around election time people talk about different things that our government in Washington is doing or should be doing. Now I would like to talk to you about some of the things that our government might do. Of course, different things are important to different people, so we don't expect everyone to have an opinion about all of these. I would like you to look at this card as I read each question and tell me how you feel about the question. If you don't have an opinion, just tell me that; if you do have an opinion, choose one of the other answers." In 1968 and 1980: "Now I'd like to read some of the things people tell us when we interview them (1968: "and ask you"; 1980: "As I read, please tell me") whether you agree or disagree with them." In 1972: "I'd like you to tell me whether you agree or disagree with each of these next six statements." In 1976: "I am going to read you two statements about U.S. foreign policy and I would like you to tell me whether you agree or disagree with each statement." In 1984–88,1992: "I am going to read a

statement about U.S. foreign policy, and I would like you to tell me whether you agree or disagree." In 1990, 1994–2000: "Do you agree or disagree with this statement?"

29. Unfortunately, the political information variable was not available until 1966. Employing this indicator would therefore necessitate dropping my 1960 observation, and thus fully half of my observations from the 1960s. Hence, for this analysis, I elected to employ education, which is available in every NES survey, as my indicator of political engagement.

30. Nevertheless, when I reran the model reported below, using network audience ratings as my indicator of the diversification of television, the substantive results were strikingly similar to those reported below. (These latter results are available from the author.)

CHAPTER EIGHT: SOFT NEWS, PUBLIC OPINION, AND AMERICAN FOREIGN POLICY

1. For instance, according the Pew Research Center (2000) survey, respondents who report following news about national politics either "very" or "somewhat" closely are about 138 percent more likely to report using the Internet as a source for news about politics than their counterparts who report following political news "not very" or "not at all" closely. And those who report following international affairs at least "somewhat" closely are twice as likely as their counterparts who follow news about international affairs "not very" or "not at all" closely to report using the Internet as a source of news about international affairs.

2. This compares to about 86 percent of those who claimed to follow government and public affairs "some of the time" or "most of the time."

3. Had the CNN tracking polls started three days earlier—and assuming the average gap remained similar during that period—the post-Oprah spike in Gore's support would be statistically significant at standard levels.

4. The first question was defined earlier in this chapter. The second question is as follows: "Some people seem to follow what's going on in government and public affairs most of the time, whether there's an election going on or not. Others aren't that interested. Would you say you follow what's going on in government and public affairs most of the time, some of the time, only now and then, or hardly at all?" Responses are coded: $0 = $ hardly at all, $1 = $ only now and then, $2 = $ some of the time, $3 = $ most of the time.

5. Voters who care about the election *could* be more likely than their less-concerned counterparts to watch talk shows. Yet given these shows' relatively apolitical audiences, there is no reason to suppose that very many viewers tuned in *due* to their interest in the election. The precise wording of the talk-show question—which asks respondents how many such shows they had watched in the *prior week*—further reduces the likelihood that talk-show viewing was, for many, a *consequence* of interest in the election. A respondent who watched a talk-show during the week prior to the NES interview *in order to see a candidate interview*, but who otherwise did not watch such shows, would score quite low on the talk show consumption scale. I also control for many of the most likely demographic correlates of talk-show viewing. Hence, while we cannot rule out the possibility of reciprocal causality, it seems highly unlikely to be a fundamental problem.

6. Unfortunately, unlike my prior statistical analysis of the Panama invasion, probability weighting produces meaningful effects on the key results. Hence, for the previously described reasons, I am unable to employ the King, Tomz, and Wittenberg (2000) methodology to derive confidence intervals. Once again, however, because the base category for soft news consumption is *nearly* statistically significant ($p < .07$), we can be

confident that the effects shown in figure 8.1 are almost certainly significant (or nearly so) among at least those respondents who did not attend high school.

7. Of course, some uninterested individuals will be exposed to presidential politics via television advertising. Yet, such individuals may elect to change channels when confronted with an unwanted political advertisement. Moreover, unlike soft news outlets, with a few notable exceptions, very little campaign advertising addresses foreign affairs, suggesting that this alternative source of political information is relatively unlikely to contribute to awareness of foreign policy. Nevertheless, properly crafted, political advertisements during soft news shows may represent an additional effective means for presidential campaigns to communicate with the soft news audience—one which does not require the physical presence of the candidates on a given program.

8. Along these lines, *Time* magazine's chief political correspondent Margaret Carlson commented in June 1999 that, while she expected President Clinton to reap a political windfall from NATO's then-imminent victory in Kosovo, "it's [the potential benefit] not as big a plus as it would have been a minus [had the conflict turned out badly for NATO]" (CNN, *The Capital Gang*, June 5, 1993). Similarly, CNN's chief political commentator, Jeff Greenfield, observed: "The engagement of Americans in harm's way usually . . . produces more of a downside threat to a president than an upside possibility of rallying around the flag" (CNN, *Larry King Live*, April 25, 1999). In fact, President Clinton's public approval remained flat following NATO's victory in Kosovo. In contrast, most political observers agreed that his public support would have plummeted had the air war in Kosovo ended in failure.

9. The strategic stakes indicator for this analysis is a dummy variable, coded 1 (i.e., high stakes) if the crisis constituted or involved a threat to a superpower's (the United States or the Soviet Union) interests or influence—as defined by Brecher and Wilkenfeld (1998)—and 0 otherwise.

10. The fatalities indicator in the MID data set is a seven-point scale with the following values: 0 = none, 1 = 1–25 deaths, 2 = 26–100 deaths, 3 = 101–250 deaths, 4 = 251–500 deaths, 5 = 501–999 deaths, and 6 = 1,000 + deaths. Statistical testing indicated that this scale was not suitable for an ordered logit estimator. Hence, I employed Ordinary Least Squares. I interpret a predicted fatality level between "1" and "2" as indicating "more than 25 deaths, but not more than 100 deaths." The strategic stakes indicator, in turn, is also a dummy variable, in this instance coded 1 (high stakes) if any one of the following five conditions holds: (1) The United States and its adversary are allies at the time of a MID, (2) the United States has more than its overall mean number of regional alliances in the data set within the region in which the MID occurs, (3) the degree of trade between the United States and its adversary exceeds the overall average U.S. level of bilateral trade in the data set, (4) the adversary possesses nuclear weapons capability, or (5) the Soviet Union is involved in the MID.

11. It is possible that lighter casualties, over time, could be an artifact of changing military technologies, such as smart bombs and cruise missiles, which have made it easier for the United States to conduct relatively low-risk military operations. If, however, technology were driving the relationships reported above, we would not expect a significant difference between low- and high-stakes conflicts. After all, presidents should prefer to employ high-tech weaponry *at least* as intensely, if not more so, in crises involving fundamental U.S. national security interests. The fact that the trend toward reduced fatalities is apparent only in low-stakes conflicts suggests that this trend is not an artifact of technological advances, but rather a product of conscious political decision making with respect to military tactics.

12. Zaller (1999) cites the example of an incident in the 1992 election, when Republican vice-presidential candidate Dan Quayle criticized the television program *Murphy Brown* for presenting a positive portrayal of a single mother. This story dominated newscasts for several days. Zaller argues that this incident produced the first serious discussion of "family values" in more than twenty years of debate over the issue.

REFERENCES

Aldrich, John H., John L. Sullivan, and Eugene Borgida. 1989. Foreign Affairs and Issue Voting: Do Presidential Candidates "Waltz before a Blind Audience"? *American Political Science Review* 83(1): 123–41.

Almond, Gabriel A. 1950. *The American People and Foreign Policy.* New York: Praeger.

American National Election Study, 1948–1994. Conducted by University of Michigan, Center for Political Studies. ICPSR CD-ROM CD0010. Ann Arbor: University of Michigan, Center for Political Studies, and Inter-university Consortium for Political and Social Research [producers], 1948–94. Ann Arbor, MI: Inter-university Consortium for Political and Social Research [distributor], May 1995.

Ansolabehere, Stephen, Roy Behr, and Shanto Iyengar. 1993. *The Media Game.* New York: Macmillan.

Asher, Herbert. 1998. *Polling and the Public.* 4th ed. Washington, D.C.: Congressional Quarterly Press.

Associated Press. 1994. U.S. Puts Off Sanctions on China and Japan. *New York Times*, (May 1), sec. 1.

Auletta, Ken. 1991. *Three Blind Mice: How the TV Networks Lost Their Way.* New York: Random House.

Ault, Michael, and James Meernik. 2000. Information Heterogeneity, Public Opinion, and Support for U.S. Presidents' Foreign Policies. Paper presented at the annual meeting of the American Political Science Association, Washington, D.C., August 31–September 3, 2000.

Banerjee, M., M. Capozzoli, L. McSweeney, and D. Sinha. 1999. Beyond Kappa: A Review of Interrater Agreement Measures. *Canadian Journal of Statistics* 27(1): 3–23.

Barber, Benjamin R. 1984. *Strong Democracy: Participatory Politics for a New Age.* Berkeley and Los Angeles: University of California Press.

Bark, Ed. 1998. For TV, 18 to 49 is Best Advertising Age. *San Diego Union-Tribune.* October 6, sec. E.

Bartels, Larry M. 1991. Constituency Opinion and Congressional Policy Making: The Reagan Defense Buildup. *American Political Science Review* 85 (June): 457–74.

———. 1993. Messages Received: The Political Impact of Media Exposure. *American Political Science Review* 87(2):267–85.

Bauder, David. 1999. News or Entertainment? The News Channels Follow Ventura. Associated Press, July 15.

Baum, Matthew A. 2000a. Foreign Policy in the Public Eye: Public Opinion, Domestic Audience Costs, and the Use of Force Abroad. Paper presented at the 1999 Meeting of the American Political Science Association, Atlanta, Ga, September 3–6.

———. 2000b. "Tabloid Wars: The Mass Media, Public Opinion, and the Decision to Use Force Abroad." Ph.D. diss. University of California, San Diego.

———. 2002a. The Constituent Foundations of the Rally-round-the-Flag Phenomenon. *International Studies Quarterly* 46 (June): 263–98.

———. 2002b. A Marriage of Convenience: Presidential Politics Hits the Talk Show Circuit. *PRG Report* (Spring): 1.

Baum, Matthew A., Michael J. Hiscox, and Angela O'Mahony. 2001. Playing to the

Crowd: Public Opinion and the Initiation of Trade Sanctions. Paper presented at the Annual Meeting of the American Political Science Association, San Francisco, Calif.

Baum, Matthew A., and Sam Kernell. 1999. Has Cable Ended the Golden Age of Presidential Television? *American Political Science Review* 93 (March): 99–114.

———. 2001. Economic Class and Popular Support for Franklin Roosevelt in War and Peace. *Public Opinion Quarterly* 65 (Summer): 198–229.

Bednarski, P.J. 2001. More Than I Can Watch: The Number of TV Channels Is Growing Faster than Our Interest. *Broadcasting and Cable*, July 9, 8.

Bennett, James. 1999. "The Cable Guys." *New York Times Magazine*. On-line edition, October 24, 1999.

Bennett, Stephen Earl. 1986. *Apathy in America, 1960–1984: Causes and Consequences of Citizen Political Indifference.* Dobbs Ferry, New York: Transnational Publishers.

———. 1995. Comparing Americans' Political Information in 1988 and 1992. *Journal of Politics* 57:521–32.

Bennett, W. Lance. 1990. Toward a Theory of Press-State Relations. *Journal of Communication* 40:103–125.

Berelson, Bernard R., Paul F. Lazarsfeld, and William N. McPhee. 1954. *Voting: A Study of Opinion Formation in a Presidential Campaign.* Chicago: University of Chicago Press.

Bernstein, Robert, Anita Chadha, and Robert Montjoy. 2001. Overreporting Voting: Why It Happens and Why It Matters. *Public Opinion Quarterly* 65 (Spring): 22–44.

Blechman, Barry M., and Stephen S. Kaplan. 1978. *Force without War: U.S. Armed Forces as a Political Instrument.* Washington, D.C.: Brookings Institution Press.

Blumler, Jay G., and Denis McQuail. 1969. *Television in Politics: Its Uses and Influence.* Chicago: University of Chicago Press.

Bogart, Leo. 1991. *Preserving the Press: How Daily Newspapers Mobilized to Keep Their Readers.* New York: Columbia University Press

Bosso, Christopher J. 1989. Setting the Agenda: Mass Media and the Discovery of Famine in Ethiopia. In *Manipulating Public Opinion: Essays on Public Opinion as a Dependent Variable*, Margolis, Michael and Gary A. Mauser. Pacific Grove, Calif.: Brooks/Cole Publishing Company.

Bovitz, Gregory L., James N. Druckman, and Arthur Lupia. 2002. When Can a News Organization Lead Public Opinion?—Ideology versus Market Forces in Decisions to Make News. *Public Choice* 113 (October): 127–55.

Bower, Robert T. 1985. *The Changing Television Audience in America.* New York: Columbia University Press.

Brecher, Michael, and Jonathan Wilkenfeld, producers. *International Crisis Behavior Project, 1918–1994.* 3rd ICPSR version. 1998. [Computer file]. College Park, Md.: University of Maryland, 1996. Distributed by Ann Arbor, Mich.: Inter-university Consortium for Political and Social Research, 1998.

Briller, Bert, R. 1990. Zooming in Closer on the News Audience. *Television Quarterly* 25 (1): 107–16.

Broder, David. 1994. War on Cynicism. *Washington Post*, July 6, sec. A.

Brody, Richard. 1991. *Assessing Presidential Character: The Media, Elite Opinion, and Public Support.* Stanford, Calif.: Stanford University Press.

———. 1994. The Media and Public Support for the President. In *Taken by Storm: The Media, Public Opinion, and U.S. Foreign Policy in the Gulf War*, edited by Lance W. Bennett, and David L. Paletz, 210–27. Chicago: University of Chicago Press.

Brody, Richard, and Catherine R. Shapiro. 1989. A Reconsideration of the Rally Phenomenon in Public Opinion. In *Political Behavior Annual*, vol. 2, edited by S. Long. Boulder, Colo.: Westview Press.

Bumiller, Elisabeth. 2002. President Notes Dissent on Iraq, Vowing to Listen. *New York Times*, August 17 late ed., sec. A.

Campbell, Angus, Philip E. Converse, Warren E. Miller, and Donald E. Stokes. 1960. *The American Voter*, New York: Wiley.

Chaffee, Steven H., and Stacey F. Kanihan. 1997. Learning about Politics from the Mass Media. *Political Communication* 14 (October–December): 421–30.

Chaiken, Shelly, and Alice H. Eagly. 1976. Communication Modality as a Determinant of Message Persuasiveness and Message Comprehensibility. *Journal of Personality and Social Psychology* 34 (October): 605–14.

Cohen, Bernard C. 1963. *The Press and Foreign Policy*. Princeton: Princeton University Press.

———. 1973. *The Public's Impact on Foreign Policy*. Boston: Little, Brown.

Cohen, Jeffrey. 1995. Presidential Rhetoric and the Public Agenda. *American Journal of Political Science* 39(1) (February): 87–107.

Committee of Concerned Journalists (CCJ). 1998a. *Changing Definitions of News*. Report. Available at: http://www.journalism.org/lastudy.html

———. 1998b. *News as Entertainment: Entertainment as News*. Symposium. Available at: http://www.journalism.org/USCreporta.html

Conover, Pamela, and Stanley Feldman. 1984. How People Organize the Political World: A Schematic Model. *American Journal of Political Science* 28 (1): 95–126.

Converse, Philip E. 1964. The Nature of Belief Systems in Mass Publics. In *Ideology and Discontent*, edited by David E. Apter. New York: Free Press.

———. 1969. Of Time and Partisan Stability. *Comparative Political Studies* 2:139–71.

Cook R. J. 1998. Kappa. In *The Encyclopedia of Biostatistics*, edited by Peter Armitage and Theodore Colton, 2160–66. New York: Wiley.

Cook, Thomas D., and Donald T. Campbell. 1979. *Quasi-Experimentation: Design and Analysis Issues for Field Settings*. Boston: Houghton Mifflin.

Daalder, Ivo H., and Michael E. O'Hanlon. 2000. *Winning Ugly: NATO's War to Save Kosovo*. Washington, D.C.: Brookings Institution Press.

Davis, Richard, and Diana Owen. 1998. *New Media and American Politics*. New York: Oxford University Press.

Decker, Cathleen. 2000. Gore's Come a Long Way with Help of Women. *Los Angeles Times*, September 18, sec. A.

Delli Carpini, Michael X., and Scott Keeter. 1996. *What Americans Know about Politics and Why It Matters*. New Haven: Yale University Press.

de Moraes, Lisa. 2002. "Reality" TV Is Marching to the Military's Tune. *Washington Post*, March 19, sec. A.

Dimock, Michael A., and Samuel L. Popkin. 1997. Political Knowledge in Comparative Perspective. In *Do The Media Govern? Politicians, Voters, and Reporters in America*, edited by Shanto Iyenar and Richard Reeves. Thousand Oaks, Calif.: Sage.

Dionne, E. J. 1991. *Why Americans Hate Politics*. New York: Simon and Schuster.

Downs, Anthony. 1972. Up and Down with Ecology: The "Issue-Attention Cycle." *Public Interest* 28:28–50.

Druckman, James N. 2001a. On the Limits of Framing Effects: Who Can Frame? *The Journal of Politics* 63 (November): 1041–1066.

———. 2001b. The Implications of Framing Effects for Citizen Competence. *Political Behavior* 23:225–56.

Edelman, Murray. 1989. *The Symbolic Use of Politics*. Urbana: University of Illinois Press.

Edwards, George C., III. 1990. *Presidential Approval: A Source Book*. Baltimore: Johns Hopkins University Press.

Edwards, George, III and Tami Swenson. 1997. Who Rallies? The Anatomy of a Rally Event. *Journal of Politics* 59 (February): 200–212.

Entman, Robert M. 1991. "Framing U.S. Coverage of International News: Contrasts in Narratives of the KAL and Iran Air Incidents." *Journal of Communication* 41:6–27.

———. 1993. Framing: Toward Clarification of a Fractured Paradigm. *Journal of Communication* 43:51–58.

Eveland, William P., and Sietram A. Scheufele. 2000. Connecting News Media Use with Gaps in Knowledge and Participation. *Political Communication* 17 (July–September): 215–37.

Fazio, Russell H. 1989. On the Power and Functionality of Attitudes: The Role of Attitude Accessibility. In *Attitude Structure and Function*, edited by Anthony R. Pratkinis, Steven J. Breckler, and Anthony G. Greenwald. Hillsdale, N.J.: Lawrence Erlbaum Associates, Publishers.

Fearon, James. 1994. Domestic Political Audiences and the Escalation of International Conflict. *American Political Science Review* 88(September): 577–92.

Feaver, Peter V., and Christopher Gelpi. 1999. A Look at . . . Casualty Aversion: How Many Deaths Are Acceptable? A Surprising Answer. *Washington Post*, November 7, sec. B.

Feder, Robert. 2000. Gore to Help Kick off New Season of *Oprah. Chicago Sun-Times*. September 1.

Federal Communications Commission (FCC). 1998. *Charting the Digital Broadcasting Future: Final Report of the Advisory Committee on Public Interest Obligations of Digital Television Broadcasters*. Washington, D.C.: Government Printing Office, December 18.

Fiske, Susan T., and Shelley E. Taylor. 1991. *Social Cognition*. 2nd ed. New York: McGraw-Hill.

Fitzsimmons, Stephen J., and Hobart G. Osburn. 1968. The Impact of Social Issues and Public Affairs Television Documentaries. *Public Opinion Quarterly* 32 (Autumn): 379–97.

Fordham, Benjamin O., and Christopher C. Sarver. 2001. Militarized Interstate Disputes and United States Uses of Force. *International Studies Quarterly* 45 (September): 455–66.

Fornier, Patrick. 1998. The Determinants of Heterogeneity in Models of Individual Behavior. Paper presented at the Annual Meeting of the Midwest Political Science Association, Chicago, Ill., April 23–25.

Gallup. 1998. *Media/Social Security Poll*. Gallup Organization. Telephone poll, July 13–14.

Gamson, William A., and Andre Modigliani. 1987. The Changing Culture of Affirmative Action. In *Research in Political Sociology*, vol. 3, edited by Richard D. Braungart, 137–77. Greenwich, Conn.: JAI.

Gaubatz, Kurt Taylor. 1999. *Elections and War: The Electoral Incentive in the Democratic Politics of War and Peace*. Stanford, Calif.: Stanford University Press.

Gelb, Leslie H., and Richard K. Betts. 1979. *The Irony of Vietnam: The System Worked*. Washington, D.C.: Brookings Institution Press.

General Social Survey. 1999. *NORC-GSS Cumulative Data File, 1972–1998* [CD-

ROM]. Storrs: The Roper Center for Public Opinion Research, University of Connect-icut.

Getlin, Josh. 2000. In Politics of Celebrity, Be Charming, Win Big Campaign. *Los Angeles Times*, September 29, sec. A.

Ginsburg, Herbert, and Sylvia Opper. 1969. *Piaget's Theory of Intellectual Development*. Saddle River, N. J.: Prentice-Hall, Inc.

Graber, Doris A. 1984. *Processing the News: How People Tame the Information Tide*. New York: Longman.

———. 1997. *Mass Media and American Politics*. Washington, D.C.: Congressional Quarterly Press.

Graebner, Normal A. 1983. Public Opinion and Foreign Policy: A Pragmatic View. In *Interaction: Foreign Policy and Public Policy*, edited by E. D. Piper and R. J. Turchik, 11–34. Washington, D.C.: American Enterprise Institute.

Graham, Jefferson. 1997. Networks Try TV movie cutback. *USA Today*, June 2, sec. D.

Green, Donald P., and Ian Shapiro. 1994. *Pathologies of Rational Choice Theory: A Critique of Applications in Political Science*. New Haven: Yale University Press.

Groeling, Tim, and Samuel Kernell. 1998. Is Network News Coverage of the President Biased? *Journal of Politics* 60 (November): 1064–86.

Grossman, Michael B., and Martha J. Kumar. 1981. *Portraying the President: The White House and the News Media*. Baltimore: Johns Hopkins University Press.

Grossman, Lawrence K. 2000. It's Time to Treat Broadcasting Like Any Other Business. *Columbia Journalism Review* (November–December).

Groves, Robert M., and Robert L. Kahn. 1979. *Surveys by Telephone: A National Comparison with Personal Interviews*. New York: Academic Press.

Hallin, Daniel. 1991. Whose Campaign Is It, Anyway? *Columbia Journalism Review* 39 (January–February): 43–46.

Hamilton, James T. 1998. *Channeling Violence: The Economic Market for Violent Television Programming*. Princeton: Princeton University Press.

———. 2003. *"All the News that's Fit to Sell. How the Market Transforms Information into News."* Princeton: Princeton University Press (forthcoming).

Hess, Stephen. 1998. The Once and Future Worlds of Presidents Communicating. *Presidential Studies Quarterly* 28 (Fall).

Hill, David B. 1985. Viewer Characteristics and Agenda Setting by Television News. *Public Opinion Quarterly* 49 (Fall): 340–50.

Hinckley, Ronald H. 1992. *People, Polls, and Policy-Makers: American Public Opinion and National Security*. New York: Lexington Books.

Hofmeister, Sallie. 1997. Networks Try to Find Niches. *Los Angeles Times*. January 23, sec. A.

Hoge, James. 1997. Foreign News: Who Gives a Damn? *Columbia Journalism Review* 36 (November–December): 48–52.

Holsti, Ole R. 1992. Public Opinion and Foreign Policy: Challenges to the Almond-Lippman Consensus. Mershon Series, Research Programs and Debates. *International Studies Quarterly* 36: 439–66.

———. 1996. *Public Opinion and American Foreign Policy*. Ann Arbor: University of Michigan Press.

Holsti, Ole R., and James N. Rosenau. 1979. Vietnam, Consensus, and the Belief Systems of American Leaders. *World Politics* 32:1–56.

Holyoak K.J., and P. Thagard. 1995. *Mental Leaps: Analogy in Creative Thought*. Cambridge: MIT Press.

Hovland, C.I., A. A. Lumsdaine, and F. D. Sheffield. 1949. *Experiments on Mass Communications*. Vol. 3. New York: John Wiley and Sons.

Hristoulas, Athanasios, Patrick James, and Jean Sebastien Rioux. 2000. Domestic And International Determinants of Presidential Rallies, 1954–1999: Fact or Fiction? Paper presented at the Annual Meeting of the International Studies Association, Los Angeles, Calif., March 14–18.

Hugick, Larry, and Alec M. Gallup. 1991. "Rally Events" and Presidential Approval. *Gallup Poll Monthly*, 39:15–27.

Hurwitz, Jon, and Mark Peffley. 1987. How Are Foreign Policy Attitudes Structured? A Hierarchical Model. *American Political Science Review* 81 (4): 1099–1120.

Iyengar, Shanto. 1990. Shortcuts to Political Knowledge: The Role of Selective Attention and Accessibility. In *Information and Democratic Processes*, edited by John A. Ferejohn and James H. Kulinski, 160–85. Urbana: University of Illinois Press.

———. 1991. *Is Anyone Responsible? How Television Frames Political Issues*. Chicago: University of Chicago Press.

———. 1992. The Accessibility Bias in Politics: Television News and Public Opinion. In *The Mass Media*, edited by Stanley Rothman, 85–101. New York: Paragon.

———. 1993. Agenda Setting and Beyond: Television News and the Strength of Political Issues. In *Agenda Formation*, edited by William H. Riker, 211–29. Ann Arbor: University of Michigan Press.

Iyengar, Shanto, and Donald R. Kinder. 1987. *News That Matters*. Chicago: University of Chicago Press.

Jacobsen, John K. 1996. Are All Politics Domestic? Perspectives on the Integration of Comparative Politics and International Relations Theories. *Comparative Politics* 29 (October): 93–111.

James, Patrick, and John R. Oneal. 1991. The Influence of Domestic and International Politics on the President's Use of Force. *Journal of Conflict Resolution* 35 (2) :307–32.

Jentleson, Bruce W. 1992. The Pretty Prudent Public: Post post-Vietnam American Opinion on the Use of Military Force. *International Studies Quarterly* 36 (March): 49–74.

Jones, Daniel M., Stuart A. Bremer, and J. David Singer, producers. 1996. *Militarized Interstate Disputes, 1816–1992*. Computer File. Produced as part of J. David Singer and Melvin Small. 1993. *Correlates of War Project: International and Civil War Data, 1870–1992*. Ann Arbor: University of Michigan, Inter-university Consortium for Political and Social Research [distributor], 1994.

Jordan, Donald L., and Benjamin I. Page. 1992. Shaping Foreign Policy Opinions: The Role of TV News. *Journal of Conflict Resolution* 36:227–41.

Kahneman, Daniel. 1973. *Attention and Effort*. Englewood Cliffs, N.J.: Prentice-Hall.

Kahneman, Daniel, and Amos Tversky. 1984. Choices, Values, and Frames. *American Psychologist* 39:341–50.

Kalb, Marvin. 1998a. Get Ready for the Really Bad News. *Los Angeles Times*. July 10, sec. B.

———. 1998b. The Rise of the "New News": A Case Study of Two Root Causes of the Modern Scandal Coverage. Discussion paper D-34. Cambridge: Harvard University. Joan Shorenstein Center on the Press, Politics, and Public Policy.

Katz, Elihu, Jay G. Blumler, and Michael Gurevitch. 1973–74. Uses and Gratifications Research. *Public Opinion Quarterly* 37 (Winter): 509–23.

Katz, Elihu, and David Foulkes. 1962. On the Use of the Mass Media as "Escape": Clarification of a Concept. *Public Opinion Quarterly* 26 (Autumn): 377–88.

Katzman, Natan. 1972. Television Soap Operas: What's Been Going on Anyway? *Public Opinion Quarterly* 36 (Summer): 200–212.

Kegley, Charles W., Jr., and Eugene R. Wittkopf. 1996. *American Foreign Policy: Pattern and Process*. 5th ed. New York: St. Martin's Press.

Kelly, Michael. 2001. A Get-Out-of-Jail-Free Card: Just Get Famous. *Los Angeles Times*, March 21, sec. B.

Kelly, Stanley, Jr., and Thad W. Mirer. 1974. The Simple Act of Voting. *American Political Science Review* 68 (January): 572–91.

Kernell, Samuel. 1975. "Presidential Popularity and Electoral Preference: A Model of Short Term Political Change." Ph.D. diss. University of California, Berkeley.

———. 1978. Explaining Presidential Popularity. *American Political Science Review* 72:506–22.

———. 1997. *Going Public*. 3rd ed. Washington, D.C.: Congressional Quarterly Press.

Kernell, Samuel, and Douglas A. Hibbs, Jr. 1981. A Critical Threshold Model of Presidential Popularity. In *Contemporary Political Economy*, edited by Douglas A. Hibbs, Jr., and H. Fassbender. Amsterdam: North-Holland Publishing Company.

Key, V. O. 1961. *Public Opinion and American Democracy*. New York: Knopf.

Kinchla, R. A. 1980. The Measurement of Attention. In *Attention and Performance VIII*, edited by Raymond S. Nickerson. Mahwah, N.J.: Lawrence Erlbaum Associates.

Kinder, Donald R. 1983. Diversity and Complexity in American Public Opinion. In *Political Science: The State of the Discipline*, edited by Ada W. Finifter. Washington, D.C.: American Political Science Association.

King, Gary. 1997. *A Solution to the Ecological Inference Problem: Reconstructing Individual Behavior from Aggregate Data*. Princeton: Princeton University Press.

King, Gary, Michael Tomz, and Jason Wittenberg. 2000. Making the Most of Statistical Analyses: Improving Interpretation and Presentation. *American Journal of Political Science* 44 (April): 341–55.

Krause, George. 1997. Voters, Information Heterogeneity, and the Dynamics of Aggregate Economic Expectations. *American Journal of Political Science* 41:1170–1200.

Krosnick, Jon A., and Laura A. Brannon. 1993. The Impact of the Gulf War on the Ingredients of Presidential Evaluations: Multidimensional Effects of Political Involvement. *American Political Science Review* 87 (December): 963–75.

Krugman, Herbert E., and Eugene L. Hartley. 1970. Passive Learning from Television. *Public Opinion Quarterly* 34 (Summer): 184–90.

Kull, Steven, and I. M. Destler. 1999. *Misreading the Public: The Myth of a New Isolationism*. Washington, D.C.: Brookings Institution Press.

Kurtz, Howard. 1999. Americans Wait for the Punch Line on Impeachment; As the Senate Trial Proceeds, Comedians Deliver the News. *Washington Post*, January 26, sec. A.

———. 2002. Despite Sept. 11, Interest Still Low In Foreign News. *Washington Post* June 10, sec. A.

LaGanga, Maria L. 2000. The Softer Side of Bush: George W. Visits Oprah. *Los Angeles Times*, September 20, sec. A.

LaMay, C. 1991. By the Numbers, II: Measuring the Coverage. In *The Media at War: The Press and the Persian Gulf Conflict*, edited by C. LaMay, M. Sahadi, and J. Sahadi, 45–50. New York: Gannett Foundation Media Center.

Larson, Deborah. 1985. *Origins of Containment: A Psychological Explanation*. Princeton: Princeton University Press.

Lazarsfeld, Paul F., Bernard Berelson, and Hazel Gaudet. 1948. *The People's Choice:*

How the Voter Makes up His Mind in a Presidential Campaign. New York: Columbia University Press

Levin, Irwin P., Sandra L. Schneider, and Gary J. Gaeth. 1998. All Frames Are Not Created Equal: A Typology and Critical Analysis of Framing Effects. *Organizational Behavior and Human Decision Process* 76 (November): 149–88.

Lian, Bradley, and John R. Oneal. 1993. Presidents, the Use of Military Force, and Public Opinion. *Journal of Conflict Resolution* 37:277–300.

Lichty, Lawrence W., and Douglas Gomery. 1992. More Is Less. In *The Future of News: Television, Newspapers, Wire Services, Newsmagazines,* edited by Philip S. Cook, Douglas Gomery, and Lawrence W. Lichty. Washington, D.C.: Woodrow Wilson Center Press.

Lippman, Walter. 1934. *The Method of Freedom.* New York: Macmillan.

Lodge, Milton, and Kathleen M. McGraw, editors. 1995. *Political Judgment: Structure and Process.* Ann Arbor: University of Michigan Press.

Lodge, Milton, Marco R. Steenbergen, and Shawn Brau. 1995. The Responsive Voter: Campaign Information and the Dynamics of Candidate Evaluation. *American Political Science Review* 89 (June):309–26.

Lowry, Brian. 1997. Cable Stations Gather Strength. *Los Angeles Times,* September 2, sec. F.

———. 1998. With Clinton under Fire, Viewers Vote for the News. *Los Angeles Times,* January 30, sec. F.

———. 1999. Networks Face a Bumpy Ride. *Los Angeles Times,* August 20, sec. F.

———. 2000. Dr. Laura's New TV Show Gets Lukewarm Reception. *Los Angeles Times,* September 13, sec. F.

Lupia, Arthur, and Matthew D. McCubbins. 1998. *The Democratic Dilemma: Can Citizens Learn What They Need to Know?* Cambridge: Cambridge University Press.

Lutz, Richard J. 1975. First-Order and Second-Order Cognitive Effects in Attitude Change. *Communication Research* 2 (July): 289–99.

Lynn, Michael, Sharon Shavitt, and Thomas Ostrom. 1985. Effects of Pictures on the Organization and Recall of Social Information. *Journal of Personality and Social Psychology* 49 (November): 1160–68.

MacKuen, Michael. 1984. Exposure to Information, Belief Integration, and Individual Responsiveness to Agenda Change. *American Political Science Review* 78 (June): 372–91.

Marketplace. 1997. Public Radio International, October 31.

McGuire, William J. 1969. The Nature of Attitudes and Attitude Change. In *The Handbook of Social Psychology,* 2nd ed., vol. 3, edited by Lindzey Gardner and Elliott Aronson, 136–314. Reading, Mass: Addison-Wesley Publishing Company.

———. 1973. Persuasion, Resistance, and Attitude Change. In *Handbook of Communication,* edited by I. De la Pool, F. Frey, W. Schramm, N. Maccoby, and E. B. Parker. Chicago: Rand McNally.

Media Monitor. 1997a. Defining Journalism Down: Visual and Verbal Images in Tabloid TV News Shows. Center for Media and Public Affairs 11 (November/December): 5.

———. 1997b. News of the Nineties. Center for Media and Public Affairs 11 (July/August): 3.

———. 2000. The Media at the Millennium. Center for Media and Public Affairs 14 (July/August): 3.

Meernik, James, and Peter Waterman. 1996. The Myth of the Diversionary Use of Force by American Presidents. *Political Research Quarterly* 49 (3): 573–90.

Miller, Arthur H. 1974. Political Issues and Trust in Government. *American Political Science Review* 68 (3): 951–72.

Miller, Joanne, and Jon Krosnick. 1996. News Media Impact on the Ingredients of Presidential Evaluations: A Program of Research on the Priming Hypothesis. In *Political Persuasion and Attitude Change*, edited by Diana C. Mutz, Paul M. Sniderman, and Richard A. Brody. Ann Arbor: University of Michigan Press.

Miller, Warren E., Donald R. Kinder, Steven J. Rosenstone, and the National Election Studies. 1993. *American National Election Study, 1992: Pre- and Post-Election Survey* [Enhanced with 1990 and 1991 Data] [Computer file]. Conducted by University of Michigan, Center for Political Studies. ICPSR ed. Ann Arbor: University of Michigan, Center for Political Studies, and Inter-university Consortium for Political and Social Research (producers), 1993; Inter-university Consortium for Political and Social Research (distributor), 1993.

Moisy, Claude. 1997. Myths of the Global Information Village. *Foreign Policy* 107 (Summer): 78–87.

Moon, David. 1990. What You Use Depends on What You Have. *American Politics Quarterly* 18 (1): 3–24.

Mueller, John E. 1970. Presidential Popularity from Truman to Johnson. *American Political Science Review* 64 (March): 18–34.

———. 1973. *War, Presidents, and Public Opinion.* New York: John Wiley and Sons.

———. 1994. *Policy and Opinion in the Gulf War.* Chicago: University of Chicago Press.

Munck, Gerardo. 2001. Game Theory and Comparative Politics: New Perspectives and Old Concerns. *World Politics* 53 (January): 173–204

Naples, Michael J. 1979. *Effective Framing.* New York: Association of National Advertisers.

Navon, David, and Daniel Gopher. 1980. Task Difficulty, Resources, and Dual-Task Performance. In *Attention and Performance VIII*, edited by Raymond S. Nickerson. Mahwah, N.J.: Lawrence Erlbaum Associates.

Neuman, Russell W. 1990 The Threshold of Public Attention. *Public Opinion Quarterly* 54 (2) (Summer): 159–76

Neuman, W. Russell, Marion R. Just, and Ann R. Crigler. 1992. *Common Knowledge: News and the Construction of Political Meaning.* Chicago: University of Chicago Press.

Neustadt, Richard E. 1990. *Presidential Power and the Modern Presidents: The Politics of Leadership from Roosevelt to Reagan.* Rev. ed. New York: Free Press.

Nicholson, S. P., G. M. Segura, and N. D. Woods. 1999. The Paradox of Presidential Approval: The Mixed Blessing of Divided Government to Presidential Success. Paper presented at the annual meeting of the Midwest Political Science Association, Chicago, Ill., April 15–17.

Niemberg, Jason. 2001. How Jay Leno's Chin Changes the Face of Presidential Campaigns. Unpublished manuscript.

Niemi, Richard G., and Jane Junn. 1998. *Civic Education: What Makes Students Learn.* New Haven: Yale University Press.

Niemi, Richard G., John Mueller, and Tom W. Smith. 1989. *Trends in Public Opinion: A Compendium of Survey Data.* Westport, Conn.: Greenwood Press.

Nisbett, Richard, and Lee Ross. 1980. *Human Inference: Strategies and Shortcomings of Social Judgment.* Englewood Cliffs, N.J.: Prentice-Hall.

Noah, Timothy 1997. Beating Swords into TV Shares. *U.S. News and World Report.* December 1.

Nye, Joseph S., Jr., Philip D. Zelikow, and David C. King, ed. 1997. *Why People Don't Trust Government*. Cambridge: Harvard University Press.

Oneal, John R., Brad Lian, and James H. Joyner, Jr. 1996. Are the American People "Pretty Prudent"? Public Responses to U.S. Uses of Force, 1950–1988. *International Studies Quarterly* 40 (June): 261–280.

Ostrom, Charles W., Jr., and Brian L. Job. 1986. The President and the Political Use of Force. *American Political Science Review* 80 (2): 541–66.

Ostrom, Charles W., and Dennis Simon. 1985. Promise and Performances: A Dynamic Model of Presidential Popularity. *American Political Science Review* 79:334–338.

Ottati, Victor C., and Robert S. Wyer, Jr. 1990. The Cognitive Mediators of Political Choice: Toward a Comprehensive Model of Political Information Processing. In *Information and Democratic Processes*, edited by John A. Ferejohn, and James H. Kuklinski, 186–218. Urbana: University of Illinois Press.

Page, Benjamin I., and Robert Y. Shapiro. 1983. Effects of Public Opinion on Policy. *American Political Science Review* 77 (1): 175–90.

———. 1992. *The Rational Public: Fifty Years of Trends in Americans' Policy Preferences*. Chicago: University of Chicago Press.

Page, Benjamin I., Robert Y. Shapiro, and Glenn R. Dempsey. 1987. What Moves Public Opinion? *American Political Science Review* 81:23–44.

Parker, Suzanne L. 1995. Toward Understanding of "Rally" Effects: Public Opinion in the Persian Gulf War. *Public Opinion Quarterly* 59:526–46.

Patterson, Thomas E. 1980. *The Mass Media Election: How Americans Choose Their President*. New York: Praeger.

———. 1996. Bad News, Period. *PS: Political Science and Politics* 29 (March): 17–20.

———. 2000. Doing Well and Doing Good. Faculty Research Working Paper Series, #RWP01-001. John F. Kennedy School of Government. Cambridge: Harvard University.

Pennington, Gail. 2002. Network News: Incredible Shrinking Audience Share. *Augusta Chronicle*, February 4. Available online at http://www.augustachronicle.com/stories/020402/fea_124-4905.shtml.

Pew Research Center for the People and the Press. 1996. *Media Consumption Survey*. Princeton Survey Research Associates, April.

———. 1998a. *Believability of Media/People*. Princeton Survey Research Associates, May.

———. 1998b. *Media Consumption 1998*. Princeton Survey Research Associates, April.

———. 1998c. *News Interest Index*. Princeton Survey Research Associates, August.

———. 1998d. *The 1998 Technology Study*. Princeton Survey Research Associates, October–December.

———. 2000. *Biennial Media Consumption Survey*. Princeton Survey Research Associates, April.

———. 2001. *Response to Terrorism Tracking Poll*. Princeton Survey Research Associates, September 21–25.

———. 2002a. *News Interest Index*. Princeton Survey Research Associates, January.

———. 2002b. *Biennial Media Consumption Survey*. Princeton Survey Research Associates, April.

Picard, Robert G. 1998. Media Concentration, Economics, and Regulation. In *The Politics of News, the News of Politics*, edited by Doris Graber, Denis McQuail, and Pippa Norris. Washington, D.C.: Congressional Quarterly Press.

Popkin, Samuel. 1994. *The Reasoning Voter*. 2nd ed. Chicago: University of Chicago Press.

Powlick, Philip J. 1995. The Sources of Public Opinion for American Foreign Policy Officials. *International Studies Quarterly* 39 (4): 427–52.

Powlick, Philip J., and Andrew Z. Katz. 1998a. Defining the American Public Opinion/ Foreign Policy Nexus. *Mershon International Studies Review* 42 (1) (May): 29–62.

———. 1998b. Testing a Model of Public Opinion–Foreign Policy Linkage: Public Opinion in Two Carter Foreign Policy Decisions. Paper presented at the 1998 Meeting of the Midwest Political Science Association, Chicago, Ill., April 23–25.

Princeton Survey Research Associates. 1991. *Times Mirror News Interest Index*, January 3–6.

Prior, Markus. 2003. Any Good News in Soft News? The Impact of Soft News Preference on Political Knowledge. *Political Communication* 20 (April): 149–71.

Public Papers of the President. 1998. American Reference Library, CD-ROM.

Putnam, Robert D. 1988. Diplomacy and Domestic Politics: The Logic of Two-Level Games. *International Organization* 42 (3): 427–60.

———. 1995. Bowling Alone: America's Declining Social Capital. *Journal of Democracy* 6 (January): 65–78

———. 2000. *Bowling Alone: The Collapse and Revival of American Community*. New York: Simon and Schuster.

Quigley, John. 1992. *The Ruses for War*. Buffalo, N.Y.: Prometheus Books.

Rao, Potluri, and Roger LeRoy Miller. 1971. *Applied Econometrics*. Belmont, Calif.: Wadsworth Publishing Company.

Reeder, Glenn D., and John M. Spores. 1983. The Attribution of Morality. *Journal of Personality and Social Psychology* 44 (April): 736–45.

Rhine, Staci L., Stephen Earl Bennett, and Richard S. Flickinger. 1998. Exposure and Attention to Electronic and Print Media and Their Impact on Democratic Citizenship. Paper presented at the Fifty-sixth annual meeting of the Midwest Political Science Association, Chicago, Ill. April 23–25.

Rielly, John E., ed. 1995. *American Public Opinion and U.S. Foreign Policy, 1995*. Chicago: Chicago Council on Foreign Relations.

———, ed. 1999. *American Public Opinion and U.S. Foreign Policy, 1999*. Chicago: Chicago Council on Foreign Relations.

Riker, William H., and Peter C. Ordeshook. 1968. A Theory of the Calculus of Voting. *American Political Science Review* 62 (March): 25–41.

Risse-Kappen, Thomas. 1991. Public Opinion, Domestic Structure, and Foreign Policy in Liberal Democracies. *World Politics* 43 (July): 479–513.

Robinson, M. 1974. The Impact of the Televised Watergate Hearings. *Journal of Communication* 24: 17–30.

Roper Center Online. 1998. TV Remains Dominant News and Product Information Source, New Poll Reveals. Available online at: http://www.roper.com/news/content/news10.htm, May 28.

Rosenau, James N. 1961. *Public Opinion and Foreign Policy*. New York: Random House.

———. 1990. *Turbulence in World Politics: A Theory of Change and Continuity*. Princeton: Princeton University Press.

———. 1997. *Along the Domestic-Foreign Frontier: Exploring Governance in a Turbulent World*. Cambridge: Cambridge University Press.

Rosenberg, Howard. 2000. Candidates on Talk-Show Circuit: If You Don't Schmooze, You Lose. *Los Angeles Times*, September 15, sec. F.

Rosengren, Karl E., Lawrence A. Wenner, and Philip Palmgreen. 1985. *Media Gratifications Research: Current Perspectives*. Beverly Hills, Calif.: Sage Publications.

Rosenstiel, Tom, Carl Gottlieb, and Lee Ann Brady. 2000. Time of Peril for TV News: Quality Sells, but Commitment and Viewership Continue to Erode. Report by the Project for Excellence in Journalism, 84–99. New York: Columbia University Graduate School of Journalism, November/December.

Rosenstone, Steven J., Donald R. Kinder, Warren E. Miller, and the National Election Studies. 1997. *American National Election Study, 1996: Pre- and Post-Election Survey* (computer file); 2nd release. Ann Arbor: University of Michigan, Center for Political Studies(producer); 1997. Ann Arbor, MI: Inter-university Consortium for Political and Social Research (distributor).

Rosenstone, Steven J., and John Mark Hansen. 1993. *Mobilization, Participation, and Democracy in America*. New York: Macmillan.

Sabato, Larry J., Mark Stencel, and S. Robert Lichter. 2000. *Peep Show: Media and Politics in an Age of Scandal*. New York: Rowman and Littlefield.

Schultz, Kenneth A. 1998. Domestic Opposition and Signaling in International Crises. *American Political Science Review* 92 (4) (December): 829–44.

Scott, David K., and R. H. Gobetz. 1992. Hard News/Soft News. *Journalism Quarterly* 69:412–26.

Scott, Janny. 1998. The President under Fire, the Media: A Media Race Enters Waters Still Uncharted. *New York Times*, February 1, late ed., final, sec. 1.

Sears, David O. 1986. College Sophomores in the Laboratory: Influences of a Narrow Data Base on Social Psychology's View of Human Nature. *Journal of Personality and Social Psychology* 51:515–30.

Shaw, David. 2001. Foreign News Shrinks in Era of Globalization. *Los Angeles Times*, September 27, sec. A.

Simon, Dennis M., and Charles W. Ostrom, Jr. 1989. The Impact of Televised Speeches and Foreign Travel on Presidential Approval. *Public Opinion Quarterly* 53 (Spring): 58–82.

Simon, Herbert A. 1979. *Models of Thought*. New Haven: Yale University Press.

Singer, David J., and Melvin Small. 1993. *Correlates of War Project: International and Civil War Data, 1870–1992*. [Computer File], Ann Arbor, MI [producers]. Inter-university Consortium for Political and Social Research [distributor], 1994.

Skowronski, John J., and Donal E. Carlston. 1987. Social Judgment and Social Memory: The Role of Cue Diagnosticity in Negativity, Positivity, and Extremity Biases. *Journal of Personality and Social Psychology* 52 (April): 689–99.

———. 1989. Negativity and Extremity Biases in Impression Formation: A Review of Explanations. *Psychological Bulletin* 103 (January): 131–42.

Smith, Alastair. 1996. Diversionary Foreign Policy in Democratic Systems. *International Studies Quarterly* 40 (1): 133–54.

———. 1998. International Crises and Domestic Politics. *American Political Science Review* 92 (3) (September): 623–38.

Smith, M. Brewster, Jerome S. Bruner, and Robert W. White. 1956. *Opinions and Personality*. New York: John Wiley and Sons.

Smith, Rogers. 1993. Beyond Tocqueville, Myrdal, and Hartz: The Multiple Traditions in America. *American Political Science Review* 87 (September): 549–66.

Smith, Terrence. 2001. Evening News Evolution. *The News Hour with Jim Lehrer* (March 9). Transcript available at: http://www.pbs.org/newshour/bb/media/jan-june01/news_3-9.html.

Sniderman, Paul. 1993. A New Look in Public Opinion Research. In *Political Science: The State of the Discipline II*, edited by Ada Finifter, 220–45. Washington, D.C.: American Political Science Association.

Sniderman, Paul, Richard Brody, and Philip Tetlock. 1991. *Reasoning and Choice: Explorations in Political Psychology*. New York: Cambridge University Press.

Sobel, Richard. 1989. A Report: Public Opinion about United States Intervention in El Salvador and Nicaragua. *Public Opinion Quarterly* 53 (Spring): 114–28.

———. 2001. *The Impact of Public Opinion on U.S. Foreign Policy since Vietnam*. New York: Oxford University Press.

Stanley, Harold W., and Richard G. Niemi. 1994. *Vital Statistics on American Politics*. 4th ed. Washington, D.C.: Congressional Quarterly Press.

Stanovich, Keith E., and Richard F. West. 1998. Individual Differences in Framing and Conjunction Effects. *Thinking and Reasoning* 4 (November):289–317.

Star Tribune. 1998. *Minnesota Poll #98008B: Clinton, Lewinsky, Scandal/Morality*, August 19–21.

Stimson, James A. 1976. Public Support for American Presidents: A Cyclical Model. *Public Opinion Quarterly* 40:1–21.

Summers, Harry G., Jr. 1995. *Persian Gulf War Almanac*. New York: Facts on File.

Tetlock, Philip E. 1984. Cognitive Style and Political Belief Systems in the British House of Commons. *Journal of Personality and Social Psychology* 46 (2): 365–75.

———. 1985. Integrative Complexity of American and Soviet Foreign Policy Rhetoric: A Time-Series Analysis. *Journal of Personality and Social Psychology* 49 (6): 1565–85.

———. 1986. A Value Pluralism Model of Ideological Reasoning. *Journal of Personality and Social Psychology* 50 (4): 819–27.

———. 1989. Structure and Function in Political Belief Systems. In *Attitude Structure and Function*, edited by Anthony R. Pratkinis, Steven J. Breckler, and Anthony G. Greenwald. Hillsdale, N.J.: Lawrence Erlbaum Associates, Publishers.

Tocqueville, Alexis de. 2000. *Democracy in America*. Translated by Harvey Claflin Mansfield and Delba Winthrop. Chicago: University of Chicago Press.

Times Mirror. 1990. *News Interest Index*, January 4–7, 1990.

———. 1993. *News Interest Index*. February 20–23, 1993.

Tomz, Michael, Jason Wittenberg, and Gary King. 1998. CLARIFY: Software for Interpreting and Presenting Statistical Results. Version 1.1.1 Cambridge: Harvard University, August 28. Available online at http://gking.harvard.edu/

Vanderbilt Television News Archives. Available online at http://tvnews.vanderbilt.edu.

Vincent, Norah. 2002. Heroes and Demons and Just Humans. *Los Angeles Times*, July 19, sec. B.

Wamsley, Gary, and Richard A. Pride. 1972. Television Network News: Rethinking the Iceburg Problem. *Western Political Quarterly* 25:434–50.

Webster, James G., and Lawrence W. Lichty. 1991. *Ratings Analysis: Theory and Practice*. Hillsdale, N.J.: Lawrence Erlbaum Associates.

Wechtel, Paul L. 1967. Conceptions of Broad and Narrow Attention. *Psychological Bulletin* 68 (6): 417–29.

Weinstein, Steve. 1998. CNN Adds Newsmagazines to the Mix. *Los Angeles Times*, June 6, 1998, sec. F.

Wickens, Christopher D. 1980. The Structure of Attentional Resources. In *Attention and Performance VIII*, edited by Raymond S. Nickerson. Hillsdale, N.J.: Lawrence Erlbaum Associates.

Wright, Gerald C. 1993. Error in Measuring Vote Choice in the National Election Studies, 1952–1988. *American Journal of Political Science* 37 (February): 291–316.

Zaller, John. 1985. Proposal for the Measurement of Political Information. Report to the NES Board of Overseers. Ann Arbor: University of Michigan, Center for Political Studies.

————. 1991. Information, Values, and Opinion. *American Political Science Review* 85 (4): 1215–1237.

————. 1992. *The Nature and Origins of Mass Opinion.* New York: Cambridge University Press.

————. 1994. Elite Leadership of Mass Opinion: New Evidence from the Gulf War. In *Taken by Storm: The Media, Public Opinion, and U.S. Foreign Policy in the Gulf War,* edited by Lance W. Bennett, and David L. Paletz, 186–209. Chicago: University of Chicago Press.

————. 1998. Monica Lewinsky's Contribution to Political Science. *PS: Political Science and Politics* 31 (June): 182–89.

————. 1999. *A Theory of Media Politics: How the Interests of Politicians, Journalists, and Citizens Shape the News.* Chicago: University of Chicago Press. Forthcoming.

Zaller, John, and Dennis Chiu. 1999. Government's Little Helper: U.S. Press Coverage of Foreign Policy Crises, 1945–1999. In *Decisionmaking in a Glass House: Mass Media, Public Opinion, and American and European Foreign Policy in the 21st Century,* edited by Brigitte L. Nacos, Robert Y. Shapiro, and Pierangelo Isernia, 61–84. Lanham, Md.: Rowman & Littlefield.

Zaller, John, and Stanley Feldman. 1992. A Simple Theory of Survey Response. *American Journal of Political Science* 36:579–616.

Zukin, Cliff (with Robin Snyder). 1984. Passive Learning: When the Media Environment is the Message. *Public Opinion Quarterly* 48 (Autumn): 629–38.

INDEX

Access Hollywood: airing of several times a day, 38; debut of, 304–5n15; Iraq, coverage of crisis with, 64; Lewinsky scandal, coverage of, 84–85; Operation Desert Fox, coverage of, 79; program coverage, rationale for, 41, 47; terrorism, coverage of, 84; viewership of, 62

activist foreign policy. *See* internationalism

A Current Affair, 37, 47, 119

advertising, revenue from, news vs. original entertainment programs, 35–37

Afghanistan: air power, reliance on, 287; missile strikes against, 1–5, 129–32, 317n32; women in, 57, 229

agenda setting, 8

Albright, Madeleine, 45, 178

Almond-Lippman Consensus, 289, 291

Al Qaeda, 57

American National Election Study (NES), 297n7; attentiveness, indicators of, 134–37; Cumulative Data File (CDF), 190–91, 254, 258, 320nn55–56; education and political information, correlation of, 114; education level of respondents, 163, 192; election of 2000, talk show coverage and, 275; government affairs, public interest in, 28–29; Gulf War Pilot Study, 165, 315n8; isolationism, popular support for, 230, 233–34, 238, 249–52, 254, 256–57, 324n5; problems facing the nation, public perception of most important, 183, 185, 190, 318–19n45; television variable in, 187–89; television watching habits, 59, 165, 295n10; Vietnam, Gulf, and Korean Wars, public opinion regarding, 20, 159–60, 163, 195; voting and political engagement levels, 274

Annan, Kofi, 63

Arafat, Yasser, 177

attention. *See* attentiveness

attentiveness: definition of, 10–12, 15–17; education and (*see* education); to force, all uses of, 172–77; to foreign crises, exposure to soft news and, 100–108, 112–18, 120–27, 167–72; framing in accessible terms, ease of and, 43–44 (*see also* framing); interest in war and, paradox of, 19–25; internationalism and (*see* internationalism); knowledge, distinguished from, 108, 132–33; to major national problems, 183–87;

television viewing habits and, 187–90; by topics, 190–94; to non-foreign crisis issues, 109–11, 118–19, 122–23, 127–29; opinionation as indicator of, 133–37; over time, limitations of tracking, 156–57; to peace talks, 177–82; personal importance and, 159–60; political awareness and, 215–16; prediction of increased, 47–48; validity of indicators, 98–99; to wars, increasing, 157–64, 167–72 (*see also* wars)

Banderas, Antonio, 83

Baum, Matthew A., 188, 326n27

Beatty, Warren, 309n14

Begin, Menachem, 177

Belfield, David, 84

Bennett, James, 274

Berk, Barry, 41–42, 100

Berlin, Mark L., 300nn39–40

Berlin Crisis (1961–62), 168–69

Berry, Jeff, 79

Betts, Richard K., 86

Bin Laden, Osama, 1, 45

Blechman, Barry M., 172, 316n28

Bosnia: attentiveness to and soft news coverage, 100–108, 112–18; casualty aversion in, 287; Dayton Peace Accords, 177–82; foreign policy in, soft news coverage and support for, 238–44; news coverage of, soft and hard compared, 77–78; soft news coverage of, 64–70

Bremer, Stuart A., 286

Brill, Steven, 18

Broadcast News, 291

Brody, Richard, 223

Brosnan, Pierce, 83

Bruner, Jerome S., 33

Buchanan, Patrick, 284

Bush, George H. W., 45, 86–87, 233, 285

Bush, George W.: election of 2000, 274–76; foreign policy decisionmaking and public opinion, 289; as internationalist, 284; public approval ratings of, 212; public support, efforts to rally, 285; rhetoric of, 233; Winfrey, women in Afghanistan and, 229

Cable News Network (CNN), 179, 275

Camp David Peace Accords, 177–82

Carlson, Margaret, 328n8
Carter, Jimmy, 137, 177, 180
causal narratives, 32–33, 41–43
CBS. *See* Columbia Broadcasting System
CDF. *See* American National Election Study, Cumulative Data File
Center for Media and Public Affairs (CMPA), 38–39, 296n17, 307n1
cheap framing, 31–33, 37, 39, 53, 109. *See also* framing
Chevy Chase Show, The, 178
Chicago Council on Foreign Relations, 298n17
Clinton, Bill: approval ratings of, 212, 249–53, 279, 328n8; Bosnia, public approval regarding, 180, 239–43; foreign policy decision-making and public opinion, 289; Lewinsky scandal and (*see* Lewinsky scandal); Milosevic, vilification of, 45; Northern Ireland and, 119; Operation Desert Fox and, 79–80, 212; pardons upon leaving office, 50; scandals during 1992 primaries, 309n14; soft media, campaign appearances on, 273; State of the Union address, Lewinsky affair and, 278–79; Whitewater investigation, 41–42
Clinton, Hillary, 84
CMPA. *See* Center for Media and Public Affairs
CNN. *See* Cable News Network
cognizance, 16–17
Columbia Broadcasting System (CBS): Camp David Peace Accords, survey regarding, 137, 179; Kosovo, coverage of, 78–79; news, changing environment for, 35; Operation Desert Fox, coverage of, 79–80; Vietnam and Persian Gulf Wars, coverage of, 90–91
Committee of Concerned Journalists, 39
congressional check-bouncing scandal, 51
Conover, Pamela, 300n33
Converse, Philip E., 290
Corvo, David, 34, 300n39
Crigler, Ann R., 7, 32, 39, 81
crisis: definition of, 49; dramatic, 49 (*see also* water-cooler events)
Crowe, Russell, 83
Cuban Missile Crisis, 168–69

Daalder, Ivo H., 286
Daily Show, 119
Dateline, 35–38, 62, 84, 301n48
daytime talk shows: Bosnia, opinions and, 240–43; foreign crises, frequency of coverage, 64–70; internationalism, impact on attitudes toward, 249–53; Japan, feelings regarding and, 248–49; Northern Ireland and, 119; presidential elections and, 273–77, 283; proliferation of, 37; viewership of, 59–62. *See also* soft news media
Dayton Peace Accords, 177–82
democracy, the soft news media and, 288–91
Dominican Republic intervention, 168–69
Donahue, Phil, 37
Downs, Anthony, 55–56
Dreyfus, Richard, 108
Drunkard's Search, parable of, 283

economy: approval of president's handling of, 249–50; soft news and attentiveness to, 118–19, 127–29
Edelman, Murray, 303n71
education: average daily hours of television viewing and, 188; Bosnia, support for foreign policy in and, 241–44; casualties in military actions, sensitivity to, 287–88; force, attentiveness to all uses of and, 174–76; foreign policy crises, attentiveness to and, 167–72; as indicator of political engagement, 113–14; international affairs, concern with and, 125–26; isolationism and, 253–58; Japan, opinions regarding and, 248–49; Korean, Vietnam, and Gulf Wars, opinions regarding and, 163–64; Lewinsky scandal and incidental learning, 130–31; major national problems: attentiveness to, television viewing habits and, 189–90; attentiveness to types of and, 192–94; NATO enlargement, support for and, 245–47; news program preferences and, 60; peace accords, attentiveness to and, 180–81; political knowledge, soft news consumption and, 280–81; presidential approval ratings and, 217–18; rally-round-the-flag phenomenon and, 218–19, 221–22; soft news consumption and, 113–23, 127–29; time of day, television watching and, 60; Vietnam and Gulf Wars, opinions regarding and, 158–59. *See also* information; political awareness/engagement
Edwards, George, III, 317n31, 321n4
Eisenhower, Dwight, 160
elections: 1996 Republican primaries, 69, 109; of 1998, 69–7, 110; strategies in, implications of the rise of the soft media for, 282–83; of 2000, 9, 50, 85–86, 273–78
elites. *See* political elites
E! News Daily, 179

Engel, Eliot, 45
Entertainment Tonight, 2, 62, 84–85, 108
ER, 35–37
expected utility model, 19; benefits of information, 26–29; costs of information, 29–33; costs vs. benefits as explanatory variable, 53–56; *P* term in, 297n5
Extra: airing of several times a day, 38; Arab-Israeli conflict, coverage of, 108; Iraq, coverage of crisis with, 63, 65; Lewinsky scandal, coverage of, 85; Operation Desert Fox, coverage of, 79–81; terrorism and 9/11, coverage of, 81–83; viewership of, 62

Fay, Bradford, 303n1
FCC. *See* Federal Communications Commission
Feaver, Peter V., 286–87
Federal Communications Commission (FCC), 34–35, 300n39
Feldman, Stanley, 300n33
Flint, Larry, 80
Fordham, Benjamin O., 172
foreign affairs. *See* foreign policy
foreign aid, 126–27
foreign crises. *See* foreign policy; wars
foreign policy: activist/multilateral (*see* internationalism); concern regarding, soft news and, 123–27; elite framing of issues and, 44–46; focus on, reasons for, 9–10; force, attentiveness to all uses of, 172–77; mass media coverage, changes in, 3–4, 296n17; partisanship and, 296n16; peace talks, attentiveness to, 177–82; presidential, implications of the rise of the soft media for, 283–88; public interest in, 21–24; public opinion and, 8–9, 222–23, 282, 318n44; rally-round-the-flag phenomenon (*see* rally-round-the-flag phenomenon); soft news coverage: compared to hard news media, 71–84; frequency of, 63–71; impact of, 229, 258; reasons for, 39–44; wars (*see* wars); water-cooler events and the soft news media, 5–8. *See also* names of specific actions/events
48 Hours, 38
framing, 5; in accessible terms, ease of and soft news coverage, 43–44; cheap, 31–33, 37, 39, 53, 109; definition of, 299n27; episodic vs. thematic, 74–76, 231, 234–35; favored by soft news media, 39–40; of the Oslo Accords signing, 179; by political leaders, 44–46; public opinion, influence on through, 8; selective and non-foreign crisis

issues, 109–10; soft and hard news media compared, illustrative examples, 79, 80–83
Franken, Al, 178–79

Gallup, Alec M., 317n33
Gallup polls: on the Camp David and Dayton Peace Accords, 179; on the most important problem facing the nation, 21–22, 298n15, 320n63; on news consumption habits and major policy issues, 119–20, 244; on presidential job performance, 173, 181–82, 212, 220; on the Vietnam and Persian Gulf Wars, 158–59, 195, 202, 298n12
Gamson, William A., 299n27
gatekeeping/Gateway Hypothesis, 33, 48, 97, 111–12, 278
Gelb, Leslie H., 86
Gelpi, Christopher, 286–87
General Social Survey (GSS), 22–24, 298n16
Gere, Richard, 108
Gonzales, Elian, 50
Gonzales, Steven, 78
Good Friday Peace Accords. *See* Northern Ireland
Gore, Al, 274–76
Graber, Doris A., 32, 302–3n66
Grand Canyon, 291
Greenfield, Jeff, 328n8
Gregorish, Lisa, 31, 33, 37, 40–42, 59, 100
GSS. *See* General Social Survey
Gulf War. *See* Persian Gulf War

Haiti, 64–70, 168–69
Hamas, 108
Hamilton, James T., 38, 114, 234, 302n55, 324n2
Hard Copy, 9, 42, 59, 63
Hart, Gary, 309n14
Hartley, Eugene L., 299n25
Hibbs, Douglas A., Jr., 214, 217, 322n7
Hill, David B., 300n32
Hristoulas, Athansios, 321n4, 322n10
Hugick, Larry, 317n33
Hume, John, 119
Hurt, William, 291
Hussein, Saddam, 45, 212

ICB. *See* International Crisis Behavior data set
incidental by-product model, 7; incidental by-product defined, 30; Lewinsky scandal, application to, 278–79; news piggybacking on entertainment, 99, 129; non-foreign policy application, 182; paradox of public opinion

incidental by-product model (*cont.*)
and foreign policy, explanation of, 269; on
political information, 53. *See also* theory
incidental learning model, 129–31
information: attentiveness to major national
problems, television viewing habits, and,
187–89; attentiveness to major national
problems and, 183–87; attitudes, impact on,
299n23; citizenship and, 288–89; costs of,
reasons for decline in, 33–39; expected benefit from, 12, 26–29, 53–56; expected costs
of, 12, 29–33, 53–56; foreign policy attitudes, impact of daytime talk shows and,
250–53; Korean, Vietnam, and Persian Gulf
Wars, opinions regarding and, 162–63; low
information rationality, 26; news program
preferences and level of, 60; Persian Gulf
War, opinions regarding and, 165–67; public
opinion and, 4; rally-round-the-flag phenomenon and, 215–16; reception-acceptance
model of public opinion and, 214–15. *See
also* education; political awareness/
engagement
infotainment, 295n4
Inside Edition, 9, 42, 79, 81–83, 108, 179
interest: attentiveness, distinguished from, 16;
attentiveness to war and, paradox of, 19–25;
personal importance of the Vietnam and
Gulf Wars, 159–60; Whitewater vs.
Lewinsky, reasons for difference in, 41–42.
See also attentiveness
International Crisis Behavior (ICB) data set,
286–87
internationalism: Bosnia, soft news consumption and opinions regarding, 238–44; daytime talk shows, impact of on attitudes
toward, 249–53; framing and opinions regarding, 235; of highly informed individuals,
234; hypotheses regarding, 235–36; isolationism, rising support for, 253–56; Japan,
soft news consumption and opinions regarding, 247–49; NATO enlargement, soft news
consumption and opinions regarding, 244–
47; rally-round-the-flag phenomenon and,
237–38; rise of the soft media and, 284; soft
news consumption and opinions regarding,
230–31, 256–58; terrorism, support for war
on and, 236–37
Internet, the, 271–72
Iraq: Operation Desert Fox, 41, 79–81; Persian
Gulf War (*see* Persian Gulf War); weapons
inspections, conflict over, 63
Ireland, conflict in Northern, 119–23

isolationism, 233–34, 250–56, 284. *See also*
internationalism
Israel-Lebanon conflict, 100–108. *See also*
Middle East peace process
issue attention cycle, 54–56
Iyengar, Shanto, 235, 299n26, 323n21

James, Patrick, 321n4, 322n10
Japan, feelings toward, 247–49
Johnson, David, 25
Johnson, Lyndon, 86–87
Jones, Daniel M., 286
Jordan, Michael H., 35
Joyner, James H., Jr., 172, 219–20, 316n28
Just, Marion R., 7, 32, 39, 81

Kalb, Marvin, 34
Kaplan, Stephen S., 172, 316n28
Kasem, Casey, 179
Kasich, John, 212
Katz, Andrew Z., 32
Kernell, Samuel, 188, 214, 217, 318n37,
322n7, 326n27
Kinchla, R. A., 11
Kinder, Donald R., 315n16
King, Gary, 175, 308n9, 309n17, 310–11n25,
311nn31–32, 312n37, 319n50, 325n15,
326n20, 326n24, 327n6
Kmetko, Steve, 24–25
knowledge: attentiveness distinguished from,
108, 132–33; information and public level
of, 26–28; learning, distinguished from,
296n2; soft news consumption and, 279–81.
See also education; information
Korean War: opinions regarding compared to
Vietnam and Gulf Wars, 160–64, 202–3;
public interest in and attentiveness to, 21–23
Kosovo: casualty aversion in, 286–88; coverage of, soft and hard news media compared,
78–79; intervention in, soft news media
coverage of, 64–70
Krugman, Herbert E., 299n25
Kurtz, Howard, 63

LaMay, C., 307n38
Larry King Live, 62
late-night talk shows: Bosnia, opinions regarding foreign policy in and, 240–43; foreign
crises, frequency of coverage, 64–70; Japan,
feelings regarding and, 248–49; Operation
Desert Fox, coverage of, 79; political humor,
tradition of, 305n18; politics, learning about
through, 63; presidential elections and, 273–

77; proliferation of, 37. *See also* soft news media

learning: knowledge, distinguished from, 296n2; passive and incidental, 298–99n21; passive and television, 299n25

Leno, Jay, 63, 273

Letterman, David, 63, 81

Lewinsky, Monica, 1–2, 42

Lewinsky scandal: analysis of, 305n19; appeal to soft news media, 41–42; avoidance of partisan elements by soft news media, 84–85; frequency of media coverage, 69, 71; incidental by-products of, 278–79; the Internet and, 271; missile strikes and, 1–2, 129–32; soft news coverage of, 9, 110, 290; soft news coverage of and public opinion, 15

Lexis-Nexis, 2, 64, 70, 78, 83–85, 88, 108, 178, 195

Lian, Brad, 172, 219–20, 316n28

Lichty, Lawrence W., 301n44

Lindh, John Walker, 43

Lindsey, Bruce, 278

Littlefield, Warren, 36

Live with Regis and Kathie Lee, 119, 178

Livingston, Bob, 80

Lopez, Jennifer, 83

Lorch, Donatella, 79–81

Los Angeles Times, 9, 43

Lutz, Richard J., 299n23

mainstreaming effect, 236, 290

Marketplace, 25

McEwen, Mark, 24

McRainey, Gerald, 25

media, the: direct marketing, revolution in, 34; entertainment vs. news, consumption decision regarding, 30–31; events (*see* watercooler events); gateway of soft to hard news, 111–12; individual uses of, 300n31; major political stories, changes in coverage of, 3–4; network evening newscasts, decline in viewership of, 59, 62; newspaper coverage of Vietnam and Persian Gulf Wars, 87–89; newspapers, replacement by television as news source, 58; public opinion and, 8–9; soft and hard news coverage of 2000 election compared, 85–86; soft and hard news coverage of foreign crises, illustrative examples, 77–84; soft and hard news coverage of foreign crises compared, 71–77; soft and hard news coverage of Lewinsky scandal compared, 84–85; soft news (*see* soft news media); television (*see* television)

Meernik, James, 223

methodology: floor and ceiling effects, testing for, 200–202; model specifications, 102–3; opinionation as indicator of attentiveness, use of, 133–37; rally-round-the-flag phenomenon, for investigating the, 219–21; rationality assumption, 7; reliability and validity of indicators, 98–99; reverse causality, testing for the possibility of, 308n12; Wald Coefficient Test, 322n14. *See also* theory

Michel, Robert, 45

MID. *See* Militarized Interstate Dispute data set

Middle East peace process, 136–37, 177–82

militainment, 25, 298n18

Militarized Interstate Dispute (MID) data set, 286–87, 319–20n54, 323n23, 328n10

Miller, Roger LeRoy, 322n12

Milosevic, Slobodan, 45

models. *See* theory

Modigliani, Andre, 299n27

morning variety programs. *See* network morning variety programs

Mueller, John E., 195, 213, 219

multilateral foreign policy. *See* internationalism

NAFTA. *See* North American Free Trade Agreement

National Association of Broadcasters, 300n39

National Broadcasting Company (NBC), 35–37

NATO. *See* North Atlantic Treaty Organization

NBC. *See* National Broadcasting Company

NES. *See* American National Election Study

network morning variety programs: Persian Gulf War, coverage of, 92; viewership of, 59. *See also* soft news media

network television soft news. *See* tabloid news programs

Neuman, Russell W.: audience attention cycle, definition of, 303n72; on audience-contingent effects, 54; crisis, definition of, 49–50; frames, identification of, 31–32; human impact frame, 39, 81; symbolic crises, identification of, 303n71; television and the audience attention barrier, 7

newsmagazines: costs to produce and viewership of, 35–37; foreign crisis coverage: compared to hard news media, 71–77; frequency of, 64–70; Northern Ireland and, 119; Operation Desert Fox, coverage of, 79; Operation Just Cause, coverage of, 113; soft

newsmagazines (*cont.*)
 news, emphasis on, 38; terrorism, coverage
 of, 84; viewership of, 59, 62. *See also* soft
 news media
New York Times, Vietnam and Persian Gulf
 Wars, coverage of, 87–89
Nielsen ratings, 60–62, 304n7
9/11, 81–83. *See also* terrorism
Nixon, Richard, 20, 273
NORC. *See* National Opinion Research Council
Noriega, Manuel, 112–13, 280–81
North American Free Trade Agreement
 (NAFTA), 70–71, 305n21
North Atlantic Treaty Organization (NATO):
 Bosnia and (*see* Bosnia); soft news con-
 sumption and opinions regarding enlarge-
 ment of, 244–47
Northern Ireland, 119–23

object relations, 302n51
O'Callaghan, Sean, 119
O'Donnell, Rosie, 25, 77, 83
O'Grady, Scott, 77–78
O'Hanlon, Michael E., 286
Oneal, John R., 172, 219–20, 316n28
Operation Desert Fox, 41, 79–81, 212, 321n2
Operation Desert Storm. *See* Persian Gulf War
Operation Just Cause, 112–18, 280–81
opinionation, 133–37
Opinion Research Group, 202
opportunity costs, 30–31, 54–55
Oprah Winfrey Show, The, 47, 62, 229, 273–
 75, 303n67. *See also* Winfrey, Oprah
Osborn, Barbara, 304n7
Oslo Accords, 177–82
Ostrom, Charles W., 320n61

Page, Benjamin I., 133
Paley, William, 34
Panama, 112–18, 280–81
partisan political issues: foreign policy as unlikely, 296n16; frequency of coverage by
 soft news media, 69–71; in Lewinsky scandal, avoidance of by soft news media, 84–
 85; primary elections, attentiveness to, 109;
 rally-round-the-flag phenomenon as, 216–19,
 221–23. *See also* elections; presidents
partisan threshold model, 217
Patterson, Thomas E., 6
Persian Gulf War: air power, reliance on and
 casualty aversion, 286–88; attentiveness to,
 135–36; entertainment media and, 24–25,
 47; frames employed in soft news media

coverage of, 81; local news media coverage
 of, 92–94; media attention compared to Operation Just Cause, 117–18; network television coverage of, 89–91; newspaper
 coverage of, 87–89; opinions regarding
 compared to Korean and Vietnam Wars,
 160–64, 202–3; presidential rhetoric regarding, 86–87; public interest in and attentiveness to, 20–25; public opinion regarding
 compared to the Vietnam War, 158–60,
 164–67; soft news media coverage of, 64,
 91–92; television as primary source of news
 regarding, 58–59; uniqueness of, potential
 problem regarding, 167–72; as water-cooler
 event, 40–41, 49
personal importance, of the Vietnam and Gulf
 Wars, 159–60
Pew Research Center for the People & the
 Press: Afghanistan-Sudan missile strikes and
 the Lewinsky scandal, public opinion regarding, 1, 129–30; campaign news, sources
 of, 303n1; Internet use by the public, 271,
 327n1; late-night talk show hosts, political
 information from, 63; Lewinsky scandal,
 public attentiveness to, 305n19; media use
 habits of the public, 99–101, 109–10; news
 consumption habits and major national problems, 123; news interest index, 41–42, 50–
 51, 117–18; television viewing habits of the
 public, 59, 165; terrorism, public opinion regarding the war on, 237
Pflug, Jackie, 108
Philbin, Regis, 178, 273
Piaget, Jean, 302n51
piggybacking, 30–33; cost of information and,
 53; of foreign affairs information on entertainment, 99–100; frames amenable to, 39;
 the Lewinsky scandal and, 278–79; non-
 foreign crisis issues and, 109–10; the Persian Gulf War and, 47; primary elections
 and, 109
political awareness/engagement: casualties in
 military actions, sensitivity to, 287–88; education as an indicator of, 113–14; election
 of 2000 and, 276–77; rally-round-the-flag
 phenomenon and attentiveness, 215–16;
 rally-round-the-flag phenomenon and partisanship, 216–19; soft news consumption
 and, 113–19. *See also* education;
 information
political elites: framing of issues by, 44–46;
 public participation in foreign affairs, disdain for, 288–89

political information. *See* information
Popkin, Samuel, 26, 32, 232, 283
Powlick, Philip J., 32
presidents: approval ratings and foreign policy
   attentiveness, 172–77, 181–82, 212, 321n2,
   328n8; electoral campaigns and the soft
   news media, 273–78, 282–83; foreign policy and the rise of the soft media, implications for, 283–88; framing of issues by, 44–
   45; rally-round-the-flag phenomenon (*see*
   rally-round-the-flag phenomenon); rhetoric
   regarding Vietnam and Persian Gulf Wars,
   86–87; threshold model of presidential
   approval, 217
Prime Time Live, 38
priming, 4–5, 8, 31–32, 183
public opinion: the Afghanistan-Sudan missile
   strikes, 2–3; attention of (*see* attentiveness);
   foreign affairs, interest in, 21–24; on foreign
   policy, soft news consumption and, 229–31
   (*see also* internationalism); foreign policy
   and, 8–9, 222–23, 282, 318n44; information
   and, 4; information gathering in the formation of (*see* information); interest and attentiveness to war, paradox of, 19–25;
   presidential approval polls, 172–77, 181–82;
   public affairs, interest in, 28; reception-
   acceptance model of, 214–15, 231, 253; on
   specific people or events (*see* names of
   individuals or events); surveys, validity of,
   98–99; traditional scholarly consensus
   regarding, 4, 26
Public Papers of the President, 87

Rabin, Yitzhak, 177
rally-round-the-flag phenomenon, 14, 212–13,
   222–23; data and methodology regarding,
   219–21; disaggregating, 213–14; duration
   of, 317n33; education, partisanship and,
   221–22; hypotheses regarding, 214–19; isolationism of politically inattentive individuals and, 237–38
Ramirez, Andrew, 78
Rao, Potluri, 322n12
Raphael, Sally Jesse, 306n36
rationality: assumption regarding, 7; low
   information, 26
reception-acceptance model, 214–15, 231,
   253
Rehnquist, William, 275
Rielly, John E., 298n17
Rioux, Jean Sebastien, 321n4, 322n10
Rivera, Geraldo, 63

Sadat, Anwar, 177
salience, 16–17
Sarver, Christopher C., 172
Savings and Loan scandal, 50–51
Schechter, Danny, 1
Schwarzkopf, Norman, 178
selective acceptance, 231–34
Serbia, 41
Shapiro, Robert Y., 133
Shaw, David, 296n17
Simon, Dennis, 320n61
Singer, J. David, 286
60 Minutes, 38, 62, 84, 119
Smith, M. Brewster, 33
Sniderman, Paul, 26
soft news media: America's addiction to, 59–
   62; attentiveness to politics and (*see* attentiveness); costs of information and, 30–33;
   defined, 6–7; democracy and, 288–91; education and (*see* education); elections and
   (*see* elections); entertainment as reason for
   watching, 99–100, 234; foreign crises and
   policy, coverage of (*see* foreign policy;
   wars); framing by (*see* framing); as gateway
   to hard news, 111–12; hypotheses regarding,
   48, 97, 124, 127, 173–74, 190, 236; implications for public opinion, theory explicating
   (*see* theory); incidental learning and, 129–
   32; information level of individuals and (*see*
   education; information); major issues, increased exposure resulting from, 46–47;
   Nielsen ratings for, 60–62; non-foreign-
   crisis issues and, 109–11, 127–29, 182–83,
   239–41, 249–50; partisan political issues,
   coverage of (*see* partisan political issues);
   political engagement, level of and, 113–23;
   political knowledge, acquisition of and,
   279–81; public policy, implications for,
   282–88; rally-round-the-flag phenomenon
   and (*see* rally-round-the-flag phenomenon);
   rise of, 37–39; topics favored by, 38–39;
   water-cooler events and, 5–8 (*see also*
   water-cooler events). *See also* daytime talk
   shows; late-night talk shows; network morning variety programs; newsmagazines; tabloid
   news programs; specific events and crises
Somalia, 64–70, 168–69
Stone, Christopher, 78
Sudan, 1–5, 129–32
Swenson, Tami, 321n4

tabloid news programs: foreign crisis coverage:
   compared to hard news media, 71–77; fre-

tabloid news programs (*cont.*)
quency of, 64–70; Operation Desert Fox, coverage of, 79; "tabloid," use of term, 302n54; viewership of, 59–62. *See also* soft news media
talk shows. *See* daytime talk shows; late-night talk shows
television: all-news cable networks, viewership of, 295n5; cable, importance of, 35; competition in and news programming, 34–37; increased viewing options and politically least informed viewers, 186–87; major national problems, attentiveness to types of, 190–94; news source, increasing reliance on as, 3, 58–62, 303n1; passive learning, ideal vehicle for, 299n25; peace talks, coverage of and attentiveness, 177–82; prime-time network audience ratings, 184–87; programs watched, factors determining, 59–62; reasons for watching, 298n20; soft news media, rise of, 37–39; status in the media, 18; technological innovation and, 34–35, 300–301n41; Vietnam and Persian Gulf Wars: coverage compared, 89–94; traditional news outlets and opinions regarding, 164–67; viewing habits and attentiveness to major national problems, 187–90. *See also* media, the; soft news media
terrorism: attentiveness to and exposure to soft news, 100–108; national trauma associated with, 309n13; 9/11, 81–83; soft and hard news media coverage compared, 81–84; soft news coverage of, 179; war on, public support for, 236–37
Tet Offensive, 86
theory: applicability beyond foreign policy, 182–83; expected utility model (*see* expected utility model); hypotheses, 48, 97, 124, 127, 173–74, 190, 214–19, 236; incidental by-product model (*see* incidental by-product model); incidental learning model, 129–31; partisan threshold model, 217; purpose of, 18–19; reception-acceptance model, 214–15, 231, 253; selective acceptance, 231–34
threshold effects, 214. *See also* partisan threshold model
Tichener, Edward B., 10–11
Tillman, Pat, 43
Times Mirror Center, 112, 303n1
tobacco regulation, media coverage of, 69–70, 110
Tocqueville, Alexis de, 273
Today, 302n65

Tomz, Michael, 175, 308n9, 309n17, 310–11n25, 311nn31–32, 312n37, 319n50, 325n15, 326n20, 326n24, 327n6
Tonight Show, The, 2
transaction costs, 30–32, 54–55
Trimble, David, 119
Trump, Donald, 309n14
20/20, 38, 62, 84, 113

United Nations: Bosnia, action regarding, 239 (*see also* Bosnia); weapons inspections in Iraq, 63
USA Today, 89

Vanderbilt Television News Archive, 90, 177–78, 318n43
Vietnam War: attentiveness to, 135–36; as failure, soft news references to, 76; fatalities in, 297n6; local television coverage of, 93–94; network television coverage of, 89–91; newspaper coverage of, 87–89; opinions regarding compared to Korean and Gulf Wars, 160–64, 202–3; presidential rhetoric regarding, 86–87; public interest in and attentiveness to, 19–23, 25; public opinion regarding compared to the Persian Gulf War, 158–60; soft news media coverage of, 91–92
View, The, 119
Vincent, Norah, 43

Wag the Dog, 2–3, 79
Walsh, John, 83
wars: attentiveness and interest, paradox of, 19–25; casualty aversion and reliance on air power, 286–87; cheap framing and, 43; comparing across time, 157–58; increasing attentiveness to, 157–64, 167–72, 318n44. *See also* foreign policy; names of wars
water-cooler events: defined, 5; as dramatic crises, 49–52; election of 2000 as, 50; foreign crises as likely, 10; Lewinsky scandal as, 42; Persian Gulf War as, 40–41, 49; presidential elections as, 275; the soft news media and, 5–8
Waterman, Peter, 223
Webster, James G., 301n44
White, Robert W., 33
Wickens, Christopher D., 11
Winfrey, Oprah, 57, 63, 77, 229, 273–74. *See also Oprah Winfrey Show, The*
Wittenberg, Jason, 175, 308n9, 309n17, 310–11n25, 311nn31–32, 312n37, 319n50, 325n15, 326n20, 326n24, 327n6

World Trade Organization (WTO), 70–71, 305n21

WTO. *See* World Trade Organization

Zaller, John: Clinton's approval ratings during Lewinsky scandal, 279; "don't know" responses to survey questions, evaluation of, 315n14; family values discussion, Quayle remarks and, 329n12; mainstreaming effect, 236; news quality index, score for *60 Minutes* on, 38; politically inattentive public, need for politicians to notice, 290; reception-acceptance model of public opinion, 214–15; Vietnam War and political awareness, 313n44